The One Year Book of Encouragement

THE ONE YEAR® BOOK OF

Encouragement

*365 Days of Inspiration and Wisdom
for Your Spiritual Journey*

HAROLD MYRA

Tyndale House Publishers, Inc., Carol Stream, Illinois

Visit Tyndale's exciting Web site at www.tyndale.com.

TYNDALE and Tyndale's quill logo are registered trademarks of Tyndale House Publishers, Inc.

The One Year is a registered trademark of Tyndale House Publishers, Inc.

The One Year Book of Encouragement: 365 Days of Inspiration and Wisdom for Your Spiritual Journey

Copyright © 2010 by Harold Myra. All rights reserved.

Cover and title page pen and ink drawing by Rembrandt van Rijn, from Rembrandt Bible Drawings copyright © 1979 by Dover Publications, Inc. All rights reserved.

Author photo copyright © 2008 by William Koechling Photography. All rights reserved.

Designed by Jessie McGrath

Scripture quotations marked NLT are taken from the *Holy Bible*, New Living Translation, copyright © 1996, 2004, 2007 by Tyndale House Foundation. Used by permission of Tyndale House Publishers, Inc., Carol Stream, Illinois 60188. All rights reserved.

Scripture quotations marked KJV are taken from the *Holy Bible*, King James Version.

Scripture quotations marked NKJV are taken from the New King James Version.® Copyright © 1982 by Thomas Nelson, Inc. Used by permission. All rights reserved. *NKJV* is a trademark of Thomas Nelson, Inc.

Scripture quotations marked NIV are taken from the Holy Bible, *New International Version,*® *NIV.*® Copyright © 1973, 1978, 1984 by Biblica, Inc.™ Used by permission of Zondervan. All rights reserved worldwide. www.zondervan.com.

Scripture quotations marked NASB are taken from the New American Standard Bible,® copyright © 1960, 1962, 1963, 1968, 1971, 1972, 1973, 1975, 1977, 1995 by The Lockman Foundation. Used by permission.

Scripture quotations marked *The Message* are taken from *The Message* by Eugene H. Peterson, copyright © 1993, 1994, 1995, 1996, 2000, 2001, 2002. Used by permission of NavPress Publishing Group. All rights reserved.

Scripture quotations marked AMP are taken from the *Amplified Bible,*® copyright © 1954, 1958, 1962, 1964, 1965, 1987 by The Lockman Foundation. Used by permission.

ISBN 978-1-4143-3428-8

Printed in the United States of America

16	15	14	13	12	11	10
7	6	5	4	3	2	1

WELCOME TO *Encouragement!*

If you probe beneath the surface of believers today, many of them will admit to anxieties and deep discouragement.

"I'm concerned about what's happening in the world. Things feel as if they're falling apart, and I fear what we may have to go through."

"Life is overwhelming—far more demanding and confusing than I ever thought it would be."

"My family has gone through so much; I'm fearful of what's next."

"I long to make a positive difference, but I've been surprised by how often I've failed—and I'm afraid I'll fail again."

Do you resonate with any of these comments? Whether or not they mirror your feelings, you'll likely agree that we're all living through sobering global disruptions and cultural chaos. We face an uncertain future, and many are in the middle of life-changing difficulties.

In crushing circumstances—or even in the ordinary, yet demanding, rhythms of life—we all need courage and encouragement. Personally, I've found marvelous refreshment and challenge in the deep, authentic rivers of our Christian heritage. From Brother Lawrence to Jill Briscoe, from John Wesley to Philip Yancey, from Martin Luther to Luci Shaw, my soul has been nourished by their scriptural wisdom hammered out on the anvil of life's realities.

My prayer is that you'll find these daily insights as bracing and compelling as I have. For years, I've underlined nuggets that, for me, were spiritual gold. For each quote selected, I've tried to unpack the meaning and provide some context so you can absorb it and apply it.

Especially today, we need spiritual meat, and the sages quoted in the pages to follow speak from demanding, real-life circumstances: Alan Paton, battling apartheid in South Africa; John Wesley, living in a tough marriage and praying on horseback; Luci Shaw, coping as a new widow; Oswald Chambers, speaking to men facing death (and soon to die himself); Amy Carmichael, rescuing young girls in India from sexual slavery; Mother Teresa, tending the dying. Three stalwart Christians—Helmut Thielicke, Ole Hallesby, and Corrie ten Boom—resisted the Nazis and paid heavy prices. Others with less dramatic experiences lived with eyes wide open to life's rugged turns and mysteries, yet they clung to a living faith.

Despite their differences from us, their longings and repentance and prayers resonate with immediacy. It's fascinating to me, for instance, how many of my friends say they often find François Fénelon's words from several hundred years ago exactly what they need for a given day.

For me, the men and women in this volume are truly soul mates. As I've read their words, they've often stung, but always with astringent healing, or they've opened a fresh way of viewing how God works. Other times, they've calmed me and lifted me to surrender and praise.

Life has been described as a crucible. The word describes what most people in the Bible endured, and we have much to endure today. Life not only is difficult but is a crucible that refines us. As we move through life, face adversity, bury our loved ones, and recognize the world's brutality and unfairness, we begin to appreciate more and more the depths of Scripture. We also realize we need guidance, fresh encouragement, and no-nonsense spiritual insight from those who have gone before us and have followed hard after Christ.

Fortunately, we have a rich heritage from which to draw.

Yet for most of us, life keeps quickening its pace, and we find too little time for soul nourishment. My hope is that this devotional will prove flexible for you. How might you use it? Start with today's date, or start anywhere. Read and pray through the daily devotions, or read several entries when you have the time. Personally, I mark the ones that hit home and copy quotes to carry with me. These challenges and prayers are for life as we meet it, in all its challenges, in all its opportunities, in all its wonder and grace from the loving Father.

Harold Myra

THE WAY TO FREEDOM

OSWALD CHAMBERS, in his famed devotional, paraphrases the apostle Paul, saying, "My determination is to be my utmost for His highest." Paul had exactly that spirit, and so did Chambers.

"Obey the call of Jesus," Chambers urges. "Keep yourself before God for this one thing only—my utmost for His highest." Then he switches to his own personal commitment: "I am determined to be absolutely and entirely for Him and Him alone."

When he declared that, Chambers was likely recalling his own inner turmoil as a young man. David McCasland's excellent biography *Oswald Chambers: Abandoned to God* reveals his intense struggles and the extraordinary dedication that resulted.

Chambers's determination resonates throughout his devotional, so it's no wonder countless Christians have read and reread his challenges and have been drawn into deeper commitment.

"We have to decide," Chambers says. "Surrender your will to Him absolutely and irrevocably." That was his challenge, and today we're faced with that opportunity.

Opportunity? Yes! Does surrendering our wills to God "absolutely and irrevocably" feel threatening and grim? Chambers didn't think so—and he was far from a grim, shackled person. For instance, he loved children and entertained them with sketches, having a sense of humor and love of life. He understood that the way to freedom—and ultimately to joy and laughter—lies through giving up our "rights" and allowing God full control.

As you begin the New Year, are you determined to hear the whispers and guidance of the Holy Spirit, who can equip you to experience God's highest? Here is Chambers's counsel: "Keep your life so constant in its contact with God that His surprising power may break out on the right hand and on the left. Live in a constant state of expectancy."

Lord, you know my struggles. Urgent duties clamor
for my attention! "Special offers" lure me to spend
time and money on superficial things. Fill me, I pray,
with the resolve to surrender myself to you.

Work hard to show the results of your salvation, obeying God with deep reverence
and fear. For God is working in you, giving you the desire and the power to do what
pleases him. PHILIPPIANS 2:12-13, NLT

WHY CRINGE? BE ENCOURAGED

MARTIN LUTHER says, "We can be sure of this: a sorrowful, timid, and frightened heart doesn't come from Christ. He came to this earth, fulfilled his mission, and ascended into heaven to take away sorrow and fearfulness from our hearts and replace them with cheerful hearts, consciences, and minds. That's why he promises to send the Holy Spirit."

The reformer wasn't always waging great historic battles; out of the doldrums of his own discouragement he spoke to the hearts of his fellow believers. Jesus says, "Don't let your hearts be troubled. Trust in God, and trust also in me" (John 14:1, NLT). Here's how Luther unpacks that: "It's as if Christ is saying to us, 'What are you doing? Why are you cringing? Be encouraged and take heart. All is not lost, even if the devil, the world, or your conscience plagues and terrifies you. You're not ruined if you don't feel my presence.'"

Sometimes we can feel ruined—when it seems the Lord is absent and the devil is near us instead. But Luther tells us that Jesus' promise of the Holy Spirit is real, even when we don't feel his presence.

We're urged to pray, whether we feel spiritually comforted or not, for the Holy Spirit is at work, whether we sense it or not.

Luther tells us that if we are Christians, the Lord speaks to us "with friendly and comforting words and actions." In addition, Luther challenges us to pray with confidence. "We think small, but the Lord is great and powerful. He expects us to ask for great things. He wants to give them to us to demonstrate his almighty power."

Holy Spirit of God, so often my feelings are flat or fearful. Grant me confidence and comfort, I pray. Thank you for your guidance and the wonderful things you've done. Help me not to cringe, but to take heart.

Jesus spoke to them at once. "Don't be afraid," he said. "Take courage. I am here!"
MATTHEW 14:27, NLT

RAGS AND BLOSSOMS

AMY CARMICHAEL chose happiness. In her later years, she wrote, "The sunshine is streaming into my little room, and I can see by twisting my head a tiny glimpse of the sky. It is a joy to feel the air coming on my face, though sometimes, and particularly in the spring, I have a big longing to get right out of doors beyond four walls, and to feel the wind and sunshine, and the rain too, upon me."

Why did she have to twist her head to see the sky, and why did she have to long for the wind, sun, and rain?

"It is twenty-one years since I could sit up, and for nineteen years it has been this one position in bed; but isn't it wonderful that He enables us to triumph, and to rejoice in Him?"

Despite being bedridden, she turned to what was good, especially the goodness of the Lord. She writes of finding pleasure in all the intricate details of the petals, stamens, and shadows in spring blossoms. In her ministry to children in India, she had experienced the dashing of many hopes; and then, for years, she endured the limitations of her body. Yet, in the ruins, she found beauty and blessed gifts from God.

Amy writes of the prisoner Jeremiah being drawn up by ropes from the miry dungeon in Jerusalem. He was grateful for the rags that kept his arms from being cut by the cords. In other words, if we look for blessings we can find them. She quotes a prayer by Stephen Phillips: "Aid me, when I cease to soar, to stand; make me Thy athlete, even in my bed."

That's what she was! In this context, we think not only of Amy Carmichael but also of Joni Eareckson Tada and many others who have lived astounding lives of faith despite extreme limitations.

"What is my heart's desire?" Carmichael asks. "Relief from fatigue? The dearth of pain? The cheery flowers of earth? Those blossoms may be given, but if not there remains the prayer, *'Make me Thy athlete, even in my bed.'*"

---

*Father, in spite of my limitations, open my eyes to
see your blessings. Fill me with your Holy Spirit.
Enable me to be your athlete when the big hurdles
and gigantic challenges stretch before me.*

Praise the LORD! Sing to the LORD a new song. . . . Let the faithful rejoice that he honors them. Let them sing for joy as they lie on their beds. PSALM 149:1, 5, NLT

HE HEARS THE PICCOLO PLAYER

JOHN HENRY JOWETT says that when we think of ourselves as insignificant in a huge world—as just one among billions, with our contributions little appreciated—we should recognize that the eyes of God are on us. He recognizes all we do and all we intend. Jowett illustrates this by the story of a piccolo player who thought he could take a little break.

"At a great orchestral rehearsal, which Sir Michael Costa was conducting, the man who played the piccolo stayed his fingers for a moment, thinking that his trifling contribution would never be missed. At once, Sir Michael raised his hand and said, 'Stop! Where's the piccolo?' He missed the individual note."

Our Lord is aware of and sees each contribution we make. Those around us may or may not appreciate us, but they need not be our reference point.

One believer, discouraged by a lack of recognition for his constant hard work and pure intentions, wrote these words in large, bold letters on a card: "FOR HIS EYES ONLY." He carried the card in his pocket, where it would show up when he reached for his pen. He would then pull it out, look at the proclamation, and smile. His efforts were seen by the one who would not only judge but encourage and bless, the one who ultimately mattered.

Jowett says the Lord uses "the note of my life to make the music of his kingdom, and if the note be absent he will miss it, and the glorious music will be broken and incomplete."

In contrast, Jowett affirms this hope: "By the power of his grace we can accomplish wonders."

---

*Lord, put me in tune with your music. Keep my
eyes on you as my Conductor, and help me move
with your rhythms. Draw me into full harmony
with you, praising you for wonders to come.*

God has given each of you a gift from his great variety of spiritual gifts. Use them well to serve one another. I PETER 4:10, NLT

EMBRACING ADVENTURE

LUCI SHAW tells us, "Each of us is at risk. And each of us must learn to live with it and even thrive on it."

Really? Thrive on risk? Isn't that for the few who long for wild adventures? But Shaw observes that in this age of terrorism, "dread is almost guaranteed"; furthermore, even ordinary tasks such as driving in traffic can make life risky indeed.

Shaw makes these assertions in her book *The Crime of Living Cautiously*, with the subtitle *Hearing God's Call to Adventure*. She highlights Jesus' parable about the timid servant burying his master's money and asserts that Jesus saw the servant's timidity as criminal neglect.

Does God call us to adventure? If so, adventure by its nature requires dangerous risk. That's one reason we like action movies! Yet it's one thing to watch an adventure film with the heroine on a grapevine dangling over crocodiles; it's another to actually face our own troubles, with their crocodilian teeth.

In these tumultuous times, how can we confront our fears?

Over and over in the Bible when an angel appears, his first words are, "Fear not." The angels bring news of what God is up to. As Luci Shaw notes in 1 John 4:18, "Perfect love casts out fear" (NKJV).

Life as adventure? It's a matter of faith. The truth is, we're all plopped down in circumstances that can threaten, dishearten, or even overwhelm us. Yet most of us also have many good things happening around us. Only as we see life as an adventure from God do we experience life's tang and purpose.

Luci Shaw asks, "Has your heart ever been blown open by the sudden exhilarating thought, *This could be my Year of Living the Adventure?* And if not, why not?"

Father, you know how my anxiety rises when I think about all that can go wrong! When life seems not an adventure but a miserable muddle, please cast out my fear. Help me to embrace my adventure.

The LORD directs the steps of the godly. He delights in every detail of their lives. Though they stumble, they will never fall, for the LORD holds them by the hand.
PSALM 37:23-24, NLT

BEARING OTHERS' DEFECTS

JOHN WESLEY writes, "God is the first object of our love: Its next office is to bear the defects of others. And we should begin the practice of this amidst our own household."

It's fascinating how bearing others' faults comes up repeatedly in the writings of spiritual guides such as Thomas à Kempis, who wrote long before Wesley. Apparently, the human condition hasn't changed for centuries—whether in homes or in monasteries. We're all human, with human defects, and sin keeps squirming like the proverbial worm in the apple.

Wesley's challenge to live a holy life and to love other people had remarkable effects. Through his small groups, which he called bands, he witnessed countless transformations. Always methodical in everything he did, he got very specific when urging listeners and readers to love others: "We should chiefly exercise our love toward those who most shock . . . our way of thinking." In other words, we should love people who have terrible ideas. Beyond that, he added, we should love those who make us really mad!

Wesley was not lecturing merely to others. He had an extremely difficult marriage, and he knew that showing love is far from child's play. To draw upon God's wisdom and strength, he made a practice of praying while traveling on horseback.

"Give to my eyes refreshing tears," he asked the Lord. "Give to my soul the love all heaven's hosts inspire." Only God could provide the love Wesley sought.

In response to the biblical admonition to "pray without ceasing," Wesley writes, "All that a Christian does, even in eating and sleeping, is prayer. Prayer continues in the desire of the heart, though the mind is on other things. In souls filled with love, the desire to please God is a continual prayer."

Heavenly Father, sometimes people frustrate me beyond patience. Please help me experience what John Wesley describes as having my soul filled with love, even when someone shakes me to the core and shocks my way of thinking.

Love is patient and kind. Love is not jealous or boastful or proud or rude. It does not demand its own way. It is not irritable, and it keeps no record of being wronged.
I CORINTHIANS 13:4-5, NLT

A FLASH OF LIGHTNING

HENRI NOUWEN confessed that when he met with Mother Teresa of Calcutta, he started explaining all his problems as soon as they sat down. For ten minutes, he tried to convince her how complicated they were.

When he was finally quiet, Mother Teresa said, "Well, when you spend one hour a day adoring your Lord and never do anything you know is wrong . . . you will be fine."

Nouwen's response? "I realized, suddenly, that she had punctured my big balloon of complex self-complaints and pointed me far beyond myself to the place of real healing. I had raised a question from below and she had given an answer from above—from God's place and not the place of my complaints. Mother Teresa's answer was like a flash of lightning in my darkness."

Our setbacks, struggles, doubts, and insecurities can enmesh us in severe complications. We want solutions. We want practical answers. A simple answer "from above" often strikes us as irrelevant to the problem, as it did at first to Henri Nouwen. After all, he was an Ivy League professor and understood the complications of life. Yet many problems cannot be "solved," and other times the solution is in our seeing the maze of difficulties through God's eyes.

Nouwen advises, "Your life, my life, is given graciously by God. Our lives are not problems to be solved but journeys to be taken with Jesus as our friend and finest guide."

Lord Jesus, my need for you to guide me is greater
than ever. My journey seems a thicket of troubles,
with no pathway out. Please grant me your perspective
and your confidence as you lead me today.

Humble yourselves under the mighty power of God, and at the right time he will lift you up in honor. Give all your worries and cares to God, for he cares about you.
I PETER 5:6-7, NLT

NO UGLY SISTERS

JILL BRISCOE describes her sister as very beautiful and says she always adored her. "It was no problem to me at all that the boys wanted to get to know me so they could get to know her! But even though I was more than grateful to bask in her glory, the inevitable happened, and I developed a very low self-image."

Family relationships and countless experiences shape us and form what we think of ourselves. Our natural self-absorption limits our capacity to transcend our actual and perceived limitations.

Briscoe is brutally honest in her confession: "I never realized how self-centered I was until I began to practice being still and quiet. There I was, filling the center of my thinking. I couldn't escape from my self-absorption. I was everywhere. I found that if I asked God to help me change my self-absorption to God-absorption and sat there long enough for him to do that renewing work within me, it actually began to happen."

Centering our thoughts on God has the remarkable effect of lifting them from ourselves. When we consider his wonderful works, his majesty, and his love for us and recognize the purpose and meaning he has built into our lives, we can become compassionate toward the concerns of others. We can lend a helping hand, oblivious for the moment to what others might think.

Jill Briscoe says of her own self-image that she had to learn that God is purposeful and has his own reasons for making us as we are. "It's hard to understand that God likes me when I don't like myself," she says. She eventually came to realize that "there are no ugly sisters in God's sight."

---

*Lord, help me not to worry about my appearance and
what others think of me. Let my identity come from
you as my heavenly Father. Thank you for loving me
and for sending your Son for our redemption.*

---

*I remember your wonderful deeds of long ago. They are constantly in my thoughts. . . .
O God, your ways are holy. . . . You are the God of great wonders!*
PSALM 77:11-14, NLT

SEASONS TO CATCH YOUR BREATH

FRANÇOIS FÉNELON encourages us by saying, "Let the ups and downs of your spiritual life come and go. If you were always down, you would become hardened and discouraged. God gives you seasons when you can catch your breath."

Then he gets personal. "Let me tell you about myself. When I suffer, I can never see an end to my trials. And when relief comes, I am so suspicious that the suffering is not really over that I hesitate to accept my rest. It seems to me that to accept both 'good' and 'bad' seasons alike is to be truly fruitful. Accept both comfort and correction from the hand of God."

Fénelon then admits, "This is all very easy for me to say to you, but I want you to know that I cringe at the very thought of the cross coming to work in me."

How very human we all are—even great heroes of the faith. We run hot and cold spiritually, for countless reasons. Remember how Elijah sank into depression right after he had vanquished Jezebel's priests in one of history's most dramatic confrontations? He was so fearful that it took an angel to buck him up, even though he had shortly before acted with the faith and power of a superhero.

Though we may experience victories in our spiritual journeys, we also trip and fall. It's then that we understand the apostle Paul's insight that when we're weak, we're strong.

One reason the writings of François Fénelon have spoken to millions over the years is his mark of authenticity. "If I sound a bit pessimistic, it is because I am writing to you in the midst of a spiritual dry spell. I don't know what tomorrow brings." Nor do we. Fénelon concludes by saying about his next-day anxieties, "God will do what seems good to him. Sometimes what he wants is hard to accept." Yet Fénelon offers this hope: "Listen to God—there is true freedom, peace, and joy in him."

Father, when storms come into my life, I get all caught up in bailing out the boat. When what I'm doing seems purposeless, I lose the sense of your energy and presence. Today, please pour your light and power into my life.

Shout with joy to the LORD, all the earth! Worship the LORD with gladness. Come before him, singing with joy. PSALM 100:1-2, NLT

TOURIST OR PILGRIM?

EUGENE PETERSON observes that millions make decisions for Christ but then are captured by a "tourist mind-set." They want instant spirituality, "adopting the lifestyle of a tourist and wanting only the high points."

That perspective contrasts sharply with developing a mature Christian life. The title of one of Peterson's books, *A Long Obedience in the Same Direction*, captures what discipleship actually requires.

An authentic spiritual journey is more than merely an enriching experience— a museum visit or getting an advanced degree. It's a rigorous adventure, in many ways as demanding of our bodies and souls as the tales told by Homer, Tolstoy, or Hemingway.

Peterson contrasts the idea of a spiritual tourist with two biblical words: *disciple* and *pilgrim*.

As disciples, we learn from our Master throughout our life's journey. Peterson says that our learning—unlike gathering information and insight in a school or an online course—is like being "at the work site of a craftsman." We learn right in the midst of our tumultuous lives, with Jesus the master carpenter and craftsman guiding and deepening us as we learn and grow.

We are also pilgrims on a lifetime journey. With a strange sense that this world is not our home—despite our firm attachment to it—we seek the way to the Father's house.

How do we find our way? Peterson tells us: "Abraham, who 'went out,' is our archetype. Jesus, answering Thomas's question, 'Lord, we do not know where you are going; how can we know the way?' gives us direction. 'I am the way, the truth, and the life. No one can come to the Father except through me.'"

Father in heaven, help me to be not a tourist but a pilgrim and a disciple. Guide me and fill my mind and spirit with your Spirit. Keep me faithful on my journey as each new challenge appears.

Let us strip off every weight that slows us down, especially the sin that so easily trips us up. And let us run with endurance the race God has set before us. HEBREWS 12:1, NLT

OUT OF DESPAIR

JONI EARECKSON TADA, paralyzed at seventeen, lay in a hospital Stryker frame at night wanting to die. For days, she had begged her friends to help her commit suicide, to bring her sleeping pills or razor blades.

"I wanted so much to die, but God wouldn't let me die. From the numb blackness of my despair, I suddenly found myself praying, *God, if I can't die, show me how to live, please!*"

Lying facedown in the Stryker frame, Tada says she knew she had nothing to bring to God. Yet her short, simple prayer started the changes in her that have led to decades of remarkable ministry and spiritual joy.

We may not be physically paralyzed, but sometimes we may feel just as constrained by our troubles and plunged into despair. Or we may face drudgery and hopeless tedium, with no sense of purpose. In some difficulties, we may not feel as if we can pray at all. Yet whatever our feelings, if we reach out to God with a simple prayer, we will start to sense his strength and presence.

Sometimes that's a lengthy process—as it was with Joni Eareckson Tada. Yet the starting point is to call in our distress. "Pray and mean it," she says. "You just might start living the impossible."

Some would say that living the impossible is what Tada has done all these years. She has written marvelous books, married, founded and led an organization, and even starred in a movie about her life—all while still paralyzed!

Joni Eareckson Tada quotes Psalm 34:18, which has encouraged so many in extreme situations: "The LORD is close to the brokenhearted and saves those who are crushed in spirit" (NIV).

---

*Lord, my troubles may not compare to Joni's, but
they're formidable. Lift me, I pray. Show me how to
live—this moment and all through the day. Begin
the fresh changes you want to bring into my life.*

---

*I prayed to the LORD, and he answered me. He freed me from all my fears. . . . In my
desperation I prayed, and the LORD listened; he saved me from all my troubles.*
PSALM 34:4, 6, NLT

OUR ACTIVE COMFORTER

CHARLES HADDON SPURGEON identifies the Holy Spirit as our Teacher, who makes dark things light and unravels mysteries—in contrast to Satan the deceiver, who runs the poisonous devil's college that leads to everlasting ruin. Spurgeon also identifies the Spirit as our Advocate, who makes intercession for us. Then he explores at length the Spirit's role as Comforter, describing him in the following terms:

A loving Comforter. Spurgeon says that a stranger's words of comfort run over us "like oil on marble"—but the words of someone who loves us deeply are like music.

A faithful Comforter. In dark days of trouble, friends may betray us, but the Holy Spirit shelters us and cares for us.

An unwearied Comforter. Sometimes, others may give up on us, but the Spirit relentlessly pursues us with his love.

A wise Comforter. Unlike Job's comforters, the Holy Spirit cuts directly to the root of the soul's trouble and applies just the right astringent or balm.

A safe Comforter. In contrast to our soul's enemy, the Spirit comforts but does not coddle, drawing us to the safety of his protection. Spurgeon adds, "He does not comfort by words, but by deeds. He intercedes with Jesus. He gives us grace and promises. He is ever-present, so you never have to send for him. Your God is always near you when you need comfort in your distress. He is an ever-present help in time of trouble."

Sometimes, our life experiences can be crushing or bewildering. Sometimes they're exhilarating and full of triumph. Whatever we experience, the Holy Spirit cares. He is ready to challenge, cleanse, celebrate, instruct, and comfort us. We need only turn to him in prayer.

Holy Spirit of God, I want to be holy, and I want to be wholly in step with you. I'm in need of your comfort and your wisdom. Keep me from buying into any ideas from "the devil's college." Fill me with your truth.

Those who are dominated by the sinful nature think about sinful things, but those who are controlled by the Holy Spirit think about things that please the Spirit.
ROMANS 8:5, NLT

IN TROUBLE? TO THE ROOFS!

ALAN PATON said that when he faced an insurmountable problem, he always thought of German aircraft dropping tons of high-explosive and incendiary bombs on London in 1940. "While Londoners sheltered in basements, strategic and historic buildings burned above their heads. If this kept going on, nothing would be left of London."

Paton remembered Winston Churchill's proclamation: "'To the basements' must be replaced by, 'To the roofs!'" The citizens of London rallied to the cause, and Churchill later said, "Many became adept, and thousands of fires were extinguished before they took hold. The experience of remaining on the roof night after night under fire, with no protection but a tin hat, became habitual."

Sometimes, we may feel hunkered down in the basement of our lives with all sorts of incendiaries exploding above us. We want protection from the fires and the explosions of our troubles. Yet, staying hunkered down may not be nearly as safe as scurrying up the stairs and onto the roof to fight the flames.

Alan Paton, author of *Cry, the Beloved Country,* was a courageous Christian who battled apartheid in South Africa. He endured persecution and bitter hostility, yet he kept the faith, like a Londoner on a burning roof. "There is only one thing I can do in times like these," he said. "I must ask to be made an instrument of God's peace, so that one more healing stream may flow into the river of hate."

Whatever our circumstances, we can either call on the Lord to help us stand firm or we can give in to our fears.

Paton prayed, "Lord, save us from a retreat into hatred or despair. Call us out of the shelters and send us up to the roofs, even if day and night we are under fire. May we remain calm in the midst of violence and panic, and may reason and love and mercy and understanding rule our lives."

Lord, please grant me courage and integrity when
I'm called to stand fast in difficult times. Equip
me for what's ahead. Fill me with your Spirit
and make me an instrument of your peace.

This is my command—be strong and courageous! Do not be afraid or discouraged. For the LORD your God is with you wherever you go. JOSHUA 1:9, NLT

ARE YOU BROKENHEARTED?

NANCY GUTHRIE asserts that "God loves brokenhearted people." She quotes Psalm 34:18: "The LORD is close to the brokenhearted; he rescues those whose spirits are crushed" (NLT).

Guthrie knows well what it's like to be crushed in spirit and brokenhearted. When she was pregnant, a doctor told her that the baby girl she was carrying had Zellweger syndrome, a rare metabolic disorder that includes severe brain damage, the inability to see or hear, and internal bleeding. Such infants usually live less than six months. Guthrie learned that, after giving birth, she would be taking her baby home to die.

You can imagine how wrenching were her pregnancy and her daughter Hope's short life. In the months following Hope's death, Nancy felt empty, disappointed, lonely, and sad.

She and her husband, David, decided they would have no more children—but then they were surprised by a new pregnancy. Tragically, they learned early on that this child, a boy they named Gabriel, also had Zellweger syndrome. Like Hope, he would live for only a short time.

"I remember when it first hit me," Nancy Guthrie says. "The depth of the cry bordering on a scream bubbled inside and then burst out of me. It scared me, and I know it scared David." Out of those unimaginable, bittersweet experiences Nancy has written thoughtful, faith-filled books. She mined the book of Job for its rich insights about both God's silence and his engagement. She embraced hope, quoting Isaiah 25:8: "The Sovereign LORD will wipe away all tears" (NLT).

Why does God love us when we are brokenhearted? The richness of Nancy's personal journey gives us clues. Her broken heart led her to discover infinite depths of love in the Father who had sent his only Son to this broken world.

Nancy Guthrie concludes that only when we're shaken to the core do we give up our own plans. "Jesus calls us to abandon our agendas so that the abundant life he offers has room to take root and grow. This is not an extreme brand of discipleship only for go-getters. This is the call for everyone."

Loving Father, bring deep into my soul the sense
that you really do love me. Lift me into your hope,
and let me share your hope with others today.
Wipe away my tears and bring me new life.

Praise the LORD! How good to sing praises to our God! . . . He heals the brokenhearted and bandages their wounds. PSALM 147:1, 3, NLT

THAT'S UNFAIR!!!

January 15

THOMAS À KEMPIS wrote centuries ago, "It's good for us that at times we have sorrows and adversities. It's good we sometimes endure opposition and are evilly and wrongly judged, when our actions are good, for then we seek God's witness in the heart."

Sorrow and adversity good for us? The idea feels both jarring and crazy. It's *good* to be *unfairly* judged?

You've probably been unfairly judged; if so, it surely didn't feel good! Unfair criticisms and attacks make us angry and determined to set the matter straight.

Yet this disturbing challenge from Thomas à Kempis carries a compelling truth: only what God thinks ultimately counts.

That truth relates to another extremely tough reality: as Christians, we are called not to *get* justice but to *give* justice.

In our culture, this is viewed as foolishness. A popular magazine runs a column titled "That's Outrageous." We love to be outraged and to demand our rights. We're often called a litigious society because our courts are clogged with lawsuits, and we'll sue the instant we think our rights have been trampled.

Righteous indignation has its place as we try to view the world's injustice through our heavenly Father's eyes. Yet Thomas à Kempis says that unfair criticism can deepen us and refine our souls. The Holy Spirit is praying for us in the process!

Jesus certainly didn't get justice. Yet in his Father's plans, out of that injustice came the wonder of the world's redemption.

Lord, I'm so human! You know that when someone accuses
or wounds me, I react. Fill me, I pray, with your Spirit.
Help me see through your eyes. If I need to learn from
my critics, let me listen, secure in your love and care.

I will rejoice in the LORD. I will be glad because he rescues me. . . . Then I will proclaim your justice, and I will praise you all day long. PSALM 35:9, 28, NLT

HOPE IN DEEP TROUBLE

ED DOBSON tells about the time his cat climbed into the dryer and onto the top of some warm clothes. Dobson's wife didn't know the cat was in there and closed the dryer door. Then she pushed the start button. When she suddenly heard terrible noises coming from the dryer as it tumbled, she opened the door. The cat staggered out with hair sticking out in every direction and a totally dazed look on its face.

Dobson compares the way his cat felt at that moment to what happened to him in a doctor's office when he was diagnosed with ALS (Lou Gehrig's disease). Before that moment, he says, he felt warm and comfortable, like the cat in the dryer. After he heard the terrible news that he had a terminal disease, he was staggered and dazed.

He draws another parallel to being dazed like that—the feelings of Jesus' disciples the evening before their Master's death. Jesus told them that, despite his leaving them, they should not be *troubled*. Not troubled? There they were, facing disaster.

Medical diagnoses. Accidents. Profound losses of all sorts. Everyone experiences disasters in this life—or we fear disasters that may come. How can we not feel troubled? Here is what Jesus said to his dazed disciples when he was soon to leave them: "Don't let your hearts be troubled. Trust in God, and trust also in me. There is more than enough room in my Father's home. If this were not so, would I have told you that I am going to prepare a place for you?" (John 14:1-2, NLT).

Although, like the disciples, we may face grim circumstances and disappointments, our ultimate hope is for the life to come. We are given many promises of God's faithfulness to us in this life, including Jesus' promise that the Holy Spirit would be our comforter and lead us into truth. Yet our ultimate hope is in what is being prepared for us beyond this world.

"Even though Jesus has gone back to the Father," Dobson says, "he has not forgotten about us."

---

*Lord, I do trust in you. Please increase my faith
when troubles come, and enable me to live in hope of
all you are preparing. When I hear news that scares
me, please grant me your courage and calm.*

I am leaving you with a gift—peace of mind and heart. And the peace I give is a gift the world cannot give. So don't be troubled or afraid. JOHN 14:27, NLT

WHEN WE CAN'T STAND
THE KITCHEN

BROTHER LAWRENCE said he was happy to pick up a piece of straw from the ground just for the love of God, not looking for anything in return, but seeking the Lord alone.

Over the centuries, readers of Brother Lawrence's letters and written conversations have been intrigued by the image of the awkward, barefoot monk bending for that straw with a wonderful sense of God's presence. What was going on? How did he find such joy and contentment in his simple daily tasks?

Even more intriguing is his confession that although he worked in the monastery kitchen for fifteen years, he had "a strong natural aversion" to it! Somehow that didn't matter. He was "always doing small things for the love of God." He had formed the habit of conversing with God, constantly practicing God's presence no matter what the circumstances.

How might we emulate this humble brother? Pick up some litter. Peel the carrots. Write a paragraph. Drive to the store. Say a kind word to someone. *All as acts of service for God.*

Is it possible to *consciously* do that, moment by moment?

Brother Lawrence worked at it, and his attitude resulted in God's giving him "endless gifts of grace."

We might dislike the tasks at hand, but doing everything we do as service for God changes our perspective. Brother Lawrence's secret was not changing what he did, but "doing for God what we commonly do for ourselves."

---

*Lord, you know my thoughts. Infuse my mind with
what Brother Lawrence practiced. When I'm distracted
from you, transform my thoughts. Father, if I wander,
please bring me back and lift me into your arms.*

---

*Work willingly at whatever you do, as though you were working for the Lord rather than
for people. Remember that the Lord will give you an inheritance as your reward, and
that the Master you are serving is Christ.* COLOSSIANS 3:23-24, NLT

CATCHING THE WIND

ROSEMARY BUDD, describing a magical moment with her young daughter, writes, "Suddenly, Susannah jerked away from me. 'I'm going to catch the wind,' she declared and whooped as she ran in imitation of its gusts and bursts. She skipped up and down the path. One of the wind's tails flipped her scarf across her eyes. She pulled it back with a laugh and a 'tut.' The wind galloped in her hair this way and that, riding it, tearing at its roots, hard and demanding. A lighter touch sent the hem of her coat into ripples. Behind the fat bole of a lime tree, I found her leaning back against the bark, eyes closed and breathless."

The Holy Spirit is described in Scripture as the wild, unpredictable desert wind. This description of Susannah reminds us of all the ways the Spirit surprises us, sometimes rattling and roughing us up—and changing everything. If only we would respond as Susannah did when that happens!

"Susannah had not caught the wind," her mother writes, "but the wind in an amazing variety of speeds and touches had caught her—hair, eyes, cheeks, legs, energy. It had caught her, bowled through her, and showed not the slightest dent in its energy for having done so."

Jesus says in John 3:8: "The wind blows wherever it wants. . . . You can hear the wind but can't tell where it comes from or where it is going" (NLT).

Not long after Jesus said that, the Spirit came to believers at Pentecost as a mighty, rushing wind. He invaded their lives and tongues and lifted them to praise and give glory to God.

It's up to the Spirit to gust his way into our lives or to ruffle our thoughts or to gently breathe his blessings on us. Our role is to respond like faithful, exuberant children.

Holy Spirit of God, you are mysterious, and I'm not always sure how I can respond to you. Let your wind have its way with me; quicken my senses so I'll be fully responsive to you, ready to feel your wind and revel in your refreshing breezes.

After this prayer, the meeting place shook, and they were all filled with the Holy Spirit.
ACTS 4:31, NLT

OUR ORIGINAL DESIGN

JOHN ORTBERG says we were created to be masterpieces. Though made in God's image, we are fallen creatures whom God longs to restore to our original condition and beauty.

Ortberg has plenty of inspired support for his assertion. He quotes the apostle Paul, who says that we are "God's workmanship" (Ephesians 2:10, NIV), his "work of art." Paul also writes about Christ being "formed" in us (Galatians 4:19, NIV) and being "transformed by the renewing of your mind" (Romans 12:2, KJV). A prayer by Søren Kierkegaard succinctly captures the idea of the original starting to become reality: "And now Lord, with your help I shall become myself."

John Ortberg sees us in a spiritual gestation process: "We are pregnant with possibilities of spiritual growth and moral beauty." To emphasize the grandeur of what this means, he quotes the familiar yet always striking words of C. S. Lewis: "It is a serious thing to live in a society of possible gods and goddesses, to remember that the dullest and most uninteresting person you talk to may one day be a creature which, if you saw it now, you would be strongly tempted to worship."

The process of becoming what Lewis and Ortberg describe starts here and now, not in some celestial birthing place after our time on earth is done. "We are called by God to live as our uniquely created selves," Ortberg says. "To grow spiritually means to live increasingly as Jesus would in our unique place—to perceive what Jesus would perceive if he looked through our eyes, to think what he would think, to feel what he would feel, and therefore to do what he would do."

The alternative is to become less and less like the original—which would be a tragedy beyond words. Lewis explains the stakes: "It is immortals whom we joke with, work with, marry, snub, and exploit—immortal horrors or everlasting splendors."

Father above, I see pregnancy and birth as a very natural process. Is a similar process taking place in me spiritually? Help me to nurture your new life within me. Restore me to your original design and purpose for me.

We will speak the truth in love, growing in every way more and more like Christ.
EPHESIANS 4:15, NLT

THE FATHER IN THE DARK FOREST January 20

HELMUT THIELICKE, as a young Lutheran pastor in Stuttgart, Germany, during World War II, resisted the Nazis and kept true to the gospel. When the Allies began to bomb German cities, Thielicke would see anxiety and fear on the faces of his congregation as they awaited the screams of the air raid sirens. Theirs was "a world in which the furies had been unleashed."

To these distressed Germans, Thielicke preached on the Lord's Prayer. In the chaos of a devastating world war, many wondered, *Where is the heavenly Father?* With their cities in ruins and their sons, fathers, and husbands in early graves, they were acutely aware of how "unfatherly" the world was.

The experiences of these German Christians in their bombed-out city may seem remote. Yet, even if we are safe in our own communities, we see on our television screens new violence and devastation every day. This world in many ways is still an "unfatherly" place.

In his Lord's Prayer message, Thielicke described people who do not believe in the heavenly Father as walking alone through a forest in the gloom of night. They are fearful and cannot suppress the deep yearning to have a Father and to know they are safe with him.

Deep within the human soul is a deep yearning for the Father. Thielicke emphasized that it was Jesus himself who taught us to pray the Our Father and that he comes to meet us in the dark forest. The Father's heart beats for us.

When we are overwhelmed by the world's chaos or by personal grief or fears, we can call on the Father who loves us. "Part of the good news of the Gospel," Thielicke writes, "is that there is a Father to whom we can tell our doubts, even our doubts whether there is a Father."

Father in heaven, when I see all the terrible things
that happen to people on every continent, it makes me
wonder how this can be your world. Help me to put my
hand in yours, to trust you, and to be your child.

Jesus said, "This is how you should pray: 'Father, may your name be kept holy. May your Kingdom come soon.'" LUKE 11:2, NLT

WHY PRAY?

PHILIP YANCEY admits that although we may live and breathe and have our being in God, his personal awareness of God's presence is sometimes "as fickle as the weather."

Some things, such as beauty in nature and encounters with authentic believers, feed Yancey's faith. Other things, such as God's seeming silence and inaction despite the world's endless atrocities, feed his doubts.

Sometimes, we may wonder why we pray—especially when we don't feel we're "connecting" with God, or when we pray earnestly and our prayers appear unanswered. Countless reasons keep us from prayer, and countless discouragements create all sorts of questions about prayer.

Yancey says that if he had to answer the question "Why pray?" in one sentence, it would be, "Because Jesus did!"

The communication between Jesus and his heavenly Father was constant. It was the source of his marching orders and his powerful sense of identity. We're invited to have that same sort of communication, to get our marching orders and identity as beloved children of the Father. At the same time, we must recognize that prayer is steeped in mystery and is far more like great literature than like mathematics.

The familiar question, "What would Jesus do?" might first be answered by knowing that he would pray.

Yancey writes of Jesus, "While on earth he became vulnerable, as we are vulnerable; rejected, as we are rejected; and tested, as we are tested. In every case his response was prayer."

Father in heaven, when I'm vulnerable, distressed,
and anxious about what's happening, let me respond
by coming to you. Help me not to react in ways that
make situations worse. Teach me your ways to peace.

Jesus prayed this prayer: "O Father, Lord of heaven and earth, thank you for hiding these things from those who think themselves wise and clever, and for revealing them to the childlike." MATTHEW 11:25, NLT

THE UBIQUITOUS KNOCK

OLE HALLESBY points us to Jesus' promise in Revelation 3:20 as the key that opens the door to holy and blessed prayer: "Look!" Jesus says. "I stand at the door and knock. If you hear my voice and open the door, I will come in, and we will share a meal together as friends" (NLT).

Hallesby believes that no other passage in the Bible throws more light on prayer than this invitation from Jesus. "To pray is to let Jesus come into our hearts," he writes. "It is not our prayer which moves the Lord Jesus. It is Jesus who moves us to pray. He knocks."

Jesus takes the initiative, and our prayers are a result of his knocking at the door of our hearts. "He knocks in order to move us by prayer to open the door and accept the gift he had already appointed for us."

Hallesby uses as an illustration the air around us that is always ready to enter our lungs. "From time immemorial, prayer has been spoken of as the breath of the soul," he says. "Air seeks to enter our bodies and exerts pressure. The air our souls need also envelops us at all times. God is round about us in Christ, with his many-sided and all-sufficient grace. All we need to do is open our parched and withered hearts."

Jesus says that if anyone opens the door, he will come in. Just as air enters our bodies when we breathe, Jesus enters our hearts when we invite him in; he loves us, bringing meaning and grace into our lives.

His promise to share a meal with us as friends when we open the door brings a spirit of celebration. Hallesby writes, "God has designed prayer as a means of intimate and joyous fellowship."

Lord Jesus, I open my heart's door to your knock. Please come in. You know all about the needs of my heart and my longings. Fill me with your presence and your love.

I will answer them before they even call to me. While they are still talking about their needs, I will go ahead and answer their prayers! ISAIAH 65:24, NLT

GOD THE HIDING PLACE

January 23

BILLY GRAHAM makes a thoughtful observation: "Sometimes life touches one person with a bouquet and another with a thorn bush. But the first may find a wasp in the flowers, and the second may discover roses among the thorns."

Bouquets, wasps, roses, thorns—they come to all of us in strange sequences and indecipherable patterns. No one gets all flowers without any wasps, though we all hope for that. The human condition is such that sorrow and grief come to every home and every person.

From long experience, Graham concluded that it's very often people with the most vital faith who experience the deepest suffering. To give an example, he tells a story about his friend Corrie ten Boom.

For sheltering Jews from the Nazis in her native Holland, Corrie and her sister Betsie were taken to Ravensbrück concentration camp, where they suffered terribly. Corrie survived the war, but Betsie died before the camp could be liberated.

By the time Corrie ten Boom was eighty-five, many good things had come to her in America, and a colleague chanced to remark about how good God was to provide for her. She answered in a way that gives us much pause for reflection: "God was good to me when I was in Ravensbrück, too."

Many of us have heard and repeated the affirmation, "God is good all the time." When we put that in the context of Corrie ten Boom's experience in the concentration camp where her sister died, it powerfully demonstrates the link between vital faith and suffering.

In solitary confinement for four months in a dark, wet cell, Corrie ten Boom heard the screams of people being tortured. She was terrified and cried out to the Lord. She noticed an ant run into its hiding place in the wall and sensed God saying to her that he was her hiding place. She could run to him.

Billy Graham often quotes Corrie ten Boom as saying, "The worst can happen, but the *best* remains."

Lord, help me in my circumstances to concentrate on the best—what you are doing and the grace you bring into my life. Let Corrie ten Boom's example of seeing your best in the worst bring forth praise from me, no matter what.

The LORD is my shepherd; I have all that I need. . . . Surely your goodness and unfailing love will pursue me all the days of my life. PSALM 23:1, 6, NLT

MINISTERING TO JESUS

MOTHER TERESA presented this challenge: "All of us, you and I, should use what God has given us, that for which God created us. For God has created us for great things: to love and to give love."

What makes things great? Mother Teresa says, "It is how much love we put in the doing that makes our offering something beautiful for God."

Billy Graham visited Mother Teresa in Calcutta. When he was introduced to her, she was holding a dying man in her arms, and Graham waited as she helped the man face death. When he died, she prayed and gently lowered him to his bed. Then "this tiny, wrinkled, radiant lady" turned to greet Graham.

They talked till dusk, and here is how Billy Graham says she explained her calling to him:

"Mother Teresa looks past the physical features of every man, woman, or child and sees the face of Jesus staring up at her through them. In every starving child she feeds, she sees Jesus. Surrounding every lonely, dying man she cradles in her arms is Jesus. When she ministers to anyone, she is ministering to her Savior and Lord."

Mother Teresa often referred to the poor and dying as being Jesus in "distressing disguise." She saw being abandoned and unwanted as the greatest poverty, and she daily ministered to people with love as if each were Jesus in distress.

Most of us will never pick up dying men or starving children from the streets, yet we must deal with the "irritable, the exacting, and the unreasonable" in our own lives. Mother Teresa demonstrated that it's a unique privilege to get beyond our frustrations and to share the joy and love of Jesus.

Impossible? "Love is a fruit," she says, "in season at all times and within the reach of every hand. Anyone may gather it, and no limit is set."

Lord Jesus, I want to sense your love today. Help me
to reach for it and see you in "distressing disguise"
in the faces of those I meet who need encouragement
and the love that comes only from you.

The King will say, "I tell you the truth, when you did it to one of the least of these my brothers and sisters, you were doing it to me!" MATTHEW 25:40, NLT

REFRESHING THEOLOGY

J. I. PACKER insists in his book *Knowing God* that the study of who God is and how we can grow to know him is a highly relevant and practical pursuit in our lives. He starts with a provocative illustration.

Suppose we were to fly a tribesman from the Amazon to London and simply dropped him in Trafalgar Square, this man with no knowledge of the language or how to survive in England. Leaving him to fend for himself would be cruel.

"So we are cruel to ourselves," Packer writes, "if we try to live in this world without knowing about the God whose world it is. The world becomes a strange, mad, painful place . . . for those who do not know about God."

Jim quotes Charles Spurgeon, who preached that the study of God humbles and expands our minds and souls. Spurgeon says that in contemplating Father, Son, and Holy Spirit we find a balm for our wounds and comfort in our grief.

"Would you lose your sorrows?" Spurgeon asks. "Would you drown your cares? Then go, plunge yourself in the Godhead's deepest sea; be lost in his immensity and you'll come forth as from a couch of rest, refreshed and invigorated. I know of nothing else that can so comfort the soul."

As we study the Scriptures and learn more and more about God's holiness and love, the more we will see *from his perspective* all that assaults us, all that weighs us down, all that tears apart our lives.

J. I. Packer says that as we gain an understanding of God's power and grace, this realization humbles us, encourages us, and reassures us. "We contemplate the unsearchable riches of divine mercy displayed in the Lord Jesus Christ. As our knowledge of God increases, so does our peace, our strength, and our joy."

Holy Spirit of God, Jesus said you would lead us to truth. Expand my thoughts about who you are and the majesty of your glory. Stretch my understanding and my soul so that I may bask in your grace and joy.

There is no one like the God of Israel. He rides across the heavens to help you, across the skies in majestic splendor. The eternal God is your refuge, and his everlasting arms are under you. DEUTERONOMY 33:26-27, NLT

EXTREME TEMPTATION

C. S. LEWIS asserts that the ultimate sin is Pride. "It is a terrible thing that the worst of all the vices can smuggle itself into the very center of our religious life." Lewis says that other vices, such as anger, greed, and drunkenness, are "mere fleabites in comparison" and come from our physical nature, but Pride, he observes, "comes direct from hell."

Direct from hell? Isn't that a bit extreme?

"It was through Pride that the devil became the devil," Lewis contends. "Pride leads to every other vice; it is the complete anti-God state of mind."

Lewis is not, of course, speaking of self-worth or of enjoying a compliment. He's referring to the pride that rises within us to be better than others, to have more than others, and to be "captains of our own fate." Who needs God when we can rise on our own?

In contrast to devilish pride, there's godly humility. Lewis emphasizes that God "wants to give you Himself." He predicts that those in touch with God "will, in fact, be humble—delightedly humble."

The pride that Satan tries to smuggle into us provides not delight but a rebel spirit. Some are puzzled about Jesus' scathing renunciations of religious leaders. He called them snakes and hypocrites and used language against them that would fit a brutal political campaign. These same leaders determined that Jesus should be crucified.

A thoughtful Christian once observed, "If I had lived in Jesus' day, I'd have been a Pharisee. I believe in the Scriptures as the Pharisees did." It sobered him to think he might be a modern counterpart to those who sent Jesus to the Cross.

It should sober us all! We who claim the Christian faith are determined to get our doctrines right, and we are often critical of those who cross our categories.

It was the Pharisees' pride that angered Jesus—and their lack of love. Jesus said the greatest commandments are to love God and love others. When we genuinely love God, we become "delightedly humble."

Lord, I'm a sinner saved by your grace. Keep me from being proud when I resist vices that have tripped up others. Let your magnificence and holiness fill my mind with awe and praise.

Seek the LORD, all who are humble, and follow his commands. ZEPHANIAH 2:3, NLT

WHO'S IN CHARGE?

BEN PATTERSON was lying on the floor in great pain from two ruptured discs. His doctor had prescribed six weeks of total rest. Bored and frustrated, Patterson decided to pray for every member of his church.

The process took about two hours each time, and day after day these times of prayer became sweet. As Patterson started getting better, he said to the Lord, "It's too bad I don't have time to do this when I'm at work."

He says that God confronted him with the fact he had twenty-four hours every day, and then the Lord nailed him with this: "The trouble with you, Ben, is when you're well, you think you're in charge; when you're sick, you know you're not."

Does it take being flat on our backs for us to realize we're not in charge? What might it take for us to genuinely believe that prayer is the essential work and that when we prioritize it, we're drawn into God's perspectives and presence?

The pace of life can squeeze out prayer; yet ironically, it is prayer that can enable us to cope with life.

Christ Jesus said, "Come to me, all of you who are weary and carry heavy burdens, and I will give you rest. Take my yoke upon you. Let me teach you, because I am humble and gentle at heart, and you will find rest for your souls" (Matthew 11:28-29, NLT).

A familiar hymn says it well:

> *What a friend we have in Jesus,*
> *All our sins and griefs to bear;*
> *What a privilege to carry,*
> *Everything to God in prayer.*

"Prayer is a discipline before it is a joy," writes Ben Patterson, "and it remains a discipline after it becomes a joy."

Lord, thank you for the privilege of prayer. I bring to you now all that troubles me, and I leave my burdens in your hands. Show me, Lord, how to make prayer and your grace the driving forces of my life.

I pray to you, O LORD, my rock. Do not turn a deaf ear to me. For if you are silent, I might as well give up and die. Listen to my prayer for mercy as I cry out to you for help. PSALM 28:1-2, NLT

WHAT LOVE DOES

FRED SMITH and JILL BRISCOE, in the book *Breakfast with Fred*, team up to illustrate that when we have someone who greatly loves us, it empowers us to adjust our attitudes and behavior.

Fred Smith remembers traveling in Europe with a nonbelieving business associate whom he expected to take advantage of the many sexual opportunities available. Yet all during the trip, the man talked only about his wife and their love for each other. Smith reports, "After attending a concert at LaScala, his only remark was, 'I wish she were here.' His response to her love became his strength."

Jill Briscoe recalls her own experiences with her father, whom she adored. When she was in high school, her boyfriend invited her to go to bed with him. She remembers her sister's saying, "Jill, if you ever get pregnant, it would kill Daddy!" Briscoe's love and reverence for her father kept her from yielding to temptation. In the same way, she says, her love for her heavenly Father helps her resist what would break his heart.

Knowing that God loves us personally gives us a sense of identity and security so we can approach life with purpose and drive. When we believe that God views us as his beloved—the way Jill Briscoe's father loved her—we become empowered to live in faith. This puts us on the path to joy.

Jill Briscoe writes of enjoying her father's company when they went fishing in the beautiful English Lake District, spending hours together trekking along the rivers. "So it has been with my heavenly Father," she writes. "Obedience without love is a miserable affair. Obedience with love is faith dancing!"

---

*Father who loves me, I pray you will bring into my
soul the assurance that you see me as your beloved.
Make my faith dance because I'm free and forgiven,
smiling because of my wonderful Father.*

We know how dearly God loves us, because he has given us the Holy Spirit to fill our hearts with his love. ROMANS 5:5, NLT

HEALING IN CHICAGO

D. L. MOODY made pastoral calls one day on homes in Chicago, and he was amazed to find grief and deep pain in every one.

In the first home, a woman with eyes red from weeping said that her only boy was addicted to alcohol and that last night he had come home drunk at midnight. In the next home, where children who attended Moody's Sunday school lived, the tearful mother showed Moody toys and little shoes that had belonged to her child who had died. In the next home, the woman's husband had left her, with winter coming on and no way for her to provide for her family. In the next home, an emotionally crushed woman told Moody that her son had left and she had no idea where he was.

"That afternoon," Moody said, "I made five calls, and in every home I found a broken heart. . . . Rich or poor," the evangelist declared, "none are exempt from broken hearts."

Moody then referred to Jesus' reading from Isaiah in Luke 4:18: "The Spirit of the Lord is upon me, because he hath anointed me to preach the gospel to the poor; he hath sent me to heal the brokenhearted, to preach deliverance to the captives, and recovering of sight to the blind, to set at liberty them that are bruised" (KJV).

In our own homes and in homes all around us are the bruised and the brokenhearted. Jesus listens as we call on him for his redemption, healing, and hope.

Lord, it's surely true that everywhere in my church and community are broken, bewildered hearts. Help me to pray and to be sensitive to what people are going through and to bring all burdens to you.

Help me understand the meaning of your commandments, and I will meditate on your wonderful deeds. I weep with sorrow; encourage me by your word.
PSALM 119:27-28, NLT

DON'T FORGET THE DEVIL

CALVIN MILLER warns that the devil is the lord of "feel-good," and he will teach us the fun of license rather than the power of self-denial. He says Satan relabels sinful acts as "gray." Then the devil asks, "Have you sinned? Certainly not!"

In our media-saturated world, we hear articulated back and forth everyone's opinion about every moral dilemma and enticement. As we sample the smorgasbord of compelling images and impassioned arguments, the devil whispers that it's all a muddle. "Don't try to figure it out—just do what feels good."

Miller offers counsel that he says he learned in the shadows: "Enjoy Christ. Bask in his love. Count his presence in your life the chief of all your joys. But never forget an opposite force is at work. The devil will circle you with gloom to obscure those moral values you learned from Christ."

So what do we do? Scripture and the Holy Spirit enable us to identify sin. When we do sin, we must not believe Satan's lie that we are always doomed to failure. We must repent and seek God's cleansing.

When we consider the hatred and terror so evident around the world and the moral degradation so evident on thousands of Web sites, it's clear that evil has a powerful foothold in the world. Scripture tells us that holy angels and wicked angels are at war—and we are right in the middle of it.

To gain victory in the battle with Satan, we must first be indwelt by the fullness of Christ in the person of his Spirit. We must clothe ourselves with his strength as described in Ephesians 6:11: "Put on all of God's armor so that you will be able to stand firm against all strategies of the devil" (NLT).

Satan is smart, subtle, and wily. More often than we might think, we need to call for spiritual reinforcements.

Spirit of God, sometimes with all that is happening, it seems the devil is winning. Please don't let him win in my thoughts or actions. Please, show me what you are thinking and planning for me. Equip me to obey.

"Get out of here, Satan," Jesus told him. "For the Scriptures say, 'You must worship the LORD your God and serve only him.'" MATTHEW 4:10, NLT

THE AUTHENTIC CHRISTIAN MARK   *January 31*

FRANCIS SCHAEFFER describes various symbols that people have displayed over the centuries to identify themselves as Christians. We're well familiar with the wearing of a cross on our clothing or on a chain around our necks. We put the fish symbol on cars and notebooks. Yet, Schaeffer writes, there's a much better sign, the universal mark that Jesus himself instituted.

The distinguishing mark of the Christian comes from Jesus' own command found in John 13:34-35: "I am giving you a new commandment: Love each other. Just as I have loved you, you should love each other. Your love for one another will prove to the world that you are my disciples" (NLT).

Why is love the ultimate identifying mark? Not only did Jesus command it, he said this would be the way people could tell whether a person is one of his disciples. The litmus test is love for one another.

Schaeffer points out that although someone may be a Christian without obeying this command, not showing the love of Christ rejects the Lord's own description of a disciple's identity.

"If you obey, you will wear the mark Christ gave," Schaeffer writes. He then expands the principle to include the other side of Jesus' teaching, as shown in the parable of the Good Samaritan: We are to love *all* persons, for all bear the image of God.

So how does the world view the way Christians treat one another? Is the mark Jesus instituted most often in evidence? Or is its opposite more common?

Research has shown that most young people view Christians as judgmental and lacking in love. Whatever the truth of their perceptions, we know what our marching orders are. Jesus commanded, "Love each other as I have loved you" (John 15:12, NIV).

---

*Lord Jesus, you know that sometimes I don't feel the
love you command. Right now I open my emotions and
my will to you. Please give me the love I lack and show
me how I can demonstrate love to others this day.*

God showed how much he loved us by sending his one and only Son into the world so that we might have eternal life through him. . . . Dear friends, since God loved us that much, we surely ought to love each other. I JOHN 4:9, 11, NLT

PRAY DESPITE DIRTY THOUGHTS

MARTIN LUTHER was an earthy guy, and he gives us some very straight talk: "Pray when you are in the heat of temptation—when your mind is preoccupied with thoughts of lust or revenge." If you feel "your dirty thoughts leave no room for prayer," Luther advises, pray anyway—and right away.

"At precisely the moment when you feel the strongest temptation, and you're least prepared to pray, go somewhere you can be alone. Pray the Lord's Prayer or any other prayer."

Never wait to pray, Luther urgently counsels. When we feel attacked and vulnerable and when we feel we don't have it in us to pray, we may find it helpful to pray prayers found in Scripture. If we have given in to temptation and sinned, we can call on both the Holy Spirit and the Lord Jesus, for we are told they intercede for us with the Father.

Luther says we must never despair when we sin, but we should seek God's mercy. "Lift your eyes upward," he urges, "where Christ intercedes for you. He pleads for you, saying, 'Father, for this person I have suffered. I am looking after this person.'"

What a remarkable reality! God the Son and God the Holy Spirit pray for us! What a magnificent reason for us not to wait to pray, no matter the circumstances.

"Christ was born for us," Luther says. "He suffered for us. He ascended into heaven for our sake, sits at the right hand of the Father, and prays for us."

Father, it's amazing that I can call on you, the same
"Abba" that Jesus called on, the Father with whom
he intercedes. I pray you'll give me a glimpse of the
wonder of all this and that you will cleanse me.

I am writing this to you so that you will not sin. But if anyone does sin, we have an advocate who pleads our case before the Father. He is Jesus Christ, the one who is truly righteous. I JOHN 2:1, NLT

DESPERATE HAVOC

OSWALD CHAMBERS, speaking to British troops in Egypt in 1916, said, "The Bible and our common sense agree that the basis of human life is tragic." He was expounding on the book of Job and observed, in light of the horrors the listening troops were facing, "Many a man through this war has lost his form of belief in God and imagines that he has thereby lost God."

The longer we live, the more we recognize the sobering reality that life is tragic. Why? In Job we see fascinating glimpses into what's really going on. We read dialogue between God and Satan that makes us realize that what's happening in our lives and around the world has spiritual dimensions far beyond what we can see.

Both our heavenly Father and the enemy of our souls are at work in the midst of our troubles and grief.

"Without any warning," Chambers writes, "Job's life is turned into desperate havoc and God keeps out of sight and never gives any sign whatever to Job that he *is*. The odds are desperately against God and it looks as if the sneer of Satan will prove to be true; but God wins in the end, Job comes out triumphant in his faith in God, and Satan is completely vanquished."

When we are bewildered by events and all we believe about God is threatened, do we stand firm? Job took the full brunt of Satan's attacks, yet refused to turn on God. "Though he slay me," he said, "yet will I trust him" (Job 13:15, KJV).

In the maddening mysteries of life, God is enigmatic yet still faithful. In turn, he calls *us* to be faithful and—when the going gets grim—to hang on to his promises and to pray.

Lord, what's really going on in this world and in my own world? So much is confusing. I want to be faithful to you! Help me understand enough to obey you and to believe that you are at work.

Give thanks to the LORD, for he is good! His faithful love endures forever.
PSALM 136:1, NLT

IN A DARK WOOD? LOOK UP!

AMY CARMICHAEL writes, "Broken hearts are everywhere. Bereavement is a very dark wood." As founder of Dohnavur Fellowship in India, Carmichael had rescued many young girls and boys from sexual servitude, and she had great empathy for people who were going through bereavement or despair. She referred to it as a dark wood that suddenly blocks our way and forbids us to go on.

In her writings, Carmichael refers to "the partings of the nursery"—the deaths of children—occurrences that in her generation were tragically common. It wasn't that long ago in American history when children were at great risk and died early of many causes. Parents often buried as many children as they raised to adulthood.

Of course, that's still true in many places in the world where parents suffer loss over and over again because of poverty and poor health care.

The dark woods differ for each of us, but the need for faith is the same. Amy Carmichael herself became a pain-wracked invalid, yet she writes, "Look up to the light that pours into the wood from high above the trees. The long, pure rays of that conquering light are interwoven with the tall stems of the trees, even as threads bright and dark are interwoven in the web of our lives."

When we are in the dark, we may forget the bright threads that give us hope, and we may not think to look up to the light above.

Despite her afflictions, Amy Carmichael kept praising God and encouraging others. Her prayer is one we can make our own when we find ourselves in the depths of a dark wood: "Look above the treetops, O my soul; from thence flow the fountains of light. See how that blessed light streams through the wood."

Heavenly Father, sometimes tall trees and ominous clouds obscure your light from penetrating my dark wood. Help me to lift my eyes off my troubles and see your light streaming through the darkness.

The LORD, my God, lights up my darkness. PSALM 18:28, NLT

ESCAPING OUR SMALL IMPRISONMENTS

JOHN HENRY JOWETT says that faith is doing God's will and "quietly leaving the results to him." This, he says, brings serenity: "He that believes shall not make haste—or, more literally, shall not get into a fuss. He shall not panic, neither fetching fears from his yesterdays nor from his tomorrows."

When we pray and then act on what we sense God leads us to do, we're urged to leave matters in his hands. Yet it's far easier said than done! We're acutely aware of what has gone wrong in the past. When we consider how fragile life can be, we dread what may devastate our hopes in the future.

Yet what choice do we have but to place our anxieties in God's hands?

Jowett says that it's enough to feel the pressure of the guiding hand. "He brings us out of our small imprisonments and sets our feet in a large place."

How can we experience this? When prayer saturates our thinking, when we "never stop praying," our prayers can open our eyes and drive out fear.

John Henry Jowett describes how God brought Abraham out of his tent and had him look toward heaven. In the same way, we have the opportunity to escape these "small imprisonments" by opening our eyes to the grandeur and love of the Creator.

Just as the sun sends away shadows, our seeing through the Father's eyes chases anxieties. Then we "exchange the tent for the sky," Jowett writes, "and live and move in great, spacious thoughts of his purposes and will."

---

*Father in heaven, you see how anxious I am about
so many things, including regrets from yesterdays
and fears about tomorrows. Open my mind,
heart, and spirit to your grandeur and love.*

Sing a new song to the LORD, for he has done wonderful deeds. PSALM 98:1, NLT

ROADSTER BLUES

SHERWOOD "WOODY" WIRT once owned a little yellow Model A Ford roadster. It was the joy of his life and he loved to drive it—but he didn't love having to maintain it. After he neglected to put oil in it, a connecting rod ripped through the block. That was the end of his little yellow roadster.

Wirt later drew the parallel that just as a car must have oil so, too, we need the "oil" of the Holy Spirit. "Without it," he writes, "we'll end up like my Model A Ford."

Being filled with the oil of the Spirit means, in part, that we're to be filled with God's love and compassion. At one time, Woody Wirt made a list of ten characteristics of the Holy Spirit that he found in the Bible. Years later, he concluded that *love* belonged in first place on that list.

We certainly see this same emphasis in the Bible. For instance, in 1 John 4:7-8 we read, "Dear friends, let us continue to love one another, for love comes from God. Anyone who loves is a child of God and knows God. But anyone who does not love does not know God, for God is love" (NLT).

This passage, and the one that follows, may be so familiar that the extreme emphasis on love doesn't adequately sink in. But these truths are ones in which we must immerse ourselves in order to awaken ourselves to God's astounding love.

"God showed how much he loved us by sending his one and only Son into the world so that we might have eternal life through him. This is real love—not that we loved God, but that he loved us and sent his Son as a sacrifice to take away our sins" (1 John 4:9-10, NLT). We receive that love as we open ourselves to the presence and power of the Lord and share it with one another.

"Do you want more love in your life?" asks Woody Wirt. "Ask the Holy Spirit to fill you with love. He will do it."

Holy Spirit of God, only you can pour love into me, for I can't generate it myself. Please make me an instrument of your love to others. Thank you for the magnificent love you have shown me.

Love is patient and kind. Love is not jealous or boastful or proud. . . . Love never gives up, never loses faith, is always hopeful, and endures through every circumstance. . . . Three things will last forever—faith, hope, and love—and the greatest of these is love.
I CORINTHIANS 13:4, 7, 13, NLT

MONEY REALISM

JOHN WESLEY's succinct advice about money has been widely quoted in magazines, books, advice columns, college classes, and the Web. "Gain all you can, save all you can, give all you can." These three phrases provide a snapshot of what Wesley called "Christian prudence" about money. They're worth closer consideration.

Gain all you can. Wesley says that in generating income we should apply ourselves with constant diligence and with all the understanding God gives us. That lays out a broad mandate for study, industry, creativity, and integrity. We are to do all this, he says, "without hurting either yourself or your neighbor, in soul or body."

Save all you can. Wesley advises cutting off every expense that indulges "foolish desire or the desires of the flesh." He quotes 1 John 2:16 as his authority: "All that is in the world, the lust of the flesh, and the lust of the eyes, and the pride of life, is not of the Father, but is of the world" (KJV).

Elsewhere, Wesley affirms that God is pleased when we enjoy the pleasures of his creation, such as eating and drinking. Wesley's emphasis is not to *waste* or *spend* on what the Spirit warns against.

Give all you can. Wesley says that we are to give all we can to God. That means whether we are spending on ourselves or donating to God's work or using money to help the needy, we are to do all in harmony with the Holy Spirit.

The use of money is a complex issue in our lives. It's a tough challenge, and gray areas abound. But grayness can be beneficial, for then we must seek the Lord's witness in our hearts as we earn, save, spend, and give.

Father in heaven, all good things come from your
hand. Help me to see money as you do and to have
great wisdom and compassion, being under the control
of your Holy Spirit in all my financial dealings.

Store your treasures in heaven, where moths and rust cannot destroy, and thieves do not break in and steal. Wherever your treasure is, there the desires of your heart will also be.
MATTHEW 6:20-21, NLT

THE LION IN THE MARBLE

HENRI NOUWEN used a familiar tale about Michelangelo to make a spiritual point:

A little boy watched as the famous sculptor hammered and chiseled at a block of marble. Pieces fell and flew away, but the child had no idea what was happening. Weeks later, the boy returned and was surprised by a large, powerful lion sitting in the place where the marble block had stood. Excited, he ran to Michelangelo and asked, "Sir, tell me, how did you know there was a lion in the marble?"

Just as Michelangelo was able to "see" the lion in the marble, so, too, God, the Master Sculptor, sees what we can become. He gradually chips away at the parts that don't belong until we finally become all that he intends for us to be.

Nouwen writes, "Spiritual direction is the interaction between the little child, the master sculptor, and the emerging, beautiful marble lion."

All that hammering and chipping, however, can be sweaty and difficult. "Living a spiritual life is far from easy," Nouwen admits. "Marble doesn't give way easily, and neither does the human spirit quickly conform to God's design. Being formed in God's likeness involves the struggle to move from *absurd living* to *obedient living.*"

Nouwen defines absurd living as deafness in which we don't hear the voice of the Creator who calls us to new life. Such living is painful because it cuts us off from the essential source of our being.

In contrast, Nouwen says, the meaning of *obedience* includes the word *audire*, which means "listening."

We seem much more wired to make requests and to talk than to listen. Yet hearing what God communicates to us through his Word and his Holy Spirit—and then responding—creates the dynamic of spiritual growth.

Henri Nouwen challenges us to listen very carefully. "Our God is a God who cares, heals, guides, directs, challenges, confronts, corrects, and forms us."

---

*Lord, I don't know what "lion" you might see in me,
but I want to be formed in your likeness. Help me
to hear what you say and to obey as you give me the
willpower. I'll then praise you for your grace.*

The Scriptures give us hope and encouragement as we wait patiently for God's promises to be fulfilled. ROMANS 15:4, NLT

PRAYING WITH BROKEN TEETH

JILL BRISCOE writes honestly about how her prayer life as a teenager was challenged when she saw some graphic images of the Holocaust. She asked God how he could allow such cruelty.

Decades later, when she learned that her son's wife had left their little family, Briscoe was devastated. "I fell on my knees. 'Lord,' I prayed. . . . Then my prayer turned into garbled words. I couldn't believe I was praying like this! Had I learned nothing in over forty years of knowing Christ and serving him? I listened to myself charging God with sleeping on the job! Suddenly I didn't want to talk about it anymore. Not with him."

Have you ever felt like that?

Briscoe quotes Jeremiah's graphic honesty in Lamentations 3:11, where the prophet compares God to a bear who "dragged me from the path and mangled me and left me without help" (NIV). Jeremiah had plenty of reasons to lament. He complains that God surrounded him with bitterness and hardship. "He drew his bow and made me the target for his arrows. . . . He has broken my teeth with gravel" (verses 12, 16).

Although we may lay the blame on God, it's not God who does the horrific things we see in death camps or brings the tragedies we endure in our families. He sent his Son because he is the God of love. Jeremiah says, "Because of the LORD's great love we are not consumed, for his compassions never fail. They are new every morning; great is your faithfulness" (verses 22-23).

Jeremiah's statement is quite a reversal from his earlier accusation that God is a marauding bear! It's all in the perspective. The prophet wisely concludes, "It is good to wait quietly for the salvation of the LORD" (verse 26).

Jill Briscoe observes, "God is a consuming fire, but because of his love he will not consume us. God is a forgiving God, full of mercy and grace."

Lord, sometimes, like Jill Briscoe, I'm dismayed by what happens in the world—and you know how my own experiences have jolted me. God of love, please help me sense your love now and to share it with others who have mangled hopes.

How gracious and merciful is our LORD! PSALM 111:4, NLT

HOW DID BROTHER LAWRENCE DO IT? *February 9*

BROTHER LAWRENCE committed mind and soul to unbroken communion with God, continuously occupied with praising, worshiping, and loving him. How could he pull that off moment by moment in a busy kitchen or while traveling?

> He persevered in training himself to do everything in the kitchen or on the road for the love of God.
> He prayed at every juncture for God's grace to do the work.
> He gave no thought to death or his sins but only to doing small things for the love of God. Great things, he said, he was unable to do.
> He realized God was intimately present within him and so he constantly asked for his help.
> He was alert to recognize God's will "in all things doubtful."
> When he saw clearly what God required, he did his very best.
> He offered what he was doing to God.
> After doing it, he gave God thanks.

In the monastery kitchen where he worked, Lawrence wasn't doing anything different from other workers, except he was constantly practicing the Lord's presence. In other words, he was constantly open to the indwelling of the Holy Spirit. His alertness to the Spirit's whispers and guidance made God his ultimate companion, no matter what Lawrence was doing.

The more we persist in directing our thoughts to God in our fast-paced lives, the more we find internal peace and joy. Brother Lawrence observes, "There is not in the world a way of life more sweet, nor more delightful than continual converse with God. Only those who practice and savor it can understand it."

Loving Father, you know how Brother Lawrence's example resonates in me—as wonderful for him, but not always for me! My life is so busy and my will so frail! Help me to avoid "things doubtful" and to listen to you.

Devote yourselves to prayer with an alert mind and a thankful heart.
COLOSSIANS 4:2, NLT

GOD'S WHOLENESS

ROSEMARY BUDD admits, "I find that prayer, more than pitching me into the world's hope, scourges me with the world's sorrow."

She describes how a video of an innocent reporter shot in cold blood haunted her. Perhaps you've had a similar experience, when, as never before, you've seen in vivid detail the anguish of the starving, the grief stricken, and the terrified.

"The world God loves is a world of senseless killings," Budd says, "of mass imprisonment, of constant exploitation, of economic wrongs, of rape and violence."

Yet she recognizes that "God takes the world's hurt into himself: it makes imprints in his hands and feet, and it thrusts itself as a spear into his side. He agonizes and he bleeds. And he dies. In prayer, God sometimes asks us to agonize and bleed a little, too."

At the same time, Budd recognizes that we must not let the sorrow swamp us. We need to place it in God's hands. She sees the Holy Spirit as inviting us to bring the world's brokenness to the wholeness of God.

Rosemary concludes her reflections in a wonderful way—by telling the familiar story of Martin Luther, who, like us, could get overwhelmed by the evil and despair in the world. At a time when he was particularly morose, his wife, Catherine, came to breakfast dressed in black mourning clothes.

Luther wanted to know why she was wearing black.

"Because God is dead," she answered.

For those of us who tend toward the melancholy, it might take a similar gambit to jolt us into realizing that God is not dead; rather, he is calling each of us to receive his compassion and redemption.

Father in heaven, a familiar song says you have the whole world in your hands, yet obviously the devil disrupts and disturbs your creation. Help me to place the world's sorrows and my own with you and to trust in your Spirit.

We now have this light shining in our hearts, but we ourselves are like fragile clay jars containing this great treasure. This makes it clear that our great power is from God, not from ourselves. 2 CORINTHIANS 4:7, NLT

GIVING GOD EXCUSES

JOHN ORTBERG puts himself in Moses' place when Moses saw the burning bush and was told by God that he was the one to rescue his people from slavery. When Moses heard God's commands to confront Pharaoh, wouldn't he have felt that God's timing was extremely strange?

Forty years earlier, Moses had been at the peak of life, living as the privileged son of the pharaoh, with powerful connections and ways of getting things done. Now he was an eighty-year-old fugitive, a nobody, living in a desert.

Moses was stunned by God's command. He objected, saying that he was not the one to confront Pharaoh. What was God thinking?

We may not see burning bushes or hear commands as dramatic as what God told Moses. Yet what we have to do and the timing of God's answers to our prayers may seem just as strange. We feel inadequate, or we feel this isn't the best time for something to happen. We feel we're trapped in circumstances or that God expects more of us than we can possibly deliver.

Just as God led Moses through incredible adventures that would change all of human history, he still leads those who stop and listen to him. Sometimes the messages seem garbled or unrealistic, but as we pray and seek the leading of his Spirit, we also become part of God's drama.

John Ortberg says that when we respond to God, "ordinary people can receive power for extraordinary change." All those excuses that Moses cast up to God so he could duck out became irrelevant. Moses obeyed and returned to Egypt, facing Pharaoh again and becoming the conduit for God's power.

We each have our pharaohs to face. When we stop and listen to God and then move at the impulse of his love, we, too, can become conduits for his work in the world.

Lord, I've stopped what I'm doing for the moment and am listening. Help me to hear you clearly and then to take courage to do what you ask. Courage and stamina must come from you, Father. Strengthen me, I pray.

It was by faith that Moses left the land of Egypt, not fearing the king's anger. He kept right on going because he kept his eyes on the one who is invisible. HEBREWS 11:27, NLT

THE SHEPHERD WITH US

HELMUT THIELICKE, preaching to his shattered congregation in Stuttgart during the chaos of World War II, described sin, suffering, and death as *hostile* powers—enemies of God. War and its horrific convulsions, he said, come from our separation from God. Yet, for people of faith, even though the dark powers are permitted their way, a transformation takes place.

The transformation this young wartime pastor pointed to is that our Father in heaven sees all. As we call on the Father, even terror and the dreadful valleys of the shadow of death become places to traverse beside our Good Shepherd.

Thielicke emphasized to his terrorized congregation in the bombed-out city that when we know the good hand of the Father is at work in our lives, we receive tremendous comfort. It was Jesus who taught us to pray, "*Our* Father"—the Father who loves us and "has great, fatherly plans for our lives."

In the midst of the absurd horrors of war or in the aftermath of the death of a loved one or in the ordinary grief and suffering of our families and communities, we may find it very hard to sense the good hand of the Father. Sometimes in our pain we ask, "Where was the Good Shepherd when this happened?"

In our questions and in our suffering, Jesus' invitation is to pray, "Our Father . . ." (Matthew 6:9, NLT).

Our Father will listen to us and walk with us and lead us.

As Helmut Thielicke preached, he knew his listening parishioners might at any moment hear the scream of air raid sirens. He told his congregation that when they prayed "*Our Father*," they could know the secret "that the Father's voice is really and truly calling our name in the dark forest and that we can answer as beloved children: 'Abba! Father!'"

Our Father in heaven, help us to hear your voice and to respond to you. Give us courage when we hear the sirens going off in our lives. Let your love, Lord, replace our fears, and help us to share your love with others.

You will keep in perfect peace all who trust in you, all whose thoughts are fixed on you!
ISAIAH 26:3, NLT

AN INCREDIBLE PRAYER
IN AUSCHWITZ

PHILIP YANCEY brings to our attention the journal of a young Jewish girl, Etty Hillesum, who wrote of her dialogue with God in the Auschwitz concentration camp. "Sometimes when I stand in some corner of the camp, my feet planted on Your earth, my eyes raised toward Your Heaven, tears run down my face, tears of deep emotion and gratitude."

Yancey says that Etty knew the horrors of the death camp, still she wrote in her journal, "I want to be right there in the thick of what people call horror and still be able to say: life is beautiful. Yes, I lie here in a corner, parched and dizzy and feverish and unable to do a thing. Yet I am also with the jasmine and the piece of sky beyond my window."

Even though many of us enjoy health, plenty of open sky, and unlimited freedom, we often express less gratitude than Etty did for the wonders of God's creation. It's hard for us to imagine this young woman's remarkable spirit and depth of prayer in her tragic situation. Yet the crucible of horrendous circumstances is what sometimes creates unusual spiritual strength.

Prison chaplains speak of prisoners finding faith in the trauma of imprisonment. Some prisoners have even said, "Thank God for prison." Thousands of believers behind bars live out their faith with passionate prayer.

Philip Yancey expresses awe at Etty Hillesum's "defiant faith," and he quotes her triumphant conclusion: "Once you have begun to walk with God, you need only keep on walking with God and all of life becomes one long stroll—a marvelous feeling."

Heavenly Father, if I were in Etty's place, it's hard to imagine how I could walk with you so that I'd see life as beautiful. Enable me to gain perspective, to walk with you each moment, responding to you with authentic faith.

This is the day the LORD has made. We will rejoice and be glad in it.
PSALM 118:24, NLT

JUST OPEN THE DOOR

OLE HALLESBY writes that to pray is simply to let Jesus into our circumstances and invite him to alleviate our distress. "To pray is to let Jesus glorify his name in the midst of our needs."

Hallesby emphasizes that our prayers' effectiveness doesn't depend on our powers. Fervent emotions, an intense will, or a clear understanding of what we're praying for are not the basis for prayers being heard and answered. In fact, we're fortunate that none of these are required, because they may well be in short supply.

When we pray, we simply open the door to Jesus and lay all our needs before him, inviting him to use his power to deal with them in his own time and way.

"He who gave us the privilege of prayer knows us very well," Hallesby observes. "He knows our frame; he remembers that we are dust. That is why he designed prayer in such a way that the most impotent can make use of it. For to pray is to open the door to Jesus, and that requires no strength. It is only a question of our wills."

Hallesby urges us simply to give Jesus access to our needs, for he sees that as "the one great and fundamental question" related to our prayers.

To pray, we look to the Savior, who stands and knocks. He knows our genuine needs far better than we do. Often it seems quite obvious to us what is desperately needed, but we need to invite Jesus in to do what he will for us. Healing and comfort come as we submit our will to him and his plans.

Lord Jesus, you know my many concerns, desires,
and needs. Help me to submit my will to yours
and to rest in the fact that your love and care will
deal with all that is so important to me.

I lie in the dust; revive me by your word. I told you my plans, and you answered. Now teach me your decrees. PSALM 119:25-26, NLT

DARK NIGHT, GOD'S LIGHT

BILLY GRAHAM for many decades has read psalms every day for strength and encouragement from God. "His love has seen me through sickness, discouragement and frustration," he writes. "His love has sustained me during times of disappointment and bewilderment."

The pressures and demands on Billy Graham have been enormous, but he is quick to point to others who have carried greater burdens or suffered in extraordinary ways while experiencing God's sustaining love. For instance, he tells of a Romanian pastor who was imprisoned by the Communists for sixteen years. He was brutally beaten and tortured and told that his family had deserted him and that Christianity in the outside world was dead. Though weakened and demoralized, the pastor continued to believe.

After his release he wrote that, alone in his cell, he had discovered a stronger belief in God and even a delight in him: "a deep and extraordinary ecstasy of happiness."

We may shake our heads at his describing ecstasy despite the horrors, but other prisoners have reported similar faith experiences. Sometimes in the darkest moments, God's light shines brightest and his joy is most vibrant.

Whatever our setbacks, bewilderments, or imprisonments, we have a loving God to turn to.

Billy Graham says that as a boy he'd never seen the ocean and couldn't imagine its size. He had to experience its vastness for himself. Likewise, he says, we are invited to experience the vastness of God's love.

George Beverly Shea, Dr. Graham's colleague, often sang the following hymn:

> *The love of God is greater far,*
> *Than tongue or pen can ever tell.*
> *It goes beyond the highest star,*
> *And reaches to the lowest hell.*
> *O love of God, how rich and pure!*
> *How measureless and strong!*
> *It shall forevermore endure,*
> *The saints' and angels' song.*

Like Billy Graham, we can read the Psalms, and we will repeatedly find the phrase "God's unfailing love." Let us welcome it into our lives.

> *Lord Jesus, bring into my mind and heart your love.*
> *It is far beyond what I can understand, but please*
> *let me experience that portion you have for me. Help*
> *me today to believe and to live in your love.*

The LORD is my strength and my song; he has given me victory. PSALM 118:14, NLT

JOY IN THE DARK

MOTHER TERESA says, "Joy is prayer; joy is strength; joy is love. God loves a cheerful giver. If you have difficulties and accept them with joy, with a big smile, others will see your good works and glorify the Father."

Mother Teresa believed and practiced what she preached. However, it did not come easy for her; in fact, it was harder for her than for most people. "Joy is not simply a matter of temperament," she said from long experience. "In the service of God and souls, it is always hard to be joyful—all the more reason why we should try to acquire it and make it grow in our hearts."

Her phrases, "not simply a matter of temperament" and "always hard to be joyful," take on huge significance in light of her personal correspondence, which was released after her death. She privately admits that she experienced "darkness, coldness, and emptiness." Many people are dismayed when they read her descriptions of her extremely deep struggles.

Yet, like Jesus her Lord, a "man of sorrows, and acquainted with grief" (Isaiah 53:3, KJV), she intentionally embraced her Lord's joy regardless of her emotional state. She quoted Jesus' words "that my joy may be in you" (John 15:11, NIV) and asked, "What is this joy of Jesus? It is the result of his continual union with God, doing the will of the Father."

She calls us to seek the same union: "Living in the presence of God fills us with joy. God is joy."

One reason she could live like this and was known as a person of joy was her practical commitment: "Joy must be one of the pivots of our life," she says and adds, "Let those who suffer find in us comforting angels."

Mother Teresa confesses that, although she experienced many human weaknesses, "[Christ] comes and uses us to be his love and compassion in the world in spite of our weaknesses and frailties."

Lord Jesus, it helps me to know that Mother Teresa didn't
feel joy all the time, even though she communicated
your joy. Help me, Lord, to understand this and to take
action with your spirit of love—no matter how I feel.

Rejoice in the LORD and be glad, all you who obey him! Shout for joy, all you whose hearts are pure! PSALM 32:11, NLT

THE VALUE OF HUMILIATION

February 17

FRANÇOIS FÉNELON writes, "Jesus' life was full of humiliation, but we are horrified by the slightest humiliation."

Horrified at humiliation? Most of us would say, "Of course! Who wouldn't be?"

We aspire to grow in *humility*, but we don't want to be humiliated! When it happens, we feel ashamed and that our self-worth has been attacked. We shudder at the idea of being humiliated in front of others.

Yet Fénelon says, "Consider the life of Jesus. He was born in a stable. He suffered hunger, thirst, and fatigue. He was poor and he was ridiculed. He was treated like a slave and betrayed. How do you expect to know Jesus if you do not seek him where he was found: in suffering."

The great French spiritual master isn't saying that we should seek suffering and humiliation—they find us on their own! The worst that life hammers us with—grief, tragedy, humiliation—can drive us to God. When we are crushed, we can remember the suffering and humiliation that Jesus endured.

Fénelon advises us not to think that we can follow Jesus in our own strength. He emphasizes that *all* our strength will have to come from God. When we realize how magnificent God is and how limited we are—and how our best intentions so often run aground—we turn in our weakness to him.

Fénelon's writing is always realistic, and he admits, "No one wants to be humiliated and put down. But it is the way of God. Seek to follow Jesus along the road of humility that he has taken. Your weakness helps you become more humble."

Lord, you know how I react when someone humiliates me. Bind up my wounds and grant me courage so I can accept suffering and humiliation—not as something devastating, but as storms beating against an oak.

Those who exalt themselves will be humbled, and those who humble themselves will be exalted. LUKE 14:11, NLT

DROWNING IN OUR CULTURE?

EUGENE PETERSON writes, "People submerged in a culture swarming with lies and malice feel like they are drowning in it."

Submerged in a culture and drowning. Are we?

Peterson says our culture is full of lies. Here's a small sampling: "We don't need the grace of God." "The next scientific breakthrough or better leadership or financial strategy will solve our problems." "People are basically good." "If we are in deep trouble, it's someone else's fault." "With just a little more time, we can fix it all."

These are lies, Peterson says, "because they claim to tell us who we are and omit everything about our origin in God and our destiny in God. They instruct us in love without telling us about the God who loves us and gave himself for us."

Are we submerged in a culture? Indeed, yes! Vivid media images constantly bombard us with scripts and spin rooted deeply in the new sacred texts that say God is only a product of our imaginations. We're told that children aren't hurt much by serial monogamy, that giving in to our passions is inevitable, and countless other rationalizations about human nature. As one concerned commentator observed, "The Ten Commandments have become the Ten Suggestions."

The lies can be appealing. They soothe us and entice us—yet they also lead to despair.

Eugene Peterson says that when someone is fed up and bewildered, "Pain penetrates through despair and stimulates a new beginning—a journey to God—the transition from a dreamy nostalgia for a better life to a rugged pilgrimage of discipleship."

Throughout our rugged pilgrimage, we must continually sort through the mélange of lies mixed with honest inquiry. We are invited to find our way by continually listening to the voice of the Holy Spirit. Jesus promised that his Spirit will lead us to truth.

Holy Spirit, please transform my thinking. Flow into my thoughts your responses to all that I am seeing and hearing. Holy Spirit of God, instruct me in your truth and fill me with your love and compassion.

When the Spirit of truth comes, he will guide you into all truth. JOHN 16:13, NLT

KNOCKING AGAIN AND AGAIN

February 19

JONI EARECKSON TADA says that in the early days of her paralysis, she was "desperate for a promise—any promise—that would bring hope into my dark and bleak world. Would I ever smile again? Would life have any meaning? Could anything good come from useless hands and feet?"

Someone pointed out Philippians 1:6, which told her she should be confident that the good work God had begun in her would be carried on to completion. She quoted the verse over and over as if it were a lifeline. She prayed repeatedly, "knocking and knocking at the door of his tenderness and mercy until he opened it."

Tada found peace through her prayers, and her depression lifted. Prayer was what made all the difference. "It was as though God pressed the fast-forward button on my walk with him," she says, "and I began growing, as they say, by leaps and bounds. Out of nowhere, I began thirsting for his Word. Surprisingly, I was hungering after his righteousness. I believe a special bond, a forged closeness, was custom-made between the Lord and me during those times of pleading in prayer."

The Scripture so helpful to Tada was Paul's message to "all of God's holy people in Philippi" (Philippians 1:1, NLT). Paul was assuring them that when God births new life in a person, he is faithful to finish what he started. Paul was therefore able to pray for them with joy at their faith and their future.

Joni Eareckson Tada's changed and miraculous life came about through her desperate yet simple prayers that believed God would be faithful, despite her paralysis. In our own most desperate experiences we can utter the same simple, earnest pleading that God will open the doors to his mercy and grace.

Father, you have been at work in my life. Please continue to carry to completion everything you have planned. Help me to hunger after your righteousness and to faithfully pray for others.

Whenever I pray, I make my requests for all of you with joy. . . . And I am certain that God, who began the good work within you, will continue his work until it is finally finished on the day when Christ Jesus returns. PHILIPPIANS 1:4, 6, NLT

DISPELLING MELANCHOLY

ALAN PATON says, "I wish to place on record that I am in unrepayable debt to Francis of Assisi."

Why would this champion of the oppressed in apartheid South Africa say that? "When I pray his prayer, or even remember it," Paton explains, "my melancholy is dispelled, my self-pity comes to an end, my faith is restored, because of this majestic conception of what the work of a disciple should be."

For most of us, the prayer of St. Francis is familiar: "Lord, make me an instrument of thy peace." Paton, facing challenges beyond most of ours, found it not just familiar but life changing.

"So majestic is this conception," he testifies, "that one dare to no longer be sorry for oneself. This world ceases to be one's enemy. Life is no longer nasty, mean, brutish, and short, but the time one needs to make it less nasty and mean. We are brought back instantaneously to the reality of our faith, that we are not passive recipients but active instruments."

St. Francis prayed,

Where there is hatred, let me sow love.
Where there is doubt, let me sow faith.
Where there is despair, let me sow hope.

We Christians, when we make becoming instruments of peace our focus, become active planters of faith, hope, and love.

This opportunity gripped Alan Paton, who prayed, "Lord, open my eyes that I may see the need of others. Show me where love and hope and faith are needed, that I may this coming day do some work of peace for you."

Father in heaven, sometimes I do feel sorry for myself.
Day after day the news is full of tragedies. Personal
troubles assault my faith. Help me, Lord, to be an
active planter of your love, faith, and hope.

If you are wise and understand God's ways, prove it by living an honorable life, doing good works with the humility that comes from wisdom. JAMES 3:13, NLT

LOVE AND WAR

CHARLES HADDON SPURGEON found it "not a little astonishing" that John's epistles, so thoroughly "soaked in love," should in 1 John 5:4 include references to war. The apostle John writes, "For whatsoever is born of God overcometh the world: and this is the victory that overcometh the world, even our faith" (KJV).

"Here are intimations of strife and battle," Spurgeon writes, "because there is something in the world antagonistic to love. Darkness broods. Who can take Satan down but by force?"

Spurgeon then preached on three elements in the quoted verse:

Great victory. Caesar, Alexander, Wellington—history chronicles many who have won renowned victories. But faith is the victory of victories that overcomes the world. "The earth is the battlefield," Spurgeon says. "Angels look on, burning to mingle in the conflict, but the slender band of soldiers of the cross must fight, and shall triumph gloriously."

Great birth. It is faith born of God that overcomes the world, faith that is an enduring, supernatural change of the Spirit. Spurgeon preaches, "The world says, 'I will give you this, I will give you that, you shall be rich and great.' But faith says, 'I have a hope laid up in heaven. A hope which fades not away, eternal, a golden hope.' The hope of glory overcomes all hope of the world."

Great grace. The world, the flesh, and the devil are formidable, and we don't overcome them by strategizing and getting more and more savvy on the battlefield. Spurgeon says, "Christians do not triumph over the world by reason. Not at all. Reason is good, but it's a candle, whereas faith is a sun. Reason is a wooden sword that snaps, while faith cuts to the dividing of soul and body."

The apostle John declares, "This is the victory that overcomes the world, even our faith."

Charles Spurgeon affirms, "Give us faith, and we can do all things."

Lord, please equip me with more than a wooden sword that snaps as I face what's before me. Grant me your wisdom, love, and power so that I can overcome the world and share your grace with others.

I will wait quietly before God, for my victory comes from him. PSALM 62:1, NLT

NURTURING YOUR HEART

NANCY GUTHRIE observed two opposite reactions when watching people go through tragic experiences. Their hearts either became hardened against the Lord, or they became "more soft and pliable to the work of God."

When our hearts are broken, in our pain we often react by putting the blame on God or someone else. We may feel deserted or betrayed or both. Whether we blame God or someone we judge guilty, we begin a process that can harden our hearts. We can become bitter and resentful, nurturing the enemy's seeds in our souls.

To avoid that and "to nurture a soft heart," Nancy Guthrie sends us to Paul's counsel in Philippians, where we find his remarkable recipe for living through extreme circumstances: "Don't worry about anything; instead, pray about everything. Tell God what you need, and thank him for all he has done. Then you will experience God's peace, which exceeds anything we can understand. His peace will guard your hearts and minds as you live in Christ Jesus. . . . Fix your thoughts on what is true, and honorable, and right, and pure, and lovely, and admirable. Think about things that are excellent and worthy of praise" (Philippians 4:6-8, NLT).

Guthrie emphasizes how thankfulness changes everything: "Gratitude plows up the ground for God's peace to grow. This is the kind of peace in the midst of pain that is foreign to the world. Peace is the gift of God, but we prepare ourselves to receive this gift as we pray about everything, cultivate gratitude, and refuse to surrender to worry."

Father, lift my eyes above my troubles so I can praise you
for your love and grace. Fill my heart with gratitude
and my mind with Paul's list of good things—for I
know they come from you, the Father of lights.

May all who are godly rejoice in the LORD and praise his holy name!
PSALM 97:12, NLT

A SHORT VISIT HERE

THOMAS À KEMPIS provides the yardstick of genuine success: "He is truly great, who is great in the love of God. He is truly great, who is humble in mind, and regards earth's honors as nothing."

We strive for "earth's honors"—sports trophies, academic degrees, career success—and that's valid and good. Yet we must keep all achievements in perspective, for life is fleeting and the bottom line is living in the Spirit and serving Christ.

"Where," à Kempis asks, "are now all those Masters and Doctors you knew so well in the full flower of their learning? Others now sit in their seats and they are hardly ever thought of. Oh, how swiftly the glory of the world passes away!"

As we engage in life with vigor and faith, we are often rewarded. In all our success we owe thanks to the Father, for all good things come from him, including our capacities and opportunities. We also recognize that time inexorably moves on. We are visitors here.

How do we deal with this transience? We are earthbound, and the truth is that earth's honors and blessings mean a great deal to us. Keeping the spiritual and temporal in balance happens only though humble and frequent prayer. As we recognize how dependent we are on God, we receive his blessings with less vanity and more joy.

Thomas à Kempis tells us that the truly great renounce their own will for the will of God. "Blessed are the single-hearted," à Kempis declares, "for they shall enjoy much peace."

Father in heaven, thank you for the capacities and blessings you've given me. Help me to "live in the present moment" yet be aware that this moment will soon be gone. Make me single-hearted in your grace and love.

Teach us to realize the brevity of life, so that we may grow in wisdom.
PSALM 90:12, NLT

COURAGE FROM THE SPIRIT

February 24

ED DOBSON, slowly dying of ALS, admits that the more he thought about what would happen to him as the disease progressed, the more afraid he became. ALS slowly reduces the capacity to swallow and to breathe, but until death comes, the brain functions normally. Through the long process, the person with Lou Gehrig's disease is fully aware of what is happening.

In his struggle, Dobson found that one Bible passage helped him more than any other: Hebrews 13:5-6. "God has said, 'I will never fail you. I will never abandon you.' So we can say with confidence, 'The LORD is my helper, so I will have no fear'" (NLT).

Especially in times of serious illness or significant loss, our fears about what may happen to us or our loved ones may grow into ominous clouds darkening our thoughts and emotions. In the same way, uncertainties create anxieties that invade and drain our spirits and our sense of God's presence.

Yet the Bible is full of passages that promise that God will be there for us when we call. We may experience extreme troubles, but we can ask the Holy Spirit to assuage our fears and give us courage that transcends what's happening to us.

Ed Dobson says that when he feels fear beginning to take over his life, he takes a time-out. For a full five minutes he repeats the verses over and over: "God has said, 'I will never fail you. I will never abandon you.' So we can say with confidence, 'The LORD is my helper, so I will have no fear.'"

Courage is not the absence of fear, but facing our fears head-on. One way to do that is to remind ourselves that the Good Shepherd is with us in each of the valleys we traverse.

Father in heaven, here are my fears and anxieties. So many things could happen to me and to those I love. May your Holy Spirit equip me to serve you and others with fresh courage.

We will not fear when earthquakes come and the mountains crumble into the sea.
PSALM 46:2, NLT

OUT OF THE BOG AND
THE BELLY OF THE FISH

J. I. PACKER writes in his professorial but warm British way, "If I had found I had driven into a bog, I should know I had missed the road. But this would not be much comfort if I then had to stand helpless watching my car sink and vanish."

Jim insists the Christian life is not like that. We may stupidly or willfully drive off the road, but God does not let us sink into the depths of the bog. We can have "confidence in the God who will not let us ruin our souls."

Temptations, conflicts, bad advice, and even devastating trials assault us. Adversity is inevitable. It may make us feel we're sinking. Yet if we see difficulties as part of the course we're on, we can press forward with hope. We can learn how to deal not only with the bad things that happen to us but with our own besetting weaknesses.

"Grace," writes Packer, "is God's drawing us sinners closer and closer to himself. How does God in grace prosecute this purpose? Not by shielding us from assault by the world, the flesh, and the devil."

Our worst moments may be when we realize that some of our gravest troubles are of our own making. We feel the guilt. We wonder how we could have done something that so displeases God. Packer says that one of the most startling applications of God's grace is how he uses our sins and mistakes. He points to men in the Scriptures who made huge mistakes—Moses (murder), David (adultery and murder), Jonah (fleeing from God)—yet, by repentance, they learned to cleave far more tightly to God.

At times, most of us will find ourselves like Jonah, living, as it were, in the darkness and stench of a great fish belly, crying out to God for forgiveness. J. I. Packer asks, "Is your trouble a sense of failure? The knowledge of having made some ghastly mistake? Go back to God; his restoring grace waits for you."

---

*Lord, fill me with your hope. Forgive all the stupid and
sinful things I've done. Dissipate my discouragements
so I can experience your grace in a fresh way that
cleanses and empowers me to reach out to others.*

May God our Father and the Lord Jesus Christ give you grace and peace.
GALATIANS 1:3, NLT

THE SLAVE MARKET

RAY STEDMAN, in a sermon on the book of Ephesians, quotes writer Dorothy Sayers: "The final tendency of the modern philosophies, hailed in their day as a release from the burden of sinfulness, has been to bind man hard and fast in the chains of an iron determinism. . . . Evil has been represented as something imposed on us from without, not made by us from within. The dreadful conclusion follows inevitably that as he is not responsible for evil; he cannot alter it." In other words, if you can't recognize guilt, you can't escape it.

The gospel says that when God convicts us of sin, we understand our guilt, and through grace we find redemption. Consider these declarations in Ephesians 1:6-7: "So we praise God for the glorious grace he has poured out on us who belong to his dear Son. He is so rich in kindness and grace that he purchased our freedom with the blood of his Son and forgave our sins" (NLT).

"The picture is that of a slave market," Stedman says, "a common sight in the Roman Empire, where human beings were offered for sale to anyone who would pay the price. Here we were, bound as slaves. Into this slave pit, Jesus came, and he struck off our fetters and set us free."

Liberation means that God accepts and loves us. We're his children, in whom he's well pleased. That becomes our identity, and we can accept ourselves. When we're beset by guilt, we need to open ourselves to God and accept his forgiveness.

Ray Stedman preaches it this way: "Once you sense you're forgiven, healed, whole in God's sight, that your sin has been set aside and you're a wholesome person made in the image of God, you want to sing and rejoice and dance and shout to the heavens that you've been set free. You never want to go back and add to that load of guilt again."

Lord Jesus, thank you for setting me free. Thank you for your love for me. When I fail, help me to quickly turn to you for fresh cleansing and a renewal of your Spirit so I can do what is pleasing in your sight.

Sin is no longer your master, for you no longer live under the requirements of the law. Instead, you live under the freedom of God's grace. ROMANS 6:14, NLT

GOURMET FOOD

BEN PATTERSON confesses to a very foolish succumbing to temptation. After missing lunch one day, he was on his way to dinner at a friend's house when he saw a fast-food restaurant specializing in hot dogs. To tide him over till dinner, he stopped to order a snack. The "snack" became a regular hot dog, a kraut dog, and a chili dog, along with a large order of fries and a large drink. By the time he arrived for dinner, he was no longer hungry and was unable to enjoy the wonderful meal his hostess had prepared.

Patterson draws a connection between his story and what it's like for us when we come to prayer with our spirits stuffed and overloaded—not with the Bread of Life, but with spiritual junk food. "Before it is anything else," he says, "lack of prayer is a lack of hunger for God."

In contrast, we read the familiar words of David, who was so passionate about seeking the Lord:

> *O God, you are my God;*
> *I earnestly search for you.*
> *My soul thirsts for you;*
> *my whole body longs for you. . . .*
> *Your unfailing love is better than life itself; . . .*
> *You satisfy me more than the richest feast. (Psalm 63:1, 3, 5, NLT)*

How can our spiritual thirst and hunger be satisfied? God the Father is ready with his feast, if only we will attend. He calls out to us:

> *Is anyone thirsty?*
> *Come and drink—even if you have no money!*
> *Come, take your choice of wine or milk—it's all free! . . .*
> *Why pay for food that does you no good?*
> *Listen to me, and you will eat what is good.*
> *You will enjoy the finest food. (Isaiah 55:1-2, NLT)*

Lord, my days are full of so much that distracts me
from a spirit of prayer and fills my mind and emotions
in ways that make me feel distant from your presence.
Help me to listen for you and to eat at your table.

Search for the LORD and for his strength; continually seek him.
I CHRONICLES 16:11, NLT

MANAGING OUR ANXIETIES

FRED SMITH maintains that perseverance requires "enemy management." He says that worry is one of the greatest enemies of holding on in tough times.

Smith often speaks to large groups of people, and when he asks them what they were worrying about this time *last year*, he typically gets a lot of laughs—most can't remember. But when he asks if they are worrying about something at that moment, he sees a roomful of nodding heads.

"The average worrier is 92 percent inefficient," he says. "Only 8 percent of what we worry about ever comes true."

So what is Smith's "enemy management" for worry? Planned action. "The moment you inject planning into confusion, it moves toward order. A plan turns your mind from worry to concrete action."

Smith would also advise dipping deeply into spiritual resources, among them the writings of François Fénelon, who says we should let our anxieties flow away like a stream. "Do not try to look too far ahead," Fénelon says, "but live moment by moment before God. Yield to God with a heart full of trust."

"Enemy management" is both a spiritual and a practical matter. When we put our troubles and failures into context, they build experience and character.

On his Web site breakfastwithfred.com, the ever-practical Smith gives this counsel: "When nothing can be done about something, dismiss it. If something can be done, do it. When real troubles come, we survive. Out of this survival we develop strength.

"Trust in God—not worry—is the answer."

---

*Father in heaven, you know my anxieties. Help
me to do all that's possible now, but then to trust
you fully. Grant me your peace within as I practice
your presence and listen for your guidance.*

---

*Don't worry about anything; instead, pray about everything. Tell God what you need,
and thank him for all he has done.* PHILIPPIANS 4:6, NLT

SLINKING AWAY?

OSWALD CHAMBERS uses the phrase "dazed and amazed" to describe the trials of Job. He finds a lesson for us in Job's powerlessness when his family, wealth, and health were shattered—showing, first of all, our complete dependence on God.

Chambers was speaking to soldiers who were facing the terrors of World War I when he said, "One thing the war has done is to knock on the head all such shallow optimism as telling people 'every cloud has a silver lining.'" He asserted some clouds are entirely dark.

Yet God comforts those who mourn. The title for Chambers's book on Job is *Baffled to Fight Better*, a fascinating phrase and challenge. "This man was buffeted and stripped of all he held dear," Chambers says, "but in the whirlwind of disaster he remained unblameable."

Would we?

Chambers quotes a poem that refers to Jesus' "heart of love and spirit of steel." The poet goes on to pray:

> *I would not to thy bosom fly*
> *To slink off till the storms go by.*

Are we tempted to "slink off till the storms go by"? In times of crisis, our natural inclination is to hope the storm will pass so we don't have to endure humiliations and loss as Job did. But storms don't always pass. We are called not to "slink off" but to endure and to believe, as Job did.

"Thank God he does give us difficult things to do!" Chambers asserts. "His salvation is a glad thing, but it is also a heroic, holy thing. It tests us for all we are worth."

Lord, when storms come, my first reaction is to
duck and seek shelter. Help me to not slink off,
but to fight, in your strength, the battles I find
before me. Enable me to stand firm in your Spirit.

Happy are those who hear the joyful call to worship, for they will walk in the light of your presence, LORD. . . . You are their glorious strength. It pleases you to make us strong.
PSALM 89:15, 17, NLT

FATHER AND CHILD

MARTIN LUTHER explored the question of how we should address God. When we present ourselves to him, how should we honor him? Luther concluded that we should use the name *Father*.

"Calling him Father," Luther writes, "is a friendly, affectionate, deep, and heartfelt way to address him. We acknowledge ourselves as children of God, which stirs God's heart. No voice is more dear to a father than his own child's."

Luther also counsels that we include "in heaven" in our references to God the Father, as in the Lord's Prayer. He reasons, "Those who pray, 'Our Father in heaven,' and do so out of the depths of their hearts, acknowledge that they have a Father and that their Father is in heaven." Luther counsels that when we feel abandoned we should tell our heavenly Father. When we do, we will "soon feel a heartfelt yearning, like a child who lives far from his father's land."

In our grief and troubles, we long for our heavenly home and the Father who loves us. Of course, not everyone has experienced the blessing of a loving father on earth, so we each approach praying in our own ways. What is true for everyone is what we read in the Scriptures: God is love, and he actively shows his love toward us. Whatever our experience with our earthly parents, we can know that we have a loving heavenly Father.

Luther describes those who come to the Father as praying like children in distress and danger, surrounded by evil forces, urgently crying out for rescue. "Those who pray in this way," he writes, "stand with pure, uplifted hearts toward God. They are able to pray and move God to mercy."

Father in heaven, my need for your mercy is great.
In my troubles, break through with your mercy. Help
me, in all my attitudes and actions, to reflect that I
am your child and to share your love with others.

Pray like this: Our Father in heaven, may your name be kept holy. May your Kingdom come soon. May your will be done on earth, as it is in heaven. MATTHEW 6:9-10, NLT

STANDING SPEECHLESS

AMY CARMICHAEL writes eloquently about two effects of light in South India: "One is seen on a clear evening when the terra cotta earth of the plains, and every brick and tile made of that earth, takes on a brief and amazing brightness. The other is never seen except in thundery weather, and then only on the hills that run down the western coast like a spine set out of place. The sun's rays striking up from the sea in sunrise are flung back by the thundercloud, and falling on mountain and forest turn the whole world to rose. You stand speechless. You can only worship. Worthy, worthy to be worshiped is the God who can imagine such beauty and command it."

We have in God's creation such wonders all over the world, revealing our Creator's magnificence. Science might be able to explain how these phenomena occur, but even knowing wouldn't diminish or detract from our amazement and enjoyment when we experience these wonders.

Carmichael observes that the beauty of a sunrise slowly changes as the daylight grows brighter. She contrasts the spectacular but brief glories with "the common sunlight that is the life of every day."

Sometimes we stand speechless when the curtain over God's wonders is flung back in a magnificent way. We savor those moments, yet we live in the ordinary; and in the ordinary, we can be on the lookout for wonders of many sorts. What might God be up to in the routines of our lives? What wonders pass unnoticed?

Amy Carmichael calls us to live in the ordinary, yet to be filled with wonder at creation and God's mighty works, embracing hope from the God of hope.

Father and Creator of all wonders, let this creature draw
breath in harmony with you. I often feel out of sync
in this fallen world. Let my "sunrise moments," when
I'm filled with awe, keep me alert to your glory.

Give thanks to him who made the heavens so skillfully. His faithful love endures forever.
PSALM 136:5, NLT

TAKING THE LANDSCAPE WITH US

JOHN HENRY JOWETT points out that we have a very high privilege. We share the spiritual resources of Abraham and the apostle Paul—what was given to them is not withheld from us. Spiritual giants may intimidate us or fill us with awe, but we "need not be dismayed." We share the same thirst-quenching waters they enjoyed from the river of God.

As we read the thoughts of so many who have followed hard after God, we can rejoice that they drank from and were refreshed by that same invigorating river. Jowett, Wesley, Briscoe, Chambers, Carmichael, Lewis, Luther, Shaw—all are soul mates of ours who have sought after the God who challenges, nourishes, demands, loves.

Jowett, while on the Scottish Isle of Arran and thinking about his departure for New York the next day, wrote that he would leave the island behind "but I shall take the landscape with me."

Perhaps you've had a similar experience, on vacation in a prime part of God's creation or in some other favorite spot. Even after you've left, you can always mentally take yourself back and enjoy that refreshing experience.

Jowett's point is that our "incorruptible inheritance" in Christ is like that. It is always with us and can be appropriated through concentration and prayer. In our "New Yorks"—that is, in our daily, workaday lives with all their stresses and strains—we can access a richness of experience that lifts us and equips us by saturating our imaginations with things of the Spirit.

"With the years, God's praise acquires new grace and beauty," Jowett writes. "It is never so fresh and flourishing as just when everything else is fading away."

Heavenly Father, in many ways and many places,
you've enriched and encouraged my spirit. Help me to
remember those moments. Let me avoid contaminated
rivers and drink fully from your life-giving stream.

As the deer longs for streams of water, so I long for you, O God. I thirst for God, the living God. PSALM 42:1-2, NLT

GIVE FEAR THE COLD SHOULDER

LUCI SHAW says that we can't deny our fears, because fear is part of our human nature. She views Jesus as calling us to adventure and risk, and that includes dealing with our fears. When we face challenges that hit us in the pit of the stomach, Shaw advises us to "Feel the fear, but do it anyway. Shoulder aside the fear, as you would a curtain in a doorway as you pass through."

Shaw is realistic about how difficult it is to walk into unknown territory and how threatening it can be to our faith. "For some," she writes, "it may even mean moving into a wilderness of the spirit, where doubts and despairs besiege us as fiercely as Jesus was besieged at the beginning of his public ministry. I have been there, where the particulars of my circumstances and the demon of depression seemed to press me down with paralyzing force, causing a wave of skepticism about God's love and care to engulf me."

Fear. Skepticism. Despair. If you were writing the script for an action movie or, for that matter, any sort of adventure film, you'd include all three. If God calls us to adventure—and the truth is, if we're alive we'll experience adventures—we're called to face these dynamics with faith.

When we hit bottom, we recognize how much we need God. Luci Shaw says she's learned from experience those are the times she's called upon to wait. "In the waiting, God will send me the gift of his presence again. I learn a lot as I wait, and my watchword in this unknown and fearful territory is, '*Continue to be faithful and obedient.*'"

In those times, Shaw says, she also sings to herself one of her favorite hymns, the old Celtic song "St. Patrick's Breastplate":

> *Christ be with me, Christ within me,*
> *Christ behind me, Christ before me,*
> *Christ beside me, Christ to win me,*
> *Christ to comfort and restore me.*

Father in heaven, let this hymn resonate in my soul.
Help me to shoulder aside my fears as I realize you're
with me no matter what happens. Grant me the will to
obey you and the courage to embrace your adventure.

Praise the LORD! How joyful are those who fear the LORD and delight in obeying his commands. PSALM 112:1, NLT

DUCK, REBUT, OR GROW

JOHN WESLEY warns us that we must watch and pray continually against pride. He saw pride as subtle and very dangerous to our spiritual health.

He points out how easily we can become falsely confident. Strong in one area, we may think wrongly we're therefore strong in another. We may be effective in one role or task, but stumble in another that demands different skills or insights.

"We often think we have no need of anyone else's advice or reproof," Wesley writes. "Always remember, much grace does not imply much enlightenment. We may be wise but have little love, or we may have love with little wisdom. God has wisely joined us all together as the parts of a body so that we cannot say to another, 'I have no need of you.'"

We must learn from one another, but often that makes us chafe. We certainly react when someone "gets in our face" and criticizes us! Yet those experiences can lead us to deeper humility and new levels of self-understanding.

Wesley writes, "Be open and honest when you are rebuked, and do not seek to evade it or disguise it. Rather, let it appear just as it is and you will thereby not hinder but adorn the gospel."

We may resolve in a quiet devotional moment to do what Wesley advises, but our natural reaction to a rebuke is a swift rebuttal. It takes prayer and determination to humbly look on criticisms as opportunities.

Here's Wesley's rugged challenge: "Oh, beware of touchiness, of testiness, of an unwillingness to be corrected. Beware of being provoked to anger at criticism."

Lord Jesus, religious leaders rebuked you, and those with training and authority rejected your teachings. Grant me your inner strength to listen and to respond in my situations with your wisdom and the strength of your Spirit.

The wise are glad to be instructed, but babbling fools fall flat on their faces.
PROVERBS 10:8, NLT

OUR IDENTITY AS THE BELOVED

HENRI NOUWEN often spoke and wrote about the decisive moment in Jesus' life when he heard the divine affirmation in his baptism, "This is my beloved Son, in whom I am well pleased" (Matthew 3:17, KJV).

Nouwen writes, "In this core experience, Jesus is reminded in a deep, deep way of who he really is."

Jesus knew his identity as the beloved of the Father, and that identity defined all his days on earth. Unlike us, he did not allow himself to be defined by others' opinions.

"When people speak well about me," Nouwen writes, "and when I do good things, and when I have a lot, I am quite up and excited. But when I suddenly find out I can't do some task anymore, when I learn that people talk against me, then I slip into the pit. This whole zigzag approach is wrong."

What, then, is our identity? Nouwen says that we are the beloved of God. He wants us to hear these words with tenderness and force so that they reverberate in every aspect of our beings: "You are the beloved."

We might feel we are beloved when we get married, or when a loving parent glows at some special moment in our lives. But it's hard for us to accept that God ever thinks of us that way—especially when we fail, or when our faith wavers. Yet our worst moments may be just the times to receive from the Lord this reality of our redemption.

Nouwen regarded Satan's strategy when he tempted Jesus as an assault on the Savior's *identity*. Instead of recognizing Jesus as the beloved of God, the devil tempted him to be the one who could turn a stone into bread or jump unharmed from the Temple. Yet, no matter what temptations or rejections came, Jesus always claimed his true identity.

Henri Nouwen warns against "the trap of being a fugitive hiding from your truest identity. The voice that speaks from above and from within whispers softly or declares loudly, 'You are my beloved son or daughter, on you my favor rests.'"

Father in heaven, is it really true that I am your beloved? I want to sense that, and I open my arms and heart to you. Enable me to find my identity in you, Lord, and to praise you for your love and grace.

God showed his great love for us by sending Christ to die for us while we were still sinners.
ROMANS 5:8, NLT

WHERE ARE THE TEARS?

JILL BRISCOE writes, "Jeremiah prayed plenty of those 'I've-had-it-with-them' prayers." Relatives, friends, and wicked authorities were making the prophet's life miserable. Yet he stayed in God's presence long enough to catch the Lord's heart of compassion for unpleasant people and was soon weeping for them.

Praying for others changes our attitudes, even about those who do outrageously hurtful things. "Jeremiah's troubles were chiseling him into the likeness of God," Jill says. "God's compassion was in Jeremiah's heart. God's tears were on Jeremiah's face." She recounts the tears of Jesus weeping over Jerusalem and the Savior's saying, "How often I have longed to gather your children together, as a hen gathers her chicks under her wings, but you were not willing" (Matthew 23:37, NIV).

We're naturally inclined to nurse our grudges. The people who make action movies know that people love to watch the bad guys squirm and to see the good guys dangle them over cliffs and then drop them to their deaths. Loving our enemies may be our marching order from Jesus, but it's not our natural human response.

Jill says she once asked the Lord to show her an area for spiritual growth. His response was unmistakable: *I want you to care.*

She responded that she did care! Didn't he know she spent every living moment attending to his work?

Where are the tears? the Lord asked her. Briscoe writes, "I had no answer, because I had no tears. It was time to let him do his work in me in the secret places of my heart."

Jill's tears spurred her to take risks, push boundaries, and enter the trenches of the world to minister to those in great pain and danger. "Prayer is what softens our hard hearts," she says. "The secret to a heart of compassion is prayer."

---

*Lord Jesus, I know that you shed tears for those not
deserving your love. When I want revenge, help me to
know that you weep for those people I may want to see
dangled over a cliff. Grant me your grace and your tears.*

When [Jesus] saw the crowds, he had compassion on them because they were confused and helpless, like sheep without a shepherd. MATTHEW 9:36, NLT

WHY SUFFER?

FRANÇOIS FÉNELON asks, "Do you wonder why God has to make it so hard on you? Why doesn't he make you good without making you miserable in the meantime?"

Whatever our view of God's role in our suffering, we've all wondered why it has to be so severe. Fénelon brings us comfort and insight: "I am awed by what suffering can produce. I agonize and cry when the cross is working within me, but when it is over I look back in admiration for what God has accomplished."

Then he gets even more personal and admits, "I am then ashamed that I bore it so poorly. I have learned so much from my foolish reactions."

Here was a man well known for his wise responses in the heat of national upheaval in France. He was a remarkable leader, yet he was always looking deep beneath the surface.

"You yourself must endure the painful process of change," he writes in a letter. "God uses your disappointments, disillusionments, and failures to take your trust away from yourself and help you put your trust in him."

That's easier said than done in the muck and mire of our daily troubles! Yet if we believe God is at work, we gain perspective. Spiritual maturity often increases in the midst of pain and suffering, but seldom in the sunny days of success.

What, indeed, is God up to? When we find ourselves trapped by health or job problems or inner distress, how do we find spiritual maturity? François Fénelon promises, "Slowly you will learn that your troubles are really cures to the poison of your old nature."

He also encourages with this counsel: "Accept the cross and you will find peace even in the middle of turmoil."

Heavenly Father, suffering may do awesome things—but you know I cringe at suffering. Help me to respond with courage. Empower me to accept change as an opportunity to grow.

My suffering was good for me, for it taught me to pay attention to your decrees. Your instructions are more valuable to me than millions in gold and silver.
PSALM 119:71-72, NLT

EARTHY AND SPIRITUAL

EUGENE PETERSON observes that King David was, among other sins and failures, a poor parent and an unfaithful husband. In many ways, David was no role model, but Peterson makes the point that even role models inevitably disappoint us.

David was clearly flawed, and yet the Bible describes him as a man after God's own heart. His relevance to us lies in his passion for God, not in his failures or his exploits.

Peterson describes David's story as "simultaneously earthy and godly." He expresses amazement that, for all David's spiritual intensity, we find no miracles in his story. Even though God is at the center of it, he is largely silent and hidden in the ordinary, the sordid, and the tragic—everything that makes up the human experience.

God sometimes dealt severely with this "man after his own heart," but the example of David's life came in his passionate pursuit of God, as seen in his many psalms. We read with wonder Psalms 23 and 51. We who must live out our own stories of the ordinary and the sordid and the tragic ponder David's exultant declaration in Psalm 18:29: "By my God I can leap over a wall" (NASB). Along with David's flaws, his passion for God continued unabated.

The Bible is brutally honest in its reporting. It records Abraham's lies, Jacob's larceny, Moses' murder, David's adultery. It's been said that the book of Genesis is one long story of a dysfunctional family.

Whatever our circumstances, sins, and successes, when we seek God with our whole hearts, he engages with us in our very personal, original sagas.

Peterson writes, "David's is a most exuberant story. Earthy spirituality characterizes his life. *Earthy*: down-to-earth, dealing with everydayness. *Spiritual*: moved and animated by the Spirit of God and therefore alive to God."

Lord, I pray you will breathe into me the kind of passion
David had for you. In my troubles, let my first thoughts
be to seek your face and your shelter. Bring from my
successes and failures your grace and meaning.

Purify me from my sins, and I will be clean; wash me, and I will be whiter than snow.
Oh, give me back my joy again; you have broken me—now let me rejoice.
PSALM 51:7-8, NLT

AVAILABLE TO ALL . . .

JONI EARECKSON TADA felt perturbed at being interrupted just before going onstage to speak. A woman was shuffling toward her, arm curled against her chest, glasses askew. Joni guessed that the woman had cerebral palsy. When told the woman had an encouragement for her, her reaction was—considering the moment—that it had better be important.

The woman's name was Mary Rose and her message was simple. Ever since she had read one of Joni's books decades before, she had prayed for her *every day*.

Stunned by this news, Joni's irritation vanished. She savored the fact that this disabled woman had prayed for her thousands of times. She thought, *Well done, thou good and faithful servant.* She surmised that this woman, despite the significance of her secret prayer closet, received few if any accolades. Yet even though Mary Rose had severe limitations, her ministry of prayer was worthy of praise.

Each of us may receive accolades, or we may feel that no one appreciates us. We may enjoy vigorous health, or we may struggle with severe problems. At various times of life we may find ourselves in very different circumstances than before. Whatever our lot, through prayer we have access to significance and success of ultimate, eternal value.

Prayer is unlimited in its scope, and it is open to everyone.

In light of Mary Rose's prayers, Joni said, "That's what I love about serving God. In His eyes there are no little people. We are all on the same playing field."

Lord, so many people around me are in need of prayer!
You know, too, how much I am in need of your
guidance, courage, and willpower. Help me to pray
for others and to be genuinely engaged in prayer.

Rejoice in our confident hope. Be patient in trouble, and keep on praying.
ROMANS 12:12, NLT

OWL OR EAGLE

CHARLES HADDON SPURGEON notes the contrast between the owl and the eagle in two verses from the Psalms: "I am like an owl of the desert" (Psalm 102:6, KJV), and "Thy youth is renewed like the eagle's!" (Psalm 103:5, KJV). Spurgeon believed that David was the author of both psalms because of their "Davidic ring."

One man, two moods. Like David, we also experience both desolation and exultation.

We may feel like a desert owl when we're weighed down by our sins and failures or overwhelmed by reversals. Spurgeon outlines situations that drag us down like that: financial troubles, illness, job loss, fears about dying. His advice? "Give up the habit of looking in and around you." He emphasizes that no matter how bad things may be, we can rejoice in our salvation.

"What a mercy it is," he writes, "to shake off depression and say with Habakkuk, 'Although the fig tree shall not blossom, neither shall fruit be in the vines; . . . the flock shall be cut off from the fold, and there shall be no herd in the stalls: Yet I will rejoice in the LORD, I will joy in the God of my salvation' [Habakkuk 3:17-18, KJV]. This is the way to leave the owl in the desert, and to let the eagle soar upwards."

Spurgeon continues in this vein by asking, "Suppose we have miseries—have we not also mercies? Is your way rough? Yet your God leads you. Do you traverse a desert? Yet the manna has fallen even there! Are you weary and footsore? Remember that 'there remaineth therefore a rest to the people of God'" (Hebrews 4:9, KJV).

Spurgeon concludes his observations by contrasting the owl's avoidance of sunlight and the eagle's soaring in it. Like the eagle, we can be lifted by the Spirit's thermals beneath our wings. "The Lord alone can change spiritual sadness into spiritual gladness," he declares. "He alone can turn the owl into an eagle."

Lord, I often feel more like an owl than an eagle.
Lift me now, I pray, by your power and grace so
that I can soar above the troubles and concerns
that make me look down instead of up to you.

He fills my life with good things. My youth is renewed like the eagle's!
PSALM 103:5, NLT

PENETRATING THE GLOOM

ALAN PATON writes, "There is no more terrible condition of the soul than despair. We continue to breathe, to eat, to drink. But we hope no more."

The author of *Cry, the Beloved Country* experienced enough firsthand tragedies in apartheid South Africa to dampen his soul. But the prayer of St. Francis persistently penetrated Paton's gloom and lifted his eyes to the light.

"When I am tempted to despair," he writes, "when I am tempted to believe in the futility of all endeavor, when I believe that the love of God is not helping me, I pray or speak or read this prayer of St. Francis. I decide to act on it, or I should rather say, *I am moved to act on it.*"

The prayer, which begins, "Lord, make me an instrument of your peace," engages us in the real world: "Where there is hatred, let me sow love; where there is darkness, light." It also gets our minds off ourselves: "Grant that I may not so much seek to be consoled, as to console." We're all interconnected, and sometimes it's the strong who need help.

We have unlimited opportunities to act as instruments of God's peace. One pastor regularly ends his messages with these words: "Remember that each person you meet this week carries a heavy load."

A young mother carrying the huge burden of her husband's new cancer diagnosis reported that everywhere she went she would want to explain, "My husband has cancer." Her pain colored everything. But then she thought, *How many others around me carry burdens like this?* It gave her a new sensitivity to see past her own pain and to pray for others.

Alan Paton points out that St. Francis himself passed through a time of despair that lasted two years. A dear friend, the leader of the Order of St. Clare, helped him. "It was Clare herself who used all her holiness and skill to restore him to himself."

"Lord, save me from despair," Paton prays, "and if I am in despair, make me do some work of peace for thee."

Father in heaven, please give me a fresh attitude
of caring for others. Let me bring comfort and
encouragement to those who carry heavy burdens.
Let the joy of the Lord be my strength.

Pure and genuine religion in the sight of God the Father means caring for orphans and widows in their distress and refusing to let the world corrupt you. JAMES 1:27, NLT

UNEXPECTED JOY

NANCY GUTHRIE, whose daughter, Hope, had been born with a metabolic disorder and lived for just six months, now found herself pregnant again. Might this new baby, just eight weeks past conception, have the same problem? She wrote in her journal that, despite her sinking feelings about getting the prenatal testing results, she wanted to say yes to whatever God had for her and her husband, David.

She writes, "If someone had asked me when I was pregnant with Hope if I wanted to experience what we did with her, I'm sure I would have said no. And yet it was the most profound experience of blessing we've ever had. She brought us so much joy."

Those who have not lived through such an experience may find it hard to imagine how it could be a blessing and a source of joy. Yet the Guthries are not the only ones to report the profound enrichment that can come from bearing and nurturing a child with severe limitations and a shortened life. So much depends on how one receives and loves the child and lives in faith.

Does that mean the fear and discomfort for Nancy and David were gone? Not at all! Yet they were determined to trust God each day—even after they learned that this new baby, too, had the disorder and they would take him home to die.

They named the new baby Gabriel. They put the future in God's hands. They continued their journey of faith, continually choosing to make a new commitment to trust the Lord and to see blessings where others might see only tragedy.

---

*Father in heaven, it's sometimes so difficult to
see blessings in tragic experiences. Help me to see
beyond the disappointments to your grace and the
bountiful ways you are at work in my life.*

I am leaving you with a gift—peace of mind and heart. And the peace I give is a gift the world cannot give. So don't be troubled or afraid.   JOHN 14:27, NLT

SERIOUS TEMPTATION

THOMAS À KEMPIS sketches for us a very unpleasant reality: "So long as we live in this world, we have trials and temptations. As Job says, 'Man's life on earth is a warfare.' We must therefore be on guard against temptations and watchful in prayer."

He repeats the Bible's warning against the devil's deceiving us, prowling and never resting as he seeks whom he may devour and then says, "No one is so perfect and holy that he is never tempted, and we can never be secure from temptation. When one temptation or trial draws to a close, another takes its place and we shall always have something to fight."

Like a football coach warning his players that three-hundred-pound opponents want to crush them into the ground, à Kempis lays the hard facts before us. But also like a coach, he challenges us to resist: "We must not despair. When tempted, earnestly pray God to grant his help."

How do we resist? "Be on guard at the very onset of temptation. Repulse [the devil] at the threshold, as soon as he knocks. First comes an evil thought; next a vivid picture; then delight, and an urge to evil, and finally consent."

In our culture of instant and constant gratification, the process can be swift indeed. Thomas à Kempis could never have dreamed of all the temptations we face today. Yet the principles and the warfare remain the same.

"Fire tempers steel," he writes, "and temptation the just. Let us humble ourselves under the hand of God in every trial and trouble, for he will save and raise up the humble in spirit."

Thomas à Kempis expands on how this works as he prays, "If I count myself to be dust, as I truly am, then your grace will come upon me and your light will enter my heart. Left to myself, I abound with frailties; but when you turn your face toward me, I suddenly gain strength and am filled with new joy."

Father, temptations of all sorts catch me unaware. When I fail, draw me back to integrity. Help me to be alert, to pray, and to experience the strength and new joy Thomas à Kempis prayed for. Take charge of my mind and spirit.

Keep watch and pray, so that you will not give in to temptation. For the spirit is willing, but the body is weak! MATTHEW 26:41, NLT

PRAYER FROM THE DEPTHS

ED DOBSON, slowly dying of ALS, says that when he started out in ministry he chose as his life verse 2 Corinthians 4:16: "Therefore do not lose heart. Though outwardly we are wasting away, yet inwardly we are being renewed day by day" (NIV).

As a young man, Dobson concentrated on the part about being renewed day by day. As an older man now terminally ill, he finds most helpful the part emphasizing the body's wasting away. The verse says that *despite* what's happening in our bodies, we can be renewed each day.

Most people have not been diagnosed with a terminal disease. At the same time, in a sense we have, for Scripture and reality tell us that our time of youth is brief and our lives are soon gone like a mist. In light of that, Paul urged the Corinthians—and us—not to lose heart, for God provides renewal.

Spiritual renewal can be a battle, especially if our bodies are failing. Sometimes we may find it physically hard to pray. That's what Ed Dobson has experienced while living with ALS—yet, paradoxically, the struggles have deepened his faith.

Blockages to prayer may range from serious illness to becoming overwhelmed by events. We may doubt that God hears and helps us. To pray in faith at those times may not feel emotionally satisfying, but prayer is just as effectual then as it is in times of joyous certitude. As happens so often in the Psalms, we call upon the Lord from the depths. Sometimes those depths include a feeling of God's absence.

In all our circumstances, it's possible to grow spiritually. "I will gladly testify that this has happened in my life," Dobson says. He believes his struggles have radically changed him and have helped him become more like Christ.

Dobson testifies to this by quoting 2 Corinthians 1:3-4: "All praise to God, the Father of our Lord Jesus Christ. God is our merciful Father and the source of all comfort. He comforts us in all our troubles so that we can comfort others" (NLT).

Holy Father, my emotions as I pray are sometimes erratic.
Pressures and new challenges can feel overwhelming. And
death, the ultimate challenge, will come someday. Please hear
my prayers now as I lay all my fears and concerns before you.

Mightier than the violent raging of the seas, mightier than the breakers on the shore—
the LORD above is mightier than these! PSALM 93:4, NLT

WHAT'S THE WORST THAT CAN HAPPEN?

BROTHER LAWRENCE was convinced he knew what the worst thing that could happen to him was. He said that for him to lose the sense of God's presence would be worse than being flayed alive.

Most of us can barely imagine the horror of being whipped to death, but Brother Lawrence lived in a time when that happened to people. Yet he said that losing the sense of God's presence would be worse.

At the same time, he didn't believe he would lose that precious sense. He felt that "the lovingkindness of God" assured him God would not completely abandon him and would give him strength to bear such evil as might befall him.

Clearly, Brother Lawrence had a friendship with God somehow more intense and real than most of us experience. Why? Lawrence explains his perspective: "We are to be pitied for being satisfied with so little. God has boundless treasures to give us." He says we're too easily contented. "We bind the hands of God, and we stem the abundance of his grace. When he finds a soul imbued with living faith, into it he pours grace on grace, a flowing stream which spreads wide with force abundantly."

Yet, he adds, "We often check this torrent for the small regard we have for it. Let us check it no more and make an open way for grace."

We may not all experience the same depths of fellowship and joy in God that Brother Lawrence did. Few people do. But we can consider his remarkable example and open our hearts to "make an open way for grace." Who knows what may then begin to happen in our souls!

Lord, help me to be "imbued with living faith." Make me sensitive to your whispers, encouragements, cautions, and shouts. Pour into me, I pray, your grace as a flowing stream.

May you experience the love of Christ, though it is too great to understand fully. Then you will be made complete with all the fullness of life and power that comes from God.
EPHESIANS 3:19, NLT

HUMILITY AS OASIS

ROSEMARY BUDD, after experiencing years of spiritual dryness, concluded, "As our emotions wither and desert us, God is burrowing away at our wills. As we journey through the dark with a growing awareness of our helplessness, we learn to trust ourselves less. Trust in God takes us on a journey into humility."

What strange and harrowing experiences can produce humility! Some people crawl along on a spiritual desert of God's silence, even though they keep on trusting and praying. The furnaces of life slowly purge and refine them toward understanding the truth about themselves—the core of humility.

In her painful, arid years, Budd determined she would not infect others with her emptiness. She kept praying, often repeating scriptural and historic prayers, offering herself to God and enduring his seeming absence. "All that remained was for the Lord to return to the temple," she says. "There was nothing more I could do."

Mother Teresa, likewise, spent most of her mature life working in difficult circumstances, praying faithfully, nursing the dying, changing the world, yet not feeling God's presence or comfort. Perhaps in caring for the dying, Mother Teresa suffered classic burnout; perhaps other dynamics were at play in her spiritual journey.

Unlike Mother Teresa, however, Rosemary Budd once again came to feel God's love and presence. She refers to the seed of God's love becoming embedded deeper in the soil of her will where it could germinate. "In coldness and silence, I learn the stickability from which God can bring harvest," she writes. "Only as I persevere can I become of more use to God and others."

Like Mother Teresa, and like Rosemary Budd, we're called to persevere despite flagging emotions. "Jesus persevered to the end," Rosemary writes. "His final cry of perseverance was also a cry of triumph. 'It is completed!'"

---

*Father in heaven, my spiritual life is so mysterious! Sometimes
I sense your presence and sometimes not at all. Help me
to lift my thoughts to you. Let me rejoice when you bring
your presence, and persevere in times of spiritual dryness.*

Pursue righteousness and a godly life, along with faith, love, perseverance, and gentleness.
I TIMOTHY 6:11, NLT

THE LORD WHO SUBMITS

JOHN ORTBERG points out that the Holy Spirit did not draw attention to himself but to Jesus. "The Spirit comes in the Son's name, bears witness to the Son, and glorifies the Son."

Jesus, on the other hand, submitted to the Spirit, who drove him into the wilderness. Jesus also submitted to the Father, saying, "Not my will, but yours be done" (Luke 22:42, NIV). And the Father? At Jesus' baptism and his transfiguration, we hear the Father say that Jesus is his priceless Son in whom he is deeply pleased.

Ortberg writes, "God exists as Father, Son, and Spirit in a community of greater humility, servanthood, mutual submission, and delight than you and I can imagine."

So what does that mean for us?

We are made in God's image. We therefore should be in the same sort of community with God and with others. What's stunning, if we think long and hard about it, is this: Jesus actually invites us to be part of this fellowship of the Trinity.

"I am praying not only for these disciples," Jesus said, "but also for all who will ever believe in me through their message. I pray that they will all be one, just as you and I are one—as you are in me, Father, and I am in you. And may they be in us" (John 17:20-21, NLT).

We can't possibly get our finite human minds around all the implications of Jesus' prayer for us. Yet we know this: When we are one with the Father, Son, and Holy Spirit, we become part of a community of love and purpose, a community of humility, mutual submission, and delight beyond our capacity to imagine.

We're invited into God's fellowship of love. Outside that fellowship, we are outside the divine community; but when we are in it, we are brought to new life and vitality.

John Ortberg brings this reality into the present moment: "Every person you see is an opportunity to live in and extend the fellowship of the Trinity. We have scores of opportunities each day."

Father, Son, and Holy Spirit, draw me into fellowship
with you and with those I'll be connecting with
today. Help me to act the way you do with each
other—with extreme respect, love, and humility.

I have loved you even as the Father has loved me. Remain in my love.
JOHN 15:9, NLT

THE CALL IN THE DARK

HELMUT THIELICKE speaks to our common spiritual quest as we experience life's demanding and often bewildering events. He says that sometimes, as we find ourselves in darkness, we sense someone is passing by. Is it an enemy or a friend?

In the mysteries of life, as we experience more thunder and rain and darkness than we anticipated, we long for something, or someone, to comfort us. Thielicke says that the someone who calls to us is the same one who called to the young prophet Samuel in the night. When we answer "Here I am" and we open ourselves to the one who calls us, we find shelter and light that comes from the Father.

Yet, in our darkness, we can be apprehensive. We may have become comfortable in the dark and wonder what the Father may require of us in the light. We may question whose voice we are hearing and how we can keep from being led astray. And we may fear that we are going to be judged.

Are we apprehensive about what will really happen to us in the next life? Thielicke gives us a wonderful picture of what people of genuine faith will experience when the time of judgment arrives. "On God's great last day of reckoning," he writes, "when the Judge will come to us suddenly, he will turn out to be our Father."

This is the same loving Father who sent his Son to die for us. He is the one who finds us in the dark.

Thielicke gives us a word picture in the context of the Prodigal Son returning home: "The lights of the Father's house are flooding out to meet me."

Loving Father above, help me to listen for your
voice and to respond with full openness to your
love and grace. Ease my fears, I pray, and replace
them with confidence and hope in you.

Don't be afraid, little flock. For it gives your Father great happiness to give you the Kingdom. LUKE 12:32, NLT

BEYOND OUR BEWILDERMENT

 March 21

PHILIP YANCEY has written eloquently on the mystery of Job's anguished questions and God's responses—responses that give no direct answers. Yancey sums it up this way: "We have different roles to play, we and God. As God made clear to Job, we humans lack the capacity to figure out providence and cosmic justice and answers to the 'why' questions. It is our role, rather, to follow in Jesus' steps by doing the work of the kingdom both by our deeds and by our prayers."

Yet Job's and our own bewilderment remains, even when we praise God for his mighty works and his magnificent creation. We pray; however, grievous things happen. Sometimes, cancer and accidents and violence seem to be all we hear about. We know wonderful people whose lives are cut short.

Spiritually, we may determine to stay fully in step with the Spirit, yet we find we fail time after time.

Yancey refers to the Bible's assurance that when we're confused or broken by what's happening in or around us, God sends the Spirit of his Son into our hearts, and he intercedes for us. We may not know how to pray, but Scripture tells us that the Holy Spirit prays for us with groans that can't be expressed in words.

"Though we feel ignorant in our prayers, the Spirit does not," Yancey writes. "Though we feel exhausted and confused, the Spirit does not. God is not so far off that we need to raise our voices to be heard. We need only groan."

Holy Spirit of God, thank you. When I hear that a
friend is praying for me, it warms me and gives me
hope. How much greater should my faith and hope be
to know that you are praying for me continuously.

The Holy Spirit helps us in our weakness. For example, we don't know what God wants us to pray for. But the Holy Spirit prays for us with groanings that cannot be expressed in words. ROMANS 8:26, NLT

OUR BEST PRAYER

OLE HALLESBY tells it to us straight: "Prayer is for the helpless."

We may consider ourselves strong, courageous, and able, but the truth when it comes to prayer is quite the contrary: "Prayer and helplessness are inseparable. Only he who is helpless can truly pray."

What does this mean?

Hallesby explains that prayer is an attitude of the heart, and this spiritual condition begins with helplessness. "Unquestionably, this is the first and surest indication of a praying heart. Prayer has been ordained for the helpless."

Hallesby recognizes that we sometimes feel as if we are at the end of our rope and don't know what to do. Or we may feel we can't bring ourselves to pray, or we may feel our minds are too full of sin and impurity to pray. We may be lukewarm and halfhearted about exposing ourselves to God in prayer, struggling about our dishonesty. We may feel overwhelmed by circumstances and helpless to live a holy Christian life.

"Listen, my friend!" Hallesby says. "Your helplessness is your best prayer. It calls from your heart to the heart of God with greater effect than all your uttered pleas. He hears it from the moment you are seized with helplessness, and he becomes actively engaged at once in hearing and answering the prayer of your helplessness. Our helplessness is one continual appeal to his Father-heart."

Our Father listens to our cries as a mother listens to her child. He is moved with compassion and brings comfort. Our Father sees our distress, and his Holy Spirit is full of concern and ready to comfort us.

Prayer is for the helpless. Prayer is for me, and for you.

Father in heaven, it's so obvious that I'm helpless to live
as an authentic Christian without your Holy Spirit.
Right now I am helpless in so many ways. I pray you'll
meet me in my low estate and answer my prayers.

My grace is all you need. My power works best in weakness.
2 CORINTHIANS 12:9, NLT

COMBAT READY?

BILLY GRAHAM describes a pathway to what he calls "mushy theological think-ing." He says that it starts in childhood when we hear about goodness, badness, rewards, and punishments. "If you're good, you get ice cream; if you're bad, you go to bed early."

As we grow older, this cause-and-effect perspective seeps into our spiritual under-standing. If we help others and faithfully attend church, we figure we'll be blessed and not experience suffering. But then we get blindsided when rough times come.

Graham acknowledges that life inevitably includes some rough times, and he refers to Marine Corps boot camp to illustrate spiritual realism.

Marine Corps drill instructors impose harsh discipline. Recruits are driven to their limits and trained to know exactly how to use and care for their weapons. They know why they must crawl and run till their bodies shake, and why they must repeatedly shoot and train till they're exhausted: they are headed for deadly combat.

As Christians we must be ready for deadly spiritual combat.

A marine in war is not surprised when he sees someone shooting at him, and we should not be surprised when we face powerful temptations and severe setbacks. The New Testament epistles present a graphic picture of what we're up against, yet they also provide the training and equipment we need to survive and thrive.

For instance, we read in 2 Corinthians 10:3-4, "We are human, but we don't wage war as humans do. We use God's mighty weapons . . . to knock down the strongholds" (NLT).

We're given drill-instructor-type instructions in 1 Corinthians 16:13-14: "Be on guard. Stand firm in the faith. Be courageous. . . . And do everything with love" (NLT).

Those orders fit Billy Graham's lifelong passion to follow Christ, including his prime goal of doing everything with love.

After describing a battalion commander's orders to his troops, Graham puts it this way: "That officer was preparing his men for combat—just as our Lord prepares us for life's combat."

Lord, equip me today for whatever battles are ahead.
Be victorious in me and through me, for I know that
my own skills and weapons aren't enough. Help me to
rise to the challenges and get in step with your Spirit.

God arms me with strength. . . . He trains my hands for battle.
PSALM 18:32, 34, NLT

A WARM HAND

MOTHER TERESA gives us this simple challenge: "See what love can do."

She tells of a day when she picked up a dying man from the gutter whose body was covered with worms. She brought him to her house, and it took three hours to clean him up. She was impressed that he didn't curse or blame someone. Instead, he said, "I've lived like an animal in the street, but I'm going to die like an angel, loved and cared for. I'm going home to God."

Mother Teresa says she has never seen such a radiant smile as she saw on his face before he died. "He went home to God. See what love can do?"

She tells another story that illustrates something most of us could do for someone. She was walking down a street in London when she saw a tall, thin man sitting huddled and miserable. She went up to him, shook his hand, and asked him how he was.

He looked up at her and said, "Oh! After such a long, long time, I feel the warmth of a human hand!"

And she says he then sat up, with a beautiful smile. "Just shaking his hand had made him feel like somebody."

Who needs to feel the warmth of a human hand today? Whom do we ignore who desperately needs a little attention?

Mother Teresa emphasizes that it's the depth of our love that counts, not our carrying out grand things. We start in our own homes and with our neighbors. She urges us to be "the good news" to someone in our sphere of influence who does not feel loved—perhaps a family member or a disgruntled neighbor.

"True love is love that causes us pain, that hurts, and yet brings joy," she says. That is why we must pray to God and ask him to give us the courage to love.

"We have been created in order to love and be loved."

Father in heaven, I get all wrapped up in my
own needs and concerns. Help me to reach out to
those who need a warm hand of encouragement.
Help me to see others through your eyes.

[Jesus said,] "'You must love the LORD your God with all your heart, all your soul, and all your mind.' This is the first and greatest commandment. A second is equally important: 'Love your neighbor as yourself.'" MATTHEW 22:37-39, NLT

SELF-TRANSFORMATION

GEORGE MACDONALD sounds as tough as a medieval monk when he writes about denying ourselves: "We must refuse, abandon, and deny self altogether as a ruling, determining, or originating element in us. We are no more to think, 'What should I like to do?' but 'What would the Living One have me do?'"

He adds, "The self will be cunning and deceitful until it is thoroughly and utterly denied."

Although severe about denying ourselves and emptying our wills, MacDonald communicates grand enthusiasm at the results. He describes our drawing fresh life from God by our "uplooking will" and says that when we deny ourselves, we're receiving God's will and can shove aside our anxieties and fears: "The life of the Father will be the joy of the child."

When we deny ourselves so we can see through God's eyes and think his thoughts—when we feel his deep concerns and his compassions—we find purpose and guidance even in grim times. We follow the Father's guidance in the same way that Jesus followed his Father all the way to his heavenly home. The will of God becomes the driving force and zest of our lives—and ultimately the source of our joy.

When we take on the yoke that Jesus invites us to bear, we carry the same yoke as he bore in fulfilling the will of the Father.

"With the Garden of Gethsemane before him," MacDonald says of Jesus, "with the hour and the power of darkness waiting for him, he declares his yoke easy, his burden light [see Matthew 11:30]. He *first* denies himself, and takes up his cross—then tells us to do the same."

His burden is only light as we shoulder it in his strength—and with his determination to follow his Father without reservation.

Father in heaven, help me to bring my will and my self
to you and to trade them in for your dynamic will and
purpose. Help me to follow you now more fully than
ever before and to be an instrument of your peace.

Jesus said to his disciples, "If any of you wants to be my follower, you must turn from your selfish ways, take up your cross, and follow me." MATTHEW 16:24, NLT

WHICH HEAVENLY FATHER DO WE WANT?

C. S. LEWIS once observed: "We want, in fact, not so much a Father in Heaven as a grandfather in heaven—a senile benevolence who, as they say, 'liked to see young people enjoying themselves' and whose plan for the universe was simply that it might be truly said at the end of each day, 'a good time was had by all.'"

Though Lewis's statement is a bit tongue-in-cheek, don't we all wish that life were more like the jolly song of Sunday school: "I'm happy, happy, happy—happy all the time"? Don't we wish that we could just listen like children, learn the lessons, and find that happiness? But we grow up to experience demands beyond our capacities. Disappointments crash in on us. We realize our life journey consists of some very serious stuff.

As we try to "trust and obey," we face tough moral and spiritual choices.

Lewis writes, "If God is Love, he is, by definition, something more than mere kindness. And it appears, from all the records, that though he has often rebuked us and condemned us, he has never regarded us with contempt. He has paid us the intolerable compliment of loving us, in the deepest, most tragic, most inexorable sense."

That's quite a statement! God pays us an *intolerable* compliment—loving us, yet in the deep, tragic context of the human condition.

"To ask that God's love should be content with us as we are," writes Lewis, "is to ask that God should cease to be God."

Instead of staying as we are, we ultimately find fulfillment and what we were made for as we respond to God's initiatives. That may require some tough adjustments, but that is the way to experience both love and happiness.

Lord, you know how much I prefer your gentle side, of being led in green pastures. Yet I know by your death on the cross that life is deeply serious. Help me accept your stern commands as well as your loving-kindness.

Patient endurance is what you need now, so that you will continue to do God's will. Then you will receive all that he has promised. HEBREWS 10:36, NLT

PRAISE NO MATTER WHAT

BEN PATTERSON, in one of his books, tells two remarkable stories of gratitude and praise in circumstances that would seem to thoroughly crush such sentiments.

During the Thirty Years War, Martin Rinkart was the only pastor left in Eilenburg after a plague killed thousands of people and the other pastors either fled or died. Rinkart conducted 4,500 funerals, including his wife's. Besieged by the Swedes, he prayerfully negotiated a settlement for the desperate town. Yet this is the man who wrote the beloved hymn "Now Thank We All Our God":

> Now thank we all our God
> With heart and hands and voices,
> Who wondrous things hath done,
> In whom his world rejoices.

Patterson's second story is of Frederick Buechner's experience on a cold, rainy night during infantry training. Buechner was hungry, and the turnip someone tossed him fell to the muddy ground. He picked it up anyway and later said, "With a lurch of the heart that is real to me still, I saw suddenly that not only was the turnip good, but the mud was good too, even the drizzle and the cold were good." Buechner saw the joy of creation even at its bleakest and felt the great need to praise someone for it.

Patterson also recounts his own story of reluctantly returning from vacation to do what he now recognizes as an oxymoron: "I grimly obeyed the will of God." He says that God spoke to him after a prayer meeting about his grimness and lack of joy. He came to realize that joy is a choice, that we can choose to give thanks in all things, which triggers gratitude and grace. He points out that Paul *commands* that we be joyful, pray continually, and give thanks.

We may not be able to generate *feelings* of joy, but we can pray and give thanks and praise the Lord. Then, we may look for joy to come "in the morning."

---

*Father in heaven, I have so much to thank you for, and
I do praise you for your love and redemption. Whatever
my circumstances today, pour into me your joy in
creation as I praise you for your wonderful works.*

I will praise the Lord at all times. I will constantly speak his praises. I will boast only in the Lord; let all who are helpless take heart. PSALM 34:1-2, NLT

FORGETTING OURSELVES

FRED SMITH declares, "The essence of joy is the willingness to give oneself into forgetfulness." Then he tells a wonderful story to illustrate his point.

A young Amish girl who had received a box of candy for Christmas decided to act on her mother's suggestion to keep it unopened until her friends came and she could share. Several weeks later, when her friends arrived, she passed the candy around so that each could have a piece. She then set the box on the table without taking a piece for herself. When her mother asked if she wanted some of the candy, she said, "Oh, I forgot I was here!"

Smith says, "How many times the deep sense of joy comes as we give ourselves into forgetfulness."

Joy comes as we absorb and act on the principles found in the Bible:

Developing an attitude of gratitude.

Incorporating the gritty realism of Proverbs about money, sex, and relationships.

Trusting God in all circumstances.

Fred Smith talks about a lifelong process of cultivating "joy for the journey," which he defines as a deep feeling of adequacy available to us as we live out our faith. "Joy is a result," he says. "It is a reward for life being well spent in hope."

Yet it does not come without discipline. When Jesus says, "Let not your heart be troubled," it is not a suggestion, but a command.

The Holy Spirit in us makes all this possible, for we will find our own strength inadequate for the long journey with its side roads and temptations. The Spirit's joy is not always effervescent, but it is the source of the capacity to forget ourselves.

"When joy overflows your cup," Smith says, "try spilling it on someone."

---

*Lord, help me open myself to your joy and do my part
in the discipline that will make joy a central part of
my life day after day. Help me to care more about the
joy of sharing than about doing my own thing.*

Don't let your hearts be troubled. Trust in God, and trust also in me. JOHN 14:1, NLT

LINCOLN AND THE LORD

D. L. MOODY told the story of a teenage boy in the Civil War who had fallen asleep at his sentry post. For his offense, he was tried and sentenced to be shot.

When the news reached his mother and father in Vermont, they were devastated. Their little daughter, who had read about Abraham Lincoln's love for his children, said that if the president knew how much her parents loved her brother, he wouldn't allow him to be shot.

Somehow, the little girl got to Washington and into the White House chamber where Lincoln was in a meeting. The president asked her what she wanted, and she told her story of how much her parents loved her brother. She said that if he were shot, it would break their hearts. Lincoln, moved with compassion, immediately sent a dispatch canceling the sentence and giving the boy a parole so he could go home and see his parents.

Moody says he told this story to show how, as Lincoln's heart was moved with compassion, so the Son of God, who loves his children, has compassion on us. When we face the worst, Jesus is there. He knows how we can be devastated by life's losses and capricious events. When we come to him, he prays for us and acts on our behalf.

Robert Murray McCheyne says, "If I could hear Christ praying for me in the next room, I would not fear a million enemies. Yet distance makes no difference. He is praying for me."

"Take your crushed, bruised heart to him," Moody urges. "He will comfort you, and bind up and heal your sorrow."

Lord Jesus, I bring all my sorrows and cares to you. I lay them before you and trust that you care, that you do pray for me, and that you will be at work in my life.

You, O Lord, are a God of compassion and mercy, slow to get angry and filled with unfailing love and faithfulness. PSALM 86:15, NLT

WATCHING WHAT THE
LORD IS DOING

JOHN HENRY JOWETT observes that to many of us "the Creator is remote from his works." We don't walk in the garden with the Lord and recognize that it is he who not only made all things but keeps the process gloriously going.

In contrast Jowett illustrates, in a man named James Smethan, the attitude of wonder that we might emulate. According to Jowett, Smethan would speak of going into his garden "to see what the Lord was doing." At other times, "he would stand at the top of Highgate Hill on a blustering night to watch the goings of the Lord in the storm."

All this meant to James Smethan that Creation was not merely a single event, but a *process* whose countless events were still going on. He watched the Lord at work!

Most of us live largely separated from nature, and when we do walk the forests or the shore, our minds are saturated with images from screens large and small. "Let us recover the sacredness of things," Jowett advises. "Let us 'practice the presence of God.'"

Everywhere we look, creation reveals the "goings of the Lord." Flip through a copy of *Smithsonian* or *National Geographic*, or study the legs of that insect crawling past, or consider the dexterity of your hands. We are called to praise God for his wonderful works.

Jowett urges, "Let us link his love and power to every flower. And so shall we be able to say, as we move amid the glories of the natural world, 'The Lord is in his holy Temple.'"

Heavenly Father, the wonders of your world and your
workings among us are beyond finding out, no matter how
much scientific equipment and insight we employ. Fill
me with your wonder at all this, Lord, and thank you.

In the beginning God created the heavens and the earth. GENESIS 1:1, NLT

LOVE IN A DYING CULTURE

FRANCIS SCHAEFFER writes in *The Mark of the Christian*: "Jesus gives the world the right to judge whether you and I are Christians on the basis of our observable love toward all Christians." That's true because Jesus commanded his disciples to love one another. Not only that, but Jesus said that *love* is the mark of being his disciple.

Schaeffer sees it as "pretty frightening" when we consider the implications. When people perceive that the mark of love is missing, he says, we ought to get on our knees and ask God whether they're right or not.

Our love for fellow Christians, he emphasizes, must not be narrow and exclusionary. It must be authentic love from God that ripples out to all people. At the same time, Schaeffer urges realism. "There will be times (and let us say it with tears) when we will fail in our love toward each other as Christians. When we fail, we must ask God's forgiveness."

At the same time, many of us would testify to finding profound love and countless acts of selflessness in our churches and homes. Those on the outside seldom see all the rich caring and concern that Christians show one another. Reconciliation generally goes unreported. Instead, stories including anger, conflict, and harsh words get wide press. Tragically, there are plenty of those stories to report.

In our prayers, we need to lay all this before the Lord. Sometimes we're filled with gratitude for the love we receive or have been privileged to give. Other times, we may be caught up in conflicts that corrupt love and invalidate our witness.

Schaeffer states, "The church is to be a loving church in a dying culture." Each day we face that challenge and opportunity.

Father in heaven, in every area where I feel anger or bitterness, pour into me your love. In all the ways in which I've received love and been able to give it, let me rejoice and continue to respond to your Holy Spirit.

Those who accept my commandments and obey them are the ones who love me. And because they love me, my Father will love them. And I will love them and reveal myself to each of them. JOHN 14:21, NLT

SURVIVING BOLDLY

LUCI SHAW writes, "The unexpected is always lurking around the bend. Most of us will undergo difficulties or distresses that bring us to our knees, overcome by despair or profound doubt. After my husband, Harold, died, I was in a place like that."

She found comfort in Scripture that encouraged her to embrace new challenges, including Isaiah 54:2-5: "Enlarge your house; build an addition. Spread out your home, . . . for you will soon be bursting at the seams. . . . You will no longer remember . . . the sorrows of widowhood. For your Creator will be your husband" (NLT). It took about eighteen months for the paralysis of grief and mourning to start lifting for Luci.

When we're hit hard by the heavy events of life, we naturally grieve and find that adjusting takes lots of both time and faith. Challenges we never anticipated loom large, and sometimes we feel disoriented. The ways we previously coped no longer apply.

Shaw was determined to approach life as a continuing adventure. She claimed the promise of Psalm 16:11, that God would reveal the path of life and bring her joy. "Surviving boldly in a complex world takes getting used to," she writes, "but I can never complain that it's dull. Painful or challenging experiences and passages confirm life's verity, the solidity and surprise of it all in God, despite its traps and pitfalls, its scares and sorrows."

We'd love to avoid the pitfalls and sorrows, but we can't. Troubles are part of any adventure and of life itself. The challenge is in how we will face our realities.

Luci ramps up the challenge: "We need God to confound us with a mission larger than we are."

Father in heaven, help me embrace your mission for me. Open my eyes to see what you see. Sometimes I'm perplexed and disturbed. Give me your peace and wisdom, Lord, as I swallow hard and trust you.

I know the LORD is always with me. I will not be shaken, for he is right beside me.
PSALM 16:8, NLT

FLOWERS IN THE RUTS

JOHN HENRY JOWETT claimed that he found "forget-me-nots in many a rutty road and wild roses behind a barricade of nettles."

Many of us see little but the rutty road in this fallen world. When we keep staring at the ruts in the road, we miss the forget-me-nots. When we avoid the nettles that sting us, we miss the wild roses.

Jowett urges us to look in the dark patches of life for "tokens of the Lord's presence." He mentions that poet Frances Ridley Havergal kept a "journal of mercies." "She crowded it with her remembrances of God's goodness. She was always on the lookout for tokens of the Lord's grace and bounty, and she found them everywhere. Many a complaining life would be changed into music and song by a journal of mercies."

We read of prisoners in solitary cells thankful for the visits of a spider that helped to relieve their boredom. We hear of starving African children who, when water and a little food arrives, shout, "Now we have everything! Now we have everything!"

Despite disappointments and shortfalls, most of us have enough for our needs. We can say with gratitude, "This is the day the LORD has made; let us rejoice and be glad in it" (Psalm 118:24, NIV). Instead of keeping our eyes on the rutty road, we can be thankful.

"Mercies abound on every hand," Jowett proclaims. "Count your blessings."

Father in heaven, you've given me material things
and rich spiritual resources. Thank you! Let me show
my gratitude with a spirit of praise. My journal
would be huge if I added up all your mercies.

Truth springs up from the earth, and righteousness smiles down from heaven. Yes, the LORD pours down his blessings. PSALM 85:11-12, NLT

DEFYING NATURAL GLOOM

April 3

AMY CARMICHAEL writes of the forbidding gloom that comes when we remember what was most precious to us but is now forever lost. She quotes Psalm 42:4: "These things will I remember, how I marched with the procession to the house of God with joy and praise—a festive crowd." Then Amy makes it personal: "Yes, we were one of a festive crowd. Was there any happy thing that we did not do? And we think of what used to be, so different from all that is now."

Many of us remember the past with deep longing. Loved ones gone . . . wonderful relationships ended . . . financial security vaporized . . . health gone—the losses can generate thick gloom.

Carmichael again quotes Psalm 42:4: "When I remember these things, I pour out my soul in me" (KJV). She then asks, "Was there ever a sad heart that did not feel like that? The psalmist is ashamed of his feelings, hopes in God and praises him, but then gives in to sadness again: 'Why art thou cast down, O my soul? and why art thou disquieted in me?'" (verse 5, KJV).

Yet the psalmist also prays that God would send his light and his truth to lead him. We see in so many of the Psalms the anguish and gloom of the human experience; yet, when the psalmist calls upon God, we see the lifting of that heaviness and the spirit of praise rising up in response to his wonders and his love for us.

"It is all true," writes Amy Carmichael. "We know that it is true, and yet our feet must walk the ways of earth down that dreary hill, past those somber trees, and into the valley, before we can press up through the mist and stand under shining skies."

Father in heaven, you know how tears come to my eyes
and heaviness to my soul when I remember what is
gone and lost. The memories are bittersweet. Draw me
into your hope and joy as you create new memories.

Why am I discouraged? Why is my heart so sad? I will put my hope in God! I will praise him again—my Savior and my God! PSALM 42:11, NLT

THE UNWORTHY WHO PRAY

MARTIN LUTHER has some advice for people who first want to live a better life before they pray: "If you don't want to pray before you feel you're worthy or qualified, you'll never pray. Prayer must not be based on or depend on your personal worthiness. It must be based on the unchanging truth of God's promise."

We make resolutions, but they slowly fade. Our faith wavers as we plow through the realities of daily life. Sometimes we approach God's presence feeling as if we've failed far too often or too greatly to sense his welcome. Yet, "We pray because we are unworthy to pray," writes Luther. "Our prayers are heard precisely because we believe that we are unworthy. So go ahead and feel unworthy."

If prayer is for the unworthy, then who else might it be for?

Prayer is for the fearful.
Prayer is for the helpless.
Prayer is for those who doubt.
Prayer is for those at the end of their rope.
Prayer is for the sinner who cries out, "God be merciful to me."

Listening for the Holy Spirit becomes the great adventure of prayer. We come with hands empty, so that he can fill them.

Impediments of many kinds can keep us from prayer, but we need never allow feelings of being unwelcome to be one of them.

Luther says that worthiness doesn't help us, nor does unworthiness hinder us. The vital thing is to honor God's truthfulness, to pray, and to have faith in his promises.

Father, it's a relief to know I don't need to get my act cleaned up to come to you. How aware I am of my weakness and failures! Help me to rest in your assurance that if I call on you, you'll redeem and equip me.

Never stop praying. I THESSALONIANS 5:17, NLT

HOLINESS AND VITALITY

OSWALD CHAMBERS makes a jarring assertion: "Life without war is impossible."

Impossible? Didn't the angels on that first Christmas promise peace to those of goodwill? Don't we constantly and desperately try to avoid war of any sort? What is Chambers talking about?

"The basis of physical, mental, moral, and spiritual life is antagonism," he writes. "This is an open fact of life. Health is the balance between physical life and external nature, and it is maintained only by sufficient vitality on the inside against things on the outside."

How starkly realistic! Countless harmful organisms constantly invade our bodies, and only the vitality of our immune system keeps us healthy. Mentally and spiritually it's the same.

In the early days of the computer, the acronym GIGO—Garbage In, Garbage Out—became popular. In other words, if you put "garbage" or nonsense into a computer, that's what you'll get back. In the same way, if you put garbage into your mind or soul, that's what you'll get back.

Just as our bodies are constantly at war with alien organisms, so, too, our souls are at war with spiritual forces that seek to debilitate and destroy us. We must have spiritual vitality in order to survive and thrive.

Chambers sounds like a rugged, no-holds-barred coach when he says, "I have to learn to score off the things that come against me, and in that way produce the balance of holiness; then it becomes a delight to meet opposition."

As in sports, we can score off the spiritual attacks against us. We gain a lift from forces that look as if they will overwhelm us. Chambers writes, "The surf that distresses the ordinary swimmer produces in the surfer the super-joy of going clean through it. Tribulation, distress, persecution, produce in us the super-joy; they are not things to fight."

We're promised that God, the source of our vitality, can make us more than conquerors.

Father in heaven, sometimes the forces against me—mental, spiritual, and physical—feel overwhelming. Bring your vitality into my soul, I pray, that I might welcome the challenges and get fully in step with your Spirit.

I pray that God, the source of hope, will fill you completely with joy and peace because you trust in him. Then you will overflow with confident hope through the power of the Holy Spirit. ROMANS 15:13, NLT

PRACTICAL FAITH

JOHN WESLEY was a very practical, organized leader, and he was equally practical in his approach to spiritual vitality. Here are three of his down-to-earth challenges:

Do all the good you possibly can. We don't hear much today about "sins of omission," but Wesley defined them as "avoiding to do good of any kind when we have the opportunity." He declared that we must be aware of these omissions as sins. We should be "zealous to do good to the bodies and souls of our neighbors." He strongly emphasized that we should avoid "pious chit-chat or religious gossip," but instead should use "every shred of time." He quoted the scriptural command that whatever our hand finds to do we should do with all our might.

Aim at pleasing God in everything. In our day of Entertainment (with a capital *E*), Wesley's stern advice may seem impossible. He said we should not be interested in any pleasure that does not bring us closer to God—that our aim should be to please God in everything. Actually, our technological world gives us vast opportunities to revel in God's creation, from access to great art and literature to ball games and simple pleasures. The principle is fully valid today, although the temptations are many.

Beware of schisms. Wesley warned against ripping holes in the church and losing our love for one another. "Beware of a dividing spirit," he said. He also urged us never to criticize one pastor against another because of inconsistencies or mistakes. "Be patient with those who disagree with you. Do not condemn those who do not see things just as you do, or who think it is their duty to contradict you, whether in a great thing or small." Here is Wesley's simple game plan for the day: "Please God. Do good. Love others."

Heavenly Father, help me to have a patient, loving spirit, both toward those who return my goodwill and toward those who rebuff it. Help me to use my time wisely with your Holy Spirit's guidance.

All of you together are Christ's body, and each of you is a part of it.
I CORINTHIANS 12:27, NLT

PRAYER AS NECESSITY

HENRI NOUWEN writes about opening our hands to God without fear and about experiencing release from festering conflicts. Through prayer, we can experience freedom—and even festive spontaneity. He confides, "You begin to suspect that to pray is to live."

What a bracing reality: "To pray is to live." The inverse is equally true: "To live is to pray."

Nouwen says that prayer is acceptance. "When we pray, we are standing with our hands open to the world. We know that God will show himself in the nature that surrounds us, in the people we meet, in the situations we run into."

Prayer is adventure. Prayer is listening for "sealed orders" from God. Prayer is waiting for his secrets to be revealed.

Prayer is as necessary for nourishing our souls and spirits as food and water are for our bodies.

To live in prayer is to become alert. We ask, What is happening now that shows God's engagement with me? What is the Holy Spirit whispering? In whom do I see signals of God's grace? If I were to fully do what the Spirit wants right now, what would it be?

We find an energizing freedom when our prayerful thinking becomes a spiritual treasure hunt.

At the same time, prayer is costly.

Henri Nouwen tells us that prayer requires our confession that we're limited and weak. He advises, "Whenever you pray, you profess that you are not God and that you wouldn't want to be, that you haven't reached your goal yet, and that you never will in this life, that you must constantly stretch out your hands and wait again for the gift which gives new life."

---

*Lord, here I am again, dependent on you and hoping
for your gifts of love and courage and faith. I long for
that freedom and spontaneity that comes from being in
step with your Spirit and your continuous new life.*

O God, you are my God; I earnestly search for you. . . . Your unfailing love is better than life itself; how I praise you! PSALM 63:1, 3, NLT

NATURAL-BORN WHINERS?

JILL BRISCOE admits that humbly submitting to God in the face of difficulty has been "incredibly hard for me. I just love to gripe and complain."

Ouch! Does her stark honesty resonate with you? Most people would never admit that.

Briscoe says our griping comes naturally—that it's part of our sinful nature. But she lays this challenge before us: "We can monitor our growth in grace by our willingness to stop it."

Stop it? But we have so many reasons to complain—so many things go so very, very wrong! Jill Briscoe understands that, yet she presents us with this stark challenge: "It's as if we feel we have an inalienable right to a charmed life! God wants us to stop whining. He wants us to humbly submit and bear the difficulty patiently."

How does she know how God views whining? "God was constantly telling the children of Israel to stop it," she says. "In fact, he is still telling us in the New Testament how he felt about all the grumbling his people did in the Old Testament: 'Do not grumble, as some of them did—and were killed by the destroying angel' (1 Corinthians 10:10, NIV)." Briscoe asks, "If the destroying angel meted out such drastic punishment today, I wonder how many of us would be left?"

To turn from whining to praise is to turn 180 degrees. Our call is to concentrate on God's compassion and mercy in the storms of life and on the rejoicing that will "come in the morning."

Are we ready for hardship and testing? From long experience, Briscoe says, "It comes down to a new willingness to be broken by the circumstances of life that God in his sovereign grace permits. When you do that, your faith distress becomes faith developed. You can have faith in the loving compassion of a merciful God who will, moment by moment and crisis by crisis, supply all the grace you need."

Father in heaven, my days are full of things to grumble
about. Change me, I pray. Let my spirit be one of
thankfulness for all the mercies you provide. Lord,
let me turn from whining to faith and praise.

Make thankfulness your sacrifice to God, and keep the vows you made to the Most High.
PSALM 50:14, NLT

GENUINE SECURITY

FRANÇOIS FÉNELON made this startling and somewhat unnerving statement: "You must lose everything to find God for himself alone. But you won't lose everything until it is ripped from you. You won't begin to let go of yourself until you have been thrown off a cliff!"

Fénelon was speaking to a particular individual, so maybe that stark advice doesn't apply to us. Then again, maybe it's just realistic, for in this time of global troubles and insecurities we may find ourselves losing just about everything. If not now, eventually we'll lose it all, for life is short and we take nothing with us. Whatever it is that's most precious to us, whatever gives us enjoyment and security, will one day be gone.

Actually, realizing that all we have is transitory and that God alone gives genuine security and joy can start to free us—and to make us realize we must seek the Lord above all.

Yet we're human. We're dependent on relationships, jobs, and the commitments of others. We enjoy the many good things that come our way. Says Fénelon, "It is rare to hold God's gifts without possessiveness." He cautions that possessive love can lead to grief, but that "God's love sets you free."

It all centers on having the attitude that Jesus described when he spoke of the Father taking care of the flowers and birds. All good comes from God, and we are called to trust him and find freedom in that trust—even when what's precious to us fades or is ripped away.

François Fénelon encourages us to "experience how *immense* God is, and how he sets his children free. Bear patiently all that God allows to pass into your life. God gives you grace to bear the cross just as he provides for your daily bread. Trust God to bring you what you need."

Lord, I want to fully trust you. Help me to find my security in you. I don't want to be so bullheaded that you have to throw me off a cliff to get my attention! Here are my mind and heart. Grant me the freedom that comes with acceptance.

Seek the Kingdom of God above all else, and live righteously, and he will give you everything you need. MATTHEW 6:33, NLT

THE TEMPTATIONS OF WORK

EUGENE PETERSON claims that "work is a far more common source of temptation than sex."

What could he possibly mean by that?

"The sin of Saul took place in the midst of doing good work," Peterson writes. "Saul was ruined as a God-anointed king in the course of doing his God-anointed work."

Peterson's insight is that Saul was much more absorbed in his work as king than in the God who had anointed him. He became more concerned with pleasing the people than with authentic worship. In fact, Saul's worship of God was undertaken so that Saul could be successful in his work, not so that God would be obeyed and glorified.

"Saul was treating God as a means, and God will not be used," Peterson cautions. "The worship was undertaken so that the work could prosper."

How common is this sin? It certainly was catastrophic for Saul, but is it a big deal in our day and age? Don't today's sexual temptations—fueled by technology—trump those related to our work?

Perhaps. But then again, as we think of all the strife and contention in religious work, we see how God is often shunted aside and his glory dragged through the mud. In church, our minds are distracted from worship. At work and school, temptations of all sorts stalk us. We're often unaware of the subtle dangers of using God to get ahead instead of worshiping him, loving him, and putting him first in our lives.

David, in contrast to Saul, passionately sought God in both work and worship. Despite his flaws and sins, David was appalled by anything less than authentic worship. Eugene Peterson says of David's robust faith that he had great awareness of God's holiness and presence. We see this over and over in David's psalms.

For instance in Psalm 57 he prays, "Be exalted, O God, above the highest heavens! May your glory shine over all the earth. . . . Wake up, my heart! Wake up, O lyre and harp! I will wake the dawn with my song. . . . For your unfailing love is as high as the heavens" (NLT).

Father, only you can ignite my spiritual passion and increase my love for you. Grant me more of what David had and less of what destroyed Saul's spiritual authenticity and leadership. God, be merciful to me, a sinner.

I will fulfill my vows to you, O God, and will offer a sacrifice of thanks for your help.
PSALM 56:12, NLT

A REMARKABLE TRANSFORMATION

JONI EARECKSON TADA is an astounding example of turning a negative into a positive. Here is what she's had to deal with: When she first became a quadriplegic, she was terrified to lie down at night. Gravity is her enemy, making her more paralyzed lying down than at any other time. In a wheelchair, she can move her arms and shrug her shoulders; in bed she can't move at all, except to turn her head on the pillow. By physical necessity, she must go to bed by 7:30 each night. Her "bed of affliction" makes her feel confined, disabled, and claustrophobic.

Despite all that, she determined that her bed would become her place of prayer. She was inspired by a challenging statement she read by Charles Haddon Spurgeon: "I believe that when we cannot pray, it is time that we prayed more than ever. And if you answer, 'But how can that be?' I would say, Pray to pray. Pray for prayer. Pray for the spirit of supplication. Do not be content to say, 'I would pray if I could.' No, but if you cannot pray, pray until you can."

Joni prayed that way long and hard. The "place of discipline" eventually became "her favorite place to be." She describes her bedroom now as "a *meeting* place," and her bedtime as "a time of praise, of waiting, of confession, Scripture, praying, watching, interceding, petitioning, thanksgiving, singing and meditating, listening, and then ending in praise."

We can all think of negative situations that weigh heavily on us and drain us of our joy. Joni Eareckson Tada's tenacity in prayer and her transformation show that, even in extreme circumstances, prayer may be an antidote beyond our expectations. Might a determined commitment to prayer somehow transform what we dread the most?

Thinking of other wives who are busy with household chores in the evening, Joni says with a touch of ironic humor, "I am paralyzed in bed. What a privilege!"

Lord, grant me the vision to see my own limitations as opportunities to draw closer to you. And help me not to take for granted the freedom you've given me in Christ.

I will praise you as long as I live, lifting up my hands to you in prayer. You satisfy me more than the richest feast. I will praise you with songs of joy. PSALM 63:4-5, NLT

DOWN TO GO UP

CHARLES HADDON SPURGEON says that as we advance in our spiritual lives, we gain a deeper understanding of our unworthiness. But far from seeing this as a reason for despondency, he sees it as a cause for joy, because it means the Holy Spirit is at work.

It is not "worm theology" to grasp our smallness before almighty God. It's simply realistic to experience an ever-deepening sense of our own sinfulness and a more profound understanding of our dependence on God.

Spurgeon preached, "They are the strongest who are the weakest in themselves. They are the richest who know how poor they are apart from God. They have the most grace who know how utterly empty of grace they would be if the Lord should ever withdraw his hand from giving it to them."

When we fully understand our enormous and complete need for grace, we move from despondency to joy as we open ourselves to God. In our deepest difficulties, we find his grace all the more potent and sustaining.

Spurgeon observes that it's in our most desperate straits we discover our most joyous revelations. He points to the apostle John as an example: "John must go to the isle that is called Patmos before he could have the wondrous revelation that was there given him."

When the Holy Spirit makes us aware of our weaknesses, it is not to push us down but to raise us up.

"A Christian has never fully realized what Christ came to make him," writes Spurgeon, "until he has grasped the joy of the Lord. Christ wishes his people to be happy. When they are perfect, as he will make them in due time, they shall also be perfectly happy."

---

*Holy Father above, as I try to live for you, it becomes
increasingly clear how much I am dependent on your
strength and grace. Help me to hold nothing back from
what you want to do in and through me today.*

For the despondent, every day brings trouble; for the happy heart, life is a continual feast.
PROVERBS 15:15, NLT

LITTLE RATS' CLAWS OF ANXIETY

ALAN PATON prayed, "O Lord, save me from anxiety, and if we are anxious, let us commit ourselves to you more fully, to be used as instruments of your peace, so that we learn to be less concerned about ourselves and more concerned about others."

As we come to God in prayer, our minds sometimes flood with all sorts of nasty scenarios. Rosemary Budd described it as experiencing "little rats' claws of anxiety scurrying up and down my spirit."

In the turmoil of apartheid South Africa, Paton observed that when we commit ourselves to pray as St. Francis did, asking to become instruments of God's peace, "we do not have much time to worry about ourselves. In the end we may cease to worry about ourselves altogether." This insight freed him to continue his life of action and reconciliation.

It's no wonder so many have placed the Prayer of St. Francis on their walls, where they can see it daily. A careful study and absorption of the prayer, clause by clause, might free us as it did the courageous Alan Paton.

> Lord, make me an instrument of thy peace. Where there is hatred, let me sow love; where there is injury, pardon; where there is doubt, faith; where there is despair, hope; where there is darkness, light; where there is sadness, joy.
>
> O Divine Master, grant that I may not so much seek to be consoled as to console; not so much to be understood as to understand; not so much to be loved, as to love. For it is in giving that we receive; it is in pardoning that we are pardoned; it is in dying that we are born again to eternal life.

Lord, help me to get my eyes off myself and to care about the burdens of others. Help me to sow love, faith, hope, and joy. Develop in me all the fruit of the Spirit, for I surely cannot produce it on my own. Work in and through me, I pray.

Don't just listen to God's word. You must do what it says. Otherwise, you are only fooling yourselves. JAMES 1:22, NLT

WHEN WE CAN'T PRAY

April 14

NANCY GUTHRIE and her husband, David, after receiving the bitter news of a fatal diagnosis for their infant daughter, Hope, cried out to God and in the following weeks prayed together often. Yet, as time passed, they found they prayed less—for many reasons, including the difficulty of not knowing *how* to pray in such circumstances.

Sometimes we intend to pray, and perhaps even long to pray, yet in the crush of life or our own internal battles, we do not or cannot. We then feel guilty and lose our spiritual vitality.

Guthrie says that in those times when we don't have the will or the capacity to pray, it's a relief to know that the Holy Spirit helps us. "When we are weak-willed and weak-minded," she writes, "when distress has consumed our energy and emotions, the Holy Spirit helps us. And his prayers are not passionless or impersonal. He prays for us with deep devotion."

Many books have been written on prayer, including its practice, its mysteries, and its vital necessity. We're familiar with a variety of prayers, from confession to intercession to supplication, and many of us find insights and helps from those who have written from their experiences in prayer. Yet we still struggle as we seek to pray our way through the demands of life.

The promises we find in Scripture about the Holy Spirit's helping us in our infirmities provide a unique perspective. No matter how stumbling or incoherent our words, the Holy Spirit transforms them into authentic and powerful prayers.

Guthrie assures us, "When we wonder if heaven hears our cries, the Holy Spirit is pleading on our behalf in a language heaven hears and understands."

Father in heaven, please take my inarticulate words
and give wings to them, that they might be heard
in heaven. May your Holy Spirit take my feeble
will and empower it to love and glorify you.

O LORD, hear me as I pray; pay attention to my groaning. Listen to my cry for help, my King and my God, for I pray to no one but you. PSALM 5:1-2, NLT

USELESS WORK, FRUITFUL WORK

April 15

THOMAS À KEMPIS says that without love, work has no value—but whatever is done out of love is fruitful. "Whoever loves much does much."

Nice sentiment, but what does it really mean? Thomas à Kempis brings it right down to reality, pulling no punches in describing our fallen human nature—which is not exactly brimming over with natural love: "We require others to be perfect but don't correct ourselves. We want others bound by rules, but we want to be free of them."

He emphasizes that none of us are without hypocrisy: "If you can't mold yourself, how can you expect others to fit your expectations? Bear with your neighbor's faults, for you have many of your own that others must bear. We rebuke small faults in others but overlook greater faults in ourselves. We are quick to resent what we suffer from others, but we fail to consider what others suffer from us."

Tough accusations! To some degree, they're true of each of us. Overcoming our self-centeredness requires God's help and a commitment to love, even when it's painful. Love does not come naturally without aid from the Holy Spirit.

At the same time, the payoff of loving much is large. Because we are not self-sufficient or wise enough in and of ourselves, à Kempis advises us to "support one another, comfort, help, teach, and advise one another. Whoever is moved by true and perfect love is not self-seeking, but desires only God's glory."

Father, I pray that you'll give me a glimpse of how I really
am with others. Root the hypocrisy out of my soul. Let
me love others in ways that encourage them. Bring your
love into my life, Lord, and help me to honor you.

I will praise you, LORD, with all my heart; I will tell of all the marvelous things you have done. I will be filled with joy because of you. PSALM 9:1-2, NLT

DOUBTS AND MIRACLES

ED DOBSON admits that in his struggles with his terminal illness, ALS, his faith has been mixed with doubts. For that reason, he says, he loves the story of the man who came to Jesus with his demon-possessed son. When Jesus asked the father about his faith, the man responded, "I do believe. Help me overcome my unbelief."

Dobson says that response is one of the most remarkable and honest statements he's found in the Gospels. Countless Christians would agree—its honesty and realism have made it a universal prayer. For instance, the King James translation, "I believe; help thou mine unbelief," has been voiced by countless strugglers for hundreds of years. That's because the life of genuine faith is nearly always accompanied at some point by doubt.

So what was Jesus' response to this man? Dobson points out that Jesus didn't say, "Come back when you have more faith." He didn't say, "Purge the doubt and then we'll talk." Instead, he answered the father's heartfelt plea and healed his son.

Knowing our Lord's response, we know we can be fully honest about all our doubts and dismay as we commune with him. We bring our smidgen of faith to him and ask him to increase it.

God listens to us and loves us. He is fully aware of our troubles, no matter that what is happening is about to crush our spirits. Even when our bodies are moving through the valley of the shadow of death, we don't have to fear evil, for the Good Shepherd is with us.

Ed Dobson says that he learned two things from this story. First, that faith is not the absence of doubt. Second, we can still pray, even when doubts and questions assail us.

"Prayer," he says, "opens up the possibility of a miracle."

*Lord, I do believe in you. Here are my doubts
and my anxieties. Enlarge my faith and grant me
wisdom so that all through this day I can serve
you and others in step with your Spirit.*

[Jesus said,] "Anything is possible if a person believes." The father instantly cried out, "I do believe, but help me overcome my unbelief!" MARK 9:23-24, NLT

NOTHING SWEETER

BROTHER LAWRENCE says, "If I were a preacher, I should preach nothing else but the practice of the presence of God. There is not in the world a way of life more sweet, nor more delightful than continual converse with God."

How did Brother Lawrence do this?

"Make a holy and firm resolution," he writes. "For the love of him, live the rest of your days in his holy presence. Never lose the vision of it. Put your hand to the task."

In the pressures of today's urgent demands, which jam every hour, we may find the good brother's preachment guilt inducing. How can we possibly keep focused on God when a baby is wailing or we're late for a crucial meeting?

We can take large comfort that keeping focused on God is called the *practice* of the presence of God. Who knows what surprising grace we might experience as we open ourselves to the Holy Spirit? We can call on him who is called the Helper to help us stay alert to his guidance in this demanding adventure called life.

Brother Lawrence says he would keep himself apart with God "at the depth and center of my soul as much as I am able."

C. S. Lewis once observed that we seem to be on an inclined plane away from God and keep rolling away from him, despite our prayers and best intentions. Instead of letting this constantly frustrate us, we might take comfort in knowing that this is reality and that we can call on the Spirit to help us "in our infirmities."

Brother Lawrence urges us to "call the soul gently and quietly back to God as soon as we find it drawn away from him."

---

*Lord, I realize I do keep rolling down that inclined
plane away from you. With all that I'm now facing,
help me to bring everything to you. Let me see
through your eyes and follow your guidance.*

Fix your thoughts on what is true, and honorable, and right, and pure, and lovely, and admirable. Think about things that are excellent and worthy of praise.
PHILIPPIANS 4:8, NLT

HUMILITY'S MUSIC

ROSEMARY BUDD once said, "The music of humility is the sound of laughter."

Humility and laughter? How do they go together?

Maybe you remember a time when you experienced great success at something, and as you were admiring your reflection in the mirror and reveling in your victory, you realized just how much other people had contributed to your success. You might have also realized how *God* made it all possible.

Perhaps at that moment you saw yourself for who you really are—in all your humanness—and a little merriment bubbled out. Or maybe you even burst out laughing.

That's the music of humility. We don't own success; we receive it as a gracious gift from God.

"The music of humility is the sound of laughter." That's so true—we can't even breathe without God's enablement. Rosemary Budd expands on the connection: "Such laughter is an echo of the laughter in heaven, the merry company of the saints."

Jesus says, "You will know the truth, and the truth will set you free" (John 8:32, NLT).

Humility is simply knowing the truth—that our skills and abilities, our success and stability, our health, and even our faith, are all gifts from the Creator. We own nothing.

"If I own nothing, then no one can take it from me," Budd writes. "From humility springs poverty; from poverty springs freedom; from freedom springs joy."

Lord Jesus, they say you had a sense of humor, using images such as camels squeezing through the eye of a needle to describe the entrance to heaven. Help me to be able to laugh at myself. Let me "get" the humor and joy of true humility.

Don't try to impress others. Be humble, thinking of others as better than yourselves. . . . You must have the same attitude that Christ Jesus had. . . . He gave up his divine privileges; he took the humble position of a slave. PHILIPPIANS 2:3, 5, 7, NLT

WHEELCHAIR POWER

JOHN ORTBERG reports on a friend's description of an old woman in a convalescent hospital filled with the smells of sickness and urine and senile people waiting to die. His friend found the woman strapped in a wheelchair, her face "an absolute horror" of distortion, with sores and with flesh eaten away by cancer.

He offered her a flower, but because she was blind she asked if she could give it to someone else. She then held out the flower to another patient and said, "Here, this is from Jesus."

This woman had been in the hospital for twenty-five years, battling pain and growing steadily weaker. Yet she became an inspiration to Ortberg's friend as the woman continually quoted Scripture and hymns and applied them to her own situation. When asked what she thought about, the woman said, "I think about my Jesus. I think about how good he's been to me."

Ortberg's friend was amazed. Year after year, unable to move or see, this woman dwelled on hymns about Jesus instead of thinking about her pain. John responded to his friend's story this way: "Here was an ordinary human being who received supernatural power to do extraordinary things. Her entire life consisted of following Jesus as best she could in her situation: patient endurance of suffering, solitude, prayer, meditation on Scripture, and worship. This is the twenty-third Psalm come to life: 'The LORD is my shepherd, I shall not want.'"

Sometimes we feel we cannot endure our circumstances one more day or one more hour. Yet the old adage is still true that an "attitude of gratitude" transforms our circumstances. We are called to do extraordinary things—not by our own power, but by the renewing and continual refreshment of our minds as we think about how good Jesus has been to us.

---

*Father in heaven, many times my circumstances
drag down my spirit. Help me to fill my mind with
songs of your Spirit and words of enrichment from
you. Remind me of how good you've been to me.*

Shout with joy to the LORD, all the earth! Worship the LORD with gladness. Come before him, singing with joy. PSALM 100:1-2, NLT

INTO THE SUNSHINE!

HELMUT THIELICKE contrasts the image of someone sitting alone in darkness, face screwed up in an artificial smile, with an image from Martin Luther to the effect that a Christian is someone who runs out of a dark house and into the sunshine.

When we are in relationship to God the Father through Jesus, we go from darkness to light, with the blessings from above shining on us. As we bask in the light of our position as the Father's beloved children, it removes us from the realm of trying to live up to expectations to become better persons. Thielicke refers to Luther's observation that one needn't command a stone lying in the sun to get warm. All it does is soak up the sun's rays.

When we're in proper relationship to God, we soak up the rays of the Father of lights. We don't start with our own holiness or spiritual progress, but God's holiness pours over us and into us.

Thielicke says it's Jesus who brings us out of the dark houses of our fatherless lives. "He is the one who tells me that the Sun is smiling at me; that God really means *me* when he says that, henceforth, nobody can accuse me; that he loves me; and that I need not be afraid."

We are invited to be warmed and soaked through by the Sun, to express praise and gratitude, and to rejoice that we can "walk in the light, as he is in the light." We can have fellowship with the Father and the Son and can be led by the Holy Spirit.

"The Son of God takes me by the hand," Thielicke says. "The Father is waiting for me. Goodbye, you dark, old house where once I lived. Now I know why you were so dark. Now I know, because now I know the light."

Father in heaven, I want to bask in your sunshine,
but sometimes everything around me is dreary.
Help me to soak up your warmth and light
today and to follow you in the sunshine.

The Word gave life to everything that was created, and his life brought light to everyone.
The light shines in the darkness, and the darkness can never extinguish it.
JOHN 1:4-5, NLT

JESUS' LIFELINE

PHILIP YANCEY writes that when Jesus taught us to pray for God's will to be done on earth as it is in heaven, he knew the differences between the two—because he had come down from heaven. For Jesus, prayer connected him to his home and to his Father. He stayed in constant contact to fully grasp his Father's will and to receive the power to carry it out.

We need that same lifeline! In our confusing and often hostile world, guidance, courage, and energy are essential. Yet we sometimes wonder about our lifeline of prayer. Is it genuinely effective? Do we receive real guidance from God when we pray? As we plead that he will heal or bless or protect, does it make a difference?

Yancey's book titled *Prayer* explores these questions, and he concludes, "I have no better answer than the example of Jesus, who knew above any of us the wisdom of the Father and yet who felt a strong need to flood the heavens with requests."

Yancey quotes Jesus' promise that if we ask we'll receive. So we ask. We lay our petitions before God, knowing that we can't dictate his responses. We may well be disappointed that a cancer is not healed or an urgent request for spiritual awakening doesn't happen. Yet we continue to ask, for Jesus says, "Ask and you will receive" (John 16:24, NIV).

Receive what? We wrestle with that question in our spiritual journeys, and we find few easy answers in life's enigmatic drama. Jesus, after all, did not simply have his Father "fix things." Despite his agonized cries for relief in Gethsemane, Jesus was led to his crucifixion.

When we cry out to the Father, at the core of our cry must be the willingness to say, as Jesus said, "Not my will, but yours be done" (Luke 22:42, NIV).

At the same time, the adventure of prayer brings about all sorts of "coincidences" and "answers." Yancey writes, "When his disciples failed in their attempts to heal an afflicted boy, Jesus had a simple explanation: lack of prayer."

Father in heaven, you know my stream of requests.
I lay them all before you and ask you to bring them
into harmony with your love and compassion. Not
my will but yours be done. Help me to praise you.

After telling everyone good-bye, [Jesus] went up into the hills by himself to pray.
MARK 6:46, NLT

WHEN GOD SEEMS SILENT

OLE HALLESBY describes a disappointment that many of us have experienced. We pray long and earnestly for something, attempting to have adequate faith, but the answer we long for never comes and our hopes are dashed. We wonder, *Why doesn't God answer?*

"He has answered your prayer," Hallesby responds. "He is doing the good work within you. You imagined you would receive an answer according to your own thinking, and that you would receive peace, assurance, or joy in your soul. Not receiving these things, you thought that God had not answered. Jesus has many things to tell us, and he has much to accomplish within us we do not understand at the time."

Hallesby quotes Jesus' remark to his disciples that later they would understand what he was doing. "From the heavenly perspective, many things look different than they do here on earth. Our prayers, too, look different when viewed from above."

He cautions us not to be anxious and not to let anything prevent us from praying—especially if we experience repeated failures or losses and we feel helpless about it all. "Helplessness is the real secret and the impelling power of prayer."

We don't generally think of "impelling power" and helplessness as synergistic. We are uncomfortable with our weaknesses. But Hallesby says, "Try to thank God for the feeling of helplessness he has given you. It is one of the greatest gifts God can impart to us. It is only when we are helpless that we open our hearts to Jesus and let Him help us in our distress, according to His grace and mercy."

Lord, you know how helpless I feel despite my strengths.
Only through you can I "do all things." Do your work
in me so that I can sense your Holy Spirit guiding
and strengthening me throughout this day.

LORD, *you know the hopes of the helpless. Surely you will hear their cries and comfort them.* PSALM 10:17, NLT

TEARS, YET JOY

BILLY GRAHAM had a great respect for missionary Amy Carmichael, who founded a ministry to rescue young girls in India and later, as a bedridden invalid, wrote many books of compelling spiritual insights.

When Graham visited Carmichael's former home in Dohnavur and stood in the simple room that had been like a prison for her, he was profoundly moved and said, "The presence of Christ was so very real to me that when I was asked to lead in prayer, I broke down and could not continue." He asked a colleague who was traveling with him, a successful German industrialist, to pray. That man started to pray and then he also broke down in tears.

Billy was aware that the spiritual depth and insights Amy had shared with so many had come out of deep suffering—her own and those of so many to whom she ministered in India. "She lived her life rejoicing in the midst of tribulation."

Amy Carmichael prayed that God would calm her when the winds blew and that when the pains came, she would be able to sing a psalm. She prayed she would not "lose the chance to prove the fullness of God's enabling love."

Billy Graham discovered that, in our suffering, God works in unexpected ways to bring us strength and joy. "For our light and momentary troubles are achieving for us an eternal glory that far outweighs them all" (2 Corinthians 4:17, NIV).

Paul endured shipwreck, attempted executions, and brutal beatings. Only contrasted with eternal glory could his troubles be thought of as "light and momentary."

---

*Loving Father, my troubles don't compare to all
that the apostle Paul or Amy Carmichael had to go
through, but my troubles don't feel light and it can be
hard to rejoice. Help me to be thankful for your grace
and to live with anticipation of the glory ahead.*

You have sorrow now, but I will see you again; then you will rejoice, and no one can rob you of that joy. JOHN 16:22, NLT

TOUGH JOY

MOTHER TERESA advised, "The best way to show our gratitude to God is to accept everything with joy. Never let everything so fill you with sorrow that you forget the joy of Christ risen."

She instructed others as if joy were a matter of the will—and she was very practical about it. "Being happy in Jesus means loving as he loves, helping as he helps, giving as he gives, serving as he serves, rescuing as he rescues, being with him twenty-four hours, touching him in his distressing disguise."

Jesus' "distressing disguise"—a phrase Mother Teresa often used—describes people who are wretched and abandoned, and perhaps obnoxious.

Does all this sound grim and not happy at all? Here's what Malcolm Muggeridge said of Mother Teresa and her sisters:

> Their life is tough and austere, yet I never met such delightful, happy women, or such an atmosphere of joy as they create. Mother Teresa, as she is fond of explaining, attaches the utmost importance to this joyousness. The poor, she says, deserve not just service and dedication, but also the joy that belongs to human love. This is what the sisters give them abundantly.

Andrew Greeley had a similar reaction to meeting Mother Teresa: "She was the happiest human being I ever met."

Mother Teresa herself said, "Cheerfulness is indeed the fruit of the Holy Spirit and a clear sign of the Kingdom within."

She was determined to be happy in the Lord *despite feelings of emptiness*—a paradox worth contemplating. She warns against being preoccupied with the future. "There's no reason to do so," she writes. "God is there."

She also warned against the longing for money that can bring endless "needs" and dissatisfaction. In this regard, she was far beyond most of us. "Poverty makes us free," she said to her sisters. "That is why we can joke and smile and keep a happy heart for Jesus."

Father, please enable me to experience the joy
you offer. Help me to act and think in ways that
generate your cheerfulness—in step with your Holy
Spirit, no matter what my feelings might be.

Don't be dejected and sad, for the joy of the LORD is your strength!
NEHEMIAH 8:10, NLT

CHILDREN IN HEAVEN

GEORGE MACDONALD, referring to his children who had died, said, "I love you, my sweet children who are gone into another mansion."

Losing a child brings unimaginably deep sorrow. MacDonald wrote these words as an old man still feeling he could "die of grief." Yet he envisioned that on his own death, "When I awake, my daughter and my son—grown sister and brother—in my arms shall fall, tenfold my girl and boy."

He held this hope because he could pray, "O Lord, when I think of my departed, I think of thee who art the death of parting, of you who crying Father breathed your last, then radiant from the sepulcher came."

MacDonald was caught like each of us in the "not yet" aspect of faith. We may be full of hope, yet at times we feel we could die of grief. He describes our condition with echoes of the apostle Paul:

> *With us the bitterness of death is past,*
> *But by the feet he holds us fast.*

When our loved ones have departed, we are filled with longing. MacDonald cries out:

> *Oh, my beloved, gone to heaven from me!*
> *I long to love you, sweet ones, perfectly.*

Yet he admits that his love is imperfect and longs for the day when he feels no boundaries, when he can "love as God loves."

No boundaries! Think of what it will mean in heaven to have no limitations on our love. MacDonald, the great novelist, envisioned hugging his departed children in glorious new realities that transcend anything we could hope for or imagine here on earth.

Heavenly Father, my soul longs for my loved ones who
have gone to you. Please grant me a strong sense of faith
and hope. Help me to rejoice in your resurrection and
the hope of reuniting in realities beyond imagination.

Our earthly bodies are planted in the ground when we die, but they will be raised to live
forever. Our bodies are buried in brokenness, but they will be raised in glory.
I CORINTHIANS 15:42-43, NLT

"JUST CAN'T FIND
THAT LOVING FEELING"

C. S. LEWIS writes, "God's love for us is a much safer subject to think about than our love for him."

Have you ever felt guilt that you just didn't love God enough? Does it sometimes make you uneasy when you hear or sing,

> *Turn your eyes upon Jesus,*
> *Look full on his wonderful face,*
> *And the things of earth will grow strangely dim,*
> *In the light of his glory and grace.*

Maybe as you sing those words, "the things of earth" don't grow dim. In fact, maybe you can't conjure up a visual image of Jesus' face at all. Maybe all you see is a kaleidoscope of culturally influenced images of Jesus that blur into nonsense.

We tend to berate ourselves for our lack of love for God and for others. We understand that love is our calling as Christians. But Lewis gets at something very important here. We're to open ourselves to the Holy Spirit, who brings God's love in his own time and way—but we ourselves can't conjure it up. We can only beseech God to provide it, for *true* love must come from him.

"Christian love, either towards God or towards man, is an affair of the will," Lewis writes. "If we are trying to do his will, we are obeying the commandment, 'Thou shalt love the Lord thy God.' He will give us feelings of love if he pleases. We cannot create them for ourselves, and we must not demand them as a right. But the great thing to remember is that, though our feelings come and go, his love for us does not."

Holy Spirit within, my soul longs to be in harmony
with you. When I fail to love, pour your love into me.
Let me never look at others with contempt. Help me
to open myself in every way to your love and grace.

God showed his great love for us by sending Christ to die for us while we were still sinners. ROMANS 5:8, NLT

DYNAMIC GRATITUDE

April 27

BEN PATTERSON was angry and bitter at God. His girlfriend, whom he had been seriously dating for five years, had broken up with him. Ever since, he had been rebelling against God by breaking his commandments. He would wake up with a hangover, drink his morning coffee, and stare blankly at magazines covering his Bible.

"The sight made me think about praying," he writes. "But about what? I chose something I naively thought safe: I began to give thanks. Big mistake."

Well, it was a big mistake if he wanted to keep rebelling. He simply started thanking God for the weather and music, coffee and cup, utensils and napkins. As he expressed his gratitude, unbidden joy began to trickle into his soul and eventually flooded his heart. He felt God's goodness, and tears came. The experience led to repentance and a balm for the bitterness in his soul.

Gratitude and praise to God are far more dynamic—and even explosive—than what happens when we say a simple thank-you to someone. Deep, elemental forces are unleashed, and we find ourselves in harmony with the wonders and joys of the one who loves us and made all things bright and beautiful.

When we stand on the rim of the Grand Canyon or stare in awe at the pistils in a flower, we feel the same wonder, and we want to share our thoughts and feelings with someone. The one who made it all—and who reaches out in love to us—walks beside us, sharing our delight in his creation and his love as we respond to him.

The Westminster Shorter Catechism teaches that our chief end is to love God and to enjoy him forever. We enjoy him as we lift our voices and spirits in praise and thanksgiving for all his works and benefits and his love in providing our salvation. As we cultivate an attitude of thanksgiving, we look for God's continuing grace, which may appear in unexpected ways.

Father in heaven, I thank you for everything around
me that you created and for your love and care
for me. Fill my mind and heart with joy in your
creation and with an expectation of your grace.

Our God, we thank you and praise your glorious name!
I CHRONICLES 29:13, NLT

THE GOLD MINE

FRED SMITH often urged others to look for divine *principles*, whether in Bible stories or the experiences of life. While bedridden, he wrote, "A principle that has been very sustaining to me in my disability is one that Oswald Chambers helped me to see. 'God will not give you strength to overcome, but will give you strength *as* you overcome.'"

Always mining for principles that he could apply to his life, Smith declared, "What a treasury of wisdom we have in the saints who have gone before us, and when we accept Scripture as God's word and authority for life."

In response to a request from Fred Smith to identify some of God's principles, his friend Jack Modesett shared two that he had found in the parable of the wise and foolish virgins: "God honors preparation" and "There is safety in surplus." Modesett also quoted pastor Ray Stedman, who preached "Truth must be acted upon," and pastor Chuck Swindoll, who concluded from the life of David that "It is devotion, not perfection, that warms the heart of God."

Jack Modesett also said, "François Fénelon is a gold mine of principles such as, 'Self-love is touchy, and when wounded it screams, "Murderer!"'"

We have great treasuries of biblical wisdom available. Discovering them and then figuring out how to apply them become delightful personal enterprises. Simply Google "Ray Stedman" or "Charles Spurgeon" or "Jill Briscoe" or "François Fénelon" or "Fred Smith."

The book of Proverbs, of course, is all about godly principles. Here are four good examples:

"Better to have little, with fear for the LORD, than to have great treasure and inner turmoil." (15:16, NLT)
"Plans go wrong for lack of advice; many advisers bring success." (15:22)
"A cheerful look brings joy to the heart; good news makes for good health." (15:30)
"Fear of the LORD teaches wisdom; humility precedes honor." (15:33)

Father in heaven, you have sent your Holy Spirit
to lead us into truth. Help me in my search for
wisdom and truth to discover your principles
for my life, and enable me to apply them.

Fear of the LORD is the foundation of true wisdom. All who obey his commandments will grow in wisdom. PSALM 111:10, NLT

WALK THROUGH THE SMOKE

April 29

D. L. MOODY saw humankind as being ruled either by Satan or by God. "We are led on by an unseen power we haven't strength to resist, or we are led by the loving Son of God."

Scripture says plenty about the devil's rule over the earth and its inhabitants. Moody describes the way Satan works like this: "Satan rules through lust, covetousness, appetite, temper. He rules, and none seek to be delivered until their eyes open and they see they've been taken captive."

Most people don't recognize the powers of the prince of darkness. In fact, most would be highly insulted at the suggestion that the devil has power over them. Yet if they were to look around at the evil in the world and the despair of millions, they might get an inkling of Satan's wiles and successes. Because common grace permeates the world as well, however, the great mixture of intertwined good and evil, like swirled concoctions of many colors, continues until God brings all to conclusion.

The devil, of course, works not only on those under his control but also on believers to weaken their liberation in Christ and to drain them of faith. For instance, here's one strategy that Moody describes: "Satan puts straws across our paths and magnifies them to make us believe they're mountains. But they're mountains of smoke. When you come up to them, they're not there."

From Jesus to Fénelon to Moody, we're told to ignore the taunts of despair and to cast our cares on the Lord.

Sometimes the mountains that threaten us turn out not to be smoke but insurmountable crags. Then more than ever we must shut our ears to the devil and listen for the whispers of hope and courage from the Holy Spirit.

Lord Jesus, you know all about Satan and how he tried to ensnare you with his deceptions. You know how he prowls around like a lion looking for my weaknesses. Help me to resist him as you did when he came after you.

"Yes," [Jesus] told them, "I saw Satan fall from heaven like lightning!"
LUKE 10:18, NLT

HAVING ULTIMATE POWER, HE . . .

JOHN HENRY JOWETT stopped in the middle of a sentence as he quoted the following passage: "Jesus, knowing that the Father had given all things into his hands, and that he was come from God, and went to God . . ." (John 13:1-15, KJV).

Jowett at that point paused to give us time to think about what he had just read—that Jesus knew he had all power and "all things" were in his hands and that he came from God and would go to God. Then Jowett asked, "How shall we expect the sentence to finish?"

In a *Star Wars* drama, the light sabers would be drawn and the ones with all the power would use them. In an adventure movie, the good guy would act decisively, unleashing his powers in cataclysmic action.

In contrast, the rest of the sentence about Jesus shows the unthinkable: "He . . . took a towel, and girded himself . . . and began to wash the disciples' feet."

Jowett observed, "The Lord of Glory girds himself with the apron of the slave, and almightiness addresses itself to menial service."

Remarkable. But here's the bite for us: We, too, are called to humble service. In fact, we may be called to sheer drudgery that seems to have no payback at all.

"We may be sure," Jowett writes, "that we are growing smaller when we disparage humble services. We may be sure we are growing larger when we love the ministries that never lift their voices in the streets."

Jowett then quotes Jesus: "I have given you an example, that ye should do as I have done to you."

---

*Lord Jesus, sometimes it feels as if most of what I do
is humble service. Help me recognize that if I am in
harmony with you—doing all for your sake—the glory
is service to you. Help me to remember your towel.*

[Jesus] got up from the table, took off his robe, wrapped a towel around his waist, and poured water into a basin. Then he began to wash the disciples' feet, drying them with the towel he had around him. JOHN 13:4-5, NLT

THE MYSTERIOUS TRUTH

ED DOBSON gets brutally honest when he writes, "If one more person tells me that all things work together for good, I'm going to scream." Dobson suffers from ALS, which is a terminal disease. When well-meaning people tell him not to worry because God will work out everything for good, Dobson tries to square that advice with the fact that he's in the process of dying.

Romans 8:28, of course, is the verse that these people are referring to: "We know that God causes everything to work together for the good of those who love God and are called according to his purpose for them" (NLT). Dobson says, "It's easy to quote this verse when things are going well. The challenge is to believe it when everything goes bad."

He is not the first Christian to question Romans 8:28. How can disasters and tragic human failures possibly be working for our good? When we experience such wrenching events, we wonder.

Dobson reads on in Romans 8:31-32: "If God is for us, who can ever be against us? Since he did not spare even his own Son but gave him up for us all, won't he also give us everything else?"

He concludes that this is the ultimate proof that God loves us. "When I am tempted to question whether God is with me," he says, "I go back to the cross."

We may not understand how God's love is working for us, but we know that he has shown the ultimate depth of love. In Romans 8:35, the apostle Paul asks, "Can anything ever separate us from Christ's love? Does it mean he no longer loves us if we have trouble or calamity, or are persecuted, or hungry, or destitute, or in danger, or threatened with death?"

What sobering situations Paul lists! Yet he goes on with this assurance: "I am convinced that nothing can ever separate us from God's love. Neither death nor life, neither angels nor demons, neither our fears for today nor our worries about tomorrow" (Romans 8:38).

Ed Dobson concludes that Romans 8:28 is "a hard truth, a mysterious truth, an inexplicable truth, but nonetheless, the truth."

---

*Lord, thank you for your love that is beyond
understanding. Help me to have faith, even in the
worst of circumstances, that you do care for me
and that I am ultimately secure in your love.*

Nothing in all creation will ever be able to separate us from the love of God that is revealed in Christ Jesus our Lord. ROMANS 8:39, NLT

NO MATTER WHAT OTHERS THINK . . . *May 2*

THOMAS À KEMPIS advises that we shouldn't get caught up in who's for us and who's against us because God is with us in everything we do. "Keep a clean conscience, and God will mightily defend you."

Yet, whether someone is for us or against us often has a huge impact on us. Thomas à Kempis recognized that life is not an easy path and that peace comes not from the absence of adversity but from humble patience. He admitted that it takes great grace "to live at peace among hard, obstinate, and undisciplined people and those who oppose us."

Challenges are unavoidable, and spiritual vigor is essential. For instance, à Kempis says, "It's often good for us that others know and expose our faults so we can be kept humble." Most of us would consider it calamitous if others were to go around exposing our faults. Yet, if they did, it surely would promote humility.

"When you humbly admit your faults," à Kempis writes, "you appease others and are reconciled to them. God loves, protects, comforts, and delivers the humble. In trouble, they remain at peace by trusting in God and not the world. Those who are peaceful bring peace to others."

Throughout our lives, troubles assault us. The person with a quiet conscience endures. What others think about us becomes irrelevant because God is the one whose opinion matters and who brings inner peace.

Thomas à Kempis declares, "The joy of the saints is *from* God and *in* God. He alone is the true comfort of the soul and joy of the heart."

Father in heaven, help me to care most about
what you think about me. Enable me to accept
criticisms and the tough things that might be said
today. Let me find my peace and joy in you.

You will keep in perfect peace all who trust in you, all whose thoughts are fixed on you!
ISAIAH 26:3, NLT

WHAT'S IT ALL ABOUT?

NANCY GUTHRIE, writing from personal experience, says, "Significant suffering leaves us with significant questions."

Most people, it seems, are content to leave the wrenching questions of life's unfairness and God's seeming silence relatively unexplored. Yet, when deep suffering invades their lives, the questions become urgent—as relevant as a hospital or police report. What's really going on? What's this all about?

"We want the truth," Nancy writes, "and this is when we need the Holy Spirit—when we're facing an uncertain future and trying to make sense of it all." She reminds us that when Jesus was leaving his disciples, he told them he would ask the Father to send the Holy Spirit, who would lead them into all truth.

Earlier, Jesus had taught these same disciples about prayer: "Keep on asking, and you will receive what you ask for. Keep on seeking, and you will find. Keep on knocking, and the door will be opened to you. For everyone who asks, receives. Everyone who seeks, finds. And to everyone who knocks, the door will be opened" (Luke 11:9-10, NLT).

Quite a promise!

Jesus concluded his teaching with a statement that puts it all in perspective: "If you sinful people know how to give good gifts to your children, how much more will your heavenly Father give the Holy Spirit to those who ask him" (Luke 11:13, NLT).

When we seek the truth and keep on knocking on God's door, he gives us the gift of the Spirit of truth.

"God's wisdom and an understanding of the big picture," writes Nancy Guthrie, "is not something that can be discovered with our minds. It is only something that can be revealed to us by the Holy Spirit."

Spirit of God, I know that in this life I can't fully comprehend the tragedies and mysteries. Help me, though, to understand enough to grow in you and to embrace your truth. Let your love define my spirit and soul today.

If you need wisdom, ask our generous God, and he will give it to you. JAMES 1:5, NLT

AM I A TERRIBLE SINNER?

ALAN PATON points out that both the apostle Paul and St. Francis considered themselves the worst of sinners. In this context he says, "No one is too weak, too vile, too unimportant to be God's instrument."

Sometimes we get all tangled up in our limitations and can't see anything else. Sometimes, when we have failed over and over again, we are ready to sink into the mire. To that, Paton says, "First, never doubt that God can use us if we are willing to be used. Second, see that God can use any other person willing to be used, and if need be, assure him of this truth."

To illustrate, he tells a story about a time when St. Francis was returning from his prayers in the woods and met Brother Masseo along the way. To test Francis's humility, Matteo asked him why all the world was flocking to him. Why did everyone want to see him, hear him, and obey him? After all, he wasn't handsome or of noble birth or great knowledge.

Hearing this, Francis was filled with joy. He raised his face toward heaven. He knelt down and gave praise and thanks to God.

Now here's the twist that says something about the making of a saint. Francis, "with great fervor of spirit," explained: "The eyes of the most high God, those most holy eyes, have not seen among sinners one more vile, nor more insufficient, nor a greater sinner than I, and therefore to do that wonderful work which he intends to do, he elected me to confound the nobility, that all may know that all virtue and all goodness are of him and that no one should glory in his presence. He who glories should glory in the Lord."

In light of this truth, Paton prays, "May my knowledge of my unworthiness never make me resist being used by thee. Open my eyes and my heart that I may this coming day be able to do some work of peace for thee."

Lord Jesus Christ, Son of God, have mercy on me, a sinner. You know how weak and needy I am. Pour into me your virtue, love, and power, that I might accept your agenda instead of my own and serve you and others.

Just as sin ruled over all people and brought them to death, now God's wonderful grace rules instead, giving us right standing with God and resulting in eternal life through Jesus Christ our Lord. ROMANS 5:21, NLT

LAME SHEEP

May 5

CHARLES HADDON SPURGEON contrasts believers who have a strong, vigorous faith with others who are weak or troubled. He concludes, "In God's flock, there are always some lame sheep."

Some of these, he says, were born to see the dark side of everything. They see in the Bible only the threats and never the promises. "For them the road is always rugged, the pastures unsavory. If there is a slough, they will fall into it, and if a thicket, they will get entangled by it."

Others aren't born that way but become lame from hearing superficial theology or responding to the devil's lures and lies. Still others have been crushed by home troubles, unable to rally their spirits, or they've been wounded by church splits and controversies.

Spurgeon saw all sorts of lame sheep and expressed great empathy for them. In fact, he also saw their strengths and said to the morose: "Some flowers must be grown in the shade, and perhaps you are one of those flowers. I have known women for whom the sunny scenes of life have no charms, but their faces have shone like angels in the chambers of the sick or the wards of the hospital." He advised those who tend toward depression to consider Jesus, the Man of Sorrows, whose spirit was not crushed.

However, he came down hard on those who treated the lame harshly. "You may be strong and vigorous and strangers to depression," he said, "but be thankful and not presumptuous. Don't despise those who suffer—your turn may come before long."

So what should be done about the lame? Spurgeon advises, "The rest of the flock should seek their healing!" and quotes Hebrews 12:13, "Make straight paths for your feet, so that what is lame may . . . be healed" (KJV).

When we see the suffering among us, we are to comfort them, assist them, and encourage them.

Charles Spurgeon says, "Consider the example of our Lord Jesus, who was always quick to spy out the lame, the blind, the crippled. His hands were always stretched out for their relief."

Lord, in many ways, I'm one of those lame sheep. Help me in my needs. And open my eyes to the troubles and limitations of others who need my understanding and loving touch.

The King will say, "I tell you the truth, when you did it to one of the least of these my brothers and sisters, you were doing it to me!" MATTHEW 25:40, NLT

BEYOND THE HAZE OF L.A.

JONI EARECKSON TADA loves the night sky. She writes with near rapturous appreciation of one night when she and her husband, Ken, drove away from the obscuring lights of Los Angeles to a distant mountain in the desert, where they could see a rare comet that was due to pass through the Big Dipper.

They were not disappointed. In the cold desert air, with no haze to obscure their view, they saw in the sparkling black of the sky a fuzzy ball of light with a long, thin tail cutting through the Big Dipper. Joni writes, "It seemed like the Lord of the universe was beckoning us, whispering, saying, 'Want to see my glory?'"

Joni and Ken sang in harmony under the stars that night, "Angels, help us to adore him . . ."

Their need to escape the lights of L.A. in order to see the wonders of God captures perfectly our daily spiritual dilemma. Our lives are full of demands and diversions that blur our vision of the Creator, whose wonders truly go beyond our imaginations.

Like no generation before us, we are able to see graphic images in vivid detail that show how vast, complex, and beautiful God's creation is. When we lift our hearts in praise at all these wonders, we sense a harmony with our Savior and Redeemer—by whom, the Bible tells us, all things consist and are held together.

We can see microscopic images of very strange creatures, and with the Hubble telescope we can view images of stunning celestial expanses. Yet the ordinary, day-to-day world in which we live is also full of God's glory. To see it, we need only look at the thin veins in a cherry blossom or the darting flight of a sparrow or the skill and dexterity of our own fingers. As poets have said in so many ways, if we have eyes to see, all creation is ablaze with God's glory.

God of all creation, open my eyes! Pour into my
spirit praise and wonder at your creation and your
love. Help me to see past the haze that blurs my
vision. Fill me with expectation and hope.

Honor the LORD, you heavenly beings; honor the LORD for his glory and strength.
PSALM 29:1, NLT

ZESTFUL LIVES

EUGENE PETERSON tells us, "The Bible makes it clear that every time there is a story of faith, it is completely original. God's creative genius is endless. Each life is a fresh canvas on which he uses lines and colors, shades and lights, textures and proportions that he has never used before."

What a marvelous thought! We may look like our relatives, and we may have similar experiences to other people. But each of us is genuinely unique, and our spiritual journeys are full of twists and turns and opportunities different from all others.

This becomes especially apparent when we embrace a sense of expectation as we respond to God's call. Our stories of faith may seem ordinary. Yet to those who love us and depend on us, our stories are unique and powerful. When we look back at what has become of our dreams and our faith, we see God's originality.

These days, when we can view videos of the striking intricacies and overwhelming grandeur of God's ever-surprising creation, we can rejoice that the Creator made us! He not only made each of us, but he will also shape each of our unique stories as we invite him to change us.

Though we may feel as if we are painfully ordinary and our stories drab and uninspiring, if we will respond to God's call, he will thrust us into the adventure of spiritual battles.

In *Run with the Horses*, Peterson declares that we can live zestful lives "that spill out of the stereotyped containers that a sin-inhibited society provides. Such lives fuse spontaneity and purpose and green the desiccated landscape with meaning. And we see *how* it is possible: by plunging into a life of faith, participating in what God initiates in each life."

Lord, what do you want the rest of my story to be? So many unexpected things could happen! Enable me to become fully engaged with you so that my story will have the unique twists and turns that only your Spirit can bring.

This is what the LORD says—the LORD who made the earth, who formed and established it, whose name is the LORD: Ask me and I will tell you remarkable secrets you do not know about things to come. JEREMIAH 33:2-3, NLT

DON'T WASTE THE PAIN!

FRANÇOIS FÉNELON wrote to someone who was enduring deep disappointment, "Do not waste the suffering. Let suffering accomplish what God wants it to in your life."

Fénelon's wisdom has endured the years. Not long ago, a spiritually vital woman was jolted and grieved to learn that her son's wife had deserted their little family. A wise Christian friend empathized with her and gave her this pungent advice: "Don't waste the pain."

What a paradoxical statement! We don't usually think of pain as valuable, even though Philip Yancey and Dr. Paul Brand have written books on how necessary pain is for the body to avoid damage. Might emotional and spiritual pain have its own unique value? How would we waste the pain? What might pain bring into our lives and souls?

We might start by pondering this observation from Fénelon: "The events of life are like a furnace for the heart."

If we're alive, we're in that furnace. As we submit to the heat, our impurities are melted and we're refined like gold and silver. That's why Fénelon tells us to embrace our circumstances, no matter how grueling—even when they seem to overwhelm us. "Allow God to mold you through the events he allows to enter your life. This will make you flexible toward the will of God."

Well, do we have any choice? We seldom can change our circumstances, but we *can* change our perspective. If we believe God is at work in our pain, we see our pain differently.

"The intrusions that God sends you will no doubt upset your plans and oppose all that you want," writes Fénelon. "But they will chase you toward God."

Lord, you know how difficult circumstances jolt me
and flood my soul with emotion. If the events of life
are a furnace, please be with me there as you were with
Daniel's friends. Purify me and rescue me from evil.

You have allowed me to suffer much hardship, but you will restore me to life again and lift me up from the depths of the earth. PSALM 71:20, NLT

HOW TO BUCK UP

OSWALD CHAMBERS puts his finger on something we've all experienced in one way or another—regret that we've missed a huge opportunity or failed to resist temptation. But before we sink into despair, we should consider the challenge Chambers offers: "Arise and go to the next thing. Let the past sleep. Go out to the irresistible future with him."

We prepare for the "irresistible future" by calling on the Lord to purify us and empower us, especially when we feel corrupted and weak. When we open ourselves to God's work in our lives, Chambers predicts, "The Spirit of God comes in and says, 'Buck up.'"

There's a mysterious alchemy here—our call and the Spirit's command and empowering. We have our part, and we need to step up to it. When we do "buck up," we often find that spiritual energy starts to flow. Chambers points out that when Jesus healed the man with the withered hand, he told him to stretch it forth.

The longer we live, the more we realize that although we may have skills, spiritual insights, and a strong commitment to following Christ, we still fall short of the Lord's example. Sometimes we fall so far short that we're amazed at the depth of the ditch we find ourselves in.

It's when we're amazed at just how weak we are to live as faithful disciples that we understand what Scripture means when it says that God gives his strength in our great weakness.

When we feel paralyzed by our failures or full of regret over lost opportunities, we might well get a grip on Oswald Chambers's stringent and practical challenge: "Never let the sense of failure corrupt your new action!"

Father in heaven, I open myself to your strength and your will. Don't allow my past sins and blunders to keep me from following your Spirit. Help me to do my part as you do your work in me today.

Listen closely to my prayer, O LORD; hear my urgent cry. I will call to you whenever I'm in trouble, and you will answer me. PSALM 86:6-7, NLT

KNOW YOUR ENEMIES

MARTIN LUTHER gets realistic and down-to-earth when he urges us not to be surprised at the conflict between the Holy Spirit and our sinful nature. He says we should take courage and be comforted at Paul's words in Galatians 5:17: "The sinful nature wants to do evil, which is just the opposite of what the Spirit wants. And the Spirit gives us desires that are the opposite of what the sinful nature desires. These two forces are constantly fighting each other, so you are not free to carry out your good intentions" (NLT).

Wait a minute! What's encouraging about that? We're not free to do the good things we want to? How does that give us comfort and courage?

Luther's point is that knowing what's going on and where our help lies keeps us from being bewildered and weaponless. When we find ourselves fighting the same old battles and—much to our chagrin—giving in, we've at least been forewarned that we're in a continuing conflict.

When we're knocked down by sin, we can keep getting up off the floor and call on the Spirit, who comforts and equips us.

"If you are aware of this battle with the sinful nature," Luther writes, "don't lose heart but resist in the Spirit and say, 'I am a sinner and feel sinful because I am still in this body. As long as I live, sin will cling to this body. I will obey the Spirit, not the sinful nature. I will grasp Christ by faith, hope in him, and find comfort in his Word.'"

Heavenly Father, you know how often I struggle
with the same old issues. Lift me out of my weakness
by your Holy Spirit. Bring your freedom into my
life, and let me share your love with others.

You have been called to live in freedom, my brothers and sisters. But don't use your freedom to satisfy your sinful nature. Instead, use your freedom to serve one another in love. GALATIANS 5:13, NLT

MUCKRAKE EXCHANGE

AMY CARMICHAEL says it straight: "Life is a journey; it is a climb; it is also and always a war. The soldier of the Lord of Hosts is always a soldier. He dare not drivel. This sounds like a rough word, but sometimes roughness helps."

The Bible is full of grim stories of warfare as well as stern counsel about the spiritual warfare in which we are all engaged. When we're tempted to coast through life, we are likely to be confronted with tough realities. A Marine Corps drill instructor is harsh because he is preparing marines for deadly battles ahead. He is determined to teach them that the enemy will do everything possible to kill them—and they shouldn't be surprised!

In the same way, we're not to be surprised when the enemy of our souls shoots to kill. We're in a spiritual war. Amy Carmichael challenges each of us: "Expose yourself to the circumstances of [God's] choice."

Our circumstances can be tough, but when we receive them from God's hand, we put on the dynamic attitude so necessary to marines and spiritual soldiers. In contrast, Carmichael describes those who "look no way but downward, and spend their time raking to themselves the straws, the small sticks, and dust of the floor, though there stands One who offers to exchange the muckrake for a crown."

Even in the dullest of circumstances, we are either gathering "wood, hay and stubble," or we are gathering priceless, eternal gems. Do we chafe at circumstances, or do we accept them as God's spiritual training for the battlefield?

Amy Carmichael emphasizes that full engagement in the circumstances God permits is "the call to the climbing soul." She sees it as a bracing, positive challenge, quoting the scriptural promise, "The joy of the LORD is your strength!" (Nehemiah 8:10, NLT).

Joy, she affirms, is "perfect acquiescence in the will of God."

Lord, the idea of life as warfare can wear me down. Only you can equip me with an attitude of "bring it on, because the Lord is my strength and shield." By your grace, help me to be an agent of positive change in the world.

O LORD, do not stay far away! You are my strength; come quickly to my aid!
PSALM 22:19, NLT

DOES "STUFF" MULTIPLY TEMPTATIONS?

JOHN HENRY JOWETT says something about money that at first may seem odd, but on reflection resonates with reality. "There is nothing more divisive than wealth."

Adequate money gives a family security and the chance for harmony; but significant riches can have the opposite effect. "As families grow richer," Jowett observes, "their members frequently become alienated." Media reports on "lucky" lottery winners who ended up miserable illustrate his point. Jowett recognized that poverty ravages families and souls—yet he presents a litany of cautions about money:

> Love rarely increases with the increase of riches.
> Luxurious possessions waken sleeping vices.
> Selfishness is quickened with success.
> Our possessions multiply our temptations.
> The bright day "brings forth the adder."

So what should we do? Jowett writes, "We need extra defenses when fortune smiles on us, God's protections against the fiery darts of success."

Whether we're wealthy or poor or "stuck in the middle," money and success have powerful spiritual dimensions. As we strive for wealth and position, we find they can become either corrosive substitutes for God or magnificent blessings from his hand.

Jowett cites Abraham as an example of someone who remained unscathed as his wealth increased because he put his faith first: He dwelled in the "secret place of the most High," and he abode in "the shadow of the Almighty" (Psalm 91:1, KJV).

Lord, you know how my life requires money! Loving Father, protect me from the blistering effects of poverty. Help me to pursue the kind of success you'll bless and to praise you for all you provide.

Wealth from get-rich-quick schemes quickly disappears; wealth from hard work grows over time. PROVERBS 13:11, NLT

LIKE GERMINATED SEEDS

LUCI SHAW asks, "Have you had your attacks of agnosticism, of not being sure of anything, of feeling lost in thick darkness? I have. I'm convinced that those who have never experienced this nadir of unbelief are out of touch with reality. God's larger purposes are sometimes too large for our sin-blinded, pain-blinkered eyes to accept."

Shaw shares a story that Henri Nouwen once told about twins waiting like seeds in the darkness of the mother's womb. They feel quite at home there and wonder about what's ahead for them. "Have you heard?" one asks. "Someday soon we'll push into the light, and there'll be this thing called a *mother*. We'll see her face."

"Our irresistible urge toward growth and freedom," writes Shaw, "pulls us, like the push of a fetus towards birth, into eternity, when we can see God face-to-face, where we'll know and be known. And the long wait in the dark will make the sighting more splendid."

We now see "through a glass, darkly" (1 Corinthians 13:12, KJV). The analogy of our being in the womb of God—as babes and not-yet babes—sparks hopes of illumination far beyond our earthbound imaginations. Our doubts and our darkness will disappear in the sudden light of God's glory.

So we move toward the light, with blurred vision, but knowing enough of God's love and the sacrifice of his Son that we can walk in the Spirit. God tells us not to be afraid, for he is here with us in our darkness.

Luci Shaw describes a germinated seed pushing up: "Think, for a moment, of its single-mindedness. All its juicy energy is channeled into launching its way up through the loam to the light. It 'knows' its task is to reach the light. That it is destined for resurrection after its long burial—that to arrive in the light will mean life and health and fruitfulness."

In this context, Shaw quotes John Polkinghorne: "Faith is not a leap into the dark, but into the light."

Father in heaven, help me to be single-minded in seeking your light. Illumine my way and fill me with your hope. Refresh me spiritually so that I can refresh others and live fully for you today.

Dear friends, we are already God's children, but he has not yet shown us what we will be like when Christ appears. But we do know that we will be like him, for we will see him as he really is. I JOHN 3:2, NLT

GOOD PLEASURES

JOHN WESLEY set very high standards of holiness for his followers. He encouraged them to ask themselves challenging questions, such as, *Have I prayed with fervor? Have I contrived ways to avoid self-denial?* He taught his followers to pray, "Let me abstain from all pleasures that don't prepare me for taking pleasure in thee."

That doesn't mean he was a killjoy. When people accused him of being dour, he replied that he was convinced "true religion or holiness cannot be without cheerfulness. True religion has nothing sour, austere, unsociable, or unfriendly in it."

Wesley countered critics with questions: "Are you for having as much cheerfulness as you can? So am I. Do you try to keep alive your taste for innocent pleasures? So do I." He insisted that he enjoyed "every pleasure that leads to my taking pleasure in [God]."

Wesley denounced the idea that knowledge of our sinfulness makes us miserable. He insisted that dealing head-on with our tendencies toward "pride, self-will and peevishness" enables one to experience "peace and joy in the Holy Ghost."

Wesley wrote prayers for daily use, including these:

> "I know you are the end for which I was created, and I can expect no happiness but in thee."

> "Let us take pleasure in your service and abound in your work, and in your love and praise evermore."

Father and Provider of all blessings, cleanse me and bring your holiness of joy and fulfillment into my life. Help me to seek you fervently and to enjoy all pleasures in your company.

You will show me the way of life, granting me the joy of your presence and the pleasures of living with you forever. PSALM 16:11, NLT

DROP THOSE WEAPONS!

HENRI NOUWEN points out a sobering dynamic: "Praying presents a problem. It requires a constant readiness to lay our weapons down."

What weapons? Nouwen refers to the common belief that we must stand firm and hold our own against those who want to take away what we have. He says that according to the natural world, "If you don't carry a weapon, if you don't make a fist, you're just asking to be threadbare and destitute. You open your hands and they pound in nails!"

Prayer changes our stance and our perspective. We live in a world in which justice requires police—and sometimes weapons and fists, but as we pray, we also begin to see the larger picture through God's eyes. We ponder Jesus' words to those who drove the nails into his hands: "Father, forgive them, for they don't know what they are doing" (Luke 23:34, NLT).

When we are in communion with God, we breathe in his air of forgiveness and grace and spiritual refreshment. We are promised strength beyond our own to endure opposition and suffering. We pray for grace to respond wisely and appropriately with love.

When we pray with "open hands," Nouwen says, we live in expectation that the God who makes everything new will constantly make us new. As we face each day, we anticipate receiving the breath of God and his renewal in our lives.

Nouwen equates the person who never prays with a person who has asthma: "Because he is short of breath, the whole world shrivels up before him. . . . But the man who prays opens himself to God and can freely breathe again, . . . free to boldly stride through the world . . . without fear."

It's true. To pray is to live. To live is to pray.

Father, sometimes I have good reasons to make a fist.
When I have to stand up for my rights, help me know
when it's "righteous indignation," in harmony with
your Spirit, or when I'm reacting in ways I'll regret.

Let the Holy Spirit guide your lives. GALATIANS 5:16, NLT

PRODDED INTO BATTLE

JILL BRISCOE describes a scene on the Bayeux Tapestry that shows a bishop with his soldiers. A frightened soldier is running away from battle toward the safety of the bishop's tent. The tapestry shows the bishop using the sharp end of his staff to poke and prod the soldier back to where he belongs. The caption for the tapestry reads, "The bishop encourages his soldier."

Briscoe admits that she has run away from hard things in life and has felt the unmistakable prodding of the Good Shepherd's crook. "This is how he 'encourages' me back into the midst of the battle to do my part."

Sometimes we long for the comfort of the bishop's tent as we face battles that fill us with anxiety and fear or that exhaust and dishearten us. Sometimes we fear the consequences of what we're called to do and want to shrink back, letting others take the heat.

Moses was reluctant to obey God's command to go back to Egypt and confront the Pharaoh. The prophet Jeremiah reacted with similar apprehension when commanded to confront the authorities in Israel. He objected that he was only a child—a stance to which we can all relate when facing weighty challenges. Yet God told Jeremiah not to say he was too young, but to go and do what God had commanded.

Jill Briscoe says we may be like Jeremiah, facing tough challenges, but that God's compassions will never fail us. "They will be 'new every morning,'" she says, "and great will be his faithfulness [see Lamentations 3:22-23, NIV]. If things are right when we are on our knees, they will be right when we are on our feet."

Lord, I want to take on the challenges before me, but sometimes they're overwhelming. Heavenly Father, when I feel like a child facing responsibilities far beyond my capabilities, please reach down and lift me up.

I cry out to the LORD; I plead for the LORD's mercy. I pour out my complaints before him and tell him all my troubles. PSALM 142:1-2, NLT

A VIVID SENSE OF MALODOROUS THINGS

BROTHER LAWRENCE—like the apostle Paul, Francis of Assisi, and many other saints—had a strong sense of his own sinfulness. "I regard myself as the most wretched of all men," he writes, "ragged with sores, full of malodorous things and guilty of all manner of crimes against God."

One would think that such an acute sense of his guilt and "crimes" would create a depressing drag on his spiritual life. Instead, seeing the glory and brightness of God in contrast to his own dark proclivities and failures did not limit his joy one bit. He was as eloquent in his praise and rejoicing as he was in expressing his conviction that he was the worst of sinners.

How was this possible?

"Touched by a live repentance," Lawrence writes, "I confess all my evil deeds to him, I implore his pardon, and give myself over to his hands to do with me what he will. This king, full of goodness and mercy, far from chastising me, embraces me lovingly, makes me eat at his table, serves me with his own hands, gives me the keys to his pleasures, and treats me just as if I were his favorite."

When a child feels like a parent's favorite, it's like supergrowth food for his or her sense of identity. Freud said that the person who wins the heart of his mother can do anything at all.

Wise parents do everything they can to make each child feel like the favorite. God does the same. "Come to me, all you who labor and are heavy laden" (Matthew 11:28, NKJV). In our failures and spiritual malaise, God reaches out to us.

Brother Lawrence somehow put all that together, seeing himself as "ever more weak and wretched, yet more cherished by God." Paul, St. Francis, and Lawrence all had an extraordinary awareness of their failures and an extraordinary joy in the Holy Spirit.

However anxious or guilty or depressed we may feel, maybe today we should think of ourselves as God's favorites!

Lord, transform my fears that my failures negate your great love for me. Let me rejoice in the wonders of your grace. Despite all my failings, let me sense the joy of your presence.

Always be full of joy in the Lord. I say it again—rejoice! PHILIPPIANS 4:4, NLT

GOODNESS LIKE FIRE

ROSEMARY BUDD declares, "God's goodness is not an absence of badness, but it is like a fire."

When we feel overwhelmed by the evil and tragedy in every part of our suffering world, we know that our Father not only weeps with those who weep, he acts! His compassion, holiness, and love enter the terrible emptiness of the fallen creation. God made the ultimate sacrifice of sending his Son to redeem the world.

As we watch the news and hear of all the heartache around us—and perhaps in our own lives—it's hard not to be overwhelmed. Yet we know that the Lord also is watching and listening. In a sense, he partners with us in bringing his grace to bear. As we pray, he enables us to endure, to listen, and to act.

Mother Teresa was asked how she coped, since her ministry in India for the dying accomplished relatively little amid oceans of needs. She said her questioner was not using the right math. Hers was the math of subtraction—if you can't help a hundred people, help one.

When we feel overwhelmed, we can think, like Mother Teresa, of what we can do in the name of Christ, not think of what isn't done.

Today, do we align ourselves with God's love that "is like a fire"? Do we have faith that he is at work and that we can be part of what he is doing?

"As we come to the God of Justice in prayer, our world grows bigger," Rosemary asserts. "God's goodness always journeys out to overcome evil. He is very alive and purposeful. God creates and recreates, restores and woos and empowers."

Father in heaven, if it's true that you watch all that happens here, and if you are the God of love, let me see through your eyes. Help me to reach out to the brokenhearted. Use your mighty arm to heal, restore, and empower.

Since we are receiving a Kingdom that is unshakable, let us be thankful and please God by worshiping him with holy fear and awe. For our God is a devouring fire.
HEBREWS 12:28-29, NLT

CAN WE LOVE GOD AND NOT OTHERS?

JOHN ORTBERG writes, "People who don't love people *can't* love God, just as people who don't know the multiplication table can't do algebra."

What does he mean by that?

Ortberg makes the case that the God revealed to us by Jesus "is constantly thinking about the people he loves so much." Scripture says that God thinks about his lost sheep, and he can no more forget his people than a nursing mother her baby. "It is simply impossible to love the Father without sharing his heart for people."

Yet we find it's easy to harden our hearts against callous sinners and against those who ridicule our beliefs. It's natural to become judgmental, even if we are trying to grow spiritually.

Ortberg cautions that we may be without scandalous sins and be thought of as spiritually mature, yet miss the essential expression of our faith. "Just as love is the ultimate expression of the law," Ortberg writes, "so lovelessness is the ultimate expression of sin."

We can't love God and despise other people—including agitators and enemies. That's why Jesus told us to love even our enemies and to judge not that we not be judged.

The teachers of the law who were critical of Jesus were so obsessed with being doctrinally correct that they couldn't show love to people who in their eyes didn't measure up. They didn't care one bit about the paralyzed man Jesus healed.

We who want to have "sound doctrine" must take to heart the ultimate mark of being a Christian—love for others. Ortberg says this is far from automatic. He confesses, "I struggle with the same self-righteousness that plagued the teachers of the law."

It all boils down to what Jesus says is the essence of the law: that we are to love God with all our hearts, souls, and minds, and our neighbor as ourselves. And who is our neighbor? Jesus told a story about that—the Good Samaritan. The Samaritan was the one with suspect theology, but he rescued the robbery victim—after all the "doctrinally correct" leaders had passed him by.

Lord, some people in my life are very hard to love.
It's also hard not to detest those who try to tear
down all I hold dear. Help me to detest sin and not
people. Put your love into my heart and soul.

Love your enemies! Pray for those who persecute you! In that way you will be acting as true children of your Father in heaven. MATTHEW 5:44-45, NLT

FAITH IN THE RUBBLE

HELMUT THIELICKE preached in Stuttgart, Germany, during World War II. Under regular bombardment from Allied aircraft, fires swept through the city, killing thousands of people and destroying or damaging tens of thousands of buildings, including many churches. The people lived with the knowledge—and fear—that bombs could fall again at any time. "Here we are gathered in a ruin," Thielicke told his listeners, "and here I am standing in my old army boots, because I no longer possess proper clothes."

He admitted that, like everyone else, he at times felt utterly stricken, his ministry in pieces amid all the churches in rubble and ashes. Yet he proclaimed, "The greatest mysteries of God are always enacted in the depths. God's rule grows mighty in the midst of terrors."

His listeners had lost sons in distant battles. In the bombings, loved ones died beside them. Their livelihoods and possessions were gone, their fears constant. Yet, Thielicke said, "We learned more, and probably also experienced more, about the kingdom of God in the crash of air raids and the terrors of our cellars and underground shelters than in those peaceful and almost utopian times of comfort and well-being."

In our day, we may not experience all-out war, yet a sense of comfort and well-being often eludes us. We see on our media screens violence erupting all over the globe. We see terrorism's victims. The world seems unstable, and we try not to think about all the ways catastrophe could shatter our own town or city.

If the worst were to happen, how would we respond? What spiritual depths might we experience? Would we find faith and hope more necessary than even food and water?

In times of crisis, we are rushed to consider issues of eternity. The transitory and superficial fade. We call on the Father to rescue, comfort, and enable us not only to endure but also to sense his presence.

Thielicke acknowledged what many of his congregation had recently experienced: "The person who has gone through nights of bombing with his hand in God's and has said to himself, when sirens were screaming and shaking, 'If we live, we live to the Lord, and if we die, we die to the Lord,' that person has experienced the hand of God with a new reality he will never forget."

Lord, help me to live in your presence, even if the worst happens. Help me to deepen my trust in you. Lead me each day so that whatever comes, I will sense your presence.

He lifted me out of the pit of despair, out of the mud and the mire. He set my feet on solid ground and steadied me as I walked along. PSALM 40:2, NLT

PRAYER AS NECESSITY

PHILIP YANCEY illustrates from the life of Bishop Desmond Tutu the necessity of praying when our spirits are battered by grievous events. For two years, Bishop Tutu chaired the Truth and Reconciliation Commission hearings in South Africa. He heard endless horror stories of gruesome beatings, torture, and "necklacing" with burning tires. The tales of the atrocities would numb anyone's soul.

When asked why he prayed, Bishop Tutu gave this response: "If your day starts off wrong, it stays skewed. What I've found is that getting up a little earlier and trying to have an hour of quiet in the presence of God, mulling over some Scripture, supports me. I try to have two, three hours of quiet per day . . . when I go on the treadmill for thirty minutes, I use that time for intercession."

Yancey says that Tutu would then put on his judicial commission robes and try to bring truth and reconciliation to the land.

What we face each day has its own pressures and discouragements, even if they don't compare to the terrible stories from postapartheid South Africa. We have the same opportunity as Bishop Tutu to seek that hour of quiet in God's presence or to pray as we exercise or wait in line. We bring our own prayer requests, confession, and praise as we deal with raw experiences.

Philip writes, "The musician Bono once asked Tutu how he managed to find time for prayer and meditation. Tutu replied, 'What are you talking about? Do you think we'd be able to do this stuff if we didn't?'"

Lord, you know both what has discouraged me in the past and what I now must deal with. Fill me with your Spirit, I pray. Enable me to have compassion without burnout, equipped for the battles ahead.

God is our refuge and strength, always ready to help in times of trouble.
PSALM 46:1, NLT

THE POWER OF HELPLESSNESS

OLE HALLESBY describes a process of spiritual growth that can be extremely uncomfortable. Since we cannot fully understand God and his ways, we can grow distressed when he doesn't seem to be coming to our aid. Why does he not answer our prayers? What's going on?

Hallesby says we can endure many things calmly if we see the reasons or purpose of our suffering. But if it seems meaningless, we don't know what to do and may feel rebellious or fearful or both.

However, even though we may feel distraught about our uncertain circumstances, if we stay in the presence of our incomprehensible God, we eventually experience a miracle of decisive importance: God breaks down our self-conceit and self-sufficiency, and we're drawn into fellowship with him.

We become reconciled to two things: our inability to understand many things about God, and our own helplessness. It's this helplessness that becomes the sustaining power of our prayer lives.

"A humble and contrite heart knows that it can merit nothing before God," writes Hallesby. "We are moved to pray every time the Spirit of God emphasizes anew to us our helplessness, and we realize how impotent we are by nature to believe, to love, to hope, to serve, to sacrifice, to suffer, to read the Bible, to pray and to struggle against our sinful desires."

The struggle is lifelong, for we often fall away from what Hallesby calls "this blessed attitude of helplessness before God." Self-conceit and self-sufficiency reassert themselves, and we again feel anxiety and perplexity—until we come once more to God as helpless sinners.

"We ask God to have mercy on us, to love and care for us. Then our helplessness re-establishes us in our right relationship to God and others."

Lord Jesus, my concerns and questions are always
bubbling within me. Help me to relax in you when
I have laid before you everything that troubles me,
and let me trust that my life is in your care.

I will boast only in the LORD; let all who are helpless take heart.   PSALM 34:2, NLT

FIRST LOVE

May 23

BILLY GRAHAM remembers the tremendous excitement he felt when he first saw his wife, Ruth. He recalls their first kiss as thrilling and says that on their honeymoon his heart was pumping and his blood boiling. "But the first flames of physical passion inevitably change," he says. "Our love has been one of commitment."

Graham compares the changes in romantic love with the changes in spiritual passion as he considers Christ's message to the church in Ephesus in Revelation 2:2-4: "I know all the things you do," Jesus declared. "I have seen your hard work and your patient endurance. . . . You have patiently suffered for me without quitting. But I have this complaint against you. You don't love me or each other as you did at first!" (NLT).

These words from the Savior can cut to the core. Many of us identify with losing spiritual steam and the authentic love that once burned brighter.

Graham, late in life, writes of sitting silently beside Ruth on their front porch, communicating with a depth of passion made possible by a lifetime of commitment, including times of great stress. Sadly, many marriages fail to end up with husband and wife rocking on a porch. Likewise, Christian discipleship is full of hazards and competing forces—with spiritual apathy always ready to seep in like a gray fog.

Jesus told the Ephesians that they must repent of losing their first love for him. Billy Graham says that Jesus wasn't asking them to return to their old *feelings*. "Love is more than feeling," Billy says. "Love is a commitment. Love is doing."

Our spiritual journeys require a constant re-igniting of our commitment—by doing *acts* of love for Christ.

First love cools. Spiritual passion may, too, as many committed Christians have experienced. Yet the call is to keep on doing those acts that show our love for Jesus, no matter what our feelings.

We may lose the emotional feeling of first love, but we can show greater love than at the first by our continuing commitment.

Loving Father, show me what you want me to do and enable me to do it. Only you can pour into me your love and the spiritual vitality to obey your guidance day by day.

Make thankfulness your sacrifice to God, and keep the vows you made to the Most High.
PSALM 50:14, NLT

THE BEAUTIFUL PENCIL

MOTHER TERESA often gave this challenge: "Now let us do something beautiful for God."

Malcolm Muggeridge received that challenge in a letter from her, and his response was, "I found the phrase enchanting, with a sparkle and gaiety very characteristic of her. Doing something beautiful for God is, for Mother Teresa, what life is about. Everything becomes beautiful. Mother Teresa and the Missionaries of Charity provide a living witness to the power and truth of what Jesus came to proclaim. His light shines in them. When I think of them in Calcutta, it is not the bare house in a dark slum conjured up in mind, but a light shining and a joy abounding."

Muggeridge later named his documentary and book about Mother Teresa *Something Beautiful for God.*

How did she maintain that beautiful spirit, and how did she accomplish so much that she won the Nobel Peace Prize? "Very often I would feel like a little pencil in God's hand," she said. "He does the writing; he does the thinking; he does the movement—I have only to be a pencil and nothing else."

A pencil. Just a little pencil. We see in that illustration her humility and also her trust in the hand that moved her and that acted through her. When we are little pencils in God's hands, we see his work appear in our circumstances.

Mother Teresa points to the Gospel of John and asks us to see how many times Jesus used the word *Father.* As Jesus totally and lovingly trusted his Father, so must we. "I must give myself completely to him," she says. "We surrender even our sins. We need humility to acknowledge our sin. The knowledge of our sin helps us to rise."

When we see ourselves like the Prodigal Son in Jesus' parable, we continually get up to go to our Father.

"We are at his disposal," Mother Teresa emphasizes. "We must say, 'I belong to you. You can do whatever you like.' This is our strength, and this is the joy of the Lord."

Father in heaven, I love the idea of being simply a little pencil in your hand. Write with me what you desire. Let all my movements today produce the words and marks that communicate your love and care.

You are the light of the world. . . . Let your good deeds shine out for all to see, so that everyone will praise your heavenly Father. MATTHEW 5:14, 16, NLT

PRAYER IN THE STORM

GEORGE MACDONALD prayed with passionate faith, even when he experienced doubts and distress. His prayers were full of vivid imagery. Read the following prayer slowly to get the picture:

> *Doubt swells and surges.*
> *My soul in storm is but a tattered sail,*
> *Streaming its ribbons on the gale.*
> *In calm, 'tis but a limp and flapping thing:*
> *Oh, swell it with thy breath; make it a wing.*

MacDonald prayed that his soul would be a wing sweeping through ocean and wind, finding its haven in God. But this would happen only if God would perform it in him.

Our minds may not turn to poetic imagery when we're swamped by troubles and doubt, but we've likely prayed with similar feelings. Doubt surges when storms destroy what we hoped would be answers to fervent prayers. Where is God when we're on the edge and about to go under? Doesn't he care?

Those are the kinds of questions and prayers we find in the Psalms: raw pain and accusations that God isn't doing his part. Yet the psalmists prayed anyway—and so did MacDonald. When "doubt, pain, anger and strife" made him feel he just couldn't pray no matter how he tried, he kept at it.

He described his fledgling prayer as a little bird barely out of the nest, "crouching, falling, flitting, flying, perching."

Ever feel your prayers are like that? When they can't seem to get airborne, pray anyway—and wait for God's wind under your wings.

Father, sometimes I'm lifted in prayer and sense
your presence. Other times I'm like that tattered sail
MacDonald describes, flapping limply in the wind.
Lift me by the mighty winds of your Spirit.

In my desperation I prayed, and the LORD listened; he saved me from all my troubles.
. . . Taste and see that the LORD is good. Oh, the joys of those who take refuge in him!
PSALM 34:6, 8, NLT

YES, BUT WHAT ABOUT BOB?

RAY STEDMAN, referring to the first chapter of Paul's letter to the Ephesians, points out from the text that "the thing that convinced Paul their faith was authentic was the evidence of their love." Stedman was greatly moved as he studied the following verses, and we would do well to read them slowly and let the implications of the italicized words sink in:

> For this reason I too, having heard of the faith in the Lord Jesus which exists among you and *your love for all the saints*, do not cease giving thanks for you, while making mention of you in my prayers; that the God of our Lord Jesus Christ, the Father of glory, may give to you a spirit of wisdom and of revelation in the knowledge of Him. I pray that the eyes of your heart may be enlightened, so that you will know what is the hope of His calling, what are the riches of the glory of His inheritance in the saints. (Ephesians 1:15-18, NASB, emphasis added)

Stedman observes, "Paul is struck by the fact that these Christians love *all* the saints, not just some of them."

Jill Briscoe, in studying these same verses, drives home a similar point when she writes, "As we make Christ at home in our hearts, he will constantly shed abroad his love, supplying us with the ability to love 'the whole family.'" Her very next sentence—and you can almost see her smile with tongue firmly in cheek—is her exclamation: "If only Paul hadn't said that!"

In other words, we're called to love even that relative we try to avoid and the person at church who grates on us . . . or worse. Says Jill Briscoe, "Paul reminds us that we are part of the 'whole family,' a family that needs loving, and that is going to take a lot more love than just mine. It's going to take Christ in the inner person—in all of us."

One of the best ways we can grow in love for others, including the unlovable, is to pray for them—as Paul here demonstrates. Some saints are easy to love, some not. When we pray for others, we call down God's blessings on them. At the same time, we smooth out the rough edges of our own attitudes.

Only prayer and the Holy Spirit can make possible our loving *all* the saints.

Holy Spirit of God, loving some people is just beyond
my capacity. I invite you to work on my emotions and
attitudes and to give me a love that is larger than
my own. Help me to love "the whole family."

You were cleansed from your sins when you obeyed the truth, so now you must show sincere love to each other as brothers and sisters. Love each other deeply with all your heart. I PETER 1:22, NLT

THE DELIGHT CYCLE

BEN PATTERSON was dusting his furniture, moving to music he had playing. He started revving it up, dancing more and more vigorously and flamboyantly. Gradually, he became aware of his four-year-old son watching—and beaming with delight. Patterson invited his son to join in, and they danced. They leaped over chairs, ran across the coffee table, jumped on the sofa, shouted, and giggled.

Ben writes, "I wish you could have seen the look of unabashed pleasure and joy on my son's face as he danced. Any exploration of joy is incomplete if we do not understand that at its deepest, joy is delight for God and with God—not unlike my dance with my son."

Psalm 37:4 tells us that when we delight ourselves in the Lord, he will give us the desires of our hearts. An obvious cycle of cause and effect leaps out from that verse. If we're delighted in the Lord, we'll be delighted with what delights him. Naturally, if we're delighted in what brings joy to the Lord, he gives us the desires of our hearts because they're in harmony with his desires and plans.

What delights God and gives him joy? Psalm 104:31 exclaims, "May the glory of the LORD continue forever! The LORD takes pleasure in all he has made!" (NLT). Throughout the Psalms we see how God delights in his creation.

At Jesus' baptism, the Father said he was delighted in his Son. God so loved the world—and you and me—that he sent his Son into the world that we might be redeemed—and so he could rejoice in our rescue.

When we find our delight in God, we share in his delights. And, incredibly, he delights in us, the same as Ben Patterson did in his son, and his son in him, and the joy of the dance.

Lord, I take refuge in you. Draw me into your
delights! Give me a heart that genuinely rejoices
in what brings joy to you instead of what lures me
to the shortcuts and "pleasures for a season."

Taste and see that the LORD is good. Oh, the joys of those who take refuge in him!
PSALM 34:8, NLT

PRAY FOR SUCCESS?

FRED SMITH says he doesn't pray for miracles or success. What does he pray for?

A willingness to join God in his process and his work.

A redemptive spirit, equipped with biblical principles, as he faces day-to-day opportunities.

Consciousness that God is present and cares.

So where does success come in? Smith says, "I believe in *working* for success much more than praying for it. Pray for maturity, and work for success. Work enthusiastically, work intelligently, work intensely, and work ethically."

The truth is, the results of all activities are in God's hands; our role is to energetically engage with life, to discern as best we can how to work and live, prayerfully seeking to be in step with the Holy Spirit.

Not that we can't lay specific requests before the Lord. Yet, in humility, we accept what happens. As Smith once pointed out, both Daniel and Stephen prayed and obeyed God, with very different results. Daniel was delivered from the lions, but Stephen was stoned to death.

Only our sovereign God sees it all and understands the meaning and his plans. It's helpful to remember that Stephen saw heaven open as he was stoned, and was ushered into glory. We pray, but we have no idea how God will answer our prayers. We trust him, we pray, and we energetically set out to do his will as we perceive it.

Most of us have areas of resistance to following through on what we know we should be doing. Fred Smith admitted he was not gifted in evangelism, yet he believed he needed to be involved with others. Each morning, therefore, he simply prayed, "Lord, today I won't duck."

So we pray for resilience, courage, hope, and wisdom. As has often been said, we then watch to see what God is up to.

Lord, do your work in me so I may do your work in the world. Help me to accept all results of prayer, including disappointments, with trust and love for you. Help me to live in your peace in your Spirit.

We can make our plans, but the LORD determines our steps. PROVERBS 16:9, NLT

TOUGH TIMES, TOUGH FAITH

D. L. MOODY says that when it comes to our spiritual lives, "We can stand affliction better than we can prosperity, for in prosperity we forget God."

No one seeks affliction as a helpful aid to spiritual growth, but it's hard to reject the truth of Moody's assertion. When things are going well and we feel prosperous and secure, we easily forget how our Father has provided for us.

Of course, Moody was painfully aware that without searching for them, troubles inevitably find us. When they do, he advises us to face them—and even, if possible, to embrace them—with courage and faith: "Let troubles come if it will drive us closer to God."

No doubt you've heard a coach say, "When the going gets tough, the tough get going." That's true, and the way to be tough and strong is to "get going" to God in our weakness.

Robert Murray McCheyne writes, "You will never find Jesus so precious as when the world is one vast wilderness. He is like a rock rising above the storm. He is like a rose blooming in the midst of desolation."

One of the troubles that keep finding us is the depth of our own waywardness. Each of us is engaged in significant spiritual battles. Moody famously admitted, "I have had more trouble with myself than with any other man."

In all our troubles, whether circumstantial or personal, it all boils down to the prayer of the old-time spiritual:

> Not the preacher who is preaching,
>   nor the deacon, Lord,
>   Standing in the need of prayer.
> It's me, it's me, it's me, O Lord,
>   Standing in the need of prayer.

We all long for peace and prosperity, health and good times. We all want spiritual vitality. These ebb and flow, but not God. He waits and listens always to hear our prayers.

Father in heaven, I do have most of my trouble with myself. Draw me so that I'm fully in step with your Spirit. Help me to face all the tough things with resilience and to depend on your strength all through the day.

O Lord, you are so good, so ready to forgive, so full of unfailing love for all who ask for your help. PSALM 86:5, NLT

BESEECHING THE FORCES OF HEAVEN

JOHN HENRY JOWETT writes about "the mighty ministry of intercession." Let's face it—the word *intercession* sounds rather bland. And *mighty*? When we do intercede for others, most of us wonder whether anything will really change.

In times of crisis, we may pour out our hearts for those in danger or those swamped with grief. But at other times we may drift away from intercession, letting it slip to the margins.

Yet praying for others—interceding on their behalf with our heavenly Father— may indeed create mighty results. In that regard, Jowett looks at the remarkable story of what Jesus said to Peter, who was soon to be assaulted by the devil. "Simon, Simon, . . . Satan hath desired to have you" (Luke 22:31, KJV).

What was going on in the spiritual realm that impinges on our own? Jesus knew that momentous spiritual battles were raging, and he said to Peter—right after telling him that Satan was after him—"But I have prayed for thee" (Luke 22:32, KJV).

Jowett says this: "That '*but*' is the massing of the forces of heaven against the subtle hordes of hell. Let me ever remember that the Lord's prayers are always the conveyers of holy power to those for whom he prays."

That's enormous comfort when we consider that, according to Scripture, Jesus prays for us even now as we struggle in our own spiritual warfare—as does the Holy Spirit "with groanings that cannot be expressed in words" (Romans 8:26, NLT).

Jowett writes, "When we invent little devices to protect us against the evil one, he laughs. It is like a child erecting sand ramparts against the sea. The only thing that makes the devil fear is the presence of God."

Jesus intercedes for us. He is present with us as we pray. And we have the golden opportunity to intercede through prayer for others, because Satan is like a lion looking for whom he may devour.

As John Henry Jowett says, "Only God can deal with devils."

Holy and almighty Father, sometimes I'm confused about what the devil may be trying to do in my life. You're not confused, and you can block his attempts to take me down. Protect me, Lord. Send your holy angels to my defense.

Are any of you suffering hardships? You should pray. JAMES 5:13, NLT

FIVE GREAT COMFORTS

FRED SMITH says his friend Ray Stedman once told him that his life turned around when he realized God was for him and not against him.

For many, the weight of sin or failures dissipates the joy of salvation. God the condemning Judge looms large.

Smith suggests that we can take comfort in five ways God shows himself to be our loving heavenly Father:

1. Our Father reaches out to us. He's the one who calls us to come to him. He takes the initiative.
2. Our Father loves us, even with all our weaknesses. "God totally knows me and yet he loves me," Smith says. "That's extremely humbling!"
3. Our Father forgives us. We're not just excused or tolerated or ignored. We are loved and forgiven.
4. Our Father is *for* us. Have we thought about how transforming it is to realize God is in our corner? For Ray Stedman, it opened new vistas, as it can for us. God's promises bring peace and vitality into our lives.
5. Our Father is always with us. We may feel lonely or neglected, but we can call to God and listen for his whispers and ask to sense his presence. Whatever our thoughts or feelings, he is there.

When we feel oppressed by our weaknesses, let's realize God is not surprised by them. He loves us just as we are. Yet he also lifts us into new life with him as we respond to his initiatives.

---

*Father in heaven, help me to soak in this reality that
you love me far more than I can imagine. When I
feel condemned or exasperated at my own failures,
draw me to your strength, renewal, and joy.*

There is no condemnation for those who belong to Christ Jesus. And because you belong to him, the power of the life-giving Spirit has freed you from the power of sin that leads to death. ROMANS 8:1-2, NLT

THE WORST PERSON CHANGED?

OSWALD CHAMBERS shakes our settled perceptions of ourselves when he writes, "Most of us love other people for what they are to us instead of what God wants them to be."

"To us" is the key phrase—our love generally is rooted in the benefits that come our way. Chambers's blunt assessment probes to the core of our relationships. Our natural instinct is to love those who love us—which in itself is a good thing. However, we are called to go beyond that. We are called to love others by seeing them through the Father's eyes, by seeing how he desires to transform them into new creatures.

That perspective comes only through fresh vision from the Holy Spirit.

Seeing others through God's eyes frees us to love the unlovable, not just those who meet our needs. Chambers, in discussing his own transformation by God from pettiness and resentment to joy, writes, "God is interested in some extraordinary people—in you and in me—and he is just as interested in the person you dislike as he is in you."

Chambers then asks us to think of the worst person we know. He cautions that it must actually be a specific person, not someone we've simply heard about. Then he asks what hope we have for that person. "Does the Holy Spirit begin to convey to your mind the wonder of that person's being presented perfect in Christ Jesus?" Chambers sees that as the test of whether we're learning to see others as Jesus does.

When we begin to see that way, we are moved to intercessory prayer. Chambers saw praying for others as the essential work of the believer. He often said it was the one thing in ministry that had no snare, and he personally prayed this way, not out of grim duty but with enthusiasm and joy.

In praying for others, we have the golden opportunity to be engaged in the work of the Holy Spirit.

Lord, it's true that I care most about the people who love me. Help me to see everyone through your eyes, and to be empowered to pray for others as you work in me.

The Holy Spirit helps us in our weakness. For example, we don't know what God wants us to pray for. But the Holy Spirit prays for us with groanings that cannot be expressed in words. ROMANS 8:26, NLT

ASKING BOLDLY

MARTIN LUTHER urges us to get beyond the habit of praying only for insignificant things and to grasp the majesty and generosity of God as we pray.

"If God wanted to give us only superficial things," Luther writes, "he wouldn't have given such a magnificent model for prayer."

He's referring, of course, to the Lord's Prayer, which asks for God's Kingdom to come and for God to be boldly at work. The great spiritual warfare that rages within us and around us has large stakes, yet we can boldly ask that God's power will prevail.

"God has plenty of resources," Luther asserts, "and he's not a tightwad. He expects that we will ask him for many things."

But what should we ask for? Everything! For our personal needs, yes, and the needs of others, and that God's grace will dominate in all situations before us—and that our prayers will be in harmony with his will. When we pray in the Spirit, we are lifted to his perspective and we receive "infinitely more than we might ask or think."

So as we pray in the spirit of the prayer Jesus taught us to pray—that God's Kingdom will come and his will be done—we get more than we ask for. King David tells us in Psalm 37:4 that when we delight ourselves in the Lord, he gives us the desires of our hearts. Of course, our desires—if we're delighting in the Lord—will be just what God wants to give us.

Luther believed that when we receive what we ask for in the Lord's Prayer, we are receiving the blessings of God both in heaven and on earth.

Prayers are far more than requests for good things to happen; they are a linkage with eternity that transcends our imaginations.

Our Father in heaven, holy is your name. Your Kingdom come, on earth and in my life. Let my delight be in you. Expand my understanding and faith to receive the full blessings you are ready to give.

All glory to God, who is able, through his mighty power at work within us, to accomplish infinitely more than we might ask or think. EPHESIANS 3:20, NLT

THE TOUCH OF HIS FINGERS

AMY CARMICHAEL, in writing about suffering and extreme poverty, uses the illustration of sand sprinkled on a metal plate. "You sprinkle sand on a brass plate fixed on a pedestal and draw a bow across the edge of the plate, touching it at the same time with two fingers. Then, because of this touch, the sand does not fall into confusion but into an ordered pattern, like music made visible. Each little grain of sand finds its place in that pattern." This pattern is known as a Chladni pattern.

Carmichael personally experienced much suffering and what appeared to be ineffective prayers. Yet the touch of God brought meaning to her life out of what could have seemed meaningless.

Everything matters—even when God seems silent and our prayers ineffectual. Amy Carmichael says, of prayers that seem smothered or scattered into nothingness, that they are "folded up in the thoughts of peace that He thinks toward us."

God is love. His plans for us are not for calamity, but for hope for the future. We can view life as a senseless ruin, or as a Chladni plate on which each grain of sand finds its place. The loving hand of God will somehow make sense of it all.

"Suffering, hunger, poverty, baffling circumstances," Carmichael writes, "cannot of themselves make anything but confusion. But if there be the touch of the Hand, all these things work together for good, not for ill, not for discord, but for something like the harmony of music."

Father in heaven, grant me faith that the shifting sand—the heartache, tragedies, and crushed hope—will all someday make for harmony and a beautiful pattern of your grace.

Let love be your highest goal! I CORINTHIANS 14:1, NLT

URGENT PRAISE IN THE WILDERNESS   *June 4*

JOHN HENRY JOWETT gives us this paradox: "The good Lord makes a dry experience the fountain of blessing."

In our experience of life, we see this paradox time and time again: that in the hardest times we can experience the greatest sense of God at work. Having observed this, Jowett writes, "Let us therefore not fear when the path turns into the wilderness."

Into the wilderness! Sometimes it may feel as if the path is turning into an unknown, scary place. Stability and security are elusive. Health problems, for example, can bring financial and emotional pressure. We are all tragically vulnerable. We long to protect our loved ones and to stand strong, but we realize that so much is out of our hands. Unforeseen events can trump our best-laid plans.

Jowett says, "Let us not fear. . . . The Lord had manna for the children of disappointment. . . . He makes water gush forth from the rock. I shall find lilies of peace in the lonely valley of humiliation."

Faith knows that the God of love will still be with us, no matter what lies ahead.

Yet we are human, and we respond as humans to disappointments and calamities. So how do we change our anxieties and fears into faith?

Jowett advises remembering God's past faithfulness. "Nothing so quickens hope as a journey among our yesterdays. The heart lays aside its fears. Now I see why the New Testament is so urgent in the matter of praise. Without praise, many other virtues and graces cannot be born. Without praise they have no breath of life. Praise quickens a radiant company of heavenly presences, and among them is the shining spirit of hope."

When I look at the future, Lord, I have all sorts of fears.
Your Word urges me to have faith, but I dread having
to go through really rough times! Father in heaven,
help me to see through your eyes and trust you.

God is our refuge and strength, always ready to help in times of trouble. So we will not fear
when earthquakes come and the mountains crumble into the sea. PSALM 46:1-2, NLT

WHERE'S THE JOY?

SHERWOOD WIRT asks the question, "Why did God create the universe?" Though recognizing the theological response that God created everything to show his glory, Wirt had an additional answer.

"If I read Scripture correctly," he writes, "God's nature expresses itself most characteristically and distinctively through joy. Thus the opening verses of Genesis could mean, 'In the beginning, for his own pleasure and joy, God created the heavens and the earth.' The second verse goes on to speak of the Spirit of God 'hovering over' the waters. But perhaps he was not just hovering; perhaps he was smiling. Perhaps he was rejoicing over the prospect of his new creation . . . an outpouring of the sheer, incredible joy which is at the heart of our loving God."

Wirt studied the theologians' long lists of God's attributes and found it curious that joy was missing from the lists. Certainly, God is holy, righteous, merciful, loving, and many other things, but what about his joy?

"For some reason, joy seems to have been muted in theological studies and writings," Wirt says. "If God is perfect holiness, is he not also perfect joy?" Wirt answers his own question with Scripture references about God's joy, including the joy of the Lord being our strength and that we should rejoice in what he has created.

Joy. Rejoice. The Bible is full of songs and admonitions that we are to rejoice in God's love and mercy and joy. Our world's brokenness seems to contradict the Bible's declaration that God is love. The desolate reaches of the galaxies seem to contradict its references to the Creator as a God of joy. And yet the Bible not only affirms these attributes but announces the good news that we can be embraced by God's love and joy.

"The cosmos we know," Wirt declares, "is an expression of joy by the Creator. The joy that caused the morning stars to sing together was the joy implanted by the Creator God acting out of love."

Father and Creator, too often it's easier for us to see the brokenness and desolation than it is to see your joy. Please put within me praises and delight at your love and care. Help me not to be a drag on others but to share your joy.

The morning stars sang together and all the angels shouted for joy. JOB 38:7, NLT

REACH OUT IN LOVE

JOHN WESLEY, in a time of intense animosities between Catholics and Protestants, wrote to a Roman Catholic acquaintance with his insistence that God's love should overcome their estrangement. His letter declared that, because God loves us, we should love one another; despite differences, we "should provoke one another to love and good works. Let the points on which we differ stand aside." He then proposed the following resolutions:

"Let us resolve in the name and strength of God not to hurt one another." Instead, he advocated kindness and loving Christian behavior.

"Let us resolve to speak nothing harsh or unkind about each other." On the contrary, he recommended that they verbalize all the good about one another, using only the language of love.

"Let us resolve to harbor no unkind thoughts about each other.

"Let us lay the ax to the root of the tree." He emphasized that we should examine everything that arises in our hearts and cut away "the very root of bitterness."

Finally he urged, "In whatever we are agreed leads to the kingdom, let us always rejoice to strengthen each other's hands in God."

This earnest reaching out by John Wesley gives us a model for our times. Would that all Catholics and Protestants in Northern Ireland had applied Wesley's words! Fortunately, many did reach out in remarkable examples of love that did bring relative peace.

Wesley's letter is a marvelous example of how the authentic mark of the Christian is love, especially toward those who share the faith. In contrast, we're all aware of acrimonious church splits and Christians harshly critical of one another.

Are we engaged with the spirit of Wesley as we reach out to those with whom we disagree? How might we right now show the authentic mark of the Christian?

Father, it's so easy for us to hurt one another with words and attitudes that don't match what Wesley called for. Deliver me from nursing bad feelings or talking about others behind their backs. Fill me with your love.

Don't just pretend to love others. Really love them. Hate what is wrong. Hold tightly to what is good. ROMANS 12:9, NLT

SHARING GOD'S BREATH

HENRI NOUWEN shares this wonderful reality: "The person who lives from God's breath can recognize with joy that the same breath sinks into the lungs of his brothers and sisters, and that they are all drawing from the same source. The fear of another disappears, a smile comes to the lips, the weapons fall, and one hand reaches out for the other."

What a wonderful image—that we are all drawing from the same source, the same spiritual oxygen, and that the same Holy Spirit comes to each of us who invite him into our lives. He then transforms our relationships.

When we pray with others, we are all breathing the same rarefied air. When we worship together, we are together confessing, rejoicing, and praising.

Nouwen speaks of the "prayerful acceptance of each other." He urges that instead of defining others, we should "always let them appear as ever new." In the Spirit, we can share our lives in ways that open fresh vistas of love and understanding.

Praying gives us access to God's blessings and resources that are new every day. God is not surprised by anything that happens, so he frees us to accept another dynamic. Tomorrow includes the unexpected—but God is engaged with us. His fresh vitality helps us accept a different reality.

Nouwen writes, "In prayer, I am constantly on the way, on pilgrimage."

Lord Jesus, accepting my fellow pilgrims is hard when their attitudes are difficult to accept. Help me to see them in a different light—in your light. Grant me new insights and energy to live in harmony with you and with others.

Encourage each other and build each other up, just as you are already doing.
I THESSALONIANS 5:11, NLT

TROUBLE

June 8

JILL BRISCOE experienced a family crisis and was shocked to hear herself praying panic prayers and indulging in angry tirades. She came to the conclusion that "trouble was going to do wonders for my prayer life."

She reports that it did. "Trouble can, in fact, jump-start our prayer life if we respond to divinely permitted trouble instead of reacting against it. If we are desperate enough, trouble forces us to spend time with God." She quotes the familiar advice from the book of James: "Is anyone in trouble? He should pray."

Truth is, all of us can respond to that advice, because trouble invades every life. When our troubles are at their most severe, we realize how totally dependent we are on God and what small power we have to set things right, or even to survive. When we are in the crucible of suffering, we enter a place that can become holy and purifying.

A time of crisis is also a time when we can experience the unexpected. Briscoe observes, "When we are driven by our naked need to cast ourselves on God, he comes to our rescue in the most unusual ways."

Have you ever experienced that?

As we constantly seek God's engagement and his help in our troubles, we may find, as Jill Briscoe did, that the most difficult times are when God does surprising things—in his own mysterious ways, and on his own timetable.

If we dread the moment we'll experience fearsome trouble or naked need, we can place our plight before God. The Scriptures promise that he will be there for us.

"Helplessness opens a door to the almighty ability of the Lord," Jill writes. "Let God provide for you in his way."

Lord, you know I don't feel ready to be purified
by deep trouble. Yet I know that, as Job said, we're
born to trouble as the sparks fly upward. Father,
help me to be alert to look for your surprises.

My heart is confident in you, O God; no wonder I can sing your praises with all my heart!
PSALM 108:1, NLT

WHEN WE'RE OVERWHELMED

FRANÇOIS FÉNELON was empathizing with his friends when he wrote, "At times, everything in life seems to be a trial and suffering. Sometimes the cross is so heavy it can neither be carried nor dragged. Then you can only fall down beneath it, overwhelmed and exhausted."

Fénelon is also quick to encourage us, saying we should embrace our trials and live by faith, trusting God even when we don't understand. Yet he's brutally honest. "God does not transform you on a bed of light, life, and grace. His transformation is done on the cross, in darkness, poverty, and death."

He buttresses his point by quoting Jesus, who said that anyone who follows him will have to deny himself. Fénelon adds, "His path winds up the side of a steep mountain."

With all this grim description, though, he turns the corner and says, "You do not yet see the lovely side of following Christ. You see what he takes away, but you do not see what he gives. You exaggerate the sacrifices and ignore the blessings."

Well, he certainly paints vivid pictures of the sacrifices! Clearly we live with both a stern call and bountiful blessings.

The mature challenge of following Christ is not like the Sunday school picture of children sitting at Jesus' feet in a gorgeous garden in which even the bees and snakes seem to be smiling. It's more like a gritty, brutal game of rugby. The spiritual forces arrayed against us loom large and threatening.

Yet, if life is like a game of rugby, we might remember that rugby players love the game! Sacrifices abound in the Christian life, but so does "the lovely side of following Christ."

Fénelon concludes by asserting, "You will be led to do things you'll find enjoyable, and you'll like them better than doing all the things that have led you astray."

Lord, I want your highest in my life, but the mountains seem very steep. Empower me with the grit and determination of a rugby player in serving you and resisting the devil! Draw me into your love.

Worry weighs a person down; an encouraging word cheers a person up.
PROVERBS 12:25, NLT

LAY IT ALL ON HIM

EUGENE PETERSON prays with these words: "God of all beginnings and all endings, I bring all my unfinished business to you—everything that I started and couldn't finish, all that I began but lost interest in, all that I began in hope and quit in despair. Make finished work of it all, by your grace. Amen."

The *Amen* may be the most important part of his prayer. He puts his concerns before the Lord and then leaves them in his hands.

When we come to God at the beginning of the day and realize all that's before us, or we come at the end of the day and review all the loose threads and undone tasks and causes for anxiety, we can lay each one before the Lord—and leave them there.

Easier said than done? Indeed! But that is the invitation open to us.

Not that we shirk our responsibilities, but Jesus told us repeatedly not to worry. The way to obey him is to ask for God's engagement, cleansing, and empowerment—and to leave our burdens at his feet.

We are then free to praise him. We can say with David in Psalm 9, "I will be filled with joy because of you. I will sing praises to your name, O Most High" (9:2, NLT).

When we praise God, we take our minds off ourselves and our troubles and into the freedom of his grace.

Gene assures us, "We can be sure of receiving audience with God in prayer. He will hear us out. We can lay our entire case before him without fear of being interrupted, or hurried, or cut off."

Lord of all creation, here I am again with my many concerns. I place them all in your hands and praise you for your compassionate care. Help me to leave them with you and to rejoice in all your provisions and your love.

Joyful are those who obey his laws and search for him with all their hearts.
PSALM 119:2, NLT

HOLDING ON FOR DEAR LIFE

JONI EARECKSON TADA asks, "Have you ever held on to something as though your life depended on it?" She then tells the story of when she was a little girl and went horseback riding. "I'm not talking about sitting on some small pony being led around a little ring," she says. "I'm talking about wild and woolly, galloping jaunts up and down hills and pastures, jumping fences, and splashing through streams. Real horseback riding."

At four, she was sitting behind her father on his big horse. She hung on to his belt with her tiny hands, and as long as she had the belt securely in hand, she knew she was safe.

She then refers to the "belt of truth" that Paul mentions in Ephesians 6:14. She says that when the going gets rough, she knows she has that belt and hangs on to truths about God: that he's in control, that he's passionate about her highest good, and that his grace is available and abundant and will sustain her.

Sometimes, as we get jolted in the saddle, it's easy to let those truths slip right out of our hands. God in control? It doesn't feel like it. God passionately caring about what's happening? He can seem so distant. We long for his grace but we do not always sense it.

A man once wrote to Joni and offered this advice: "Many believers gaze at their problems and glance at the Lord. But I tell you to gaze at the Lord and glance at your problems."

Her response? "Great advice!"

Joni has found it a "wonderful thing" to depend on prayer and to remind herself of the truths about the God who loves us. At the same time, she admits she is still learning in her communion with God. "He and I are still in this adventure of life together."

Father in heaven, help me to saturate my thinking
with the great truths you reveal about yourself in your
Word. Open my eyes to see your majesty and glory,
instead of being all caught up in my concerns.

I rise early, before the sun is up; I cry out for help and put my hope in your words.
PSALM 119:147, NLT

WHEN GOD DELAYS

CHARLES HADDON SPURGEON assures us, "God blesses us by his temporary delays, as well as his prompt replies." Spurgeon cautions us not to consider delays in prayer as denial: "God's long-dated bills will be punctually honored. We are dealing with a Being whose years are without end. Unanswered petitions are not unheard."

We come to God with many burdens and requests—and with earnest faith we leave them with him to act as he wills. Sometimes we sense we are in step with the Spirit and receive one answer after another that seem clearly to come from the Lord's hands. Other times great volumes of prayer go up, sometimes by many believers, and there's no answer—in fact, the situation grows worse!

We feel in those cases a severe testing of our faith.

Spurgeon says bluntly, "Beggars must not be choosers, and especially they must not be choosers when they have to deal with infinite wisdom and sovereignty."

We don't like being reminded we're beggars, but our human limitations make us beggars indeed as we pray for health, protection, spiritual vitality, and a host of other necessities. We come in our weakness asking for strength. We come devastated and ask for God's hope. Then, we express gratitude and praise for what God chooses to provide.

Spurgeon tells us that prayer doesn't alter God's purposes, but prayer is part of his purpose and plan. "We do not expect to change the will of God, but we believe our prayer to be part of his will."

Here is how he says we should pray: "As supplicants we come; joyful but not presumptuous; familiar as children before a father, yet reverential as creatures before their Maker. Our God not only hears prayer but also loves to hear it."

Heavenly Father, I place before you the mysteries
of prayer and your answering our anguished pleas.
Thank you for all you have provided and every prayer
I see answered. Help me to rest in your grace.

From the depths of despair, O LORD, I call for your help. Hear my cry, O Lord. Pay attention to my prayer. PSALM 130:1-2, NLT

OUR INSTINCT FOR ADVENTURE

PAUL TOURNIER writes that we all have an inborn thirst for adventure and that each age has its own distinct adventure. "The Holy Spirit," he counsels, "is always calling us to look forward, not back."

Tournier encourages us to engage more boldly and enthusiastically in each succeeding adventure throughout our lives. The spirit of adventure must be continually awakened, for knowledge, repetition, and routine tend to stifle it. He observes, "One must grow in adventure at the same time one grows in knowledge. We must always try to retain that indefinable freshness of outlook."

Dr. Tournier wrote many substantial, refreshing books on the role of the spiritual and moral life in health, disease, and healing. Before publishing his first book, he shared his manuscript with six friends. They made valid criticisms, but he didn't feel he could make the changes they suggested. In addition, not one encouraged him to publish the book. "I was paralyzed," he writes, and then cautions, "Do not depend too much on others to assume responsibility for your adventure."

If we are wise, we seek counselors, but we also need the zest that comes from making our own choices and plunging in. It's crucial that those choices resonate with the call of the Holy Spirit. When we are aided by him and make choices with much prayer, we often find that our adventures crystallize with clarity.

In speaking of all manner of enterprise and common toil, Tournier concludes, "The meaning of our work is the satisfaction of the instinct for adventure that God has implanted in our hearts."

Father in heaven, help me to view what's ahead as the adventure you are calling me to instead of focusing on the difficulties I must face. Grant me your grace and energy to encourage others in their adventures.

It is pleasant to see dreams come true. . . . Walk with the wise and become wise.
PROVERBS 13:19-20, NLT

THE PARADOX OF GOD'S PROTECTION

June 14

NANCY GUTHRIE asks her readers if, when plagued by doubt, it's helpful to know that the person Jesus said was "the greatest man" also dealt with doubt and endured imprisonment. Jesus said that, of everyone who had ever lived, none was greater than John the Baptist. Yet John doubted, suffered in prison, and was eventually executed.

Guthrie says she always wanted to think a "great" man or woman would be blessed with a comfortable life and not have to suffer. Isn't that how it's supposed to work when we please God? Doesn't God protect us from bad things?

Actually, as we see throughout the Bible, God's choice servants were ones who suffered greatly. David in the Psalms repeatedly cries out for relief in his pits of despair. Joseph was betrayed. Paul was beaten and imprisoned. Guthrie points out that Job was chosen to suffer *because* of his great faith, for it was God who brought up his name in conversation with Satan.

We live with a paradox: having God as our refuge and high tower of protection, as David says in the Psalms, contrasted with the reality that this refuge does not mean we are free from accidents, cancer, or the loss of loved ones. We live in a fallen creation.

Nancy Guthrie confesses that at times she has found herself "in a prison of doubt and disappointment" because she believed that if God loved her, he would make her life free of the deepest pain. Yet, suffering has deepened her understanding. Now she brings her questions and doubts to the Lord and finds comfort in knowing that she can trust him.

Her prayer is that the pain in her life not be wasted—that each disappointment would deepen and nurture her spiritual growth.

Father in heaven, when suffering comes my way,
help me to trust you completely. I pray you'll enable
me not only to endure but also to grow and deepen
in my faith as you bring your grace into my life.

Trust in the LORD always, for the LORD GOD is the eternal Rock.   ISAIAH 26:4, NLT

THE NEED FOR PATIENCE AND GRIT

THOMAS À KEMPIS tells us that no matter how hard we work at arranging our lives or trying to avoid troubles and suffering, they will find us anyway. He holds nothing back: "Do you think you can escape what no mortal has ever escaped? Prepare yourself to endure many trials and obstacles in this vale of tears, for such will be your lot wherever you are, no matter how much you try to hide from them."

Thomas à Kempis doesn't sugarcoat reality. Everyone commends patience, he tells us, but very few are ready to suffer. Yet the more we accept suffering and die to self, the more we live to God.

Does all this sound morbid and depressing? We can view it that way, for the realities of life are painful. Or we can realize that the great challenges of life require extraordinary effort. The greatest and most universal challenge is to embrace whatever comes our way with patience and trust in God.

When buffeted and nearly broken, do we rise to the ultimate challenge and grow in grace, knowledge, patience, and grit? Do we come in our weakness to the Savior and find our strength in him?

Thomas à Kempis says, "If you steel yourself to suffer, all will go better for you and you will find peace. Set yourself to endure trials, 'for the sufferings of this present time are not worthy to be compared with the glory to come.'"

---

*Heavenly Father, your Son endured great suffering
here on earth, yet he was always in harmony with you
and experienced your joy. Help me to follow in his way
and to accept what comes with courage from you.*

Dear children, remain in fellowship with Christ so that when he returns, you will be full of courage and not shrink back from him in shame. I JOHN 2:28, NLT

COUNTING THE BENEFITS

ED DOBSON, suffering from the terminal disease ALS, makes the distinction of giving thanks *in* circumstances, not necessarily *for* them. In whatever state we find ourselves, even living with a dreaded illness such as Lou Gehrig's disease, we can be thankful.

Dobson challenges us to "consider the benefit package." Personally, he has taken the time to look meticulously through his bedroom, giving thanks for everything in it: sheets, blankets, pillows, shirts, shoes, socks, lamps, furniture—every single item.

Many of us fortunate enough to live in a home could spend the larger part of a day giving thanks for countless items—things we seldom think about but depend on or find useful. Physical items are just the start. We also can give thanks for streets and fire protection and for our loved ones and others around us. The list is endless.

Most of all, we can praise the Lord for all his spiritual blessings, starting with his sending his Son to redeem us. The Holy Spirit prays for us and brings into our lives his fruits when we are open to receive them: "love, joy, peace, patience, kindness, goodness, faithfulness, gentleness, and self-control" (Galatians 5:22-23, NLT).

The old song goes, "Count your many blessings, name them one by one, and it will surprise you what the Lord has done."

When we are caught up in deep troubles or exasperated by what's going on, gratitude and thanksgiving can get us in step with the Spirit.

"Thanking God for all his benefits helps put disease into perspective," Dobson says. "I do not want my whole life to be consumed by this disease, nor do I want to lose my perspective of what God has done for me, is doing for me, and will do for me."

Father above, it's true that if I started counting all my blessings, I could go on and on and on. I praise you for all your benefits. Please enable me to live in a spirit of praise.

Give thanks to the LORD, for he is good! His faithful love endures forever.
PSALM 136:1, NLT

LIFTED ABOVE FEAR

BROTHER LAWRENCE was known for "an extraordinary firmness, which in another walk of life would have been termed fearlessness. It revealed a great soul, lifted above the fear and the hope of all that was not God. Nothing astonished him; he feared nothing."

What made his fearless faith possible?

He saw God as infinitely just. He was convinced that God would never deceive him but only bring him good. His part was not to displease God, and for the love of God, to endure whatever came.

It was said that as Lawrence's death drew near, his patience grew even stronger. A contemporary wrote, "He seemed never to have a moment of sorrow, even in the greatest violence of his malady. Joy was evident not only on his face, but also in his manner of speaking, so much so that members of the Community who went to visit him asked whether he was actually in pain. 'Pardon,' he said, 'I *am* in pain. The place in my side hurts. But my soul is content.'

"When the hour came for his departure from this world he cried again and again, 'Faith, Faith.' By the light of faith he already saw something of this intimate presence. He said he feared neither death, hell, nor the judgment of God, nor the efforts of the devil."

When asked at the last what was occupying his spirit, Lawrence replied, "I am doing what I shall do through all eternity. I am blessing God, praising him, worshiping him, and loving him with all my heart."

Brother Lawrence was so used to praising God, and so accustomed to the joy of it, that he could enjoy God's presence on his deathbed.

What better time could there be to get started following his example than when we are relatively healthy?

Lord Jesus, in the garden before your crucifixion, you agonized in prayer to your Father—and then you faced it all with firmness. When death comes for me or for my loved ones, grant us the gifts of faith and courage.

Faith comes from hearing, that is, hearing the Good News about Christ.
ROMANS 10:17, NLT

HOLY LEVITY

ROSEMARY BUDD writes, "The closer we are drawn by the wholeness of God, the greater is our horror at our own fracture. We can only lie flat on our faces in awe."

Seeing ourselves as we really are can be quite a jolt. Isaiah, when he saw the Lord high and lifted up, cried out, "Woe is me. I am lost, for I am a man of unclean lips."

"When we come closer to God," Budd asserts, "we start to understand why some of the people we think of as the greatest saints felt themselves to be full of sin." Yet she affirms that God, instead of showing disgust at our uncleanness, is ready to purify and restore. "The Lord picks us up, caresses us, cleanses us and accepts us. Our love leaps in response."

Isaiah's trembling guilt or the self-repugnance of saints who get a whiff of the blazing holiness of God—such realizations are the core of spiritual transformation. Then God, in compassion, purifies, redeems, banishes fear, and brings joy.

When angels in the Bible appeared to people struck with awe at their own unworthiness, the celestials declared, "Fear not!" And then came their announcements leading to joy.

Rosemary writes that our love and gratitude for God's cleansing is the "small, fragile seed from which humility will grow. Those who see their sins by the light of the Holy Spirit are characterized by a reverence for God and a kind of holy levity that doesn't take itself too seriously. Heaven is reserved for the joyful."

Father, I wish I didn't identify so much with Isaiah, but I, too, dwell among a people of unclean lips. Maybe my world is more corrupt than his! Purify me, Lord. Pour into my mind and soul your refreshing holiness.

She is clothed with strength and dignity, and she laughs without fear of the future.
PROVERBS 31:25, NLT

THE LIMITS OF WILLPOWER

JOHN ORTBERG contends that if we want to grow toward a healthier, more vibrant spiritual life, we must be well aware of the limitations of willpower. The first of the Twelve Steps of Alcoholics Anonymous, he reminds us, is to acknowledge that we cannot overcome addictive behaviors by willpower alone.

To illustrate, he sketches a scene from the children's book *Frog and Toad Together*, in which Frog bakes cookies. "We ought to stop eating," the two say as they keep eating. They discuss their need for willpower and ways to help it along by putting the cookies elsewhere, but they don't stop eating.

Frog finally dumps the cookies on the ground for the birds. "Now we have no more cookies," says Toad. Frog replies that now they have lots and lots of willpower, but Toad counters that he is going home to bake a cake.

If not through willpower, how should we engage in what some people call "spiritual transformation"? Ortberg suggests that there's a big difference between trying and training. He quotes Paul's advice to Timothy to *train* himself in godliness. Paul also wrote to the church at Corinth, "Everyone who competes in the games goes into *strict training*" (1 Corinthians 9:25, NIV, emphasis added).

Rich resources on spiritual formation abound. Are we ready to approach spiritual training as Paul urged, with the intensity of an Olympic athlete?

Ortberg emphasizes that this is not a guilt-inducing, burdensome challenge, but a golden opportunity to get beyond willpower and invite the Holy Spirit to deepen and strengthen us. In Ortberg's vulnerable, highly readable prose, he makes spiritual disciplines come alive, and it's instructive that he starts with *celebration* before exploring prayer, confession, following the Spirit, and studying the Scriptures.

The spiritual disciplines and tools used will differ from person to person and season to season, but training in godliness makes continuous growth possible.

---

*Lord Jesus, I've found it true that my willpower takes
me only so far. Your Word tells me that I need to rely on
your strength and determination. Here I am. Cleanse
and empower me now to live in your joy and grace.*

It is not by force nor by strength, but by my Spirit, says the LORD of Heaven's Armies.
ZECHARIAH 4:6, NLT

COMING HOME

HELMUT THIELICKE, in preaching about the Prodigal Son, said, "That he should have wanted to separate himself from his father seems as ridiculous as a person's fretting over being dependent on air and then holding his breath to assert his freedom."

What were the results of the Prodigal's cutting himself off from his father to become liberated? Said Thielicke, "Bitter laughter goes up from the pigsty." He had found only chains and deprivation.

Both Thielicke and Martin Luther emphasized a familiar biblical reality: we are not free agents who determine our own fate. We are battlefields on which God and Satan vie for our souls. The great variety of lures that the devil insinuates into our thoughts and experiences have hooks that lead to slavery and the pigsty. In contrast, the Father reaches out for us through Jesus Christ to respond to his love and to live as his children.

Actually, the spiritual pigsty of being cut off from the Father may find us physically in pleasant, prosperous surroundings. We may be unaware of the corruption eating away at our souls, and we may think ourselves happy. Yet if we are cut off from the Father, we are separated from the Source of our happiness. When we come to our senses, we see our emptiness and need, and we long for the Father's house.

Thielicke said that Jesus is "the very voice of the Father's heart that overtakes us in the far country and tells us that incredibly joyful news, 'You can come home. Come home!'"

That is indeed good news. And what did Thielicke say was the ultimate secret of the story of the Prodigal Son? "There is a homecoming for us all because there is a home."

Father in heaven, help me to be acutely aware of those times when I'm not in harmony with you. Don't let me live in the pigsty of my own selfish desires, but help me to seek you each day and to celebrate your welcoming embrace.

[Jesus said,] "I have loved you even as the Father has loved me. Remain in my love. When you obey my commandments, you remain in my love, just as I obey my Father's commandments and remain in his love." JOHN 15:9-10, NLT

THE RISKS OF PRAYER

PHILIP YANCEY writes that "praying can be a risky enterprise." He found that as he prayed for others he would be convicted to do something about their needs. Sometimes, he says, we ask God for things we should be doing ourselves.

As we pray, we often experience the tension between prayer and action. We cannot respond to every need. We cannot change every reality, and the evil in the world is so vast that we can't begin to address it personally. Yet we are called to both prayer and action.

As we consider the mountain of challenges and needs around us, we pray for them. We also pray that God would show us where to "put in our pick"—where to take action that may make a difference.

Dietrich Bonhoeffer was a man of prayer who took action against Hitler, and the Nazis ultimately executed him. He considered essential both morning and evening prayers and personal intercessions. Yancey says that Bonhoeffer saw prayer as partnership with what God was doing and believed that both prayer and prayerful action against the forces of evil are necessary.

He then illustrates the same principle with another theologian who was oppressed by Hitler's regime. "Karl Barth, living in the crisis days of Nazi rule, declared prayer to be 'the true and proper work of the Christian,' and observed that 'the most active workers and thinkers and fighters in the divine service in this world have at the same time been the most active in prayer.'"

Father in heaven, help me to care about what's
happening, and then light your fires of prayer in
my soul. If you want me to act, please give me clear
guidance so that your Holy Spirit leads all that I do.

Jesus replied, "This kind can be cast out only by prayer." MARK 9:29, NLT

HELPLESS FAITH

OLE HALLESBY writes, "I never grow weary of emphasizing our helplessness." Why?

He asks us to recall the words of Jesus—that without him we can do nothing. With those words "he tells us what it takes us a whole lifetime to learn."

Hallesby says of our helplessness, "It is the decisive factor not only in our prayer life, but in our relationship to God."

How does this square with our need to have faith? We're all aware of Jesus' declaration that if we had faith the size of a mustard seed we could move a mountain. The Bible calls for faith that gets results.

Hallesby says that those statements have caused many to despair about their lack of faith. They know they should ask in faith, doubting nothing, but they feel they do just the opposite—doubting before, during, and after prayer.

"My doubting friend," Hallesby says, "you have more faith than you think you have. You have enough faith to pray."

He then considers those to whom Jesus said, "Your faith has saved you." All they did was come to Jesus and plead their distress.

How much faith do we need? "We have faith enough when we in our helplessness turn to Jesus. True prayer is a fruit of helplessness and faith. More faith than this is not necessary. Prayer is simply opening the door when Jesus knocks.

"He does not need any help; all he needs is access."

Lord Jesus, my door is wide open to you. Here I am,
with all my cares and concerns. Please bring to me
and to those around me your strength and your peace.
Fill us, I pray, with the fruit of your Spirit.

The eyes of the Lord watch over those who do right, and his ears are open to their prayers.
I PETER 3:12, NLT

PROMISCUOUS CHURCHES

BILLY GRAHAM describes two of the churches that Christ rebuked in Revelation 2 as "victims of runaway physical passion." They had compromised with their culture's beliefs and winked at sexual promiscuity.

The churches at Pergamum and Thyatira hadn't completely caved in spiritually. In fact, Jesus had some positive things to say to them:

> To Pergamum: "I know that you live in the city where Satan has his throne, yet you have remained loyal to me." (Revelation 2:13, NLT)

> To Thyatira: "I know all the things you do. I have seen your love, your faith, your service, and your patient endurance. And I can see your constant improvement in all these things." (Revelation 2:19, NLT)

Yet Jesus came down hard on the pagan beliefs and sexual sin in which both churches were entangled. He demanded repentance.

In our own day and age, we face many of the same challenges as these ancient churches did. Everywhere we look, libidinous images vie for our attention and sexual obsessions disrupt and destroy people's lives.

Centuries before Jesus came, Isaiah, in the presence of God's holiness, cried out that he lived among people of unclean lips. The early Christians could have said the same, and in our century, hostile belief systems and promiscuity infiltrate our minds from every angle.

Spiritual battles remain the same, in Bible times and ours, but here is what Jesus said: "Repent of your sin. . . . Anyone who has ears to hear must listen to the Spirit and understand what he is saying to the churches. To everyone who is victorious I will give some of the manna that has been hidden away in heaven" (Revelation 2:16-17, NLT).

Lord, you know that to be alive in our culture is
to be constantly confronted with all sorts of sexual
temptations. Empower me, I pray, to see life through
your eyes and to avoid impurity. Help me to listen
to your Spirit and follow his guidance.

With an appeal to twisted sexual desires, they lure back into sin those who have barely escaped from a lifestyle of deception. They promise freedom, but they themselves are slaves of sin and corruption. For you are a slave to whatever controls you.
2 PETER 2:18-19, NLT

THE TEACHER OF LOVE

MOTHER TERESA said of prayer, "The essential thing is not what we say but what God says to us and through us. In our silence, he will listen to us, he will speak to our soul, and we will hear his voice. We must learn to listen."

She urged practice of inner silence in four ways:

Through your eyes. Look for the beauty of God's creation and his goodness everywhere. Shut your eyes to others' faults and what disturbs your soul.

Through your ears. Listen to God's voice and those in need. Close your ears to gossip and mean talk.

Through your tongue. Praise God. Speak from his Word with peace, hope, and joy. Refrain from self-defensive and destructive talk.

Through your mind. Pray. Ponder God's marvels. Reject revengeful, destructive thoughts and rash judgments or suspicions. Love God and avoid envy and greed.

Mother Teresa said that there's a terrible longing throughout the world to know the loving Father in heaven. "I never tire of saying that God loves us," she said. "It is a wonderful thing that God himself loves me tenderly."

Two stories about Mother Teresa illustrate the love that God has for us:

> The youngest of twelve children was terribly mutilated, and to lighten the family load, Mother Teresa offered to take the child. The mother began to cry. "For God's sake, Mother, don't tell me that." Her child, she said, was God's greatest gift to her and her family. All their love was focused on her.
>
> In Venezuela, when she visited a family that had given her a lamb, she discovered they had a badly crippled child. When she asked his name, the mother replied, "We call him 'Teacher of Love,' because he keeps on teaching us how to love." The family saw all they did for the boy as putting God's love into action.

Mother Teresa asked, "Do we have a love like that? Do we realize our child, our husband, our wife, our father, our mother, our sister, our brother, has a need for that understanding, for the warmth of our hand?"

Father, teach me to be silent before you and to
learn how to love others as you have loved me.

Love is patient and kind. . . . Love never gives up, never loses faith, is always hopeful, and endures through every circumstance. I CORINTHIANS 13:4, 7, NLT

THE HIGHEST DYNAMIC
IN THE UNIVERSE

GEORGE MACDONALD describes love as what is most precious in the Godhead. He writes that love is "a higher thing than the making of worlds and the things in them." He says this in exploring the many implications of the first chapter of John with its reference to Christ: "He existed in the beginning with God. God created everything through him. . . . The Word gave life to everything that was created, and his life brought light to everyone" (NLT).

For MacDonald, the deepest essence of God is the dynamic love between the Father and the Son.

We find plenty of scriptural support for that, including 1 John 4:8, which states it simply and plainly: "God is love" (NLT).

The mystery of how we could be drawn into this love goes far beyond our grasp. Yet the way Jesus stayed in constant prayer to his Father gives us a clue. The astounding promise that we can become children of the heavenly Father means we can pray as Jesus prayed and invite his Spirit of love and truth to become dynamic in us.

If we are to be like Jesus, we will naturally love the Father.

This comes, of course, with requirements. Obeying his Father cost Jesus the Cross. To obey our loving heavenly Father may cost us many things, starting with our self-will and our natural bent to run our own lives without interference. Praying like a child means obeying like a child, with both love and respect.

MacDonald emphasizes that Jesus loved the Father with his whole being. As his redeemed children, we are now from "the same birth home" as Jesus. His Father is our Father. What a wonderful reality to savor!

Loving Father above, fill my mind and heart, I pray,
with the realization and conviction that you are love
and that you love me. Pour your love into me that I
might, in some small way, love you back as Jesus does.

We love each other because he loved us first. . . . And he has given us this command: Those who love God must also love their Christian brothers and sisters.
I JOHN 4:19, 21, NLT

A BETTER WAY TO SLEEP

RAY STEDMAN tells of a converted South American Indian who said, "When I was living in the jungle, we never knew a day without fear. When we woke up in the morning, we were afraid. When we went out of our houses, we were afraid. When we walked along the river, we were afraid. We saw an evil spirit in every stone and tree and waterfall. And when night fell, fear came into our huts and slept with us all night long."

The believing Christian's experience stands in sharp contrast, as illustrated in Ephesians 2:12-13: "You lived in this world without God and without hope. But now you have been united with Christ Jesus. Once you were far away from God, but now you have been brought near to him through the blood of Christ" (NLT).

Instead of living in darkness and fear, we have been reconciled to God, the one who in love sent his Son into our fallen world.

The price for this redemption was extreme—the blood of Christ—and Ray Stedman says it's significant that Paul uses that phrase. We don't like to think of Jesus' death as bloody, but it was.

"The death of Jesus was violent," writes Stedman, "a bloody, gory, revolting scene—a man hanging torn and wretched upon a cross. God wants us to remember that when humanity had done its worst, had vented its anger in the utter wretchedness and violence and blood of the cross, his love reached down to that very place and began to redeem—to call back those who were far off and bring them near."

That doesn't mean we are immune to fear. Evil still stalks. Evil spirits may assault us. But evil has been conquered through the blood of Jesus Christ our Lord, who is Lord of all.

What amazing grace! Unlike the pagan in the forest, even when we feel fear and even when we confront evil, we know that God is the ultimate victor, and he is ready to come to our aid.

Lord Jesus Christ, Son of God, have mercy on me, a sinner. When I fear, please come to my aid and grant your confidence and courage. Transform my difficulties into opportunities to serve and love you and others.

Christ himself has brought peace to us. EPHESIANS 2:14, NLT

DEFIANT PRAISE

BEN PATTERSON asserts that our giving thanks to God no matter what is "a spiritual discipline and habit of joy that is profoundly transforming." He quotes two verses: "Always be full of joy in the Lord. I say it again—rejoice!" (Philippians 4:4, NLT) and "Never stop praying. Be thankful in all circumstances" (1 Thessalonians 5:17-18, NLT).

Patterson cites three reasons why doing what these verses say "powerfully works joy in us."

First, it releases us from the sin of ingratitude, that root of evil and rebellion against God. When the Israelites kept bitterly complaining about God's provisions, they cut themselves off from his blessing and from the Promised Land. Our complaints and ingratitude are far more than peccadilloes—they're deep offenses against God's sacrificial care and redemption.

Second, giving thanks affirms *hope*. We may find ourselves in difficult or even dreadful circumstances, but like a dark or even terrifying movie that ends with a glorious finale, we look forward with *hope*. We read in 2 Corinthians 4:17 that our present troubles produce in us a glory that vastly outweighs those troubles and will last forever. We look forward to a new heaven and a new earth. There, all we have gone through will be put into perspective.

Third, praising in all circumstances is defiance against the forces arrayed against us. God defiantly triumphed over guilt and death in the Resurrection.

"If God's grace is defiant," writes Patterson, "then our gratitude should also be defiant."

Lord, sometimes it takes defiance to praise you in the midst of all the pressures and difficulties. Help me to see the long view—your view—and to rejoice in what you have done and are about to do.

Rejoice in the LORD and be glad, all you who obey him! PSALM 32:11, NLT

BLESSINGS FROM ENEMIES

FRED SMITH says that not only are we Christians to love our enemies as Christ commanded, but we should also see the blessing in our *having* enemies.

Enemies are a *blessing*? Enemies threaten us, attack us, belittle us, and even ruin us. What could be good about those things?

All of life includes opposition and competition. Opposition refines us and toughens us. The football team with ferocious adversaries will take stock and train with intense discipline. The fact that the players have "enemies" takes them to a whole new level of performance.

"Loving an enemy is not the sugary, sweet, syrupy love people talk about," Smith says. "It's a tough love—a disciplined love. It is the love that is best defined as 'willing the ultimate good for the other person.'"

Enemies can do terrible things to us, but Smith quotes Robert Browning as saying that when we see the good that can come, we can "welcome each rebuff that turns life's smoothness rough." Smith adds that Aleksandr Solzhenitsyn was thankful for the "stinking straw" of his enemies that brought him to his maturity.

Enemies shove us off the props of our superficial securities and into the sufficiency of God's grace. Opposition makes us realize that we must find our strength, wisdom, and courage in God. Only he can supply the love that transcends the pain.

In contrast, hatred and revenge can burn in us like fire and destroy our spiritual vitality.

Fred lists ways in which enemy opposition can refine us and concludes, "The best use of our enemies is to develop our forgiveness toward them. This is the purification of our souls and develops our ability to accept forgiveness in turn."

Lord Jesus, you had tough words for your enemies, but you loved them and said they didn't know what they were doing. Give me your spirit of love so that I can grow and see the blessings in the conflicts, victories, and defeats.

I wait quietly before God, for my victory comes from him. PSALM 62:1, NLT

WORLD-CHANGING PRAYERS

THE APOSTLE JOHN, in Revelation 8, describes the breaking of the seventh seal and the silence throughout heaven. We can only imagine what all the angels and heavenly beings were thinking and experiencing during that silence.

Then John describes one of the most intriguing scenes in the Scriptures. An angel mixed a great amount of incense with the prayers of God's people. The angel placed this remarkable incense as an offering on the golden altar before God's throne. Following this, "the smoke of the incense, mixed with the prayers of God's holy people, ascended up to God from the altar where the angel had poured them out. Then the angel filled the incense burner with fire from the altar and threw it down upon the earth; and thunder crashed, lightning flashed, and there was a terrible earthquake" (NLT).

What a picture! Prayers of the saints with heavenly incense thrown "down upon the earth." What does all that mean?

Many have written about this extraordinary, vivid description of prayer. In total contrast to the idea that prayer is only a helpful form of meditation, we see that prayers are taken with extreme seriousness in heaven. Somehow they also have a powerful, mysterious effect on earth.

Just before describing this scene, John quotes the elder's promise that God will wipe away every tear from the eyes of those who experienced the Great Tribulation. We find in the Bible countless prayers of tears and anguish. We also find many of joyous praise, and those, too, are valued in heaven. Jude ends with these verses:

> All glory to God, who is able to keep you from falling away and will bring you with great joy into his glorious presence. . . . All glory to him who alone is God, our Savior through Jesus Christ our Lord. All glory, majesty, power, and authority are his before all time, and in the present, and beyond all time! Amen. (NLT)

Father, here is my feeble prayer. Give me glimpses of your magnificent glory today, and let my prayers be in harmony with your Spirit. Let them accomplish your will in both earth and heaven.

Always be joyful. Never stop praying. I THESSALONIANS 5:16-17, NLT

THE FLYER AND THE CATCHER

HENRI NOUWEN could not get enough of watching the Flying Rodleighs, trapeze artists in a German circus. He introduced himself to them as one of their great fans and traveled with them for a week.

What the leader of the troupe told him about the flyer and the catcher touched something deep within Nouwen's soul and set him on a new spiritual journey. He was told that the flyer may be thought of as the great star, but the real star is the catcher. "He has to be there for me with split-second precision and grab me out of the air."

Nouwen asked how it worked.

"The secret is that the flyer does nothing and the catcher does everything."

"You do nothing?"

"Nothing. It's Joe's task to catch me. If I grab Joe's wrists, I might break them or he mine. A flyer must fly, and a catcher must catch. The flyer must trust, with outstretched arms."

Clearly there's a powerful analogy here. We may think we're stars, but we are always in need of being caught and saved. We must trust the Lord, and so with outstretched arms we commit ourselves and our loved ones to his mighty arms.

Even though Nouwen attended dozens of Flying Rodleigh shows, he often found himself crying as he watched the trapeze artists flying and catching under the big top. He loved the choreography and originality.

If we have eyes to see, the same could be said about life. The beauty of a trapeze performance parallels the beauty and meaning of our own soaring and being caught in our remarkable human adventures, which are ultimately adventures of the spirit. The Creator has made a world of vast originality and challenge. Through effective prayer, we are guided and energized—and we may find unique opportunities to soar.

Henri Nouwen speaks of the body in its beauty and elegance expressing this spirit and concludes, "I want to live trusting the Catcher."

Father of all creation, wake me up to the drama and beauty of life and free me from being stuck in the sawdust under the big top. Help me to trust that when I'm suspended in air, you're there to catch me.

Let us hold tightly without wavering to the hope we affirm, for God can be trusted to keep his promise. HEBREWS 10:23, NLT

SHORT PRAYERS, LONG PRAYERS

CHARLES HADDON SPURGEON says we can be certain that God made prayer so prominent in the Bible because he intends it to be conspicuous in our lives. "If God has said much about prayer, it is because he knows we have much need of it."

Spurgeon also looked closely at Jesus' statement that we ought always to pray and not to faint and concluded that Jesus was warning us that, without prayer, we surely *would* faint.

Spurgeon, the "prince of preachers," believed fervently in prayer and said it was as essential to him as breathing. Yet he also said something unexpected about prayer, something quite different from others such as Martin Luther and John Wesley, who reported the need for hours of prayer each day. Spurgeon said, "Not length but strength is desirable. A sense of need is a mighty teacher of brevity."

Associates of evangelist Dwight L. Moody said he did not pray long prayers, but spontaneous ones. Moody, as a man of action, was "always in prayer"—he'd stop to pray, leave it with God, and move on.

Spurgeon was similar. He said that though he was aware of people who prayed for hours, and was pleased they did, he seldom saw the need for it himself. "It's like a person going into a bank with a check and stopping for an hour. The clerks would wonder." Spurgeon said that prayer is like cashing a check. "You so believe in God that you present the promise, obtain the blessing, and go about your Master's business. The prayers of the Bible are nearly all short ones: they are short and strong."

Luther, Wesley, Moody, Spurgeon, and countless others had rich, fervent prayer lives. Yet each was unique, and their passionate prayers took on many forms. At different times of their lives, their prayer experiences changed. Spurgeon, for instance, went through times of deep depression, during which he likely did not experience a "check-cashing" style of prayer.

Prayer is an integral part of our spiritual adventure. It's not a set of rules, but rather an invitation to come to Jesus, whatever our circumstances and whatever our heart's condition. As the hymn puts it:

> *What a friend we have in Jesus,*
> *All our sins and griefs to bear;*
> *What a privilege to carry,*
> *Everything to God in prayer.*

Lord Jesus Christ, help me to be constant in prayer
whatever my feelings. Help me to have faith that you
are ready to "cash my checks," yet draw me also to
love being with you and to enjoy your presence.

The earnest prayer of a righteous person has great power and produces wonderful results.
JAMES 5:16, NLT

WORK AS ADVENTURE

PAUL TOURNIER, in considering God's words to Adam to be fruitful and multiply and fill the earth and subdue it, concluded that God has endowed us with his spirit of creative adventure. "But man wished to conduct his adventure on his own, in his own way, instead of entering into God's adventure."

Despite the consequences of the Fall, which turned adventure and labor into harsh toil and troubles, Tournier maintains that work is still God's good gift to us, incomparably therapeutic and essential.

According to Tournier, the poet Rainer Maria Rilke once asked Auguste Rodin how we are to live. Rodin's reply: "Through work."

Rodin was the brilliant sculptor whose iconic works are seen in museums and countless reproductions. Oswald Chambers, as a young man, was much taken with Rodin and, since he had significant artistic talents himself, wanted to emulate him. But the door to work in the arts never opened to Chambers. Nevertheless, Chambers's words inspired millions through the books edited by his wife and published after his death at age forty-three.

Rodin said we live by work, and Tournier points to the many instances in Scripture that affirm work's value. "The book of Proverbs is full of the praise of labor," he writes. "The Bible speaks of the skill of goldsmiths and weavers, the patience of peasants and vinedressers, and the wisdom and intelligence of scholars as talents given by God."

Work is a core element of adventure. Says Tournier, "A new adventure springs into being every time a person listens to God and faithfully obeys him."

Our Father in heaven, help me to listen right now to what you are saying to me. Give me light on my path and your energy in my spirit. Grant me a sense of your adventure even in the humdrum of my work.

Godliness guards the path of the blameless. . . . The life of the godly is full of light and joy.
PROVERBS 13:6, 9, NLT

GOD'S GRACE IS ENOUGH

NANCY GUTHRIE describes how assuring someone that "God is enough" can ring hollow in the face of deep suffering. She said those words to a woman with ALS (Lou Gehrig's disease) who had to endure the taunts of a cruel husband and the despair of a daughter who had begun cutting herself. The woman had a long, frightening process of dying ahead of her, and even as Nancy voiced what she hoped would be comforting words, she apologized for their perhaps sounding simplistic.

Yet, deep in her soul, she knew they were not simplistic.

Through her personal experiences of grief and loss, she had come to thoroughly believe that God provides the grace necessary to endure hardship. She had found that God's grace enabled her to continue believing in God's goodness and his love.

"It is enough to generate joy in the midst of great sorrow," she writes, using the story of Job to illustrate ways in which we can respond to extreme hardship. Satan intended the suffering he brought to Job to break him down and force him to renounce God. But Job did not lose his faith. The devastation he endured served to deepen his understanding of God.

What Satan wants to do in our lives and what God wants to do are extreme opposites. Guthrie says that a hammer can be used to build something or to break it apart, so the intent of the person using it determines the result.

The hammer of suffering can crush our spirits and fill us with dark thoughts. Yet when the hammer is endured as part of God's permissive will, we can look for his hope. Through the furnace of affliction, we can pray that our faith will grow and deepen and that his joy will emerge.

God is enough—if we trust and receive the grace he has promised.

Father, help me to see the hope that transcends my circumstances. Fill me with the hope that comes from your Holy Spirit, and help me through all my troubles to listen for your wisdom and encouragement.

I love the LORD because he hears my voice and my prayer for mercy. Because he bends down to listen, I will pray as long as I have breath! PSALM 116:1-2, NLT

TRUE DELIGHTS

THOMAS À KEMPIS heard the argument that giving in to temptation has its plus side. He grappled with the question, What about those who find pleasure and delight when they give in to temptation?

He admitted they do find pleasure but countered: "How long does it last? It is like smoke—it vanishes quickly. Soon even the memory is gone. They will never find rest, and they will live in bitterness and weariness and fear."

Examples of the downside of temptation quickly come to mind. Giving in to the temptation to cheat on one's spouse creates waves of anger and feelings of betrayal—and families are shattered. Pilfering "just a little" of the unguarded money at work can destroy not just one life but many. In today's culture, cheating and all sorts of "recreational" pleasures are viewed as grabbing life's gusto, but the gusto, before long, turns rancid.

Thomas à Kempis writes, "The very thing they think will bring them joy will bring them sorrow; that which they think will bring them pleasure will bring them pain." He recognizes they may be blind to their own misery and numbness, unaware that "their souls are slowly dying."

How do we recognize temptation? When we sense that what we're tempted to do will quench the Holy Spirit within us. To resist, we can invite the Holy Spirit to empower us.

Thomas à Kempis adds that if we want true delight, we need to stop loving the wrong things and persevere in resisting bad habits. Over time, we will vanquish them. "Then you will find consolations from God much more sweet and potent."

Heavenly Father, you know so well the temptations
I struggle against. Take up the battle for me, I pray.
May your Holy Spirit create in me the energy and
power to embrace your will and your delights.

Show me the right path, O LORD; point out the road for me to follow.
PSALM 25:4, NLT

CLOTHING TO DISPEL THE GLOOM

JONI EARECKSON TADA writes of "dry and dusty days in my soul; sometimes a coldness in my spirit. A cloud of doom will hang heavily over me and no matter what I do or whom I see, everything is an effort."

Most of us have had times like that. What did Joni find that changed it for her? Praise.

Those moments when we don't feel at all like praising God may be just the times to do it. Joni imagines King David with clenched jaw as he writes Psalm 57, determined to pray no matter what: "My heart is fixed, O God, my heart is fixed: I will sing and give praise" (verse 7, KJV).

Joni also quotes Isaiah 61: "He has sent me to bind up the brokenhearted . . . to bestow on them a crown of beauty . . . instead of mourning, and *a garment of praise instead of a spirit of despair*" (verses 1, 3, NIV, emphasis added).

Interesting clothes to put on! Most people experience a lift when they find an item of clothing that fits just right, with pleasing colors and textures. Praise becomes a garment like that, lifting our spirits.

On our spiritual journeys, we will trek through many a discouraging desert. At those times we can repeat Psalm 42:5-6: "Why are you downcast, O my soul? Why so disturbed within me? Put your hope in God, for I will yet praise him, my Savior and my God" (NIV).

Joni says that praise is not something that comes naturally to us, but at times feels more like a duty. Yet it refocuses our emotions and realigns our thoughts. "David taught himself that praise was good for his soul, as well as glorifying to God."

---

*Holy and loving Lord, I have so much to praise you
for. You entered our broken world to redeem us,
and you pray for us now as we live in danger and
opportunity. Let my heart be full of praise today.*

Praise the LORD! Praise the LORD from the heavens! Praise him from the skies! Praise him, all his angels! Praise him, all the armies of heaven! PSALM 148:1-2, NLT

COOL IN CALAMITY

JILL BRISCOE tells the story of racing to a friend's business complex in downtown Belfast that had just been blown up by IRA bombs. At the scene, she found dense smoke and turmoil as people dashed in and out of charred rooms to salvage things while loud alarms kept ringing.

How was her friend dealing with the catastrophe? He stood in the midst of his ruined business with a spirit of peace and tranquility. When a fireman came by, he thanked him for his help and said, "Don't stay too late. Take your men home. Tomorrow is the Lord's Day, and we all need to be ready to worship him."

Briscoe was stunned, humbled, and grateful to God for his evident grace in this man.

Catastrophes of many sorts can suddenly rip into our lives. Highway accidents. Cancer. Divorce. How do we experience the depth of faith that Jill's friend showed in crisis? Clearly, the man had his spiritual priorities in place. Not even calamity could keep him from worship or from encouraging others in the faith.

Consistency in prayer, worship, and fellowship—despite all the pressures we feel—can daily prepare us for crises. It also enables us to endure the drip, drip, drip of constant irritations. Every day has its share of troubles, but also new opportunities for spiritual growth. The more we seek God daily, the more likely it is that peace and tranquility will override our anxieties and fears.

Sometimes calamity rouses our fears, but even in the best of times we can feel afraid. For instance, Jill says that on her wedding day, she froze in fear, paralyzed. For a long time, her mother and sister were unable to snap her out of it.

Who knows all the reasons brides can get paralyzed, but in that context, Jill says this: "Fear points its finger at all the things that are bound to go wrong, but faith directs our attention toward a Father who tells us, 'Jesus is there.' Faith lends us words to call on the Holy Spirit to release us from panic."

Lord, I pray that you'll fill me with your Holy Spirit of peace when I experience calamity or when I fear what's about to happen. Grant me the courage that comes only from your presence.

This is my command—be strong and courageous! Do not be afraid or discouraged. For the LORD your God is with you wherever you go. JOSHUA 1:9, NLT

FEARFUL OF SANTA CLAUS

July 1

HENRI NOUWEN gives us a vivid image of a person of little faith. That person prays like a child who wants a present from Santa Claus, but as soon as the gift is received, the child runs away. He or she wants nothing more to do with Santa. Says Nouwen, "All the attention is on the gift and none on the giver."

Jesus used the phrase "little faith" to describe some followers. Nouwen says "little faith" is praying without genuine hope in God and his providence.

We pray for many concrete things: safe travel; success in school or work; a bicycle, car, or house. Nouwen doesn't downgrade those prayers of petition as somehow inferior to prayers of thanksgiving and praise, but he does say this: "The prayer of little faith is where you hold fast to the concrete of the present situation in order to win a certain security." He refers to this as a kind of "Santa Claus naiveté." When you don't get the present you wanted, you're disappointed or maybe even bitter.

Are our prayers ones of hope, or of little faith?

When we pray with little faith, we feel anxiety, and when we don't get just what we prayed for, we're disappointed. We pray for very specific things, but Nouwen says that such a narrow focus eliminates the possibility for hope because we're trying to be certain about what's uncertain.

Prayers of little faith contrast sharply with prayers directed toward the Giver with the attitude that, whatever comes or doesn't come, we have faith in his goodness.

If we are to exercise genuine faith, we must learn to trust God in life's adventure, with all its shocks, spills, and reversals. Lots of things go wrong, but God is still faithful. He chooses the gifts. We are called to have faith that he loves us and will reward our faith with his bounty and grace.

Heavenly Father, I lay all my concerns before you.
Help me to understand that you are sovereign. When
my prayers are not answered in ways I hoped for, help
me to keep on believing in your goodness and love.

I am praying to you because I know you will answer, O God. Bend down and listen as I pray. Show me your unfailing love in wonderful ways. PSALM 17:6-7, NLT

DEFIANT PRAYER?

JOHN WESLEY took Jesus' command to love our enemies with utmost seriousness. He looked at the litany of commands in Matthew 5:44 that would stretch us far beyond our comfort zones and affirmed that we must actually do these superhuman things.

For "love your enemies," he writes that we should have "tender goodwill to those who wish us evil and are most bitter against us."

For "bless them that curse you," he says that we're to bless other people and talk to them, whether they're saying things behind your back or in your face. "Say all the good you can without violating rules of truth and justice."

For "do good to them that hate you," he says we should by our actions "show you are as real in love as they are in hatred."

For "pray for them which despitefully use you," he says that all their malice or even violence cannot hinder us from pouring out our souls to God for them.

When we come across Jesus' words about loving our enemies, we often gloss over them, not applying them to our own situations. We may think they're hyperbole or need interpretation. But Wesley took them at face value. He did the same with Jesus' warnings about unforgiving prayer. Jesus said if we don't forgive, our Father won't forgive us. First forgive, and then ask for forgiveness.

Wesley says that a Christian's refusing to forgive is the same as a spirit of rebellion. "What manner of prayer are we offering to God?" From Wesley's perspective, not forgiving someone is open defiance, as if we are praying, "Don't forgive us. Keep remembering our sins. Let your wrath abide on us."

"Can we seriously offer such prayers to God?" Wesley asks. "By his grace, forgive as you would be forgiven! Have compassion, as God has pity on you."

In a world with enemies, haters, and persecutors, such love seems impossible. Unaided by the Spirit, it is. However, we can call on the Holy Spirit to guide us into truth about how to love our enemies—and to give us the power to do it!

---

*Lord, I want to forgive and love my enemies, but I need
your transforming power to do it. Empower me to forgive!
And forgive me all my sins against you and others.*

---

*If you forgive those who sin against you, your heavenly Father will forgive you. But if you
refuse to forgive others, your Father will not forgive your sins.*
MATTHEW 6:14-15, NLT

GREAT GLORY, GREAT JOY

July 9

SHERWOOD WIRT makes the case that Jesus was a "man of joy" and wrote a book with that title.

He asks—regarding the verse in Hebrews 12 about Jesus enduring the cross for the joy set before him—"Joy? What joy?"

His answer? "The joy of heaven, of course! Heaven is a place not only of great glory but also of great joy."

Woody notes that Jesus brought the same joy to his time on earth. "Because of the presence of the Holy Spirit in him, he could carry the buoyancy of his eternal joy with him into the time zone of Palestine, sharing it with others while carrying out his Father's will. 'Be of good cheer,' he told his disciples. 'Brighten up! There are tribulations in this life, but I have overcome the world.'"

Jesus was a "man of sorrows, and acquainted with grief" (Isaiah 53:3, KJV), and we marvel at the depths of his suffering. We also identify with his struggles to endure. We call on him to help us in our own grief and troubles. Yet, as he told his disciples, he also came that we might have joy and have it abundantly.

Jesus could promise joy because he was the source of redemption and peace. He told them not to worry, because their heavenly Father knew their needs.

Often, joy comes not because of circumstances but in knowing we are the beloved of the Father and that all manner of things will be well.

Sherwood Wirt says that Jesus "saw the worst all too clearly, but he also foresaw the great future rewards of his harsh assignments. He would be restored to his rightful place amid the glorious joys and music and laughter of heaven."

---

*Father, I long for your music and joy, and I know
that you want to bring them into my life through
your Son. Help me to open myself to all you would
do, and let me bring some joy to others this day.*

[Jesus said,] "I have told you these things so that you will be filled with my joy. Yes, your joy will overflow!" JOHN 15:11, NLT

THE BETTER TO HEAR HIM BY

July 10

JOHN HENRY JOWETT writes, "Every time I hear his voice, I sharpen my sense of hearing." He recognizes that hearing God's voice is far from automatic, but he says that our spiritual hearing improves as we listen and grow. "It is the skill of the saint to catch 'the still small voice' amid all the selfish clamors of the day, and amid the far more subtle callings of the heart. It needs a good ear to catch the voice of the Lord in our sorrows and a better ear to discern the voice amid our joys."

Hearing takes concentration. Then not only must we hear, but we must act. "The one condition of the saint," Jowett says, "is to follow the immediate call. Every faculty and function will be vitalized when I follow the Lord of life and glory."

Jesus said, "My sheep hear my voice" (John 10:27, KJV). Discipleship calls for constant listening.

Often we're distracted, and that's especially true when things are going well. In the same way we can turn off a cell phone, we can tune out the quiet voice of the Spirit. When we don't sense an urgent need, we may think we can live in our own strength and by our own wits.

We need a constant alertness to hear God's voice, whether we're in trouble or in a wonderful time of life when it seems we don't need him.

Jesus said we are his disciples when we do what he commands. We each have a lifetime of daily and hourly perking up our ears and opening our hearts to his love and power.

Says Jowett, "Life is found in the ways of a listening obedience."

Holy Spirit, please sharpen my ears and soften my heart. Let me hear your "still, small voice" and do what you say. Let me bring joy to your heart because I'm listening and obedient.

Let the Holy Spirit guide your lives. Then you won't be doing what your sinful nature craves. GALATIANS 5:16, NLT

THE BEST IS COMING

AMY CARMICHAEL saw in a cemetery a small gray headstone engraved with a question and an answer that, to her, fit perfectly:

> Master, where dwellest thou?
> He saith, Come and see.

What an invitation! Yet this "come and see," through death, to where Jesus is requires that we leave all that is precious here. We all age, and we all must approach the bittersweet end of our lives. But instead of age and decay ahead, as God's children we know that in heaven we will come into our prime and begin to truly live.

Even if we live to a very old age on earth, our time here is but a moment contrasted with eternity. As the lyrics of "Amazing Grace" celebrate, "When we've been there ten thousand years, . . . we've no less days to sing God's praise than when we'd first begun."

Carmichael completes her book *Gold by Moonlight* with this personal story of envisioning the moment of "come and see":

> One evening, as we sat at the end of India on the rocks of Cape Comorin, a little fishing boat sailed into the sunset. It was only a rough thing made of three logs tied together, and its sail was a mere rag, but it was transfigured. Usually a speck of earth entangled in such glory would show dark against the glory, but that evening, so mighty were the powers of the golden air, that all of earth was swallowed up. It held us speechless.
>
> To see it so was like seeing the mortal put on immortality, the temporal take on the beauty of the eternal. What we call sunset the heavenly people call sunrise, and the Joy of the Lord, and the Morning of God.

Heavenly Father, pour into my mind and spirit faith
and high expectations of what's ahead. When I come
to the valley of the shadow of death, be with me
and show me, I pray, your light and your glory.

He has made all of this plain to us by the appearing of Christ Jesus, our Savior. He broke the power of death and illuminated the way to life and immortality through the Good News. 2 TIMOTHY 1:10, NLT

WHEN BAD THINGS HAPPEN

July 12

MARTIN LUTHER illustrates the ways in which our faith is tested by looking at what Joseph and his father, Jacob, endured. God had promised his care for Jacob and his family, but then the older brothers threw Joseph into a pit, sold him into slavery, and lied to their father by telling him that an animal had killed his favorite son. Where was God when all this happened?

"You would think that God would show some concern," Luther writes, "but God didn't send an angel, or even so much as the leaf of a tree, to stop the devil or force him away. Instead, he opened all the doors and windows to let the devil rant and rave, attacking both father and son in horrible ways."

We believe in God's promise that, when we come to him in faith and obedience, he will be with us and protect us. Yet terrible things happen. People of faith are far from immune to cancer, fatal accidents, war, and even famine and starvation. Our own families can bring us devastating troubles. When we find ourselves in chasms of pain, we wonder about the promises we read all through the Scriptures.

Luther affirms that God didn't desert Jacob and Joseph, and he doesn't desert us. God's promises are firm. Luther quotes Isaiah 49, which shows God's compassion for his people in their suffering and his love that is as strong as a mother's for the nursing child at her breast. "See," God declares with compassion, "I have written your name on the palms of my hands" (verse 16, NLT).

God works in the lives of his people, Luther tells us, and we need wisdom beyond our natural understanding to grasp even a portion of his plans.

"God won't lie to me or deceive me," Luther promises, "though at times, nothing in life will seem to make sense."

Father in heaven, it's true that sometimes nothing
seems to make sense and the suffering seems to have
no purpose. Please give me faith to believe, hope, and
endure—with a touch of joy from you this day.

I have called you by name; you are mine. When you go through deep waters, I will be with you. When you go through rivers of difficulty, you will not drown.
ISAIAH 43:1-2, NLT

THE AFTERMATH OF TEMPTATION

OSWALD CHAMBERS holds out this promise: "When temptation comes, stand absolutely true to God and you will find the onslaught leaves you with affinities higher and purer than ever before. Temptation overcome is the transfiguration of the natural into the spiritual." He sees that the Holy Spirit is transforming us through obedience and that a victory over temptation gives us greater affinity "with the purest and best."

Chambers also makes what would seem like a contradictory statement: "The knowledge that God is a consuming fire is the greatest comfort to the saint."

A comfort? Why would that be a comfort? Chambers says it's because God's love is at work within us—cleaning out the impurities.

Whether we are comforted or made nervous by the observation that God is a consuming fire, it's clear that the dynamics of temptation and spiritual growth are serious realities. We can't just relax and sidestep them. The media delight in reporting in great detail the endless stories of people ruining their lives by giving in to temptation. They also cover with equal delight stories about believers who violate their own commitments. In that light, it's a comfort that God takes his work in us seriously, for it's done with far more love than the dentist who must extract a rotten tooth.

Chambers says that because Jesus was tempted in all points as we are, yet without sin, "he knows how terrific are the onslaughts of the devil against human nature unaided."

Fortunately, we don't have to face temptation alone. The Holy Spirit gives us the strength to turn temptation into opportunity—if we turn to him at the critical moment.

Father, I know you can find plenty of impurities within me to purge. Cleanse me, Lord, and let me sense your joy within as I live today in full harmony with you.

Purify me from my sins, and I will be clean; wash me, and I will be whiter than snow.
PSALM 51:7, NLT

THE ROAD AHEAD

FRANÇOIS FÉNELON urges, "Leave everything in God's hands without look-ing at tomorrow. Often what you imagine to be so terrible and unbearable is not so bad when it actually happens."

Isn't that the truth! We fret about what will happen to us—and to our loved ones, and to our country and the world—but when we look back, we realize how much of our fretting was needless. Bad things do happen, yet worrying changes nothing except to disturb our peace and drain our spirits.

Fénelon advised a friend, "I know you want to see the road ahead rather than trusting God. Leave everything in his hands without looking at tomorrow. Walk humbly with God."

He also gave this deceptively simple yet powerful advice: "Find out what God expects of you in any given situation and stick strictly to doing that."

Each of us might well ask on a particularly challenging day, "What does God expect? How can I stick strictly to doing that?" In a family crisis, at work or school, at a party or church service, or on a long trip, what does God expect? How can I focus on doing *strictly* that?

When we focus as Fénelon advises, it frees us from all sorts of confusion and the feeling—so common today—of being overwhelmed in our electronic world.

We often hear that the way to find peace is to "live in the moment." That's true if the moment is centered on Christ.

In the same way that Jesus advises us to consider the lilies and the birds when wor-ried, François Fénelon brings the practical and the spiritual together: "All moments are in God's hands. Give yourself as completely as you can to God. Do so until your final breath, and he will never desert you."

---

*Heavenly Father, I'm often anxious about what might
happen in the days ahead. Help me to trust you. Fill
me with praise for all you have done, all you are
doing now, and what you will do in the future.*

---

*I have hidden your word in my heart, that I might not sin against you. . . . I have
rejoiced in your laws as much as in riches.* PSALM 119:11, 14, NLT

THE BLEND OF PRAISE AND SUFFERING *July 15*

EUGENE PETERSON warns us that escape, for the Christian, is faithless. Trying to escape means we've succumbed to despair. In contrast, he paraphrases from Psalm 11 the psalmist's determination to not give in to despair: "Since God is involved in the world, I will be also."

Praise music has become a major part of many worship services today. Clearly, the Bible urges us over and over to give joyful praise to God and to fully honor him. At the same time, Peterson points out that the Psalms include as many references to suffering as to praise. As the original hymnbook of Israel, the Psalms resonate with the glory and the joy of worship, yet are intersected throughout with depths of anguish and dismay.

Praise. Suffering. We need a biblical sense deep in our bones of how they work together. If, when suffering comes, we are to resist our longing to escape, we need to understand that Christians will be mired in suffering the same as everyone else. Endurance and strength come from the Holy Spirit.

Ultimately, as we see in the Psalms, praise is uttered in the midst of suffering, even as God's might and his love are proclaimed.

When we read Thomas à Kempis, François Fénelon, or Oswald Chambers, we're quickly made aware of how much suffering is part of spiritual growth and the journey to the Father. When we see our time on earth as a rugged—even extreme—adventure, with enormous meaning and consequences, we are on the path to spiritual growth.

Eugene Peterson says that he does not want to be like the disciples who, when danger came, forsook Jesus and fled. He shares this personal prayer: "When I feel like escaping, avoiding the difficulties and challenges in life, give me the strength to stand fast, in the name of Jesus who is my rock and my salvation."

Father, you know how many things make me want
to pull the covers over my head and escape. Help me
to rise up in your power to take on what's before me.
Fill me with your encouragement and courage.

I lie in the dust; revive me by your word. PSALM 119:25, NLT

PRAYING ON THE ASH HEAP

JONI EARECKSON TADA describes Job as a godly and humble man who lost his goods and children and was covered with boils, sitting on a pile of ashes, surrounded by critical friends and a nagging wife. Joni writes, "He had a lot to talk to God about."

We may not be sitting on ashes, but we often find ourselves with deep grief and calamities to talk to God about. A verse in the book of Job eloquently describes the human condition: "Man is born to trouble, as the sparks fly upward" (Job 5:7, NKJV).

Joni points out that Job didn't pray for healing or for relief from his critical friends. "His desire was to 'see the Father's face and to feel his smile.'"

"Job said, 'If only I knew where to find him! I would state my case before him,' . . . and consider what he would say."

In the book of Job and in the Psalms, we repeatedly see these gritty prayers and questions. They are like our own prayers as we experience the unfairness and frustrations of life. The psalmists lay all sorts of excruciating urgencies before God and implore him to act. Such brutal honesty is the nature of genuine prayer.

In his crisis, Job showed the depths of his desire for God by longing to find him.

When bad things happen to us, we're full of questions and attempts to deal with the pain and bewilderment. When our securities evaporate, we look for new ways to steady our feet. That's natural. Yet we also have the opportunity to express our longings to the Lord and to seek him in new ways.

If anyone had reasons to have doubts about God, it was Job. Joni, who has been paralyzed since her teens, sees as the beginning point of our spiritual journeys that we desire God the intense way Job did. "He did not lose his grip on those things about God he knew to be true."

Father in heaven, help me to keep my grip on your love and care for me, despite my circumstances. Help me to be in vital union with you as I deal with what's on my plate and with what may be coming.

O LORD, I give my life to you. I trust in you, my God! Do not let me be disgraced.
PSALM 25:1-2, NLT

NOT GREAT, MAYBE NOT PLEASANT

BROTHER LAWRENCE explains that "it's not necessary to do great things. I turn my little omelet in the pan for the love of God. When it is finished, if I have nothing to do, I prostrate myself on the ground and worship my God, who gave me the grace to make it, after which I arise happier than a king."

Lawrence wasn't concerned about how important his task was. He cared only that he could do it for God—whether repairing shoes or praying with the community.

Like all of us, he liked doing some things better than others. Because it was God he was serving, he knew the more a task was against his natural inclinations, the greater his love was in offering it to God. And if it was a very little thing he was doing, that didn't diminish the love with which he offered it.

We're seldom inclined to clean up a mess. Yet if we're doing it for God, if we praise him for the capacity to do it, and if we think about the wonder of his love and grace while tackling our tasks—whatever they are—we just may feel better than standing before an adulating crowd.

At least that's what Brother Lawrence experienced. He was determined to fulfill his duties where God put him, without longing for what might be more pleasant or fulfilling.

Lawrence's love for doing God's will dominated him to the extent that he saw the plan of God in everything that happened. This kept him in unbroken peace and freedom from anxiety.

"The time of action does not differ from that of prayer," he writes. "I possess God as peacefully in the bustle of my kitchen, where sometimes several people are asking me for different things at the same time, as I do upon my knees."

---

*Holy Spirit of God, you are the Helper, and if I am
to practice your presence the way Brother Lawrence
did, I need you to fully invade my mind and heart.
Please engage me in your thoughts about my tasks.*

You will keep in perfect peace all who trust in you, all whose thoughts are fixed on you!
ISAIAH 26:3, NLT

OUR LONGING AND RESTLESSNESS   *July 18*

ROSEMARY BUDD affirms that "God is love. The Father is always offering love to the Son, and this gift of love is the Son's glory, which he in turn perpetually offers to the Father. God lives in a relationship of love."

How can we get a picture of that? In literature and in life we might see powerful love between a father and son transcend great obstacles and radiate love in a magnificent way. This dynamic of love between Jesus and his Father goes far beyond the best human love we know.

When we read about Jesus praying all night and declaring he does nothing without the Father—or when we hear that "God loved the world so much that he gave his one and only Son"—we get a glimpse of the transforming love at the center of all that exists. It's the kind of love we long for.

Budd says that all God's creations carry an imprint of this love. "Our lives echo with a restlessness that is a longing for completion. We're most ourselves when we give and accept love, for his Spirit puts this within us."

As we pray, we're drawn to respond to the dynamic love that exists among the Father, Son, and Spirit. We receive their love and then are called to share it with others. "Because we are all fired in the love of God," she maintains, "love is the hallmark of our humanity. Our longing for the depths of love is the craftsman's signature on his craft."

Now there's an intriguing thought. If we were statues sculpted by Michelangelo, with his mark on us, our value would be priceless. Yet one far greater than Michelangelo has made us. His signature is seen in our restlessness and longing for the depths of his love.

To authenticate the signature, to turn our longing into completion, we are invited to open ourselves to God so that he can fulfill his purpose in our lives.

Father in heaven, because I am your handiwork, please don't let me disappoint you. You've said that you work best when I am weak. I confess that I'm unable to live in an authentic way unless your love and grace permeate my life.

God loved the world so much that he gave his one and only Son, so that everyone who believes in him will not perish but have eternal life. JOHN 3:16, NLT

MOTORBOATS AND SAILBOATS

July 19

JOHN ORTBERG writes, "One of the most basic laws of life is rhythm."

He describes a young mother who regrets that she isn't able to carve out times of solitude with the Lord as she once did, now that she has responsibility for the daily care of two young children. Yet, Ortberg says, caring for her children with prayers and gratitude "might become a kind of school for transformation into powerful servant-hood beyond anything she had ever known."

Life is rhythm. The seasons of life continue.

In our ever-changing circumstances, we find seasons within our souls as well. We experience times of desolation and consolation. At times we feel dry spiritually. Other times we sense the presence of the Lord in even the tiniest details of life.

Ortberg quotes C. S. Lewis on the seasons when God withdraws his presence: "He leaves the creature to stand up on its own legs—to carry out from the will alone duties which have lost all relish."

That's when, we're told by many spiritual guides, growth is most likely to occur.

Life is rhythm. Life is adventure. Life is catching the wind in our sails, the wind that comes when it pleases.

Ortberg contrasts a motorboat and a sailboat. Piloting a motorboat, we're in control. In a sailboat, we're completely dependent on the wind. If the wind doesn't come, we stay put. We have to catch the wind. It's the same with spiritual transformation.

Everything depends on catching the wind of the Spirit. "Moses didn't ask for or arrange for the burning bush," Ortberg writes. "But once it was there, he had to make a choice. God's responsibility is to provide the burning bush. Ours is to turn aside and pay attention to the work of God."

---

*Holy Spirit, I long to feel your breeze on my face,
refreshing me and lifting me into your purposes and
plan. Let me be alert to whatever you are doing in me,
and to obey, whether I feel your presence or not.*

[Jesus said,] "I am with you always, even to the end of the age."
MATTHEW 28:20, NLT

SEED FOR THE KINGDOM

HELMUT THIELICKE tells an intriguing story on himself. As a young pastor in Nazi Germany, he was determined to appropriate Jesus' statement, "All power is given me in heaven and earth." In the nation at that time, Adolf Hitler held sway, but the young Thielicke repeated in his mind Christ's audacious words. He thereby assured himself that Hitler and his dreadful Nazi machine "were merely puppets hanging by strings in the hands of the mighty Lord."

At his first Bible study, however, he found himself facing two old ladies and a still older organist with palsied fingers. Was this what the Lord with all power in heaven and earth was about? Outside marched battalions of youth who were subject to totally different lords.

That evening, he wondered what God offered. Didn't this "utterly miserable response" refute Jesus' declaration?

Thielicke compares his feelings that evening to those of the disciples when Jesus announced his coming Kingdom. They knew the Romans still occupied the seats of power.

But the disciples' hope that Jesus would usher in the "kingdom"—rising as a conquering Messiah and booting out the Romans—was not what Jesus intended. His Kingdom was not of this world. Instead, he revealed the nature of his Kingdom in the parable of the mustard seed—the tiny seed that would become a great tree the birds could nest in.

Thielicke says of the parable, "The Word of God, which has fallen like seed into our hearts, contains within it a tremendous explosive power; it wants to get out, it yearns to become a tree and bear fruit."

We who are privileged to have the Word simply need to be good soil in which it can grow. The seed in us has the power to change everything, for God is at work in us to do his will. In one sense we need do nothing but let the seed germinate and flourish within us. In other words, we simply grow into ever-deeper fellowship with Christ.

Lord, let the seed of your Word flourish in me.
Enable me to nurture your Spirit within me
and bear fruit as you create the growth.

The seed that fell on good soil represents those who truly hear and understand God's word and produce a harvest of thirty, sixty, or even a hundred times as much as had been planted! MATTHEW 13:23, NLT

FATHOMLESS MYSTERY

PHILIP YANCEY admits to often feeling besieged as he prays. He sees in the news the endless reports of poverty, injustice, human cruelty, and terrorism. He feels the distress of relatives and others who face illness, divorce, and money troubles. Personal pressures crowd in on him.

Yet he keeps at prayer, trying to get his mind off himself and asking God to refresh and renew his soul. "In prayer I ask for, and gradually gain, trust in God's love and justice and mercy and holiness, despite all that might call those traits into question."

How? Yancey writes about viewing prayer as asking a timeless God to act in our time-bound lives—but also viewing prayer "from the other side, as a way of entering into the rhythms of eternity and aligning myself with God's 'view from above,' a way to harmonize my own desires with God's and then to help effect, while on earth, what God has willed for all eternity."

In this broken, often merciless world, Yancey thinks of Mother Teresa's nuns kneeling before dawn, asking for the strength to help the dying in Calcutta. He thinks of hospice workers and military chaplains and others with massive challenges. And he thinks of Jesus "facing the darkest day in human history, pausing to pray the longest prayer recorded in the Gospels."

What happens when we kneel to pray goes far beyond our understanding. As we pray, we're joined in fathomless mysteries with our Creator and Redeemer. We are connected with God's will being done in both heaven and earth—something far more significant than we can see in this earthly dimension.

---

*Lord Jesus Christ, as I bring all things to you, I can identify
with Philip Yancey's sense of being besieged by needs and
tragedies. Draw me into your concerns and rhythms.
Show me how to harmonize my desires with yours.*

Pray like this: Our Father in heaven, may your name be kept holy. May your Kingdom come soon. May your will be done on earth, as it is in heaven. MATTHEW 6:9-10, NLT

DOUBTING FAITH

OLE HALLESBY cautions that we can avoid a lot of pain and confusion if we understand the differences between doubt and unbelief. When we experience doubt, which we all do, and we consider it the same as unbelief, we endanger our prayer lives.

Unbelief is the refusal to believe, the hardening of our hearts, the refusal to open the door when Jesus knocks. But doubt, Hallesby assures us, is not harmful to prayer. In fact, it serves to render us helpless and prompts us to admit our need.

Nevertheless, Hallesby says, these thoughts seem to contradict the plain words of Scripture—that if we pray doubting, we can't expect to be heard.

To get this straight, we must consider context and other Scriptures. Hallesby points especially to the story of the father who came to Jesus when the disciples couldn't cast an evil spirit out of his son. When Jesus questioned him about his faith, the father exclaimed, "I believe! Help my unbelief!" (Mark 9:24, NKJV).

Hallesby says it was the man himself who condemned his doubts as unbelief. But actually he was exhibiting a doubting faith—which is coming to Jesus in our distress. Jesus took it as faith, which Hallesby says is evident from the fact that Jesus healed the boy. He points to other times when unbelief kept Jesus from doing his mighty works; but this boy was healed.

For this father, everything had seemed hopeless. He wasn't sure that Jesus could succeed where the disciples had failed. He vacillated between faith and doubt—as we often do.

"We have faith enough when we bring our needs to Jesus and leave them with him," Hallesby assures us. "We do as the father did, telling him about our doubts and weak faith. I can bring everything to Jesus, no matter how difficult. I have let Jesus into my heart, and he will fulfill my heart's desire."

Lord Jesus, I bring all my doubts to you and all the concerns that cause me such distress. Thank you for the assurance that your favor doesn't depend on the depth of my belief. Please do your work of healing and comfort.

Why am I discouraged? Why is my heart so sad? I will put my hope in God! I will praise him again—my Savior and my God! PSALM 43:5, NLT

WHY ME?

BILLY GRAHAM sees "a mysterious, unknown component" in that some believers in Scripture suffer greatly while others do not.

In Hebrews 11, we see the striking contrast between heroes of the faith whom God delivered and those who were tortured and executed.

In Revelation, we read about two churches, one in Philadelphia and one in Smyrna. Both apparently were faithful congregations, but one was to go through terrible suffering and the other was not.

All over the world, it's the same today. Some Christians suffer terribly; others do not. Scripture simply accepts the fact of suffering. Only God, who sees the whole picture, knows what's really going on—and we know that he cares.

In wrestling with this unanswered question, Graham makes these suggestions:

Asking "Why me?" doesn't help. As C. S. Lewis observes, we could just as well ask, "Why me?" when we are experiencing great blessings. The truth is, we all suffer at various times and in various ways. We may not be tortured or "sawn asunder," but we will know grief and distress.

Stay faithful. Christ said to the church at Smyrna, "Don't be afraid of what you are about to suffer. . . . If you remain faithful even when facing death, I will give you the crown of life" (Revelation 2:10, NLT).

Keep your eyes on the prize. It doesn't help to be envious of the good fortunes of others when tough times come our way. We are called to press on for the high calling in Christ.

Endure with patience. The Bible is full of exhortations to patience and endurance. For instance, 2 Thessalonians 3:5 reads, "May the Lord lead your hearts into a full understanding and expression of the love of God and the patient endurance that comes from Christ" (NLT).

Never be bitter. In times of terrible trouble or betrayal, we have a choice: to call on the Holy Spirit for his peace or to savor bitterness.

---

*Lord, help me to walk with you and to constantly
listen for your voice so that in times of prosperity and
peace or pain and trouble, I'll be in step with your
Spirit. Empower me to be faithful day after day.*

The Lord is faithful; he will strengthen you and guard you from the evil one.
2 THESSALONIANS 3:3, NLT

THAT HEAVENLY CONCERT

July 24

A. W. TOZER, describing how everything within us longs to stay alive, shares this image: "Life is a short and fevered rehearsal for a concert we cannot stay to give. Just when we gain some proficiency, we are forced to lay our instruments down."

We feel the truth of Tozer's remarks with full force when a talented young person dies. Yet even when we live to a ripe old age, we don't feel "ripe" or completed at all. One woman in her seventies lamented, "You just learn how to live, and it's time to go!"

The Bible often reminds us we're here a very short time; it compares our lives to the morning mist that quickly disappears. On the other hand, the Bible also declares that we are eternal. The promise from Jesus that we will live forever with him resonates in our souls.

We may die today. We may be forced to leave this world before we can give an earthly concert of one sort or another. But we will have all eternity to give and hear concerts and to travel God's universe to exult in his music and his harmonies.

As the hymn "Amazing Grace" puts it,

> When we've been there ten thousand years,
>   bright shining as the sun,
> We've no less days to sing God's praise,
>   than when we'd first begun.

When we come to Christ and experience the new birth, we no longer have to fret about how much time we have left and what we will leave behind. This life is just the beginning, the entryway to glory.

Tozer captures this truth with a vivid, hopeful metaphor: "For those out of Christ, time is a devouring beast; before the sons of the new creation, time crouches and purrs and licks their hands."

Father above, you know all the many reasons I don't want to die right now. Grant me your peace about the brevity of my life and how my absence would affect my loved ones. Help me to trust them to your care.

We believers also groan, even though we have the Holy Spirit within us as a foretaste of future glory, for we long for our bodies to be released from sin and suffering.
ROMANS 8:23, NLT

THE DARK INTRUDER

GEORGE MACDONALD reports in his diary, "Yesterday, Death came, and knocked at my thin door."

For each of us, the door between us and death is thin indeed. Hearing that knock can chill us to the bone. Despite his great faith and love for God, MacDonald felt chilled when he heard that knock.

"I was disturbed not with awe but fear," he confessed to God. "Ashamed, I instantly roused my will to seek thee—only to fear the more: I could not find thee in the house."

Will we feel God's presence when our time comes? We can't know for sure. MacDonald felt he was like Peter walking on the water—about to sink. The experience birthed a new prayer in him: "That when death in earnest comes to my door, thou thyself would go when the latch clinks and lead him to my room, up to my cot. Then hold thy child's hand, hold and don't leave! Death comes—and goes—to leave me in thy arms, nearer thy heart, oh, nearer than before—to lay thy child, naked, new-born again."

Every day, we hear of death taking other people. Sometimes it takes someone very close. Sometimes our own bodies give us a scare. We know that someday—perhaps soon—death will come knocking at our door.

MacDonald's prayers, after his own scare, resonate with burgeoning faith as he says, "Come to me, Lord. I won't speculate how nor think at which door. Doors, windows, I throw all wide; my head I bow."

---

*Lord of all comfort, instead of dread, give me a
taste of joy and anticipation for when I hear the
knock at my door. Let me have no regrets. Lead me
to rest in your forgiveness and redemption.*

I heard a voice from heaven saying, "Write this down: Blessed are those who die in the Lord. . . . Yes, says the Spirit, they are blessed indeed, for they will rest from their hard work; for their good deeds follow them!" REVELATION 14:13, NLT

START WITH THE PEACE

RAY STEDMAN, as a pastor, had many come to him angry, troubled, and distraught over conflicts with others. They told him all the terrible things done by others and all the reasons they were so angry and despondent.

In response, Stedman would point them to a deeper peace beyond mere cessation of hostilities. He guided them to Ephesians 2:14: "Christ himself has brought peace to us" (NLT). We read in that chapter that God breaks down walls of hostility, and he reconciles.

"True peace is oneness," Stedman writes. "If you merely agree not to fight, it's not peace. That invariably results in a new outbreak, with all the previous animosity surging to the surface again. The secret of peace is oneness with a Person."

When we have peace with Christ—when we abide in his peace—we can work on the temporal conflicts that crush our spirits or fill us with anger and the desire to lash back. We can be released from the emotions that make reconciliation seem impossible.

That's not to say all conflicts can be resolved into sweetness and light. Yet the peace of Christ within our hearts changes us. Whatever progress or lack of progress we make toward reconciliation with another person, we know we have the peace most vital to our souls. God's peace can enable us to withstand even injustice and betrayal.

Once our attitudes have been changed through our surrender to him, whatever concerns us can be put into God's hands.

As we continually invite the Holy Spirit to bring us peace, we may gain fresh insights. We can apply thoughtful remedies. Perhaps we will see problems worked out in ways we never could have anticipated.

"There is profound psychological insight," writes Stedman, "in the fact the apostle begins with the declaration that Christ is our peace."

Father in heaven, it's so discouraging that conflict and even bitterness among us seem inevitable. Help me to be an instrument of your peace rather than someone who stokes the fires of discord. Grant me your wisdom and peace.

[God's] peace will guard your hearts and minds as you live in Christ Jesus.
PHILIPPIANS 4:7, NLT

IT'S GONNA BE ALL RIGHT

July 27

BEN PATTERSON was driving one evening when a song on the radio reminded him of his final year in college and all the great friends he'd had. But then he remembered how miserable he'd been during his senior year. The girl he loved had jilted him, he was tired of school, and he was fearful of the future. But now, with the perspective of years, he realized that his life had been good since then, and it was too bad he hadn't known that back then so he could have enjoyed his senior year.

It was at that moment, Patterson says, that something glorious happened to him. He thought, *I can live from now on knowing that my life is going to turn out fine.*

What a great perspective for all of us who are concerned about what lies ahead.

The world seems in upheaval in more ways than we can list. Our personal circumstances may be in precarious balance. All sorts of misfortunes or illness could swallow up our security. As Pascal puts it, "A draft of air can kill you." Yet, at the end of our lives, we are going to look back, and no matter what has happened, if we have walked with the Lord, our lives will have turned out fine.

We may have gone through deep and even horrific tragedy, and we may have seen the dissolution of much that we love. But in the brief span of time we're here, we have a faithful God who walks with us and guides us. Like Christian in *The Pilgrim's Progress*, we may have lions and giants to face and sloughs of despond to struggle through, but eventually we will see it all in God's perspective. Our lives will have been God's adventures, full of meaning and glory.

For all that, we can thank our Lord now. And as we thank and praise him, we will feel ourselves drawn away from anxiety and toward his joy.

Father in heaven, when I feel as if I'm having a miserable year, open my eyes to your grace and give me your assurance that everything is going to "turn out fine." Align my will to yours that I might walk in your Spirit.

The LORD God is our sun and our shield. He gives us grace and glory. The LORD will withhold no good thing from those who do what is right. PSALM 84:11, NLT

GETTING AERATED

FRED SMITH points out what many of us have experienced: "Life needs continual aeration. When life gets heavy, it settles down on us and needs to be lightened up." Smith recognizes that the majority of people who sit in church on a Sunday carry major hurts, and he calls for us to discover inspiration and joy in our faith, whatever our circumstances.

"The 'blessed hope' is not guilt but grace," he emphasizes. "We are forgiven, we are free, we have fellowship and an inheritance immortal. We have talents and gifts. Each of us can make a difference. Exult in it! Breathe it in."

Smith challenges us to find lilt and buoyancy in life, through wonderment, reverence, and gratitude.

We can feel wonder by looking with fresh eyes at our world and universe. "It's easy to become jaded and say, 'So what?' But that's not the biblical spirit. Paul seemed to say in the Scriptures not 'So *what?*' but 'So *that.*' Paul had a vision and a sense of wonder in what God was doing."

Smith tells us that reverence for others aerates his spirit—and he takes his own advice. In heavy traffic, for example, he resolves to do favors for other motorists instead of blowing his horn at them. Doing so lifts his spirit as he drives to the office.

Psychologists say that gratitude is the healthiest emotion of all, and the Bible is full of admonitions to be thankful. Yet, in the United States, many refer to Thanksgiving as "turkey day," avoiding the holiday's meaning. What a loss! To be thankful is to live with spiritual and physical vitality.

"Gratitude puts a lilt in life," Smith says. "Each morning I need to say, 'I am part of this marvelous human race which, though fallen, is so greatly loved by God that Jesus Christ died for it.' Talk about gratitude! If we think of the magnificent work of God on our behalf, and all of his works of wonder, we will be aerated in such a way that we can genuinely glorify our Creator."

---

*Lord, so often things go wrong, and tragedies
around me overwhelm any lilt I feel. Aerate my
spirit. Help me to focus my eyes on your greatness
and to experience your inspiration and joy.*

Praise the LORD! How good to sing praises to our God! How delightful and how fitting!
PSALM 147:1, NLT

NOT MOODY, BUT GOD

D. L. MOODY wasn't just being humble when he emphasized that it was God who brought the power and fruitfulness to his ministry. He saw clearly, and he believed fully, that God was the one working through him. "It wasn't David or the sling, but it was the God of David," he preached. "It wasn't Samson, but the God of Samson. It wasn't Joshua, but the God of Joshua."

He would surely have added, "It's not Moody, but the God of Moody." Billy Graham has exactly the same attitude, ever careful, when personally honored, to declare—with intense authenticity—that God alone is the source of his fruitful leadership.

Spiritual leaders have often emphasized that our roles are like pipes that carry the blessings—we're not the source but the conveyors of God's grace. We rejoice when God's power and fruitfulness flow through us. When we're blessed with skills and giftedness, we rightly enjoy them and express our gratitude to our Creator.

We're free to realistically assess and celebrate what God is doing in and through us.

Fred Smith once described a talented young woman who sang a beautiful solo at a meeting. Her singing had been superb, but when Smith complimented her on it, she became flustered. In her attempt to sound humble, she awkwardly dismissed her solo as not being very good.

This young woman needed to enjoy and acknowledge the talent she'd received and developed. We're not called to whisper, "Aw, shucks" to downplay our talents and spiritual fruit.

God is the Father of lights. He is the Giver of all good gifts. Scripture tells us that it's God who works in us for his good pleasure—and ultimately for ours.

That's why praise and gratitude, even for our own abilities and accomplishments, are thoroughly biblical. They release us to rejoice in all that God has done and is doing.

Father and Creator, thank you for all the magnificence
of your creation—including the skills and capacities
you've given to me. Help me, I pray, to use them wisely
with a spirit of both responsibility and thanksgiving.

There are different kinds of spiritual gifts, but the same Spirit is the source of them all.
I CORINTHIANS 12:4, NLT

ADVENTURES IN SOLITUDE

HENRI NOUWEN advocates that we seek solitude in our worried, pressured lives. "Without solitude," he writes, "it is virtually impossible to live a spiritual life. Solitude begins with a time and place for God, and him alone."

Nouwen admits that bringing solitude into our lives is difficult. Time pressures crowd it out. Some seekers find "chaos opens up" when they finally do get alone—for them, instead of solitude providing calm and escape from dysfunctions, it may foster dark thoughts.

Not everyone feels chaos in solitude, but most people will discover plenty of distractions and the need for self-discipline—both to schedule solitude and then to focus their thoughts heavenward. Simply getting alone and shutting out the world is only the first step in the discipline of solitude. We also need to be patient with the process.

For some, solitude may need to start out in short doses.

As we probe the Scriptures in solitude and employ spiritual disciplines, we often find they lead us into fresh spiritual adventures. Solitude can give us the capacity to cope with life's stresses and surprises and serve as essential "fueling stops for the road."

Even if we feel we can't find time for solitude, we can remember the example of Brother Lawrence and in our activities practice God's presence throughout the day. Whether the baby is crying or customers are demanding, we still can lift our prayers to God.

Lord, life is genuinely pressured and at times
overwhelming. Help me to be creative in finding time
to be exclusively with you. When I simply can't find that
time, help me to creatively practice your presence.

He will take delight in you with gladness. With his love, he will calm all your fears. He will rejoice over you with joyful songs. ZEPHANIAH 3:17, NLT

BEYOND BITTERNESS

FRANCIS SCHAEFFER laments that, in contrast to Jesus' command that we are to love as he loved, Christians have often said bitter things to one another—so bitter they stick in the mind and emotions for decades. Tragically, Schaeffer sees offering apologies, asking forgiveness, and working through bitterness as rare events.

However, he gives us a beautiful, ringing, positive example: the Brethren groups in Germany. During the days of the Third Reich, Hitler had required all religious groups to function together. Half the Brethren had accepted Hitler's command and half had refused. Those who refused remained spiritually vibrant, but many of them died in Nazi concentration camps.

Schaeffer asks us to imagine the tension between the two groups after the war. For instance, one man's father had died in a camp and his mother had been dragged away. "These things are not just pebbles on the beach," Schaeffer says. "They reach into the deep wellsprings of human emotions. But these people understood the command of Christ."

The Brethren met together, and several days were set aside for each man to do nothing but search his own heart and the commands of Christ.

"What happened then?" Schaeffer asked a participant.

"We just were one," he replied.

The Brethren demonstrated that, even with extreme obstacles, we can determine to obey Jesus' command to love one another. Reconciliation requires commitment and determination, and sometimes significant creativity, to find a way to overcome the difficulties of the past. The human condition is such that we often find ourselves at odds with others and have before us these enormous challenges and opportunities.

"Love," writes Schaeffer, "is the mark Christ gave to *wear* before the world. Only with this mark may the world know that Jesus was sent by the Father."

Lord Jesus, I know you have commanded us to love one another. Often I don't find the love within my heart, and I don't know how to generate it. Empower me to be your disciple in this and to show and experience your love.

May the Lord make your love for one another and for all people grow and overflow, just as our love for you overflows. I THESSALONIANS 3:12, NLT

BELIEVE, AND WORK HARD

MARTIN LUTHER quoted two proverbs to show both sides of the life of faith—our efforts, and the help of the Lord:

Lazy people are soon poor; hard workers get rich. (Proverbs 10:4, NLT)
The blessing of the LORD makes a person rich. (Proverbs 10:22, NLT)

So it's both/and, not either/or; yet those two quotes describing how life works best raise a lot of questions. Some hard workers get rich, but millions work very hard and barely survive. Some even starve. And God blesses many with prosperity, but other believers with great faith live desperate, impoverished lives.

The book of Proverbs is right that all good things come from the Lord and that generally we must work hard to become prosperous. But beyond those principles are questions about the mysterious ways of God that defy our logic and reason.

We don't have to figure it all out—nobody can. Our option is to concentrate on making sure we are in harmony with the works of God.

"If God isn't with us," Luther writes, "we are nothing at all, no matter how great our gifts may be. If he doesn't constantly uphold us, the greatest amount of knowledge will be useless, even if we are experts in theology. In the hour of temptation, the devil can tear away all the comforting Bible verses from us and leave us with threatening ones that crush our spirits."

Luther advises us to have a humble view of our spiritual progress and our talents, coming to God in faith and at the same time praying as his disciples did, "Increase our faith."

Father in heaven, sorting through the significance
of all the troubles around me and around the world
does seem hopeless. Let me see through your eyes,
and let me move at the impulse of your love.

Faith comes from hearing, that is, hearing the Good News about Christ.
ROMANS 10:17, NLT

A CANDLE AND BRIGHT LIGHT

JAY KESLER asks us to imagine standing in a basement when everything suddenly goes dark. Disoriented, we stumble toward a drawer we hope has some candles in it. Banging into boxes and barking our shins on sharp corners, we locate the drawer and light a candle. Its small, flickering light is reassuring. Just then, the power surges back on and the room fills with light. The candle becomes a mere pinprick of flame, barely noticeable in our hands.

Kesler uses this story to illustrate how our earliest experiences of faith often begin as small flickers of understanding. Though tiny, these flickers of insight are very important in the darkness. But as we grow in our faith and continually seek wisdom and truth from many sources, we move from candlelit basement to lighted room. "Yet," Kesler writes, "just as I think the Christian life has been fully illuminated, I stumble into a larger, floodlighted room yet to be explored."

In addition to the Scriptures, we have unlimited sources of illumination available to us—including thousands of years of testimonies and writings by men and women who pressed hard after God, believers who lived out their faith in difficult and challenging circumstances, and others who bring fresh bursts of insight and illumination to the at-large faith community.

As we journey through the mountains and valleys and days and nights of our lives, we uncover wisdom and find illumination in unexpected places.

The illustration of the candle can also be used another way. It vividly portrays the moment when we will move, with our flickering candles, from the dark basement of our temporal world into the glorious eternal light of heaven. All that we have learned here will amount to tiny flickers of the greater illumination of heaven, as we see with new eyes and say, "Ah! Of course! That's what it all means!"

---

*Father of lights, lead me into every lighted room that
you want me to enter. May your Holy Spirit of truth
guide me with light from above, and let me then
walk with assurance the path of doing your will.*

The apostles said to the Lord, "Show us how to increase our faith." LUKE 17:5, NLT

THE GREATER WORK

August 8

OSWALD CHAMBERS asserts, "Prayer does not fit us for the greater works; prayer is the greater work."

Now that's something to think long and hard about. Do we believe that our prayers are more strategically important than our activities?

Chambers tells us that prayer isn't just preparation for the battle; it *is* the battle. Wherever we are, whatever we're doing, whatever the challenges before us, prayer is our opportunity to join with God in fulfilling his work on earth. Prayer is our linkage to the grace and love and power of God.

"Wherever God has dumped you down in circumstances," Chambers tells us, "pray." He urges us to pray all the time. He says that as we work at prayer, important things are already happening, from God's standpoint. We will likely be astonished in the life to come when we see what has really been going on when we pray.

Did Chambers say "work" at prayer? What's work got to do with it? Isn't prayer a joy and a time for meditation and recovery from life's stresses—the solitude that restores and energizes?

Yes, it can be, but it's also work. In many ways, the kind of prayer that Chambers has in mind is more like an athlete's training than a meditative retreat. Athletic training has its benefits of producing endorphins and peak fitness and preparation for the big challenges ahead. But those workouts require significant discipline and sweat.

Prayer that changes us and the world doesn't just happen. It takes commitment and a deep belief that it is the greater work—that we are engaging with the Almighty in *his* ultimate work.

Let's not view the work side of prayer as a source of guilt. Rather, it's an invitation to spiritual fitness. Just as athletes show up to work out as the coach instructs, so we are invited to develop spiritual strength and endurance.

Lord, here I am. Teach me to pray. Enable me to pray.
Show me how prayer can be central to my life. Help me
come alive to what you are ready to do in my prayer life.

Morning, noon, and night I cry out in my distress, and the LORD hears my voice.
PSALM 55:17, NLT

YES, GET ANGRY

JOHN HENRY JOWETT asks an intriguing question: "What is the quality of our anger? Our anger reveals our character. What kindles it?"

When slapped on the face, we feel anger. We react to insults with body chemistry as automatic as gravity. Anger erupts from jealousy, spite, or hatred, but also from love and righteous indignation. The apostle Paul said, "Be ye angry, and sin not" (Ephesians 4:26, KJV).

How does all that work?

Jowett says, "My power of anger is not to be destroyed, it is to be transformed and purified. Worldly anger is set on the fire of hell; holy anger borrows flame from the altar fires of God."

Jowett describes Paul's anger by quoting his words from 2 Corinthians 11:29: "Who is made to stumble, and I do not burn?"(NKJV). He points out that Paul's "holy anger" was ignited by seeing oppression and cruelty against others.

Jesus had severe, even extreme, words for those who made children stumble—it's obvious he felt angry. His anger at the money changers in the Temple caused him to grab a whip and drive them out.

Holy anger at exploitation of children and a host of other injustices can result in redemptive work. Holy anger at our own sins and selfishness can lead to holy lives that truly change things. Yet that sort of anger is rare, for most of us find it much more satisfying to simply condemn the sins of others.

Jowett concludes that we need the anger that comes from God's redemptive compassion. "We must seek to be baptized with the Holy Ghost *and with fire.*"

Lord Jesus, your scathing anger was directed against what grieved your holy love. My anger is often just a reaction to what hurts me. Help me, Lord, to feel anger only at what needs a dose of "righteous indignation" and action on my part.

Get rid of all bitterness, rage, anger, harsh words, and slander, as well as all types of evil behavior. EPHESIANS 4:31, NLT

OBEDIENCE AND JOY

SHERWOOD WIRT writes that the joy Jesus had when he was ministering in Galilee was "the kind of joy that cannot be compartmentalized. It suffuses the whole of existence and blows the dismal clouds of unbelief out to sea."

He goes on to say, "By a miracle of grace, the Holy Spirit continues to make it available to us today. What Jesus brought with him from heaven was something more than a new start for humanity; it was a clear, bubbling, unpolluted delight in God and God's creation, his redemption, his new creation, and his promise of eternal life."

That's an amazing description of an amazing promise. Yet the truth is, we long to sense the Lord's delight much more than we actually experience it. Part of the gap may have to do with the issue of our obedience to what Jesus commands. Wirt turns right to that issue and shares two quotes:

Elisabeth Elliot: "Obedience always leads finally to joy."
Ed Wheat: "Obedience takes on the bright colors of joy."

Interesting! The hinge to joy, the gateway to joy, is the simple, annoying issue of obedience to what Christ commands. Obedience to the whispers of the Holy Spirit. Obedience as God leads us through the valleys and deep swamps and over the mountains.

Of course, it was Jesus' continuous obedience to his heavenly Father that made redemption possible.

On Easter morning, the two Marys who learned at the empty tomb that Jesus had risen were running with fear and "great joy" to tell the disciples—when suddenly Jesus appeared. His first word to the women was recorded in Greek as *chairete*. Wirt says that means, literally, "Oh, joy!"

"The agony was finished," Wirt writes, "the arrest, the trial, the conviction, the sentencing, the mocking, the beating, the torture, the crucifixion. From the risen Jesus, we hear the word that tells us rejoicing had returned: 'Oh, joy!'"

Father in heaven, as Jesus was always in contact with
you and obedient to you, help me to be alert for your
thoughts and obedient to your commands. Help me to
find your joy this day and to share it with others.

Weeping may last through the night, but joy comes with the morning.
PSALM 30:5, NLT

THE HOUSE AND THE TREE

JOHN WESLEY, reflecting on Jesus' words that every good tree brings forth good fruit, describes how this applies to our lives: "As the Christian loves God, he keeps his commandments. He avoids what God has forbidden and does what he has ordained, whether little or great, hard or easy, joyous or grievous. He runs the way of God's commandments, knowing it is the highest privilege. Loving God with all his heart, he serves him with all his strength."

Turning to Jesus' description of the wise man who built his house on a rock, Wesley describes a Christian as one who rests the whole weight of his soul on the cornerstone of Christ's sacrifice. According to Wesley, the Christian says, "I live by faith in him who loved me and gave himself for me. I live a life of love both to God and man, a life of holiness and happiness, praising God, and doing all things to his glory."

Wesley then warns that the authentic Christians he's describing are not beyond temptation. They will be "tried as gold in the fire." He reminds us that the winds blew and beat upon that house built on the rock. "Satan will not fail to try to the uttermost those he is unable to destroy."

We who have built on the rock know from experience that nothing insulates us from temptation and troubles. We know, as Wesley expresses it, that we mustn't think we won't see war. However, he maintains that winds and rain and Satan's fiery darts cannot destroy the house on the solid rock.

Quoting phrases from Scripture, he says of the believer, "He shall not fear, though the earth be moved, and though the hills be carried into the midst of the sea. Though the waters rage and swell, and the mountains shake, still he dwells under the defense of the Most High and is safe under the shadow of the Almighty."

Lord Jesus, I want to be fully committed to responding to your commands and living in your love. Protect me from all that would wrench me from your arms of mercy.

O LORD, I have come to you for protection; don't let me be disgraced. Save me, for you do what is right. PSALM 31:1, NLT

PRAYING PAST THE ULTIMATE BARRIER

August 7

HENRI NOUWEN states, "Only if you pray with hope can you break through the barriers of death."

What might he mean by that?

We don't know what's coming the next hour, day, or year. We might well be amazed at how different life will be from our expectations. It's the same with life after death. When you pray with authentic hope, Nouwen says, "no longer do you want to know what it will be like after you die, what heaven exactly will mean, how you will be eternal, or how the risen Lord will show himself. When you pray with hope, you turn yourself toward a God who will bring forth his promises; it is enough to know he is a faithful God."

In our prayers, we may ask for many things. When we pray with hope for all sorts of things, we're showing that we trust God, that he is good and good to us, and that he will fulfill his promises.

When we face death or economic calamity or family turmoil, we may feel all sorts of anxieties about what will unfold. But Nouwen says that praying in hope brings a new freedom as we thank God for his promises and praise him.

With this attitude, all our prayers—including those for specifics such as a job or a child's safety—become prayers of thanksgiving and praise.

We can either think with mixed dread about what's ahead of us, in this life and the next, or we can embrace the expectation that "the best is yet to come."

Living in Christian hope means believing that, despite plenty of rocky patches in this life and much that will attack our faith, we have much to look forward to. God's unfailing love will suffice, and we can anticipate our redemption in glory.

Father in heaven, how is it possible that I will actually be "up there" with you one of these days? When I think of leaving all I hold dear, my emotions are mixed. Give me peace about all that lies ahead.

Sing praises to God and to his name! Sing loud praises to him who rides the clouds. His name is the LORD—rejoice in his presence! PSALM 68:4, NLT

MORE HELP THAN EXPECTED

JILL BRISCOE writes, "It's hard to learn dependence when you've done a halfway decent job without it."

She's referring, of course, to dependence on the Lord. She illustrates her point by alluding to her work as a schoolteacher. Considering her exceptional talents, she most likely was doing far better than "a halfway decent job." Yet her teaching at school was quite different from her weekend youth work when she would "pray hard, trust God, and make sure I was in my Bible." She relied more on herself when she was teaching, but "then it dawned on me that Jesus wanted to be fully involved in my classroom. I began to 'trust and obey' at school and I was amazed at the results."

School, work, ball games, family visits, driving the freeway—in every situation, we have the golden opportunity to invite the Lord not only to come with us but to call the shots. When we do that, we don't feel limited; rather, we're freed up to see God at work.

As we increasingly practice the presence of Christ, we find ourselves looking for his surprise visits. Whether eating with colleagues or friends, writing a letter, or texting, we cultivate a readiness to obey and an expectancy that opens the way to fresh spiritual insights.

Calling on God deepens and stretches us. At the same time, it makes us aware of our need for his help and inspiration.

Two well-known songs many of us have sung may sum it up: "Trust and obey, for there's no other way, to be happy in Jesus," and "I need thee every hour."

Jill says when she learned in her teaching to allow God to direct her in all her activities, "the difference was astonishing. So many wonderful things began happening."

Father, as I go through my day, help me to check in with
you and to be aware of your presence. Bring me to the
point where, instead of just plunging ahead, I'm relying
on you to call the shots and guide my thoughts.

Let the Spirit renew your thoughts and attitudes. Put on your new nature, created to be like God—truly righteous and holy. EPHESIANS 4:23-24, NLT

A BIGHEARTED SPIRIT

FRANÇOIS FÉNELON observes, "Sometimes we find the most surprising faults in otherwise good people. I've found God leaves, even in the most spiritual people, certain weaknesses, which seem to be entirely out of place."

How true! We're disappointed when someone who genuinely loves God fails significantly or shows distressing faults. We're surprised and sometimes disillusioned by what seems hypocritical in someone serving the Lord.

Fénelon says we shouldn't be surprised—because such faults are true of everyone. We need to be quick to recognize our own failures and to let God deal with the flaws in others.

When asked what his definition of a hypocrite was, Swiss physician and author Paul Tournier replied, "*C'est moi.*" It is I. Here was an erudite, committed Christian who grasped the painful reality of sin.

What Fénelon calls us to is a bighearted spirit toward others' imperfections. We can't help but see them, and they may frustrate us. But, always aware of our own imperfections, we learn patience as we wisely deal with the faults of others.

"If there is a mark of perfection," Fénelon says, "it's being able to tolerate the imperfections of others. Labor to be patient with the weaknesses of other people. You know from experience how bitterly it hurts to be corrected. So work hard to make it less bitter for others."

He advises us not to reject or avoid others because of their faults. In a spirit of humility, we are to let God deal with them. Perhaps we should also add a bit of humor at how seriously we view the faults of others when at the same time we give a pass to ourselves.

Father, help me to see through your eyes those who disappoint me. Grant me wisdom and a humble spirit instead of a natural reaction to judge them. Help me to be compassionate and an instrument of your grace.

May God, who gives this patience and encouragement, help you live in complete harmony with each other, as is fitting for followers of Christ Jesus. ROMANS 15:5, NLT

THE CORRUPTED CREATION

EUGENE PETERSON succinctly captures a core reality of our faith: "We live in a creation and not a madhouse."

It's not hard to see why it often seems a madhouse—in fact, an ugly madhouse of unthinkable cruelty. What's it really like for the world's millions of sexual slaves and terrorized villagers? What about desperate refugees fleeing their homes, and corrupt governments starving families? It makes us wince when we're confronted with what has happened to so many innocent people. Hopes dashed, lives cut short, poverty grinding the poor and oppressed into starvation and degradation. A madhouse.

Peterson's eyes are wide open to such realities. In fact, he quotes a statement from Martin Luther that describes Luther's acid test of a pastor: "Does he know of death and the devil?"

The results of sin and evil have been visited with a vengeance on God's good creation, and we are engaged in spiritual battles beyond our own capacities.

This is our Father's world, but the forces of Satan and the evil in the human heart make it a fallen world. Those who see no Creator and no destiny for creation may well conclude that it is a madhouse. But Peterson proclaims, "Our existence is derived from God and destined for God," and that is what transforms our bewilderment into hope.

Gene writes of those faithful ones "who dare to live by the great invisibles of grace, who accept forgiveness, who believe promises, who pray. These people daily and dangerously decide to live by faith and not by works, in hope and not despair."

Creator and Sustainer, when I am dismayed by the troubles around me and throughout the world, grant me a vision of your great purpose for creation and your love for the world. Fill me with your hope.

Why am I discouraged? Why is my heart so sad? I will put my hope in God! I will praise him again—my Savior and my God! PSALM 43:5, NLT

HOW NOT TO SINK IN THE RIVER

August 11

JONI EARECKSON TADA writes that she loved horseback riding as a child and was determined, on her little pony, to keep up with her older sisters. As their horses waded toward midstream in a river swollen by rain, she stared at the rushing waters that swirled around the shaking legs of her pony. "Mesmerized by the circling waters, I felt dizzy," she recalls. "I was frightened and began to lose my balance in the saddle."

A sister called back, "Look up, Joni—keep looking up!"

When Joni took her eyes off the water and focused on her sister, she regained her balance and finished the river crossing. She writes that Peter had the same problem when he was walking on the water toward the Lord Jesus. He looked down, and because he took his eyes off the Lord, he began to sink.

"We are so much like Peter!" she laments. "We let our circumstances transfix us. We lose our spiritual equilibrium. We become dizzy with fear and anxiety. Before we know it, we've lost our balance."

Every day when we wake up, we never know what awaits us. Events might crash into our lives, shaking and disorienting us. But when we keep our eyes on the Lord, we can expect he will be there for us. Little surprises throughout the day become blessings that can nurture us.

"It's hard to look up when you feel like you're sinking," Joni says. "But I made it across the river, and Peter made it back to his boat."

The implications for us are obvious. When we're deeply mired in trouble, when it feels as if we're going under, we need to lift our eyes from the deep waters. When we concentrate on God's majesty and the wonders of his creation, remembering that he is preparing a place for us, we can make it through the day, and we can make it across the deep rivers ahead.

Lord Jesus, help me to look to you as I swim in
this ever-changing, demanding, dangerous culture.
Temptations seem to accompany every opportunity.
May my faith be strong and my eyes be on you.

[Peter] was terrified and began to sink. "Save me, Lord!" he shouted. Jesus immediately reached out and grabbed him. "You have so little faith," Jesus said. "Why did you doubt me?" MATTHEW 14:30-31, NLT

THE DIVINE PLUS

OLE HALLESBY wrote in the 1930s in Norway, "The stress of economic difficulty darkens many a home." He mentioned families who had been relatively rich but in one year became poor.

As then, financial losses and pressures weigh on many of us today, with negative news making us question how we'll avoid hunger and homelessness in the future.

For Hallesby and his neighbors, things got much worse—in April 1940, the Nazis invaded. Hallesby was a leader among those who resisted, and he was sent to a concentration camp for two years.

He experienced what we dread.

What if everything we're counting on for security is swept away? What if we lose our jobs or health? What if the worst happens here—the way it has happened to innocent people elsewhere in the world?

We get a bracing view of money and security in 1 Timothy 6:6-8: "True godliness with contentment is itself great wealth. After all, we brought nothing with us when we came into the world, and we can't take anything with us when we leave it. So if we have enough food and clothing, let us be content" (NLT).

Content even when the food is plain and the clothes old and threadbare? Content even when the future is uncertain? Content in a concentration camp?

God's grace has brought godly contentment to many in extreme circumstances.

We bring our anxieties and needs to the Father, with prayer and thanksgiving. In Paul's second letter to Timothy, he tells his young protégé not to be afraid of suffering.

Hallesby writes the following about times when it seemed there just wasn't enough money and resources to cover basic necessities: "God quietly added his divine plus, and there was enough. He has not *removed* our difficulties, he has transformed them so that we can see his purpose and his grace."

---

*Lord, please help me to have a spirit of contentment
about what I have and what I lack. In poverty or
prosperity, in peace or danger, pour into my soul
the confidence that you care and will provide.*

Teach those who are rich in this world not to be proud and not to trust in their money, which is so unreliable. Their trust should be in God. I TIMOTHY 6:17, NLT

THE BOOK OF ADVENTURE

PAUL TOURNIER saw the God of the Bible as the ultimate Adventurer—and as "the God who acts."

In the Old Testament, God confronts and intervenes, chooses instruments of salvation, and grieves over the suffering and stubbornness of his people. He sends them prophets, but they continue in rebellion until one prophet cries out, "Oh, that you would rend the heavens and come down . . . !" (Isaiah 64:1, NIV).

Tournier writes, "And God did come down, in person! This was the supreme adventure. This was the earthly adventure of Jesus, who said, 'My Father is working still, and I am working.'"

God's work continues even now, and we who are made in his image are called to join in his work—our participation made possible by his supreme adventure.

Yet for all the stirring words about adventures, we know that they are never simple walks in the park. They include risks, dull routines, harrowing scrapes, high moments, low disappointments, and narrow escapes. Slogging through all that, we need to constantly rediscover the vision and fresh fellowship of the Holy Spirit.

Adventure movies always keep us guessing what catastrophe will happen next. As we continue our spiritual journey, we're at times apprehensive about what we will face. But uncertainty is what makes life an adventure, and despite the trauma and turmoil, our spiritual journey ends on a very high note.

The apostle Paul, in Philippians, describes the mind-set we're to have in times of uncertainty. He zeroes in on just one thing: forgetting all the slogging that's behind him, he keeps pressing forward to finish the race.

"The Bible is the book of adventure and must be read as such," Tournier says, adding that it informs "the personal adventure of each man and woman whom God touches, calls, and sends into action."

Lord Jesus Christ, help me to embrace the adventures
before me rather than resenting them or wishing the hard
things would go away. Bring into my spirit your strength
and joy that I might be an instrument of your peace.

Pursue righteousness and a godly life, along with faith, love, perseverance, and gentleness.
Fight the good fight for the true faith. I TIMOTHY 6:11-12, NLT

YEARNING FOR HEAVEN

August 14

NANCY GUTHRIE writes that Isaiah 57 gave her new insight into the way God views things, and it changed her perspective. Here are the first two verses of that chapter:

> Good people pass away; the godly often die before their time. But no one seems to care or wonder why. No one seems to understand that God is protecting them from the evil to come. For those who follow godly paths will rest in peace when they die (NLT).

Nancy says after her baby daughter died she began to understand why so many people found such comfort in knowing their loved one was in heaven. Out of grief came a yearning for heaven. "I never had this yearning before, but I do now," she says. "A piece of me is there. I now see in a much fuller way that this life is just a shadow of our real life—of eternal life in the presence of God."

The truth is, it often takes the death of a loved one to turn our thoughts to the brevity of this life and the promises of the next. Many of us have a good life here, and even if we don't have much, we generally think and live as if this life is all there is. We may believe in the promises of eternal life, but they seem very far off.

Our culture, with its medical breakthroughs and medications for every ailment, fights death at every turn. In fact, despite faith in heaven, believers are among those who go to extreme lengths to stay alive just one more week or one more month.

Guthrie admits that her fresh insights about grief have not entirely changed how she *feels*. And this is what we all face. We may believe, and we ask for more faith to believe—but our feelings may be stuck in grief.

Nancy challenges us to consider Eugene Peterson's translation of 2 Corinthians 5:5 in *The Message*: "We've been given a glimpse of the real thing, our true home, our resurrection bodies! The Spirit of God whets our appetite by giving us a taste of what's ahead. He puts a little of heaven in our hearts so that we'll never settle for less."

---

*Lord Jesus, wash away all dread I may feel about
leaving this life someday. Grant me glimpses of the
joy and glory ahead. Help me to live today with
a sense of your majesty and love and care.*

We are always confident, even though we know that as long as we live in these bodies we are not at home with the Lord. For we live by believing and not by seeing.
2 CORINTHIANS 5:6-7, NLT

CORRECTING THE OTHER GUY

August 15

THOMAS À KEMPIS advises that if someone is being stubborn, we shouldn't argue but commit the person and the issues to God, who knows how to bring good out of evil. "Strive to be patient," he writes, "bear with the faults and frailties of others since you have faults others must bear."

He then asks an interesting question: If we can't mold ourselves as we wish, how can we expect others to meet our expectations? We often fail at rooting out our own stubbornness or bad habits, and we want mercy from God and from others. Yet our tendency is to come down hard on others who fail. We want them to shape up or pay the consequences.

Always a keen observer of human nature, à Kempis notes that we don't want to be bound by rules, but we want others to be corrected and restricted. He then asks another interesting question: If all men were perfect, what should we have to bear with in others for Christ's sake?

He urges us to bear each others' burdens, for no one is free of burdens or faults. None of us in ourselves are wise enough or sufficient enough. "Therefore we must support each other, comfort, help, teach, and advise one another," he writes.

Bearing with others is more difficult in tough times, but that's the challenge we often face. "Times of trouble best discover our true worth and our true nature."

That's all the more reason in rugged times to call on the Lord, who alone is sufficient and will supply what we lack.

Father in heaven, you know those who frustrate me and make me react. Help me, Lord, to see them through your eyes. Help me to want the best for them because you love them as you love me.

Be joyful. Grow to maturity. Encourage each other. Live in harmony and peace. Then the God of love and peace will be with you. 2 CORINTHIANS 13:11, NLT

PRAISE IN TIMES OF HEARTACHE

August 16

JONI EARECKSON, a teenager in the hospital and paralyzed, was asked by a friend to do something she immediately refused to do.

The friend had read to her 1 Thessalonians 5:18: "Give thanks in all circumstances, for this is God's will for you in Christ Jesus" (NIV). He then said, "Joni, it's about time you got around to giving thanks in that wheelchair of yours."

Joni strongly objected. She hated her life. She couldn't understand how God had allowed her accident to happen. She had given up on prayer. She savored anger and resentment. She complained. Praise was the furthest thing from her mind.

Then her friend asked her to read the verse again.

"But I don't *feel* thankful."

"The verse doesn't say 'feel thankful.' It says 'give thanks.' There's a big difference."

Joni gritted her teeth and with tears found things to thank God for. It was a turning point. Giving thanks started changing her, until eventually she was able to express and feel gratitude.

In Hebrews 13:15 we're challenged to "continually offer to God a sacrifice of praise" (NIV). Just what is a "sacrifice of praise"?

Joni unpacks that rather puzzling phrase by pointing out that it was people enduring crushing difficulties who wrote the verses in the Bible calling for praise. The sacrifices of praise created new dynamics that made spiritual victories possible. These people praised God despite harrowing circumstances—even though complaints would have been much more natural.

Like these heroes of the faith, we're called to sacrifice our natural responses and give thanks anyway. And that generates gratitude in our souls.

If Joni as a quadriplegic could be transformed by giving thanks, it may give us some perspective in our own rugged circumstances.

"When I think of a sacrifice of praise," she says, "I think of the word *embrace*. Embracing the will of God, even when the feelings aren't there, is offering to God your heart."

Words of praise have a unique power. The times we least feel like expressing gratitude may be when we most need to.

Thank you, heavenly Father, for all your countless
blessings. Help me to live beyond my difficulties today
by praising you for your goodness and love and by
responding to the whispers of your Holy Spirit.

Let them offer sacrifices of thanksgiving and sing joyfully about his glorious acts.
PSALM 107:22, NLT

THE ADVENTUROUS LIFE

August 17

BROTHER LAWRENCE's writing is full of encouragements for those of us who struggle to experience the joy and the constant sense of God's presence. Here are a few examples:

> We shouldn't be discouraged by our sins. Simply pray for the Lord's grace with perfect confidence, relying on the infinite mercies of the Lord Jesus Christ. God never fails to offer us his grace.

> God gives us light in our doubt when we have no other design except to please him.

> God does not regard the greatness of the work but the love with which it is performed.

> The whole substance of religion is simply faith, hope, and love. By practicing these, we become united to the will of God.

> All things are possible to those who believe, hope, and love.

> Troubles, temptations, oppositions, and contradictions happen to us. We ought to bear them as long as God pleases, for they are highly advantageous to us.

His statement about our troubles being advantageous appears dead wrong. They never seem that way—until we have gone through them and looked back at what God did in the midst of them.

Brother Lawrence calls living this way an adventure and then concludes, "No other life in the world is as sweet and as delightful as the life lived in continual walk with God. The only ones who can comprehend it are those who have practiced and experienced it."

---

*Lord Jesus, I want to comprehend and experience your
adventure as Brother Lawrence describes it. By your
grace, let me practice faith, hope, and love. Give me
light in my doubt and strength in my weakness.*

---

*Praise the LORD! How joyful are those who fear the LORD and delight in obeying his
commands.* PSALM 112:1, NLT

CELEBRATE US?

ROSEMARY BUDD describes the father in Jesus' parable of the Prodigal Son as "too busy rejoicing" to be concerned about his son's past sins. "We come with our past, our stupidities, our pettiness, our daydreams," she says. "We come to be celebrated. God rejoices in us, his creation."

What a strange paradox! We come to God full of our anxieties and failures, but he is ready to celebrate. Most of us don't think of it that way. Yet God sees us in light of our redemption and the love he has poured out on us. He is fulfilling his purposes in each of our lives as we open ourselves to the Holy Spirit.

In unpacking Jesus' parable, she says the Father wants to run toward us with love "to pour out freely and to celebrate what he's creating. We have to allow our Father such a generosity, to rejoice in us not for anything we have carved out but because we are God's own creation."

Of course, when Budd says we must "allow" our Father to do this, she's simply saying that giving is a two-way street. As we allow someone to give us a stupendous gift without phony resistance, so we should celebrate this most bodacious gift of all and enjoy the celebration with the Giver.

When we think of standing before God with nervous thoughts about Jesus' descriptions of sheep and goats being judged, we might remember this celebration and what Jesus said to Nicodemus in that most familiar of Bible verses, John 3:16: "For God loved the world so much that he gave his one and only Son, so that everyone who believes in him will not perish but have eternal life" (NLT).

Rosemary urges us to believe and to open ourselves to celebration in ways we might not have previously imagined. "Look up at God. God delights in you. Let him enjoy you."

---

*Heavenly Father, sometimes it's easier for me to see myself
as the prodigal coming home to you in failure than to
see the festive nature of your embrace. Let me praise you
and rejoice in you, full of delight at your welcome.*

He led me to a place of safety; he rescued me because he delights in me.
PSALM 18:19, NLT

DESPERATE PRAYERS

KING DAVID in Psalm 34 says with joy and relief, "Let all who are helpless take heart. . . . I prayed to the LORD, and he answered me. He freed me from all my fears" (verses 2, 4, NLT).

As we read David's words, we may or may not identify with them. Perhaps we're not fearful or helpless—we have good skills and abilities or a stable family and connections. Yet if we're realistic, we know that things can happen to wipe away what we count on. Even if things continue to go well, eventually we grow to realize we simply can't live up to our own deepest intentions and desires.

It's when we hit bottom that prayer becomes essential—and the cause for joy. When we're self-sufficient, prayer can be something on the margins we keep trying to get around to. When we're fearful and helpless, we cling to it and find it sustains us.

David reports, "In my desperation I prayed, and the LORD listened; he saved me from all my troubles" (verse 6, NLT).

When we are desperate, the Lord listens to our prayers. Whatever our current situation, we need him, at all times, more than we might realize—and he is at all times ready to respond to us.

From his own experience, David records lots more encouragement in Psalm 34 for those who pray. Here's more:

Taste and see that the LORD is good. Oh, the joys of those who take refuge in him! (verse 8, NLT)

The eyes of the LORD watch over those who do right; his ears are open to their cries for help. (verse 15, NLT)

The LORD is close to the brokenhearted; he rescues those whose spirits are crushed. (verse 18, NLT)

Lord, you know my troubles. I lay all of them before you. Help me to do the right and wise things and to see your hand of mercy right now. Lead me into your ways of obedience and joy.

The angel of the LORD is a guard; he surrounds and defends all who fear him.
PSALM 34:7, NLT

BLESSED ARE THE HUNGRY?

HELMUT THIELICKE asks how Jesus in the Beatitudes could call the poor and suffering "blessed." Why single out the oppressed, hungry, and thirsty and say that they are blessed? Is this some form of irony?

Thielicke answers his own question by first pointing to the one who calls them blessed. Jesus is in the midst of the people, and if they are suffering, he has his own bitter cup to drink. He is among the poor and the homeless as one of them, extending his blessings to them.

Thielicke's second point is that by the Savior's sufferings and sacrifice, heaven has been opened to the poor and the suffering. Yes, they may be in dire straits, but Jesus has come to bring freedom to the captives and bread for the hungry—bread they do not know about. Those who have nothing can come with empty hands to have them filled by the Father.

Thielicke is not referring to hands empty of material things, but to the emptiness of life without the Father. In a brutal world, we suffer in countless ways from its unfairness, but we also suffer from our own sinfulness and spiritual rebellion. When we hit bottom and recognize our emptiness without God, we can come to him with open hands.

When we recognize our deep need, heaven is opened to us. We're urged to always be alert to see God's work in the world—as we live in prayerful expectation. "He who dares to live this way," Thielicke says, "will wait with the joyful expectancy of a child for the Father's surprises. God is always positive. He makes all things new."

We are not blessed because we're poor or because our dreams have gone up in smoke, but because heaven is opened to us through Christ. The Father's hand is stretched out to us, in this life and the next.

---

*Lord Jesus Christ, Son of God, have mercy on me, a
sinner. I come to you with all my emptiness. Please
fill me with your Holy Spirit and wake me up to your
surprises. Give me a sense of positive expectation.*

God blesses those who are merciful, for they will be shown mercy. MATTHEW 5:7, NLT

EXTREME LOVE

PHILIP YANCEY asks, "Why pray?" He then answers his own question: "Evidently, God likes to be asked. God certainly does not need our wisdom or our knowledge, nor even the information contained in our prayers. But by inviting us into the partnership of creation, God also invites us into relationship."

What a remarkable reassurance! We're told that "God is love" (1 John 4:8, 16, NLT), and we see the extreme expression of his love in sending his Son to redeem us. God is love, and God wants to be in a loving relationship with us. That's the ultimate foundation of our reason for praying.

A brief look into history or sociology reveals how the love of a parent has transformed children into inspirational leaders. Examples are legion. The extreme love of a mother or father empowers a daughter or son, providing identity and purpose. Great and wonderful things can happen.

If we truly grasp that we are loved by God—if we believe he loves us as a parent passionately loves a child—we receive identity and purpose. We embrace the relationship. Great and wonderful things can happen.

Why pray? We pray because God loves us.

God not only loves us but acts on our behalf. Yancey quotes Karl Barth: "He is not deaf, he listens; more than that, he acts. He does not act in the same way whether we pray or not. The fact that God yields to man's petitions, changing his intentions in response to man's prayer, is not a sign of weakness. He himself, in the glory of his majesty and power, has so willed it."

Father in heaven, it is surely very good news
that you love me. Help me, I pray, to sense that
deep within my soul. Let the reality of your love
embrace me and empower me to do your will.

You are the light of the world—like a city on a hilltop that cannot be hidden.
MATTHEW 5:14, NLT

THE SOURCE OF RICH JOY

OLE HALLESBY says that Jesus never tired of inviting, prompting, encouraging, and even commanding us to pray.

Jesus once said, "Apart from me you can do nothing" (John 15:5, NLT). Hallesby says of Jesus, "He knew how literally true these words are, how entirely helpless we are without him. But at the same time he said, 'Ask, and it shall be given you' [Matthew 7:7, KJV; Luke 11:9, KJV]. All that you need, and more besides."

Hallesby goes on to add other encouragement to pray from Jesus:

> Seek, and ye shall find; knock, and it shall be opened unto you: for every one that asketh receiveth; and he that seeketh findeth; and to him that knocketh it shall be opened. (Matthew 7:7-8, KJV)

> If ye abide in me, and my words abide in you, ye shall ask what ye will, and it shall be done unto you. (John 15:7, KJV)

Hallesby tells us that if he were to express what Jesus is saying, he would put it this way: "Come now, I am going with you all the way and will bring you safe home to heaven. If you ever get into trouble or difficulty, just tell me about it. I will give you, without reproach, everything you need, and more besides, day by day, as long as you live."

Jesus desires to answer our prayers graciously and abundantly. Since that's true, Hallesby says, our neglect of prayer grieves him. Of course, when we drift from prayer, we are the ones who ultimately lose out.

Hallesby concludes, "Prayer should be the means by which I, at all times, receive all that I need and, for this reason, be my daily refuge, my daily consolation, my source of rich and inexhaustible joy in life."

Lord Jesus, I want to have the rich and rewarding
prayer life that you describe. Help me in my
weakness to continually open the door of my heart
to you and to share all my concerns and hopes.

O God, you know how foolish I am; my sins cannot be hidden from you. Don't let those who trust in you be ashamed because of me. PSALM 69:5-6, NLT

THE ULTIMATE INVITATION

BILLY GRAHAM describes Jesus' invitation in Revelation 3 as the most beautiful and powerful in the Bible: "Look! I stand at the door and knock. If you hear my voice and open the door, I will come in, and we will share a meal together as friends" (Revelation 3:20, NLT).

Billy calls this invitation "these wonderful words" and urges us not to miss out on our remarkable opportunity to spend time with Jesus. "He is waiting to enjoy a meal with us, waiting to share our sorrows, to renew our courage. We are not alone."

At the same time, Graham is well aware that Jesus says in Revelation 3:19, "I correct and discipline everyone I love. So be diligent and turn from your indifference. (NLT). Elsewhere in his Revelation messages to the seven churches, Jesus threatens severe retributions.

The risen Christ in Revelation is not only the gentle, loving dinner companion, he is also the Lamb of God who evokes awe, with millions of angels and other celestial beings singing, "Worthy is the Lamb who was slaughtered—to receive power and riches and wisdom and strength. . . . Blessing and honor and glory and power belong to the one sitting on the throne and to the Lamb forever and ever" (Revelation 5:12-13, NLT).

This full-orbed view of Jesus is consistent with what we see of him in the Gospels. Throughout his years of ministry, he showed great compassion, healing the sick, loving children, and weeping over Jerusalem. At the same time, he was outraged by hypocrisy and prideful religion; he resisted evil in resolute unity with his Father.

The holy God who is beyond our imaginations and the loving Savior who knocks at the door of our hearts—both are the one we worship and praise, the one we invite in as we hear him knocking.

Lord Jesus Christ, purify me by your Holy Spirit and forgive my sins. Purge me of all that would incur your wrath, and let me welcome you into my heart and soul to truly be your friend.

Jesus said, "Come to me, all of you who are weary and carry heavy burdens, and I will give you rest." MATTHEW 11:28, NLT

LIGHT AND DARK

A. W. TOZER observes, "Most of us go through life praying a little, planning a little, hoping but never certain of anything, and secretly afraid that we'll miss the way."

If that describes our outlook on life, Tozer urges us instead to "believe actively" that our heavenly Father is providing for us in ways that bring blessings to our souls. We want to see ahead and we worry about what's coming. Yet when through earnest prayer we exchange our natural concerns for trust in God's care, we breathe a sigh of relief. We won't miss his best if we place our worries in his hands.

We find many promises of God's guidance and care in the Scriptures. For instance, the Amplified Bible translates portions of Isaiah 42:16 and 45:2 this way: "I will bring the blind by a way that they know not; I will lead them in paths that they have not known. I will make darkness into light before them and make uneven places into a plain. . . . I will go before you and level the mountains [to make the crooked places straight]."

This is the intention God has toward his people who call on him and who follow him. What's ahead for each of us? As we move into the future with what Tozer calls "active believing," God illuminates the way.

Jesus says in John 8:12, "I am the light of the world. If you follow me, you won't have to walk in darkness, because you will have the light that leads to life" (NLT).

Paul declares in Ephesians 1:18, "I pray that your hearts will be flooded with light so that you can understand the confident hope he has given to those he called" (NLT).

Our circumstances may be dark, and our faith may be dim. But we ask the Lord to light our pathway one step at a time. Tozer says this is always the challenge as we face our troubles: "God constantly encourages us to trust him in the dark."

Lord, I trust you, for you have been faithful in so many ways.
Help me to pray and trust even more so that my confidence
in you is strong and I can help others to trust in your care.

Your word is a lamp to guide my feet and a light for my path. PSALM 119:105, NLT

GOD AS THE BANK

GEORGE MACDONALD had significant health issues and struggled financially. He wrote in his diary, "My harvest withers. Health, my income to life—all things seem rushing straight into the dark."

Many experience that numbing reality. We may have worked hard and tried to do all the right things, but then circumstances beyond our control dramatically change. Perhaps our income withers. To cope, we listen to financial advice and read Proverbs and focus on finding a wise path. But when no path is visible and we run out of options and money, we face grim choices.

Those are the times our faith is tested. We understand that God does not always answer our prayers with solutions. We learn that many other believers have endured hard circumstances.

In those times, with desperation rising in our hearts, we're driven to earnest prayer. We hope for tangible "answers," but as we go through difficult times, we often find that the answers to our prayers are seen more in a deepening of our faith and understanding. We learn to abide in Christ through the storms.

MacDonald believed that, despite his feelings of paralysis about money, God was there for him in the dark. "Am I not a spark of him who is the light?" he asked. "Thy will be done."

He then savored the words of Jesus that life is more than meat and clothes or even health. "Thou art my life," MacDonald prayed, "I the brook, thou the spring. Thou art my life, my health, my bank—and from all other gods you plainly warn."

Father in heaven, you are the Source of all that sustains
me. Pour into my heart faith that your love is unfailing
and that you will provide for me, in your time and
in your way. Help me to persevere and believe.

LORD, sustain me as you promised, that I may live! Do not let my hope be crushed.
PSALM 119:116, NLT

THE BELOVED CHILD

RAY STEDMAN asserts that a child outranks ambassadors, governors, or members of the president's Cabinet.

He tells the story of a time when Abraham Lincoln was in a crucial meeting with his Cabinet and someone knocked on the door. There stood Willy, the president's ten-year-old son, wanting to see his father. Lincoln excused himself from the meeting to find out what his boy wanted.

Biographies of other U.S. presidents reveal similar examples.

"Willy outranked all the others," Stedman says. "This is the truth Paul is trying to bring to our hearts—we have access to the King who has authority and power in the world."

The apostle Paul declares, "You are members of God's family" and "You are his dear children" (Ephesians 2:19; 5:1, NLT).

Just as any father's beloved child, we can come to God with our needs and concerns. We know that not only will he listen, but as our heavenly Father he will act in our best interests.

In Luke 18:15-17, we read a familiar story that further assures us of our welcome when we come to God as his children:

> One day some parents brought their little children to Jesus so he could touch and bless them. But when the disciples saw this, they scolded the parents for bothering him.
>
> Then Jesus called for the children and said to the disciples, "Let the children come to me. Don't stop them! For the Kingdom of God belongs to those who are like these children. I tell you the truth, anyone who doesn't receive the Kingdom of God like a child will never enter it." (NLT)

Jesus also says, "Keep on asking, and you will receive what you ask for. Keep on seeking, and you will find. Keep on knocking, and the door will be opened to you. For everyone who asks, receives. Everyone who seeks, finds. And to everyone who knocks, the door will be opened. . . . If you sinful people know how to give good gifts to your children, how much more will your heavenly Father give good gifts to those who ask him" (Matthew 7:7-8, 11, NLT).

Father in heaven, help me to ask for the right things
and to be so in step with your Spirit that you are
delighted to answer me. Let me praise you and thank
you for all the gifts that come from your hand.

I pray with all my heart; answer me, LORD! I will obey your decrees.
PSALM 119:145, NLT

GREATER THAN THE GRAND CANYON *August 27*

BEN PATTERSON tells two stories that illustrate how we should view every person, because they are made in the image of God:

In the fifth grade, Ben was determined to beat up a boy named Dennis, and he had told Dennis just when he would do it. But as he walked to school the next morning, he saw Dennis and his father getting out of their car. The dad knelt to give his son a hug. He kissed the boy on the cheek, ran his hand playfully over his head, and then drove away.

Ben says he was forced to see Dennis through his father's eyes. He was his dad's son, precious and beloved.

Many years later, Ben was at the Grand Canyon with his own son. They were dazzled by the Canyon's grandeur, and his son spoke of how it showed God's glory. But Ben said there was something there that showed God's glory even better than the Grand Canyon. He pointed to his son and said, "There is no canyon or river or mountain or ocean that better shows the majesty of God than you."

How can we possibly think that we are grander than the Grand Canyon? Obviously, each of us is just one of billions of humans on the planet, and we often seem to disgrace God's creation rather than enhance it. Yet, we are eternal! When the canyons and rivers and oceans are gone, we will still be praising God for his continuing creativity and joy. As the Scriptures put it, the Almighty has knit us together in the womb, and he has made us in his image.

Ben says, "To see yourself in this way is to be humbled and dazzled by the God who made you. Thank God for yourself and for the mystery and depth of your neighbor. Look at yourself in the mirror and say out loud to God, 'I praise you for I am fearfully and wonderfully made.'"

---

*Father and Creator, I don't always feel wonderfully made,
but I realize that I am when I learn about my body and
the complexities of my being. Help me to praise you and to
pray for all others, because they are made in your image.*

The LORD delights in his people; he crowns the humble with victory. Let the faithful rejoice that he honors them. Let them sing for joy as they lie on their beds.
PSALM 149:4-5, NLT

CHEER UP AND BE FREE

FRED SMITH, always practical, observes, "Grace was genuine, real, personal, and palpable to the great saints. Brother Lawrence, Frank Laubach, François Fénelon—these Christian mystics never doubted they were the constant recipients of God's amazing grace. Grace was a practical part of their everyday lives."

We usually think of grace as a theological term or as a reassurance found in hymns of the faith. But when we genuinely believe in and embrace God's grace, it has very practical effects.

For instance, Fred Smith found it freeing to read that Brother Lawrence spent no time worrying about mistakes but confessed them and moved on. Prior to reading that, Smith had been trapped by guilt, feeling that immediate grace was too good to be true.

Steve Brown, in responding to Smith's insights about grace, provides a definition: "Grace is doing good for someone when there is no compelling reason to do so and every reason not to."

That's the biblical picture of God's actions on our behalf. His love is what moves him to do good for us, and he is not looking down from heaven ready to smack us for every infraction.

Smith cautions that we often see negative events as punishments rather than simply consequences. "We feel we deserve judgment rather than grace," he says. "Grace brings freedom. Grace cannot be deserved. If we accept grace fully then we, like Brother Lawrence, have the freedom to admit failure and move on."

We are called to holiness and obedience, yet we are prone to wander. God's grace is greater than our wanderings and failures.

Steve Brown often quotes this audacious, puckish statement: "Cheer up, you're a lot worse than you think you are. Cheer up, God's grace is a lot bigger than you think it is."

> *Amazing grace, how sweet the sound,*
> *that saved a wretch like me.*
> *I once was lost, but now am found,*
> *was blind but now I see.*

Heavenly Father, thank you for your grace and love. Thank you for your forgiveness. Cleanse me now and enable me to live today full of your grace and willing to extend grace to others.

Just as sin ruled over all people and brought them to death, now God's wonderful grace rules instead. ROMANS 5:21, NLT

FROM BONDAGE TO FREEDOM

D. L. MOODY, as a young man ministering in England, was electrified when he heard evangelist Henry Varley state, "The world has yet to see what God will do with and for and through and in and by the man who is fully and wholly consecrated to him."

The words jolted and inspired Moody. He was poorly educated, with many limitations. He mused, *Varley said "a man." He did not say a great man, nor a learned man, nor a rich man, nor a wise man, nor an eloquent man. I am a man, and it lies with the man himself whether he will or will not make that entire and full consecration. I will try my uttermost to be that man.*

Try to his uttermost he did. He considered his firm commitment a core element of his remarkable ministry. He said he considered it a "sweet lesson" to learn to surrender his will to God and to let him plan and rule his life. "I cannot look a day into the future," Moody writes. "I cannot choose for myself as well as God can choose for me."

Moody learned what many have found: that letting God rule over us is not a limitation but the very best kind of freedom. God gives us purpose and direction, and the more fully we commit ourselves to him, the more fully he can work in and through us to bring the joy that Jesus promised.

Yet it's no simple, easy formula. Moody admitted that the hardest thing was getting to the end of himself—a lifelong process.

On this subject, François Fénelon and D. L. Moody were on the same page. Fénelon writes candidly of the bondage of the self, with all its anxieties and doubts. Like Moody, Fénelon points to breaking free to the blessings that come from total commitment. "The comfort that comes from knowing you're in God's hands is inexhaustible," he declares. "When you're in God's care, nothing else matters. How blessed you are when you're cut off from your own will to follow God's will."

Lord, help me to want your will more than my own, and then open my eyes day by day and hour by hour to see just what your will is for me. Help me to open myself to your Spirit's guidance.

Let me live forever in your sanctuary, safe beneath the shelter of your wings! For you have heard my vows, O God. You have given me an inheritance reserved for those who fear your name. PSALM 61:4-5, NLT

AVOID THE ABSURD

HENRY NOUWEN pondered this paradox of the spiritual life: it's at once a wonderful gift God gives us, yet we must work hard at it. The Holy Spirit lifts us, says Nouwen, "into the kingdom of God's love, yet forces keep pulling us back into a worry-filled life."

Because of this struggle, we are called to the discipline of constantly listening for the quiet voice of the Spirit, and then to the commitment to obey that voice.

Noise of all sorts in our crowded lives can make us deaf to God's voice. The danger is if we don't detect the nudges and whispers of the Holy Spirit, our lives may become what Nouwen calls "absurd," based on the Latin word for "deaf," *surdus.*

Absurd is a relevant word for modern times. Countless plays, books, and movies depict our lives as Shakespeare described them: "full of sound and fury, signifying nothing"—in a word, absurd.

Jesus, in stark contrast, lived a life of extreme significance. Far from living as if he were deaf, Jesus maintained constant communion with his Father. He was always listening and always obedient. He was fully in harmony with his Father's will.

If we are not in harmony with God, what is the meaning of all our efforts? What does it matter if our plans thrive or fail? Only as we listen for the voice of the Spirit do we sense that everything matters and that we are part of something far beyond what can be measured by the world's standards.

"Jesus was 'all ear,'" writes Henri Nouwen. "That is true prayer: being all ear for God."

Father in heaven, to be honest, I often do seem deaf.
Yet, I want to hear your voice. Right now I invite you
to whisper or shout or do whatever it takes to get me to
hear you. And help me, I pray, to respond and obey.

Search for the LORD and for his strength; continually seek him.   PSALM 105:4, NLT

THE OTHER SIDE OF JESUS

OSWALD CHAMBERS writes, "There is an aspect of Jesus that chills the heart of a disciple to the core and makes the whole spiritual life gasp for breath. This strange Being with his face 'set like flint' and his striding determination strikes terror into me. He is no longer Counselor and Comrade. He is taken up with a point of view I know nothing about, and I am amazed at him."

Chambers writes this in connection with the drama of Mark 10, which includes this story:

> They were now on the way up to Jerusalem, and Jesus was walking ahead of them. The disciples were filled with awe, and the people following behind were overwhelmed with fear. Taking the twelve disciples aside, Jesus once more began to describe everything that was about to happen to him. "Listen," he said, "we're going up to Jerusalem, where the Son of Man will be betrayed. . . . [The priests and teachers of religious law] will sentence him to die. . . . They will mock him, spit on him, flog him with a whip, and kill him, but after three days he will rise again." (verses 32-34, NLT)

Hearing what Jesus said must have been overwhelming. Yet James and John seemed oblivious. In fact, they chose that very moment to ask Jesus for a favor—and a self-centered one at that. When you come into power, they asked, would you please give us the places of highest honor? When Jesus asked if they could suffer what he was about to suffer, they said yes.

Their response reminds us of adolescents wearing T-shirts with images of a smiling Jesus. Do they know anything about his being more than buddy and best friend? Do they know what's ahead? Sometimes we're like James and John, not concerned with Jesus' agenda but wanting him to give us what we want.

Chambers talks about our feeling distant from this strange being with the steely resolve. "Jesus Christ had to fathom every sin and every sorrow man could experience. When we see him in this aspect we do not know him, and we do not know how to begin to follow him."

He then gives us something to ponder: "The discipline of dismay is essential in the life of discipleship."

Lord, help me to "get it." Engage me in your agenda, not mine. Open my eyes to what you want me to think and do, and then put within me the capacity to see clearly and to obey.

Whoever wants to be a leader among you must be your servant. MARK 10:43, NLT

"THE COMING CRISIS"

JOHN HENRY JOWETT, pondering the promise of Jesus that in the hour of disaster his peace will be given, declares, "And so I am not to worry about the coming crisis!"

"The coming crisis." Sometimes we wonder what dreadful things could be ahead. Whatever they may be, we are urged not to worry.

Jesus said a great deal about not worrying, even though he predicted terrible things to come. In the past hundred years, horrific crises have afflicted the world and torn people's lives apart. Right now, plenty of disasters loom, and the media stand ready to tell us about them. We dread what might happen not only to us but to our loved ones and our neighbors, to communities and churches, and throughout the world.

The song says, "What a friend we have in Jesus, all our sins and griefs to bear." Yet it also laments, "Oh what needless pain we bear, . . . all because we do not carry everything to God in prayer."

Jowett assures us that no matter what happens, God will be with us. "We irritate and excite our souls about the coming emergency, and we approach it with worn and feverish spirits. When the crisis comes, he will tell me what to do.

"The orders are not given until the appointed day. Why should I fume and fret and worry as to what the sealed envelope contains? 'It is enough that he knows all,' and when the hour strikes the secrets shall be revealed."

Father in heaven, the news is full of dire predictions. Here are all my worries. Please take them and grant me your peace and comfort and the confidence of your Holy Spirit.

Christ has brought us into this place of undeserved privilege where we now stand, and we confidently and joyfully look forward to sharing God's glory. We can rejoice, too, when we run into problems and trials, for we know that they help us develop endurance.
ROMANS 5:2-3, NLT

GRACE

JAY KESLER admits that he once thought God loved him for his performance. He says we tend to judge people and their worth by what they do. If on a plane we meet a stranger who says he's a janitor, we think of him differently than we would the president of a prestigious organization.

"God does not see people like that," Jay says. "He made us with intrinsic worth."

That means it's all about grace. We have the assurance of God's grace, and we gain new appreciation for how God views the weak and the foolish among us. God loves everyone—top performers and failures, the disciplined and the self-indulgent. God knows we're all full of both contradictions and potential.

God's grace and love for the world also frees us to leave its crushing tragedies in his hands. We are called to be instruments of his love and peace, but at the same time we cannot fix the world on our own, and we need not feel that everything depends on us.

We must let God be God.

Kesler emphasizes that God's grace frees us from our ego problems and enables us to take risks. "I had expected this idea of grace to make me feel lower, less worthy," he says. "But something marvelous happened. Along with the realization of my human-ness came a flooding, cleansing experience of God's forgiveness. I was loved! I didn't have to be constantly rescuing the world. God is awake and at work. Finally I could rest from trying to be God and let him love me."

Lord, help me not to presume on your grace but to receive it with both joy and sober responsibility. Help me to see others as you see them and to be a channel for your grace to flow into their lives.

Not to us, O LORD, not to us, but to your name goes all the glory for your unfailing love and faithfulness. PSALM 115:1, NLT

HOW TO RUIN EVERYTHING

MARTIN LUTHER expressed great doubts about his capacity to handle all the challenges before him. Although he was a bishop and a pastor, he prayed, "You see how unsuited I am to meet so great and difficult a task. Without your help, I would have ruined everything long ago."

We all know Luther had great capacities, yet he was intensely aware of his weaknesses. He didn't view as abstract theologies the apostle Paul's descriptions of our warring natures and our tendencies to break our resolutions. He understood in a visceral way that those descriptions applied to him personally.

Do we have the same sensitivity Luther had? Is it natural for us to realize that without God's help we'd have ruined everything?

If we do realize our limitations, good. In fact, very good! We need to understand that, on our own, we're dangerous. We're perhaps clever or greatly gifted, but at the same time we're ineffective. Oh, we might be *efficient*, but on our own we're not *effective* in our call to serve the Lord and fulfill his purposes.

How did Luther handle his sense of weakness and looming failure? He made a firm commitment to devote his mouth and heart to God.

"I shall teach the people," he said. "I myself will learn and diligently ponder your Word. Use me as your instrument—but do not forsake me, for if ever I should be on my own, I would easily wreck it all."

Only when we know that we could wreck everything if left to our own devices will we understand and experience what Paul was saying: "I can do all things through Christ who strengthens me" (Philippians 4:13, NKJV).

Father above, more and more I see that my need for you is greater than ever. Help me to see my strengths and gifts from your perspective and to open myself to your power and grace.

Who can be compared with the LORD our God, who is enthroned on high? . . . He lifts the poor from the dust and the needy from the garbage dump. PSALM 113:5, 7, NLT

CHILD WONDER

OSWALD CHAMBERS gives us this warning: "Beware of posing as a profound person; God became a baby."

Chambers is pointing out that the simple things of life, our daily tasks and eating and drinking, are ordained of God and that we have to live in "a common-sense way." He cautions us not to be intent on impressing others. He also urges us to be so engaged with the Lord that we live with a sense of "child wonder."

When we pray to our heavenly Father as Jesus taught, we come as his children. No matter how educated, savvy, or experienced, we come with child wonder at his creation, at his redemption, and at what he may do next in our lives. We ask for the Father to unfold his will all through the day, and we look for his surprises.

Child wonder. Child expectations. Child trust. We have a heavenly Father, and no matter what our age or circumstance, we come to him best as his children—with open hands and obedient hearts.

Chambers says that Jesus never worked from his own viewpoint but always that of his Father. With childlike faith, we ask the Father to educate us, to reveal his viewpoint about all that's coming at us. We equally need his perspective about all the consternation and turmoil that may be going on within our minds and souls.

"Bring your imagination into captivity to the obedience of Christ," Chambers advises. He says that in spiritual matters, when we rely on our own wisdom, we don't see clearly. How do we clear up the fog? He says simply, "When we see like children."

Father in heaven, I come to you in simplicity as your child. Thank you for your love and care for me and for my loved ones. Help me to be full of expectations that you will be visiting me today in new and fresh ways.

You are all children of God through faith in Christ Jesus. GALATIANS 3:26, NLT

SHERWOOD WIRT declares, "If Jesus wept, he also laughed."

Wirt strongly objects to burying our Lord's sense of humor "in the sludge of religious sobriety so often mistaken for reverence. Jesus' memorable sallies were forever bobbing to the surface in the sacred writings."

What is he talking about? Woody comes up with quite a list.

For example, Jesus described the teachers of the law as straining out a gnat and swallowing a camel. He said it was easier for a camel to walk through the eye of a needle than for a rich man to enter the Kingdom of God.

Jesus described religious leaders washing the outside of their cups with care but leaving the inside dirty. He warned against trying to pick a speck of dirt out of someone else's eye when you have a plank in your own eye, and against casting pearls before swine. He talked of the blind leading the blind, dead people burying dead people, picking figs off a thistle bush, and hiding a lamp under a bed.

Jesus' humor obviously had a bite to it and made sharp points. Yet Woody maintains that Jesus' humor was rooted in the joy of heaven. His warmth toward children probably included gentle humor, and his back and forth with the woman who said that even puppies get to eat the crumbs under the table was likely repartee with a smile.

What does all this mean to us? Wirt quotes Elton Trueblood: "If Christ laughed a great deal, as the evidence shows, and if he is what he claimed to be, we cannot avoid the logical conclusion that there is laughter and gaiety in the heart of God."

Father in heaven, let my laughter have you as its source,
and let it always please you. Help me to always be aware
of the plank in my own eye before probing for someone
else's speck. Bring your joy and laughter into my life.

You thrill me, LORD, with all you have done for me! I sing for joy because of what you have done. PSALM 92:4, NLT

CHOOSING HOPE

LEWIS SMEDES chose a provocative subtitle for his book *Standing on the Promises*: "Keeping Hope Alive for a Tomorrow We Cannot Control."

The seeds for the book were sown after the 1992 riots in Los Angeles, when Smedes was led "from charred ruin to charred ruin, from burned-out hope to burned-out hope, each sad scene seducing closer to the gully of despair." A few weeks later, while driving, Smedes was jolted by seeing above him a brilliant billboard above Airport Boulevard with three words in arresting red: "KEEP HOPE ALIVE."

To the L.A. residents with burned-out homes and businesses, despair often trumped hope. Anyone who has endured the tragic consequences of a degenerating culture and incessant world crises knows that hopelessness is a tempting option. But it doesn't have to be that way.

Smedes asks, "Why do some people always abound in hope and others always slouch to despair? How can we become more hopeful persons? How can we keep on hoping when our fondest hopes crash on the rugged edges of tragedy?"

The apostle Paul, who himself experienced plenty of tragedy, was one who always abounded in hope. We see how he confronted disaster with irrepressible hope when he wrote to the Romans, "We can rejoice, too, when we run into problems and trials, for we know that they help us develop endurance. And endurance develops strength of character, and character strengthens our confident hope of salvation" (Romans 5:3-4, NLT). He went on to say, "Rejoice in our confident hope. Be patient in trouble, and keep on praying" (Romans 12:12, NLT).

Though in deep trouble, Paul emphasized hope.

Smedes says, "Choosing to keep on struggling against despair and to keep on choosing for hope—this is to take responsibility to write our life story empowered by hope."

Lord, you know it's often hard for me to feel hopeful.
More and more I realize I can't create my own hope! It
comes only from you. Help me get my eyes off my troubles
and onto your grace and compassion for others.

The Scriptures give us hope and encouragement as we wait patiently for God's promises to be fulfilled. . . . I pray that God, the source of hope, will fill you completely with joy and peace because you trust in him. ROMANS 15:4, 13, NLT

THE BELOVED VOICE

HENRI NOUWEN, in his lifelong spiritual quest, came to a conclusion that should powerfully draw us toward prayer. He defined prayer as listening to the voice of the one who calls us the beloved.

We are always eager to hear the voice of a loved one who passionately considers us to be his or her beloved. Whether a parent, spouse, sibling, child, or dearest friend, when we hear from one full of love for us, we respond with warmth, joy, and a powerful sense of privileged identity.

What a thought, that God would call us his beloved! And, Nouwen would insist, what a reality.

Yet we wonder—is God really like people here on earth who love us the most?

We're told in Scripture that God is love and that God so loved the world that he sent his only Son to redeem it. Jesus said to his disciples that the mark of their belonging to him was their love, which flowed from him to them.

Nouwen emphasized that God is love, that we are God's beloved, and that in prayer we constantly claim our spiritual identity.

Yet it's not merely an emotional rush. The discipline of prayer is daily going back to hear God's voice and respond to it.

"I've said it often that prayer is listening with obedience," Nouwen writes. "Jesus listens with obedience to the Father, he keeps listening to the Father's affirmation. Prayer doesn't mean that you have loving, tender feelings as you listen to God's voice. Sometimes you do and sometimes you don't. Prayer is a discipline."

Discipline includes work; to receive the benefits of prayer, we must pray intentionally, whether we feel like it or not, whether it's satisfying or not. We go to our place of solitude, or we lift our hearts to God in our busyness, and we claim our identity as God's beloved children.

Yes, but *how* do we do that? Henri suggests that we repeat each day the words Jesus heard from heaven at his baptism: "You are my beloved. With you I am well pleased."

Father in heaven, I'm not at all sure you're pleased
with me, but repeating what Jesus heard makes me
want to please you and receive your love. Help me
today to rejoice and to hear and obey your Spirit.

Those who accept my commandments and obey them are the ones who love me. And because they love me, my Father will love them. And I will love them and reveal myself to each of them. JOHN 14:21, NLT

UP FROM FAILURE

JILL BRISCOE admits that, early in her Christian life, she was a bit cocky about her capacity to stay true to the Lord. After all, hadn't he promised his power to help her obey? Yet over the years she found many occasions when she needed to confess her failures, and she saw many other Christians fail as well. She came to the conclusion that, "at some point in our lives, we all fall flat on our faces."

Because that's true, she calls for daily confession and cleansing, as described in Isaiah's experience when he cried out, "I am a man of unclean lips" (Isaiah 6:5, NIV). He then received cleansing from the altar of God.

Jill reminds us a primary reason for failure is that we're up against a wily, powerful enemy. Jesus told Simon Peter that Satan wanted to sift him like wheat. Peter later wrote that the devil prowls around like a roaring lion looking for someone to devour. Peter had learned all about his own failures and what had caused him to deny Christ.

Though we may fall prey to some of Satan's attacks, Jill assures us that the Lord uses these sifting experiences in our lives. "God's answer to the reality that we *will* fail him from time to time is to turn our failures around. Satan is limited. God and Satan are not beings of equal force battling over my soul."

At the same time, identifying our malicious foe and his devious tactics may persuade us to pray more and to call upon our Advocate, the Holy Spirit.

Jill concludes, "Jesus wants us to know he gives us the freedom to fail and also the faith to pick ourselves up, dust ourselves off, and try again. And this will probably go on until eventually we see him as he is and be like him."

Lord, I get discouraged when I fail to keep my commitments to you. I pray today that, when I'm blindsided by the devil's subtle lures or tempted to ignore you, you will fill me with your Holy Spirit.

See how very much our Father loves us, for he calls us his children, and that is what we are! I JOHN 3:1, NLT

TWO VOICES

FRANÇOIS FÉNELON writes that within every person is a "vain, complaining babbler—self-love." He tells us we can identify it because it "always wants to entertain itself and never feels sufficiently attended to."

He adds, "I beg you not to listen. Self-love whispers in one ear and the love of God in the other."

Whatever the image before us—a holy angel on one shoulder and a demon on the other, or warring voices within us—we all know the truth of Fénelon's words. The self, he says, is grasping and impulsive, whereas the love of God is peaceful and simple. When we listen to the self, we no longer hear the whispering of the Spirit.

This tension, this constant choosing whom we'll listen to and what we will do, is the lifetime dynamic of determining to love God despite all the distractions and temptations.

We contend, of course, not only with self-love, but also with the evil tempter, who entices us with his crafty allurements and rationalizations. "Your sins are not really so bad," the devil insists, "and you deserve this . . ."

Fénelon says that our spiritual success depends not on our emotional intensity but on the direction of our wills—which we must give to God without reservation. "Love him more than yourself," he advises. Yet, in saying that, he is realistic enough to know that it doesn't come easy. Self keeps up its babbling.

So what are we to do? Only God can give us the love for him we must have.

We continually turn to the Lord in prayer. As we ask for his love to replace our self-love, Fénelon predicts, "He will pour out upon you that special peace only his children know."

---

*Lord Jesus Christ, be merciful to me and grant me
alertness and grace to hear your Spirit's whispers and
to reject all others. Help me to respond with joy to your
guidance and welcome your control of my life.*

Everyone who sins is breaking God's law, for all sin is contrary to the law of God. And you know that Jesus came to take away our sins. I JOHN 3:4-5, NLT

VAGABOND KING

EUGENE PETERSON describes the life of Jesus this way: "He talked like a king and acted like a slave."

Jesus indeed talked like a king. He said he could call down legions of angels. He declared that he and his Father were one. He said he had come to free the captives. Yet he washed his disciples' feet.

Peterson adds, "He preached with high authority and lived like a vagabond."

What Would Jesus Do? Though the question has been somewhat trivialized by its use as a bracelet and T-shirt slogan, it nonetheless strikes at the heart of what is essential in our following Jesus Christ.

What *did* Jesus do? If he had the power to call down angels and conquer Rome or to do whatever he wished, why did he act like a slave and a vagabond? Instead of taking the opportunities to conquer and control, he purposely passed them all by.

What was his strategy?

Jesus was very clear that his will and his actions were in tune with his heavenly Father's. In fact, he said he could do nothing without the Father. What did Jesus do? He prayed to the Father—and we can do the same.

If we want to know what Jesus would do in our circumstances, we should first do what he did—fervently pray to our Father in heaven. We should share our concerns, confess our dependence, and seek his guidance.

Will the Father guide us to great success? Perhaps. But maybe he will guide us to a success unrecognized by the world or by our friends. We may find that our success looks more like the success that Jesus had—in self-sacrifice, concern for others, and obedience to God the Father.

Heavenly Father, so many times I wonder what I should do. Help me now to listen intently to what your Spirit is saying. Give me the strength and courage to act on what you command and to share your love.

Just as Christ was raised from the dead by the glorious power of the Father, now we also may live new lives. ROMANS 6:4, NLT

BE NOT DISMAYED

September 11

BILLY GRAHAM, addressing the nation from the National Cathedral after the tragedy of September 11, 2001, quoted Psalm 46:1-2: "God is our refuge and strength, an ever-present help in trouble. Therefore we will not fear, though the earth give way and the mountains fall into the heart of the sea" (NIV). At that critical hour, Graham's message of hope reached millions around the world. Here are some brief excerpts of his remarks:

> I've been asked hundreds of times why God allows tragedy and suffering. I have to confess I don't know the answer totally. . . . I . . . accept by faith that God is sovereign, and he is a God of love and mercy and compassion in the midst of suffering.

> The Bible . . . speaks of evil as a "mystery." In 2 Thessalonians 2:7, it talks about the mystery of iniquity. The Old Testament prophet Jeremiah said, "The heart is deceitful above all things and beyond cure. Who can understand it?" He asked that question, "Who can understand it?" And that is one reason we need God in our lives.

> Difficult as it may be for us to see right now, this event can give a message of hope. . . . Here in this majestic National Cathedral we see all around us the symbols of the Cross. For the Christian, . . . the Cross tells us that God understands our sin and our suffering, for he took them upon himself in the person of Jesus Christ. . . . And from the Cross, God declares, "I love you. I know the heartaches and the sorrows and the pains that you feel. But I love you."

> The story does not end with the Cross, for Easter points us beyond the tragedy of the Cross to the empty tomb that tells us that there is hope for eternal life, for Christ has conquered evil and death, and hell. Yes, there is hope.

Father in heaven, Billy Graham is right when he says the deep tragedies are a mystery we can't fully understand. Thank you for entering our world of dark mystery to redeem it. Help me to live in your hope today.

Jesus [said], "I am the resurrection and the life. Anyone who believes in me will live, even after dying." JOHN 11:25, NLT

THE FATHER-SMILE

OLE HALLESBY presents us with a paradox: "Many believers pray for the fullness of the Spirit, but receive instead a fullness of *sinfulness*. And they do not see that this is a fulfillment of their prayer."

What could he possibly mean by that?

Hallesby points out that Jesus told us the Spirit would convict us of sin. He sees *a sensitive conscience* as a sure sign of the fullness of the Spirit.

When we're aware of our impurity and lack of holiness, we hunger for grace and turn to God for cleansing. Yet this is not a onetime thing. Hallesby cautions us to be realistic about our condition. Old habits do not die easily. We may have a tender conscience that helps us see our temptations for what they are, yet we still at times suffer defeat.

God gives grace to the humble and to the helpless. He cleanses and encourages us as we pray without ceasing. Sometimes we are wounded in battle or make foolish decisions. The Spirit is always there to cleanse and heal and to enable us to overcome temptation.

For those who may be discouraged at their progress as spiritual warriors, Hallesby says that God accepts us as his children not because we are holy, pure, and spiritual, but because—when our hearts condemn us and we don't know what else to do—we come in confession and repentance to Jesus Christ.

When we come, we are welcomed. Hallesby paints a wonderful picture to illustrate this point: "God's kindly Father-smile shines upon you in your daily life every time he looks at you. Thank him, both for his love, and for his smile!"

Lord, thank you that no matter what is happening in
my life, I can come to you as your child. Help me to sense
your smile when I'm feeling less like your obedient child
and more like a prodigal. Cleanse me and bring me joy.

If your instructions hadn't sustained me with joy, I would have died in my misery.
I will never forget your commandments, for by them you give me life.
PSALM 119:92-93, NLT

THE ULTIMATE MEANING

PAUL TOURNIER declares that God is a terrific inventor and that we should realize he's interested in everything—not just religion.

Of course, that's obvious when we think about it. After all, God is the one who thought up all the fine-tuned intricacies and far-flung galaxies of the universe. Talk about brilliance, creativity, and attention to detail!

Tournier adds that God's adventure of creation is also characterized by coherence and a sense of purpose. He tells of a colleague who was converted by reading Arnold Toynbee's *Civilization on Trial*. The book made the man realize that events move in irreversible progression, and it put a stark choice before him. Either everything was absurd or it had meaning—"a beginning and an end, because God is engaged in an adventure into which are filled all the adventures of men."

Whether we realize it or not, our lives are full of meaning, and they can be full of purpose as we respond to God's call to believe and to act. What is the meaning of our lives? "The meaning of the whole of God's adventure," writes Tournier, "is love. It was for love that God created the world."

That, of course, is the Bible's ultimate revelation. Yet, as many have pointed out, including Oswald Chambers in his fine book titled *The Love of God*, that's not apparent as we look around at our world full of agony.

When we think of the Holocaust, when we remember the millions of men and women in prison and the despair felt by refugees, we wonder about the almighty God who allows all this. Against that backdrop, it is only revelation that tells us that God acts out of love. Against the creation's "groanings," the familiar John 3:16 is like lightning flashing across a dark sky: "God loved the world so much that he gave his one and only Son, so that everyone who believes in him will not perish but have eternal life" (NLT).

We don't always realize that it was Jesus himself who said those words! He was with the Father at Creation and is with him now, praying for us because of his love for us.

Father in heaven, thank you for your love, which was so great that you sent your Son to redeem us. Please redeem my day, now, that I might walk in step with your Spirit and show your love to others.

We know what real love is because Jesus gave up his life for us. So we also ought to give up our lives for our brothers and sisters. I JOHN 3:16, NLT

PRAISE IN OUR PAIN?

NANCY GUTHRIE asks a provocative question: Would you be willing to thank God for a gift he gave you and has now taken away?

We live our lives grateful for God's gifts of loved ones, health, and security. All we have is a gift—but everything is also transitory, including the gift of life.

Guthrie considered her terminally ill daughter, Hope, a gift. Even though Hope died as a baby, her mother believes that the appropriate response to a gift is gratitude. She was impressed that Job, in response to all his grievous losses, fell down to worship God. Despite losing everything, Job was still grateful.

Of course, that doesn't mean we don't express our grief when we lose someone we love. Jesus wept at the tomb of his friend Lazarus. Yet the Bible urges, "No matter what happens, always be thankful."

That can be hard to imagine in our times of grief!

The mystery of a life of gratitude means praising the Lord not only at times of peace and safety but at all times. We see this repeatedly in the Psalms, in which laments rising from the depths of devastation are mixed with praises to the God of unfailing love.

How can this be? How can we live a life of gratitude, no matter what happens?

"Job recognized that everything he had was a gift from God," Nancy writes. She says it's hard to even think about being grateful in the midst of loss. "Yet when God takes away, if we're able to focus on the joy of what was given, if only for a time, we take another step down the pathway to the heart of God."

Lord, I want to be constantly moving toward your heart. Even in the worst of times, please release within me a spirit of gratitude. Help me to see what you have given and what you are doing to bless me.

Let the peace that comes from Christ rule in your hearts. For as members of one body you are called to live in peace. And always be thankful. COLOSSIANS 3:15, NLT

THE BLESSING OF "MORBID" THOUGHTS

THOMAS À KEMPIS says that if we keep the hour of our death always in mind and daily prepare ourselves to die, then we are blessed.

Blessed? Most of us think we'd be just the opposite. Keeping our own death always in mind sounds like a surefire path to anxiety—a greased chute toward depression.

Yet à Kempis insists that in the morning we should remember we may not live until evening; then we shouldn't count on living yet another day. He warns us not to promise ourselves a long life and goes on to describe all the ways people can be "unexpectedly snatched from life": "one killed by the sword, another drowned, one fell and broke his neck, another died at the table, and yet others from fire, disease or robbers."

Death is the end of all of us, he reminds us, and life disappears like a shadow.

Of course, à Kempis is echoing passages of Scripture that give the same counsel and describe life as a brief mist. It's sobering, but realistic, to realize how quickly we could find ourselves in the next world.

Billy Graham was once asked what he found the most surprising about life. His answer? "Its brevity."

As we try to embrace the joys and challenges of life, preparing ourselves for death may seem morbid and perhaps even foolish. But Thomas à Kempis sees it as a positive pursuit and advises, "Apply yourself so to live now, that at the hour of death, you may be glad and unafraid."

---

*Father in heaven, I want to someday be in heaven
with you, yet I'm afraid for what I would leave
behind. Please fill me with your peace about what lies
ahead, and let me rejoice in the prospect of glory.*

Since you have been raised to new life with Christ, set your sights on the realities of heaven, where Christ sits in the place of honor at God's right hand. Think about the things of heaven, not the things of earth. COLOSSIANS 3:1-2, NLT

PRAISE AND POWER

JONI EARECKSON TADA believes in the power of praise. "Victory is found in praise," she says, recalling the example of her hospital roommate, Denise.

Seventeen, blind, and paralyzed, Denise never complained. "Even though she was dying," Joni writes, "her mouth was full of prayers and thanksgiving." In contrast, Joni was bitterly angry she was paralyzed and trapped in the unpleasant hospital. Yet as months went by, the spirit of gratitude from Denise became a comfort to her. She became convinced Denise's "sweet sacrifice of praise cleansed the room of the dark spirits of resentment, anger, and self-destruction."

Joni says that singing the doxology, the "church's anthem of victorious praise," helps keep her life in focus:

> *Praise God from whom all blessings flow,*
> *Praise him all creatures here below.*
> *Praise him above, ye heavenly hosts,*
> *Praise Father, Son, and Holy Ghost.*

"I like to think that my prayers of praise are like one or two small drops in a vast ocean of joyful adorations that have gone up before God for countless ages."

Many of us who sing the doxology understand what she means. We are lifted from our distress and our cramped circumstances to heavenly dimensions. Instead of feeling submerged under the weight of the world's evil, we sing our praise to God for his wonders and for his power over the forces of evil. Phillips Brooks writes,

> Do not pray for easy lives.
> Pray to be stronger men.
> Do not pray for tasks equal to your powers.
> Pray for powers equal to your tasks.

When we express gratitude to God and praise him for his wonderful works, we acknowledge our weakness and invite his power.

"In praising the Lord," Joni writes, "Denise was winning a battle that you and I only glimpse now and then. Her life was the battleground upon which the mightiest forces of the universe converged in warfare. And she gained the victory through her praise to God."

> *Father of lights, illumine my life today. Praise to*
> *you for your bringing light, not darkness, into my*
> *life. Praise to you for blessing me with rich spiritual*
> *resources from believers like Joni Eareckson Tada.*

Praise the LORD! Sing to the LORD a new song. Sing his praises in the assembly of the faithful. PSALM 149:1, NLT

HABITS FOR HOLY FREEDOM

BROTHER LAWRENCE said he gave himself wholly to God and renounced everything else, seeking to live "as though there were only the Lord and me in the whole world." He had firm convictions about what that meant:

"Our being set apart for him does not depend on changing our works, but in doing for God's sake all those things we commonly do for our own. The most excellent method I have found of going to God is that of doing common business without any view to pleasing men, and as far as I am capable, doing it purely for the love of God."

How did he do that? "I made it my business to be in the Lord's presence just as much throughout the day as I did when I came to my appointed time of prayer. I drove everything from my mind that might interrupt my thought of God. I did this all the time, every hour, every minute, even in the height of my daily business. Certainly I have done this imperfectly, yet I have found a great advantage in this pursuit."

Notice he uses the word *pursuit*, for the life of spiritual adventure is indeed a pursuit and not an arrival.

"By often repeating these acts they become habit," he explained, "giving us a holy freedom and familiarity with God. The presence of God becomes natural to us. May all things praise him!"

We may feel a bit intimidated as we read his words, but they should be viewed not as an onerous duty but as an invitation to something very, very good.

"Not to advance in the spiritual life is to retreat," Lawrence said. "But those who feel the strong wind of the Holy Spirit go forward even in their sleep."

Holy Spirit, I truly want to feel your "strong wind"
as I face what's before me. Free me, I pray, to be
your instrument of peace and love. Let me do all
for your love, because you have loved me.

All glory to God, who is able to keep you from falling away and will bring you with great joy into his glorious presence without a single fault. JUDE 1:24, NLT

ELEMENTS OF PRAYER

September 18

KING DAVID, in Psalm 25, prays in a way we might emulate in our own devotions. First, he prays in full abandonment to God: "O LORD, I give my life to you. I trust in you, my God! Do not let me be disgraced" (verses 1-2, NLT).

How will he avoid disgrace? He prays with a firm intention to obey God, resting in his compassion and love: "Show me the right path, O LORD; point out the road for me to follow. Lead me by your truth and teach me, for you are the God who saves me. All day long I put my hope in you. Remember, O LORD, your compassion and unfailing love, which you have shown from long ages past" (verses 4-6, NLT).

David then readily admits that he is in need of God's mercy: "Do not remember the rebellious sins of my youth. Remember me in the light of your unfailing love, for you are merciful, O LORD" (verse 7, NLT).

David reveals confidence that his prayers are heard and that God will guide him: "The LORD is good and does what is right; he shows the proper path to those who go astray. He leads the humble in doing right, teaching them his way. The LORD leads with unfailing love and faithfulness all who keep his covenant and obey his demands" (verses 8-10, NLT).

We can envision David pausing to think about what he's just written about God's demands. He has asked forgiveness for the rebellious sins of his youth, but remembrance of other sins well up in his mind. He prays: "For the honor of your name, O LORD, forgive my many, many sins" (verse 11, NLT).

During the time he was king, God confronted David for serious sins with serious consequences. Yet his immediate repentance and humbling himself before the Lord set him apart as a man after God's own heart and enabled him to lead his nation to greatness despite his failures.

"Turn to me and have mercy, . . ." David prayed, "for I put my hope in you" (verses 16, 21, NLT).

Father in heaven, help me to have David's passionate
love for you and his honesty about my need for your
mercy. Cleanse me and fill me with hope.

The LORD is a friend to those who fear him. . . . My eyes are always on the LORD.
PSALM 25:14-15, NLT

THE DARK, GLADDENING MYSTERY  *September 19*

HELMUT THIELICKE asks how Jesus could ever have gained any disciples at all when he described the grim prospects of their going out as sheep among wolves, homeless and receiving hatred and persecution. Yet they should rejoice and be glad! Thielicke asks if there is some great mystery here we can't see.

Speaking to Christians who had courageously endured persecution under the Nazis, he asked, "Did not all of us sense something of this dark, yet gladdening, mystery during the days when the church was being persecuted? Were not all of us who suffered with Jesus Christ incredibly blessed in a way that we would never have dared to dream was possible?"

We read of saints and martyrs who made ultimate sacrifices with songs of joy on their lips. We remember Paul and Silas, beaten and shackled in prison yet singing praises to God. Thielicke says of this mysterious happiness, "Cross-bearing is full of hidden blessings." In contrast, those without faith find that the worst part of suffering for them is its meaninglessness.

Christians understand that God is not thwarted by world events. His plans for redemption through Christ will continue through all the travail. Jesus, who suffered for us, prays for us, as does the Holy Spirit.

Thielicke testifies to the "gladdening" reward of living in faith during the time of Nazi terrors. "How often during the worst times," he says, having "summoned God into the fray, I was able to say joyfully, almost exultantly: 'I'm through, I've made it! Now what comes of it is God's responsibility.'"

Whatever we face, now or later, we have the same opportunity to cast all our deepest troubles and even desperations on God and to let him do his work his way.

Thielicke says that when we step aside, "God himself rises up to perform his mighty works, in the midst of the earth, where the powers clash and the terrible battle rages."

---

*Lord, I mostly feel dread when I think of the kind of
persecution that happened in Hitler's Germany or right
now in Asia and Africa. You know all my concerns;
grant me, I pray, the joy of fully trusting you.*

You will keep in perfect peace all who trust in you, all whose thoughts are fixed on you!
ISAIAH 26:3, NLT

CAUGHT BY SURPRISE

PHILIP YANCEY writes of shooting "arrow prayers" throughout the day. Sometimes they are as brief as, "Help, Lord!" Other times they may be biblical prayers, such as "Create in me a clean heart, O God" (Psalm 51:10, NLT) or "Restore to me the joy of your salvation" (Psalm 51:12, NLT).

If we are to "pray without ceasing," and if we are to "practice the presence of Christ" as Brother Lawrence urged, we need to do so in the flow of our activities. How can we remember to turn often to the Lord throughout the day? Yancey says he "looks for the spaces, the interstices," and gives as examples such times as when lying awake at night, driving, waiting for a computer to reboot, exercising, or standing in line. "Instead of fidgeting or staring at my watch during a lull, I pray."

He finds that turning otherwise wasted moments into prayer sometimes produces interesting results. "I find myself more aware of the old woman in front of me fumbling through her change purse. I pray for the people inside as I pass a neighbor's house, a church, a bar. I pray while watching the news."

Our opportunities for such prayer are individual and unique, but we can all watch for opportune moments. We can send up an "arrow prayer" or pause to meditate on a verse of Scripture and—if only for a moment—bring ourselves into God's presence.

When we actively look for God during all the ordinary events of our lives, we find reasons for gratitude and objects for compassion. We see people to pray for, and we see God's handiwork and praise him for his remarkable creation.

But to see these opportunities for prayer, we need to be looking for them. When we're aware and turning our thoughts to the Lord, it's amazing how many things we see to pray about.

Heavenly Father, I get all caught up in the pace
of the day, and my mind is often far from you.
Please help me to constantly connect with you.

Keep watch and pray. MATTHEW 26:41, NLT

BEYOND FAILURE

OLE HALLESBY asks, "Why do most of us fail so miserably in prayer?"

This renowned Christian teacher and author of a book about prayer confesses his own failures in prayer. He admits that one of his greatest sins was his neglect of prayer.

"This neglect is the cause of my many other sins of omission as well as commission. The countless opportunities for prayer I failed to make use of, the many answers to prayer God would have given me if I only had prayed, accuse me more and more violently the more I become acquainted with the holy realm of prayer."

Hallesby says he had been pondering the question of failure in prayer ever since he began to pray. His conclusion? "Prayer is difficult." At the same time, it doesn't require special gifts but is open to all. It does, however, take two things: practice and perseverance. Hallesby advises us to admit our weaknesses in prayer and to realize we face a problem that can't be solved by our own efforts alone. "To move in prayer as though one were in one's element, to pray daily with a willing spirit, with joy, with gratitude and with adoration is something far beyond our human capacities. A miracle of God is necessary every day for this."

We therefore ask to receive the Spirit of prayer, for the Spirit teaches us to pray.

Writes Hallesby, "Through the Word and the daily exercise of prayer, he gives us the practice and divine insight into the prayer life and its laws in order to make us real men and women of prayer."

Holy Spirit, I want to pray with gratitude and perseverance and joy. Only you can teach me and enable me to fully engage in prayer. Please enliven my soul and bolster my faith.

Jesus went up on a mountain to pray, and he prayed to God all night. At daybreak he called together all of his disciples and chose twelve of them to be apostles.
LUKE 6:12-13, NLT

CONTINUOUS CLEANSING

September 22

BILLY GRAHAM says Christian believers are human and vulnerable to sin and asks, "Why can't we simply admit it?" He points out no one lives without occasional sin, and though we must never grow complacent, "It is hypocritical to say otherwise."

Billy has plenty of support in Scripture that speaks to this complex issue. Paul admits in Romans he does what he hates, and John says if we say we don't sin we lie. Yet many other verses proclaim that we can have victory over sin. It's a lifelong struggle, and it's worth a thoughtful look at Scripture.

> God's law was given so that all people could see how sinful they were. But as people sinned more and more, God's wonderful grace became more abundant. So just as sin ruled over all people and brought them to death, now God's wonderful grace rules instead, giving us right standing with God and resulting in eternal life through Jesus Christ our Lord. . . .
>
> Well then, should we keep on sinning so that God can show us more and more of his wonderful grace? Of course not! Since we have died to sin, how can we continue to live in it? . . .
>
> Do not let sin control the way you live; do not give in to sinful desires. . . . Instead, give yourselves completely to God, for you were dead, but now you have new life. . . . You live under the freedom of God's grace. (Romans 5:20-21; 6:1-2, 12-14, NLT)

The apostle John writes in his first epistle, "If we are living in the light, as God is in the light, then we have fellowship with each other, and the blood of Jesus, his Son, cleanses us from all sin. If we claim we have no sin, we are only fooling ourselves and not living in the truth. But if we confess our sins to him, he is faithful and just to forgive us our sins and to cleanse us from all wickedness" (1 John 1:7-9, NLT).

Billy Graham says his wife, Ruth, reminded him that people who lived in the mountains near where the Grahams live used to put laundry in wooden cradles and then place them in a running creek for continuous cleansing.

Continuous cleansing. Something we all need.

Lord, you know everything about me, including all my thoughts and deeds. Let your cleansing stream flow through me so that what I see and what I think become fully in harmony with your thoughts and perspectives.

Create in me a clean heart, O God. Renew a loyal spirit within me. . . . Restore to me the joy of your salvation. PSALM 51:10, 12, NLT

LOVE BEYOND WORDS

A. W. TOZER says we must speak of God's love, though we "can no more do justice to that awesome and wonder-filled theme than a child can grasp a star."

Of course, a child can't grasp a star. Yet Tozer says that by reaching toward it, a child can call attention to a star and show us where to look for it. In that humble frame of mind, a Christian calls attention to God's love. Tozer says he "stretches his heart toward the high, shining love of God to encourage others to look up and have hope."

How does this apply to our lives? Tozer quotes the apostle John's insight that perfect love casts out fear and notes that it is obviously God's magnificent love that is perfect.

So, if we are responding to God's love, we need not fear.

Tozer also says that God's love is active and creative. We need look no further than the familiar John 3:16 for an affirmation of that: "For God loved the world so much that he gave his one and only Son" (NLT). What love could be more active and "wonder-filled" than that?

If we believe in Jesus, we will experience this awesome love forever.

Another stunning aspect of God's love is the biblical revelation that he loves *us* in a big way. Julian of Norwich said we're so personally and specially loved that we couldn't even come close to grasping the marvel of it. God loves *us*!

So, we are objects of God's love, as a beloved child is the object of his or her parents' love. Tozer concludes, "The love of God is one of the great realities of the universe, a pillar on which the hope of the world rests."

Father in heaven, it's hard to imagine how much you love me. Help me to sense your love today. Put your love within me, and help me live so that others can sense your love.

You must love the LORD your God with all your heart, all your soul, and all your strength. DEUTERONOMY 6:5, NLT

INVITATION TO LOVE

GEORGE MACDONALD describes God the Father as devoted to his Son "and to all his sons and daughters, with a perfect and eternal devotion." He then envisions Jesus saying this to us: "I know your Father, for he is my Father. He is just like me. He only is the true, original good. I am true because I seek nothing but his will. I am the son in whom his heart of love is satisfied. Come home with me. Together we will do his will and be glad in him."

It's astounding to realize we're invited into the love relationship between Jesus Christ and his Father. We're invited into the dynamic love that forged creation and sent the Son to redeem it. We can be drawn into the glory and the love that is at the center of all existence.

At the same time, it means we give up our own prerogatives. We give up living on our own terms. This spiritual life comes through obedience.

That shouldn't surprise or discourage us. It was Jesus himself who said he could do nothing without the Father. If that was true of Jesus, then what about us?

When we think we can do things without God, we're not living as Jesus did. In contrast, when we say with Jesus, "Thy will be done," the life of the Trinity flows through us.

Jesus prayed, "Thy will be done," in the extreme moments in Gethsemane. He was obedient in order to gain the joy set before him. When we pray those words, we accept the will of the Father that binds us to his love as his sons and daughters.

Jesus prayed that his disciples would all be one in him and in his Father's love. That happens as we continually seek to discern and obey his will.

In light of all this, MacDonald challenges us, "Let us arise and live!"

Father, that you love me as you love your Son is too wonderful
for me to absorb. Help me to always be seeking your will so
that I might be an instrument of your peace and your love.

Live a life filled with love, following the example of Christ. EPHESIANS 5:2, NLT

LIFE EMERGING IN THE COCOON

RAY STEDMAN found in the Scriptures the core reason we cannot solve our ecological and societal problems: "The old creation that has existed since the beginning of time is gripped by what Paul calls 'the bondage of decay.' Everything is deteriorating."

Yet, writes Stedman, "The breakthrough has occurred. God is beginning a new creation, one that lives by a wholly different principle."

Why can't we step up to our ecological disasters?

Why can't we get along with one another?

Why can't we stop the massacres that drive millions of families into refugee camps?

So long as we still live in the old creation, we experience this bondage of decay. Yet, in Christ, in one sense everything has already changed. A new day is coming.

In the meantime, we are invited to walk in the Spirit. We can love and forgive. We can work for peace and justice. We can swallow our self-centeredness and care for the poor and oppressed.

Earth is still a spiritual battleground, and the new creation has experienced the breakthrough. But it has not yet been realized.

Ray Stedman uses the analogy of our civilization being like a cocoon "clinging lifelessly to the branch of history. One of these days, that cocoon will open in the springtime of the world."

We don't have to wait to be part of the new life being formed in that cocoon. In the midst of the old, we have the stirrings of new life. We're told in Romans 8:23 that we have "a foretaste of future glory" through the Holy Spirit.

"All creation is waiting eagerly for that future day when God will reveal who his children really are. Against its will, all creation was subjected to God's curse. But with eager hope, the creation looks forward to the day when it will join God's children in glorious freedom from death and decay" (Romans 8:19-21, NLT).

Father and Creator, help me to act in harmony with
your new creation that is coming (and in some ways
is already here). Let your will be done on earth as
it is in heaven, and help me be part of that.

What we suffer now is nothing compared to the glory he will reveal to us later.
ROMANS 8:18, NLT

WHEN RIVERS CLAP

September 26

JILL BRISCOE says that many of us need a new song. She quotes Psalm 98:1: "Sing a new song to the LORD."

We need a new song because our lives keep changing, sometimes in happy ways and other times in testing and disappointment.

Jill says that God gave her a new song when her children got married. He gave her a new song when her husband had to be away, at a time when she faced sobering surgery. She says, "New situations require new songs."

Some new songs will be full of praise and joy, while others will rise in the soul with minor chords resonating with our sorrows.

The exuberance of Psalm 98 should lift our souls, whatever is going on in our lives. From the start its tone is upbeat: "Sing a new song to the LORD, for he has done wonderful deeds" (NLT).

We're not just to sing a new song, but we are to sing it *to the Lord*. He gives us the song and we sing the song back to him.

Are we talking about actual music here? The psalm says we're to shout and sing praise with the harp and trumpets and to make a joyful symphony—so in one sense, yes. But it also says, "Let the sea and everything in it shout his praise! . . . Let the rivers clap their hands in glee! Let the hills sing out their songs of joy before the LORD" (verses 7-9, NLT).

Obviously, we're talking about a spirit of praise that permeates our souls and all creation. When we praise God in the spirit of this psalm, we find, even in the worst of circumstances, that we start to gain a new perspective.

Jill urges us to sing new songs in each new situation of life—songs of faith and hope. "God is never stuck for a tune," she says. "New songs are the Spirit's business—ask him to give you one."

Lord, if ever I needed a new song, it's now. So many
changes in my life have made my need for your
encouragement and Spirit greater than ever. Please bring
into my heart and soul your song and your harmonies.

Shout to the LORD, all the earth; break out in praise and sing for joy!
PSALM 98:4, NLT

TOUGH FAITH

September 27

FRED SMITH, in a time of personal economic uncertainty, wrote that, no matter how financial matters rise or fall, "I like to believe we are eagles driven to soar when we are most sore."

Many have experienced the gut-wrenching loss of financial security and wondered how to cope and pay the bills. Smith says that, from his experience, we may need to "zig and zag," but as we do, we need to focus on doing all things God's way. Then we're able to claim 2 Timothy 1:7, which tells us God has not given us the spirit of fear, but of love, power, and a sound mind.

We need such encouragement, not only for financial reversals but also for the many global threats that seem to darken the future and make us more than ever concerned for our children and grandchildren.

Sometimes it looks as if darkness keeps expanding and will envelop all we hold dear. Yet Smith reminds us that the light of Christ burns brightest in the darkness and that it cannot be extinguished.

When darkness comes, the smallest candle provides light. We may think that our candle is flickering in the wind, but it won't go out if we walk with the Spirit.

"Ours is not a fragile faith," Smith insists. "It is tough stuff. It is faith that grows stronger under pressure.

"Remember the Good News when the bad news shouts. It is real. It is strong. It is eternal."

Lord Jesus, I pray that you will fill me with your Holy Spirit of courage and love and purpose. As difficult things happen to me and to those I love, help me show the "love, power, and sound mind" you supply.

Be strong and courageous! Do not be afraid and do not panic.
DEUTERONOMY 31:6, NLT

LEAKY VESSELS, FRESH SUPPLY *September 28*

D. L. MOODY called for a very high standard for prayer, starting with the confession of sin. "As long as we have unconfessed sin in our soul," he said, "we are not going to have power with God in prayer. He says if we regard iniquity in our hearts he will not hear us, much less answer."

Moody urged us to empty our hearts of pride, selfish ambition, self-seeking, and wrongful pleasures in order to experience the Holy Spirit's presence. Otherwise, he said, there's no room for the Spirit of God. "Before we pray that God will fill us, we ought to pray him to empty us."

Moody was unbending on what authentic prayer demanded. "Let it be God's glory and not our own that we seek. There is no room for self, unholy ambitions, and unholy desires."

For all his passion for full consecration, however, Moody was far from glum. He was simply sharing the way to the power and presence of the Spirit he had himself experienced.

He was also far from naive about the battles we all face. "The fact is, we're all leaky vessels," he admitted, "and we have to keep right under the fountain all the time to keep full of Christ, and so have a fresh supply." He lamented the fact that many believers try to make do with the grace they received from God years ago. "What we need is a fresh supply, a fresh anointing and fresh power, and if we seek it with all our hearts, we will obtain it."

To illustrate, Moody described a farm in California he had visited. He was amazed at how green everything was, from trees and flowers to crops. Yet just beyond the hedge, everything was dreary and dried up. Constant irrigation had brought the green life. He made the point that God pours water on those who are thirsty and they become full of the Spirit, "like a green bay tree."

Father, empty me, I pray, of all the things that block your
fresh waters of spiritual vitality from flowing through
me. Bring your fresh cleansing and energy so that I can
serve you and pray for and serve others effectively.

I am about to do something new. See, I have already begun! Do you not see it? I will
make a pathway through the wilderness. I will create rivers in the dry wasteland.
ISAIAH 43:19, NLT

FREE TO FLY

FRANÇOIS FÉNELON describes two persons—one happy and free, the other like a tethered bird.

We find ourselves like that bird, he tells us, easily captured if we allow the world to keep us from doing God's will. A bird tethered to the ground may look free. The string may not be visible if it's thin enough. If the tether is long enough, the bird may be able to do a little flying. Yet it's a prisoner—as we will be if we're snared by the world's powerful influences.

How can the string be cut? Fénelon says, "Only the Son of God can make us really free. He breaks every fetter."

When we call on Jesus to take charge, we experience a freedom that protects us from the world's enticements. It's a constant battle. At the same time, writes Fénelon, "There is not a person in the world who can be allowed to hinder us from doing the will of God."

No one can hinder us. When the Son of God breaks the fetters, we are free! Free to continually choose what pleases God.

Fénelon strongly warns against placing too much trust in our intellect. Those who do, he says, "quench the promptings of their conscience by reasoning away what they know to be right. I'm convinced that everything we do should be under the guidance of God."

He points us to Matthew 11:25-26, in which Jesus prayed, "O Father, Lord of heaven and earth, thank you for hiding these things from those who think themselves wise and clever, and for revealing them to the childlike. Yes, Father, it pleased you to do it this way!" (NLT).

Jesus then says, "My Father has entrusted everything to me. No one truly knows the Son except the Father, and no one truly knows the Father except the Son and those to whom the Son chooses to reveal him" (Matthew 11:27, NLT).

Lord Jesus, set me free and enable me to continually respond to your Spirit and to walk in step with your will. Cut the fetters that keep me back, and guide all my thoughts as I diligently apply myself.

Jesus said, "Come to me, all of you who are weary and carry heavy burdens, and I will give you rest." MATTHEW 11:28, NLT

EVEN ARMIES OF ANGELS

September 30

KING DAVID declares in Psalm 103:8-11, "The LORD is compassionate and merciful, slow to get angry and filled with unfailing love. He will not constantly accuse us, nor remain angry forever. He does not punish us for all our sins; he does not deal harshly with us, as we deserve. For his unfailing love toward those who fear him is as great as the height of the heavens above the earth" (NLT).

David's words throughout this psalm bring comfort and refreshment to those in distress. So many people today need that comfort and refreshment. A father has lost his job and has no other prospects. A young woman has been diagnosed with aggressive breast cancer. A family has just been informed their daughter was killed in a car accident. An alcoholic mother has once again given in to temptation and her children have been taken away from her.

We hear tragic stories from every quarter. David, too, experienced great grief and sorrow, as is so evident in many of his psalms. He's thoroughly realistic about the brevity of life, yet affirms the love of God for us:

> The LORD is like a father to his children, tender and compassionate to those who fear him. For he knows how weak we are; he remembers we are only dust. Our days on earth are like grass; like wildflowers, we bloom and die. The wind blows, and we are gone—as though we had never been here. But the love of the LORD remains forever with those who fear him. (Psalm 103:13-17, NLT)

Despite his troubles, David lifts his heart in praise:

> Praise the LORD, you angels, you mighty ones who carry out his plans, listening for each of his commands. Yes, praise the LORD, you armies of angels who serve him and do his will! Praise the LORD, everything he has created, everything in all his kingdom. Let all that I am praise the LORD. (Psalm 103:20-22, NLT)

Creator God of all glory, I do praise you for your magnificent creation and for your salvation. Help me to obey you always so that my heart is full of praise and my soul resonates with your Holy Spirit.

Great is the LORD! He is most worthy of praise! No one can measure his greatness.
PSALM 145:3, NLT

SURPRISE!

OSWALD CHAMBERS says that Jesus doesn't come when and where we expect him. In fact, he asserts, Jesus comes in times and places where we least expect him.

"Jesus appears in the most illogical connections," Chambers says. He urges us to be ready for surprise visits. "It is this intense reality of expecting him at every turn that gives life the attitude of child wonder Jesus wants it to have. When we are rightly related to God, life is full of spontaneous joyful uncertainty and expectancy."

Most people don't associate uncertainty with joy. In fact, it typically generates anxiety. When we experience financial challenges, whether our own or national/global ones that threaten our way of life, we worry. When our loved ones face a serious medical diagnosis, we feel great anxiety.

Let's face it—life is tentative. We are vulnerable in more ways than we could list. Still, Jesus tells us not to worry but to consider the birds and the lilies in the fields. Chambers ramps that up with his call not only to relax in faith but to embrace joyful expectancy. Whatever happens, if we are alert and watching, Jesus will surprise us.

Relaxing in faith is a tall order, considering our biological reactions to danger and crises. We can't control the way our complex biology responds to crisis and threat. That, of course, means events become calls to prayer, for only the Lord can give us a sense of joyful expectancy rather than feelings of dread. We can pray for a sense of God's presence in the center of whatever's ahead by inviting the Spirit to create that sense within us.

"The element of surprise is always the note of the life of the Holy Ghost in us," Chambers declares. "We are born again by the great surprise. Be ready for the sudden surprise visits of our Lord."

Lord Jesus, let my eyes be alert and my soul receptive to your coming. Ease my anxieties. Help me not to be asleep at the switch or to nod off just when you're about to appear.

Come and see what our God has done, what awesome miracles he performs for people!
PSALM 66:5, NLT

DEVILISH STRATEGIES

MARTIN LUTHER confessed that the devil often tried to trick him into not praying by distracting him. He prompted him to think, "I'm not yet prepared to pray. I should wait until I'm more prepared or until I've taken care of some things."

Putting off prayer or letting the press of duties squeeze it out, Luther warned, can result in many days of prayerlessness. Endless distractions keep us from prayer.

Luther also emphasized that our awareness of our sins can keep us from coming to God—just when we most need to. We put it off until we feel we've made spiritual progress. From personal experience he said, "This serious obstacle weighs on us like a heavy stone."

Guilt and prayer are regular companions. When guilt is confessed in prayer, the combination is a way to freedom and joy. In contrast, when guilt from failures and sins persists, our guilt increases. Luther would tell us the devil is having his way with us.

The demands of life and changes that dismay us can drain our prayer lives. On the other hand, those are the very things that can drive us to prayer and help us cope and find meaning and hope.

The gift of prayer is that we can bring our complex feelings and our sense of unworthiness to the Lord. He promises he will clean them all out like a murky closet full of junk.

Luther advised that, whatever our feelings and guilt, we must "freely approach God and call upon him."

Father in heaven, here I am with my feelings of guilt and frustration. Please cleanse my soul from all that displeases you or is unworthy. Thank you for your promise that you will lead me into freedom and joy.

Let us go right into the presence of God with sincere hearts fully trusting him.
HEBREWS 10:22, NLT

PATIENTLY WAITING

JAY KESLER admits that although patience is part of the fruit of the Spirit, "Everything about my personality fights against the idea of patience."

Many of us resonate with Jay's honesty; our internal engines just naturally rev up to override patience. We want to experience the next thing. We want to get things done, and we feel we *need* to get them done *now*.

Our culture gives us no help. As the pace of technology accelerates, so does the pace of our lives. Our expectations quicken as we see all that is open to us. For many, the prospect of wedging in time for spiritual reflection, let alone the practice of patience, floats overhead like an elusive cloud of nagging guilt.

The Bible records much about believers and the need for patience. We've all heard the phrase "the patience of Job." Well, consider Abraham.

Abraham was already seventy-five when God told him his descendants would be as numerous as the stars. Then came the interminable waiting and the need for extreme patience. When Abraham was nearly one hundred, God affirmed his very old promise that Abraham would be the "father of many nations." Abraham inwardly laughed, and his wife, Sarah, laughed out loud.

Yet even after so many years, the child of promise was born. They named him Isaac. A meaning for Isaac is "He laughs."

Job and Abraham simply had to wait. Despite our fast-paced lives, the irony is that patience is often required. It may not come naturally to us, but it's very natural as a fruit of the Spirit.

To grow spiritually, we need patience.

Jay illustrates with Annie Dillard's story about a moth. When she was in fifth grade, in January, Annie's teacher allowed her students to pass around a cocoon. They delightedly held it and squeezed it in their warm hands. It started stirring and heaving, but they kept passing it around. Back in the jar, January or not, the moth emerged, but it was sodden, with wings crumpled and stuck on its back.

Sometimes we must wait. "God's way is patience," Kesler says. "The proof is the incredible patience he demonstrates in the process of making me in his image."

---

*Lord, please help me to be as patient as you are
with me in all my limitations and failures. Help
me to wait even when waiting is hard, and help me
to be patient with those who are impatient.*

---

*Patient endurance is what you need now, so that you will continue to do God's will.
Then you will receive all that he has promised.* HEBREWS 10:36, NLT

EMBRACE THE BLESSINGS, BUT HEED THE CURSES

JOHN HENRY JOWETT jars us with his take on the command in Joshua to read *all* the words of the law, not just the blessings but also the curses. He lays a heavy hand on our feel-good proclivities with one challenge after another:

> We love the passages that speak of our Master's gentleness, but we turn away from those that reveal his severity.

> We recount the promises, but we shut our ears to the rebukes.

> We read what pleases us, to hug the blessings and ignore the warnings.

> We become spiritually soft and anemic. We lack moral stamina. We are incapable of holy scorn. We are invertebrate, and on the evil day we are not able to stand.

How much do Jowett's accusations strike home?

There's nothing wrong with embracing our blessings. The promises of God are sure, and with the heavy load each person carries in this demanding, confusing world, it's natural to want to emphasize the positive. We should! Yet evil also exists, and enemy forces are out to seduce us in the heavenly warfare waged against our souls.

Jowett affirms that we must take to heart all the words of the law: "We must let the Lord brace us with his severities. We must gaze steadily upon the appalling fearfulness of sin. At all costs, we must get rid of the spurious gentleness that holds compromise with uncleanness."

As we watch our culture sink further and further into degradation, as we see the tragic results of sin blindsiding the ignorant, we sense the importance of emphasizing both the positive Good News and the call to holiness.

Jowett throws out a challenge: "We must seek the love that burns everlastingly against all sin. We must seek the gentleness that can fiercely grip a poisonous growth and tear it out."

Holy Spirit, cleanse from my soul any poisonous growth
you find there. Help me to recognize the poison I
sometimes swallow without a thought. Purify my heart.

Work at living in peace with everyone, and work at living a holy life, for those who are not holy will not see the Lord. HEBREWS 12:14, NLT

JOY SHINING THROUGH TEARS

SHERWOOD WIRT writes that the Greek word *makarios* loses some of its meaning when it is translated as *blessed* in the Beatitudes. Just what is Jesus saying when he uses the word *blessed*? Why would those who are poor in spirit, those who mourn, and those who are meek be blessed? What nuances of meaning can be found in these statements that Jesus made?

Woody turns to the writings of William Barclay:

> The blessedness which belongs to the Christian is not a blessedness postponed to some future world of glory; it is a blessedness for here and now. It is a present reality to be enjoyed. The Beatitudes in effect say, "O the bliss of being a Christian! O the joy of following Christ! O the sheer happiness of knowing Jesus Christ as Master, Savior and Lord!"
>
> The Beatitudes speak of that joy which seeks us through our pain, that joy which sorrow and loss, pain and grief are powerless to touch, that joy which shines through tears, and which nothing in life or death can take away. The world can win its joys and can lose its joys. But the Christian has the joy which comes from walking forever in the company and presence of Jesus Christ.

Barclay's description illustrates our being filled with the Spirit. Sherwood Wirt adds that being filled with the Spirit means being filled with love. "Love is the first fruit of the Spirit, and the second fruit is joy."

To be alive in God is to be controlled by him. We're "poor in spirit," but if the Holy Spirit lives within us, we're not poor at all.

Woody declares, "Jesus taught that for us to feel that love and have that joy, we must be poor in spirit. It is when we let go of the rope that we discover that underneath are the everlasting arms."

Our Father, these promises go far beyond anything I can feel or do. My spirit is inadequate for the challenges and troubles ahead of me. Help me let go of the rope and trust you to make me blessed in your way.

God blesses those whose hearts are pure, for they will see God. MATTHEW 5:8, NLT

WHEN WORK FEELS HOPELESS

LEWIS SMEDES tells a remarkable story about Michelangelo: "One early evening, as dusk darkened the Sistine Chapel, Michelangelo, weary, sore, and doubtful, climbed down the ladder from his scaffolding where he had been lying on his back since dawn painting the chapel ceiling. After eating a lonely supper, he wrote a sonnet to his aching body." The last line of his sonnet astonished me when I first came upon it, and the memory of it has comforted me in my times of self-doubt: "I am no painter."

Michelangelo no painter? No wonder Smedes was astonished. Many have seen the master painter's vision of God creating Adam. Michelangelo's magnificent visions on the Sistine Chapel ceiling have filled generations with awe and wonder.

Smedes says that Michelangelo's words have comforted him in times of self-doubt about his own labors.

Self-doubt sneaks in at odd moments. Even when we're at the peak of our skills and capacities, we can feel those doubts. Then there are the times when we really aren't very good at what we are doing—circumstances force us into work that fits us like a foot fits into a glove!

Smedes tells us that Vaclav Havel, living under Communist rule in Czechoslovakia, spent half his days in jail and half at a menial job in the state brewery. When Czechoslovakia was freed, Havel became its first president. Asked how he had kept going during those grim decades under Soviet domination, he said, "I am not an optimist. I am a person of hope."

We live by hope. Vaclav Havel, the poet of hope, and Michelangelo, painter extraordinaire, created enduring, magnificent words and images. When we're in step with the Creator, we may be discouraged, but Scripture tells us, "God is working in you, giving you the desire and the power to do what pleases him" (Philippians 2:13, NLT).

Father, let me see through your eyes what you're doing
in and through me. At times I feel so stuck in my
circumstances that I can't be of use to you. When I feel
hopeless about myself, Lord, give me your fresh hope.

In times of trouble, may the LORD answer your cry. . . . May he grant your heart's desires and make all your plans succeed. PSALM 20:1, 4, NLT

WHO'S THE HUNTER?

HENRI NOUWEN confesses that for most of his life he struggled to find and love God. He says he tried hard by praying, working for others, reading the Scriptures, and avoiding temptations. He admits he failed many times but always kept trying, even when close to despair.

Eventually, he says, he came to realize he hadn't sufficiently understood that all the time he was trying so hard, God was reaching out to love him.

"The question," Nouwen asks, "is not 'How am I to find God?' but 'How am I to let myself be found by him?' . . . 'How am I to let myself be loved by God?'"

We might ask, What is he talking about? What's the difference? We still need to pray, to help others, and to live as disciples. What does it mean to be "found" by God?

Part of the answer can be found in an observation by Ole Hallesby that "prayer is for the helpless." When we are on the hunt for a spiritual lift, when we are trying to discipline ourselves and find the Lord, we may be blocking his Spirit by relying on our own efforts. There's plenty of paradox here, but also a core principle that it is God who gives us "the desire and the power to do what pleases him" (Philippians 2:13, NLT).

We first must grasp the full truth of our complete need for God. And then, what a wonderful realization: we don't have to be on the hunt for him, because he is on the hunt for us!

"The good news," Henri says, "is that God is scanning the horizon for me, trying to find me, and longing to bring me home. In the same way, God is looking for you."

Father in heaven, I want to be found by you. More and more I recognize my own weakness. Bring me home, Lord, in the sense that you have full access to me. Let us enjoy eternity together, starting right now.

I will boast only in the LORD; let all who are helpless take heart. PSALM 34:2, NLT

JOSTLING OR PRAYING?

JILL BRISCOE describes Jesus' disciples at the Last Supper as each hoping some-one else would do the dirty job of washing the others' feet. *Why me?* each man thought. *Why not one of these other disciples?* Before this they had been squabbling among them-selves about who was greater and elbowing each other for their personal rights.

How amazing, then, that Jesus took off his outer garments and, like a slave in a loincloth, washed the disciples' feet. Even though he knew Judas would betray him and Peter would deny him, he washed their feet. Even though he was the Lord and Master who was facing the horrors of the next day and had every reason to be self-centered and self-absorbed, he knelt in a demonstration of humility and service.

Are we like the disciples, self-absorbed, jostling for position and power and applause? Or are we like Jesus, who was constantly connecting with his Father and intent on serving him and others?

If we're honest, we have to admit that we're more like the disciples, self-absorbed in our own agendas and scrambling to meet our needs and fulfill our responsibilities. As Jill says, "Humility is a tough assignment for all of us."

The way to grow in humility and service is to communicate constantly with the Father, as Jesus did. That's not easy when most of those around us are acting like the disciples.

Jill points to someone who, the Bible notes, pleased God despite what others were doing. "Noah was a pleasure to the Lord," she says. Usually we're more interested in how God can please us than in how we can bring pleasure to him. Noah, on the other hand, was pleasing to the Lord because he sought to live with integrity as God intended, no matter what was going on around him.

When God looked at Noah, he was pleased. When God looks at us, is he pleased, the way he was with Noah and with Jesus?

Father, I get caught up in my world of constant concerns. Help me to function effectively with my agenda and at the same time respond to the needs around me as you give me insight and strength.

Noah found favor with the LORD. . . . Noah did everything exactly as God had commanded him. GENESIS 6:8, 22, NLT

THE WELLSPRINGS OF LOVE

FRANÇOIS FÉNELON advises, "Love God. Everything will come by love."

When we read this, and when we remember that Jesus said that the greatest commandment is to love the Lord our God with all our hearts, souls, and minds, we may wonder—do we really know how to love God? In some ways, we know more about loving a spouse, child, or neighbor than we do about loving God.

Fénelon is quick to dispel a common misperception—that it's all about our feelings. He tells us not to be overly concerned with feelings. "God is not expecting any particular kind of emotion from you. All he asks is that you remain faithful."

With the same insight that C. S. Lewis adapted years later, Fénelon adds, "I rather think faithfulness unsustained by pleasant emotions is far purer and more reliable than one dependent on tender feelings."

Emotions come and go; we may feel God's love one day and doubt he cares for us the next.

Loving God is all about the will. Fénelon says, "Please understand about love. All I ask is that your will lean toward love. Regardless of how you feel, make up your mind to love God."

He adds, knowing the reality of our fallen condition, "No matter what corrupt desires you find in your heart, decide to love God more than self. Ask for such a love."

That, of course, is where the Holy Spirit comes in. The truth is, even when we commit our wills, we're helpless to love God on our own.

Jesus said we love him when we obey his commands. As we study the Scriptures and listen to the Spirit, we have ample guidance on the specifics of how to love God.

---

*Father in heaven, you are the source of love, and
your love is magnificently dynamic within the Holy
Trinity. Such love is far beyond my thoughts. Please
touch me with your love and presence today.*

[Jesus said,] "I have loved you even as the Father has loved me. Remain in my love."
JOHN 15:9, NLT

BLANK READING

EUGENE PETERSON tells a story about his seven-year-old grandson and the way we read the Bible. Gene's wife had taken little Hans to a park to eat their lunches. The boy talked nonstop while he ate his lunch, and then he stopped and pulled from his bag a New Testament his pastor had given him. For a long moment, he silently moved his eyes back and forth across the page. Then he returned the New Testament to the bag and announced that he was ready to go.

Peterson's wife was amused by this display because she knew Hans didn't know how to read. He was simply going through the motions without comprehension.

When Gene's wife told him this story, it developed in his mind as a parable describing how people often approach their reading of the Scriptures. *How,* we might ask ourselves, *are we like Hans in our own reading of the Bible?* In contrast, how might we read the Bible as it was intended?

Elsewhere, Peterson describes the subversion of God's Word as a satanic assault that has been "an enormously successful strategy: millions of people use the Bible to condemn people they do not approve of; millions more read the Word of God daily and within ten minutes are speaking words to spouses, neighbors, children and colleagues that are contemptuous, irritable, manipulative and misleading."

Gene asks, "How does this happen? The enemy subverted the words. They go through the minds of readers like water through a pipe."

Those chilling words are a caution to us all. Even worse than reading the Bible with no comprehension are the tragic instances throughout history when God's Word has been used as license to persecute and humiliate.

We are thoroughly dependent on the Holy Spirit to lead us into the truth of the Scriptures. We must approach God's Word with humility, expectation, and fervent prayer.

Lord, how is it possible to read your Word but end up causing you grief? Protect me, I pray, from Satan's attempts to subvert your message. Keep me from sugarcoating your hard demands and ignoring your calls for compassion.

[Jesus] opened their minds to understand the Scriptures. LUKE 24:45, NLT

THE PRIVILEGE OF DUST AND ASHES

JONI EARECKSON TADA lets us in on what she calls a "personal secret." She says, "There are times in prayer when I feel too overwhelmed by sin, too earth-stained, too dry or dull to even approach the Father."

Many of us, even if we're far along in our prayer journey, have experienced similar feelings. Joni confesses, "Sometimes I don't even have the nerve to speak to the Son. I'm too humiliated, too grieved, too dust-dirty to speak to Jesus. *Fairest Lord Jesus, you have died on the cross for me. You have given me everything. But—I'm sorry, Lord—you shouldn't even be seeing me like this.*"

At such times, she turns to the Holy Spirit, who is the Comforter, and asks him to sit next to her. She prays: "Here I am, Holy Spirit. In dust and ashes. Licking the dirt. Face down. Covered with soot. Stained. Marred. Like the psalmist before me, 'My soul cleaves to the dust.' Hear my prayer, dear Counselor."

Joni counts her coming to God in such humility as a profound, extraordinary privilege. In fact, she says that it's when we pray in that way that we experience the greatest treasures from God.

When we sense deep in our souls the holiness of God, contrasted with our own impurities, we experience the transformation of dust and ashes. In our faith journey, we discover more and more our own weaknesses. Yet we also discover the great reality that God draws us into his glory as we call on him.

Joni quotes Andrew Murray, who wrote many enduring books on prayer: "In praying, we are often occupied with ourselves, with our own needs, and our own efforts in the presentation of them. God longs to reveal himself, to fill us with himself. Be still before him and allow his Holy Spirit to waken and stir up in your soul the childlike disposition of absolute dependence and confident expectation."

Holy Spirit of God, we're told you pray for us with
"groanings that cannot be uttered." You know
how I can identify with "cleaving to the dust."
Please cleanse my soul and revive my spirit.

Have mercy on me, O God, because of your unfailing love. Because of your great compassion, blot out the stain of my sins. PSALM 51:1, NLT

WORRIED? OR FREE?

OLE HALLESBY asks, "How do you feel as Jesus looks at you?"

Perhaps you're full of joy at the thought, with gratitude for all he's done for you. Perhaps the very thought makes you smile and you think of the words of the song, "Why should I feel discouraged? Why should the shadows come? . . . His eye is on the sparrow, and I know he watches me."

Or perhaps not. Maybe his watching makes you uneasy.

Hallesby says that many people become fearful at the thought of Jesus looking at them. In fact, they can think of nothing more frightening, and so they hide.

When we sin, we're like Adam and Eve in the Garden, weighed down by our failures. Yet Jesus is the one who is ready and able to help. We read that when he saw the multitudes, he had compassion on them. Likewise, he has compassion on us when we come to him, weak and sinful, and ask for his help.

When a blind man was brought to him, Jesus asked the man, "What do you want me to do for you?"

Jesus asks each of us the same question. He is not watching us to condemn us, but to heal us and empower us.

The blind man answered Jesus' question, "Lord, I want to see!"

"All right," Jesus said. "Receive your sight! Your faith has healed you." (See Mark 10:46-52.)

And what was his faith? Hallesby tells us all the faith needed is simply coming to Jesus in our helplessness and asking him to free us.

"I sing because I'm happy," the song goes, "I sing because I'm free. His eye is on the sparrow, and I know he watches me."

Jesus watches. He stands at the door and knocks. He asks, "What do you want me to do for you?"

Lord, I open the door to my heart and welcome you
to come in. Make yourself at home in every room.
Change what you need to change. I rejoice that you
watch me and that you desire to be a part of my life.

O LORD, if you heal me, I will be truly healed; if you save me, I will be truly saved. My praises are for you alone! JEREMIAH 17:14, NLT

WATCH OUT FOR SUCCESS

PAUL TOURNIER, from his long experience as a medical doctor and philosopher, says that although we may think we are solving our problems, we can never fully free ourselves from them. "We think we have solved a problem one day only to find it is still with us on the morrow. Faith does not make life easier. Believers have as many difficulties as skeptics."

We all find ourselves in this human condition, and Tournier tells us it's in our problems and "real-life stories" we encounter God. He speaks to us in our predicaments, and what he says is often far different from what we expected.

Job wanted answers from God about his undeserved suffering, but he didn't get answers to his questions. Instead he received the experience of encountering God and of having his understanding of God vastly expanded.

We live with questions. We live with success and failure all our lives! God speaks to us as we confess our weakness and our need for him. In both the psychological and the spiritual realms, failure often produces more fruit than success. "The hard road of failure and disappointment," Tournier asserts, "takes us farther than our success. Nothing is more dangerous for a person than unlimited success."

That assertion may jar us, for we would all prefer unlimited success. We envy those who have it. But, Tournier explains, "The privileged ones to whom success comes early suffer from a serious lack of human understanding."

The issue is not success or failure, prosperity or poverty, but whether or not we are fulfilling God's purpose. We are adventurers either for or against him, and the great success in life is to be engaged in his adventures.

Lord, you know how important success is for me. Obviously, success is good and necessary in life, but grant me your perspective about it. Let my drives be in sync with your will and my reactions tempered by your Spirit.

What joy for those whose strength comes from the LORD. PSALM 84:5, NLT

COSMIC MYSTERY

NANCY GUTHRIE writes, "Sometimes what causes us the most pain and confusion is not what God says to us but the fact that in the midst of difficulty, he seems to say nothing at all."

God's silence. This was a major issue for Job, who in his extreme circumstances asked for answers from the Almighty.

The silence of God has been explored by many novelists, playwrights, and theologians—and by most people who have gone through deep waters. We may not eloquently articulate our questions, but they roil deep within us. The answers we receive can feel inadequate to provide comfort or to genuinely explain what weighs on us and bewilders us. We long to know why devastating things happen to us. Like Job, we long for understanding so we can bear the pain.

Did God answer Job? He did, but with his own questions and a long, dramatic romp describing birds, beasts, mountains, and storms—all the wonders of his creation. Where was Job when God made all this?.

"God doesn't explain," Guthrie writes. "Instead he reveals himself, and in the midst of his awesome presence, Job's questions are not answered—they simply disappear."

Magnificence and mystery—those are the two "answers" the book of Job reveals to us. We find much wisdom, guidance, and truth in God's Word. We also find much mystery. Our minds cannot even frame the right questions.

We'll never solve all the mysteries, but we know all that happens is weighted with significance. "Job had no idea he was a player in a cosmic confrontation," Nancy says. "He had no idea his faithfulness in extreme difficulty mattered so much. But it did."

It does for us as well, as we worship God in his grandeur and pray that he will keep us faithful. Each follower of God is a key player in this magnificent mystery.

God of all creation, I am in awe of all you have made. Help me to leave my questions with you and walk in your light as you illuminate my path. Protect me from all that wages war against my soul.

Listen to my voice in the morning, LORD. Each morning I bring my requests to you and wait expectantly. PSALM 5:3, NLT

HOW WEAK ARE WE?

THOMAS À KEMPIS confronts us with this blunt statement: "Remember that you are a sinner, entangled and enchained by many passions. You are much weaker than you realize."

As we fight the good fight of faith, we may experience wonderful victories. Yet, just as the apostle Paul admitted that he didn't do the good he wanted to do, we sometimes find our passions are stronger than our commitments. As the months and years go by, we discover that, yes, we are weaker than we realized—*much* weaker than we realized!

As we experience personal failures, the slow dawning of that reality can be crushing. Yet there's good news as well. Scripture repeatedly tells us that God can do his best work in us when we fully realize our weakness and draw our strength from him. Entangled and enchained, limping and struggling, we call out to God—and he promises to hear us and to come to our aid.

Sometimes addictions and circumstances are so difficult that it seems God does not answer at all. Yet we are to keep on calling and patiently persist in our dependence on him. In our weakness, God ultimately brings his grace and hope.

Thomas à Kempis points us to the Holy Spirit, the Comforter. He prays that the Spirit will visit him often: "Set me free from evil passions, and heal my heart— that cleansed in spirit, I may become able to love, strong to endure, and steadfast to persevere."

Father, here I am again, weak and in complete need of your Holy Spirit to cleanse and empower me. Here is my will and all that I am. Enable me to live the life you desire for me today.

Come and show me your mercy, as you do for all who love your name.
PSALM 119:132, NLT

FAMILIAR, BUT ASTOUNDING

October 16

JESUS, in John 3, said to Nicodemus, "No one has ever gone to heaven and returned. But the Son of Man has come down from heaven" (verse 13, NLT).

What an astounding statement! Jesus was, of course, referring to himself, and we can only imagine the reaction of Nicodemus during that nighttime visit.

Jesus then said something even more astounding: "For God loved the world so much that he gave his one and only Son, so that everyone who believes in him will not perish but have eternal life" (NLT).

When we see the familiar reference to John 3:16 on billboards and barns, placards and tracts, we might forget that it wasn't a theologian or evangelist who made that famous statement—it was Jesus, who said it about himself. He followed up with another declaration about the Father's compassion and love: "God sent his Son into the world not to judge the world, but to save the world through him" (John 3:17, NLT).

These statements are so familiar that we need to pause and ponder them, taking time to let them soak in. What marvelous good news! Jesus says that his Father's goal in sending him was not judgment but salvation. We who believe are the recipients of the love that goes beyond mortal understanding.

"I tell you the truth," Jesus says, "those who listen to my message and believe in God who sent me have eternal life. They will never be condemned for their sins, but they have already passed from death into life" (John 5:24, NLT).

His invitation is extended to everyone. Jesus says that all who are thirsty, burdened, and heavy laden should come to him.

Father in heaven, thank you for your great love in sending Jesus to redeem us. Fill me with praise for this most wonderful work of all. Help us to share your invitation with those who are thirsty, burdened, and heavy laden.

Humans can reproduce only human life, but the Holy Spirit gives birth to spiritual life.
JOHN 3:6, NLT

JUDGING OUR UBIQUITOUS SCREENS *October 17*

BROTHER LAWRENCE advises, "All things hinge on your hearty renunciation of everything you are aware does not lead to God."

Wow! With that thought in mind, consider the culture we live in.

What leads us to God? What draws us away? What things, as soon as we open the door to them, clamp right onto our spirits like a spider sucking God's vitality right out of us?

We might make a personal list with two categories. First, what leads us to God? The list might include the wonders of creation, watching films of powerful authenticity, showing love to family members, studying diligently, and working effectively—the list could and should be long.

Second, what draws us away? What "innocent" things fritter away our time and keep us from staying in step with the Holy Spirit? What sucks the Spirit right out of our lives? This category should also be large. It's a perfect opportunity to ask for the Holy Spirit's wisdom in sorting things out.

Making such lists might reduce the gray areas in our lives. Actually, we might find plenty of *good* on the large and small electronic screens that are so ubiquitous in our lives. In contrast, what on those screens draws us away from God?

Notice Brother Lawrence's *hearty* renunciation of *everything* that doesn't enhance his practicing God's presence. That sounds severe, and it is. Yet this comes from a man extraordinarily happy and blessed. He made these distinctions and choices, and yet it didn't result in deprivation.

Accustom yourself to continual conversation with God. Lawrence urges, a conversation that is free and simple. He is intimately present with us.

"In things doubtful," we need to ask his assistance to know his will. And the things we plainly see he requires of us, we should perform. Simply offer all things to him, and give him thanks. "We are also employed in praising, adoring, and loving Him incessantly, for His infinite goodness and perfection."

Lord, I praise you for your goodness and love. In all my choices, help me to discern what saddens you and what makes you smile. Let my will be fused with yours so that I can get fully in step with your Spirit.

Seek his will in all you do, and he will show you which path to take.
PROVERBS 3:6, NLT

NEVER ABANDONED

October 18

KING DAVID, in Psalm 27, gives us a remarkable example of praying with vulnerability, repentance, and faith. He senses God's warm invitation: "Hear me as I pray, O LORD. Be merciful and answer me! My heart has heard you say, 'Come and talk with me.' And my heart responds, 'LORD, I am coming'" (verses 7-8, NLT).

Yet, as soon as David prays these words, he seems disturbed by memories of his sins or things he's done that he fears displeased the Lord. He abruptly shifts his prayers to pleading: "Do not turn your back on me. Do not reject your servant in anger. You have always been my helper. Don't leave me now; don't abandon me, O God of my salvation!" (verse 9, NLT).

Apparently, as he prayed, he received full assurance that God would answer that pleading, for he proclaims: "Even if my father and mother abandon me, the LORD will hold me close" (verse 10, NLT).

David then gets down to the business at hand of talking to the Lord about his current troubles: "Teach me how to live, O LORD. Lead me along the right path, for my enemies are waiting for me. Do not let me fall into their hands. For they accuse me of things I've never done; with every breath they threaten me with violence. Yet I am confident I will see the LORD's goodness while I am here in the land of the living" (verses 11-13, NLT).

David gets specific about his predicaments, lays them before the Lord, and leaves them there, confident in him. He then turns to us and advises from long and hard experience: "Wait patiently for the LORD. Be brave and courageous. Yes, wait patiently for the LORD" (verse 14, NLT).

In Psalm 28, he bursts out in exultant song: "Praise the LORD! For he has heard my cry for mercy. The LORD is my strength and shield. I trust him with all my heart. He helps me, and my heart is filled with joy. I burst out in songs of thanksgiving" (verses 6-7, NLT).

David in these psalms gives us a model of God's warm invitation to come talk to him, to throw ourselves on his mercy, to tell him of our troubles, and then to leave them with him and rejoice in his love and care.

Lord, I am grateful for your invitation to talk to you. It's a privilege, and I ask that you'll make our conversation right now authentic. May your Spirit open my mind and speed wisdom and courage into all my thoughts.

The LORD is my light and my salvation—so why should I be afraid?
PSALM 27:1, NLT

THE POWER OF SALT AND LIGHT

October 19

HELMUT THIELICKE, in preaching on Jesus' statement that his followers are the salt of the earth, wondered if his listeners grasped the enormity of what Jesus said. Helmut unpacked the thrust of Jesus' words this way: "You disciples, you inconspicuous little crowd, you wretched little troop—you are the salt of the earth, and the light of the world."

He hastened to point out Jesus did not say the disciples *should* be salt and light, but that they *were*. Why? Because their Father in heaven had called them to be salt and light.

We, too, are called to be salt and light in our troubled world. And just like the disciples, we, too, are a "wretched little troop."

It's hard to grasp the enormity of Jesus' words. The needs are so vast, it's like looking up at the stars on a cloudless night and realizing its not just millions of stars up there but billions of *galaxies!* When we see the needs in our families and communities, the full prisons in our nation, and refugees worldwide torn from their homes, we are confronted by endless, tragic complexities and hatreds. How can we begin to be salt and light?

Yet the point of Jesus' challenge is that even a tiny pinch of salt flavors a meal and a pinprick of light in the darkness is very bright indeed. God can make salt and light out of our weakness and wretchedness if we will let him.

"He who does the will of God," Thielicke says, "is more than world history, more than nature, more than all the peaks of intellect, more than the whole cosmos. He is more than all of this—do you understand? Even though he be one of the 'nobodies,' he dwells beneath the Father's good pleasure."

Father in heaven, sometimes I don't feel at all like salt or light. By myself, I can't season or illuminate anything. Please cleanse me, pour your salt and light into me, and fill me with your love.

Salt is good for seasoning. But if it loses its flavor, how do you make it salty again?
LUKE 14:34, NLT

WHEN THE WORST COMES

KING DAVID, in Psalm 11, asks a probing question millions of people around the world would no doubt like to ask: "The foundations of law and order have collapsed. What can the righteous do?" (verse 3, NLT).

Even though we may be privileged to live in a nation ruled by law and order, others have not been as fortunate. And as we see world events unfolding, we realize our own security is not guaranteed.

If banks fail and jobs disappear and desperate men rampage in the streets of our neighborhoods, what would we do? If criminals come to our homes with guns and we couldn't call the police—what would we do? If the foundations of law and order collapse, where would we turn?

When some advised David to flee to the mountains and hide, he rejected their advice and declared, "I trust in the LORD for protection. . . . The LORD is in his holy Temple; the LORD still rules from heaven. He watches everyone closely, examining every person on earth. The LORD examines both the righteous and the wicked" (verses 1, 4-5, NLT).

David trusted God for protection and received it, but we know that many Christians have been martyred. In the book of Acts, Stephen was full of the Holy Spirit—but he was stoned to death.

David, throughout his life, passionately sought the Lord. In many extreme circumstances, he received protection and inspiration from God. At times, he also received a rebuke and then forgiveness for his sins. As we pray, we become engaged with the God who shows his love and concern for us through Christ.

We may see miraculous answers of protection, but we may not. God is sovereign, and he undertakes in ways beyond our comprehension. Yet we are assured he will walk with us through the darkest valleys.

David ends Psalm 11 with an affirmation of hope: "For the righteous LORD loves justice. The virtuous will see his face" (verse 7, NLT).

---

*Father in heaven, I pray for the leaders of our nation,
that they will listen to you. Help them to make wise
decisions. Defeat the forces of evil. Help me to do
my part to contribute to peace and justice.*

The LORD is in his holy Temple; the LORD still rules from heaven. He watches everyone closely, examining every person on earth. PSALM 11:4, NLT

THE MARY MODEL

October 21

OLE HALLESBY says that in reading "the delightful little account of the wedding in Cana of Galilee," some secrets of prayer became plain to him. He saw Mary, the mother of Jesus, as a model of true prayer. Here's why:

"In the first place, she went to the right place with the need. She goes to Jesus and tells him everything."

Hallesby's next insight was that Mary used just a few simple words: "They have no wine." He observed, "To pray is to tell Jesus what we lack. Intercession is to tell Jesus what we see that others lack."

Third, Mary did nothing more. She told Jesus about her friends' need and left it in his hands. Having done her part, she didn't worry about how he would handle the situation.

The fact is, what Jesus did in changing water into wine was a surprise to Mary. Who knows what surprises may come when we pray?

"Our prayer lives will become restful," Hallesby says, "when it really dawns on us that we've done all we're supposed to do when we've spoken to him about it. We have left the matter in the hands of Jesus, and, like the mother of Jesus, we can go back to our duties secure and happy."

Yes, back to our duties. Our leaving our concerns and distress in Jesus' hands does not mean prayer eliminates the need to take action and to work in harmony with the Holy Spirit. But we work with the assurance we're in his care: all is being done that must be done.

Hallesby says we can experience "a certain childlike inquisitiveness, having left the matter in the hands of Jesus. We say to ourselves, 'It will be interesting now to see how he solves this difficulty.'"

Lord Jesus, I leave in your care everything that gives me such concern. Help me to stop being anxious and to have a childlike spirit of anticipation about what you will do.

Each day the LORD pours his unfailing love upon me, and through each night I sing his songs, praying to God who gives me life. PSALM 42:8, NLT

HELPING THE POOR

BILLY GRAHAM says in regard to poverty and hunger, "By my reading of Scripture, I am convinced that we are called to action, not apathy."

His conclusion is sound. Hundreds of Bible verses show God's special compassion for the poor and the Lord's commands for us to act on their behalf. In fact, in God's pronouncements of judgment in the Bible, he often condemns callous treatment of the impoverished.

Here are a few relevant verses:

> Give justice to the poor and the orphan; uphold the rights of the oppressed and the destitute. Rescue the poor and helpless. (Psalm 82:3-4, NLT)

> Give generously to the poor, not grudgingly, for the LORD your God will bless you in everything you do. . . . I am commanding you to share freely with the poor. (Deuteronomy 15:10-11, NLT)

> It is a sin to belittle one's neighbor; blessed are those who help the poor. (Proverbs 14:21, NLT)

> If you help the poor, you are lending to the LORD—and he will repay you! (Proverbs 19:17, NLT)

Billy Graham took Scripture to heart. He spoke to hundreds in the U.S. Congress about the biblical mandates. He helped make a documentary about the poor in Appalachia. He reported to President Eisenhower on the severe hunger and destitution he'd encountered around the world and conferred with Secretary of State John Foster Dulles on sharing America's surpluses.

Graham could do things most of us cannot. But we can do things that others cannot.

This, of course, is where the Holy Spirit comes in. We are to live in vital union with him. As we ask, he will guide us to our personal responses to Scripture.

The bottom line? Consider Micah 6:8: "The LORD has told you what is good, and this is what he requires of you: to do what is right, to love mercy, and to walk humbly with your God" (NLT).

Lord, as I see the needs in my community and around the world, help me not to be overwhelmed but to ask you what I can do. Set my priorities for me, Lord, and help me to grab hold of the opportunities you give me.

Honor the LORD with your wealth and with the best part of everything you produce.
PROVERBS 3:9, NLT

GOD'S DELIGHTS

A. W. TOZER writes, "Many think of God as far removed, gloomy and mightily displeased with everything!" He then vigorously declares that view erroneous. "True, God hates sin, but now in Christ, all believing souls are objects of God's delight."

Tozer goes on to quote Zephaniah as capturing this aspect of God's personality: "The LORD thy God in the midst of thee is mighty; he will save, he will rejoice over thee with joy; he will rest in his love, he will joy over thee with singing" (3:17, KJV).

He points out the Bible emphasizes God enjoys his creation. For instance, in Psalm 104, we read at great length about God's greatness: "You are dressed in a robe of light. You stretch out the starry curtain of the heavens. . . . You placed the world on its foundation. . . . You make springs pour water into the ravines, so streams gush down from the mountains. They provide water for all the animals. . . . Birds nest beside the streams and sing among the branches" (verses 2, 5, 10-11, 12, NLT).

In describing and celebrating all of God's creation in this exuberant chapter of Holy Scripture, the psalmist declares, "May the glory of the LORD continue forever! The LORD takes pleasure in all he has made!" (verse 31, NLT).

God enjoys his creation, and that includes us.

God loves us and delights in us and prepares a place for us. What a hope!

Tozer tells us, "Heaven is full of music because it is the place where the pleasures of holy love abound."

Lord, it's delightful you're delighted in your creation.
You certainly have unlimited wonders to celebrate!
I pray you'll bring me into full harmony with
your Spirit so that I can live in your delight.

The LORD's delight is in those who fear him, those who put their hope in his unfailing love. PSALM 147:11, NLT

FROM RAGS TO GOD

GEORGE MACDONALD was unusually sensitive to the way his actions affected others. He knew when we "stand up for our rights" we can violate the spirit of Christ.

"Lord, I have fallen again—a human clod!" he lamented. "Selfish I was and stood on my rights."

MacDonald well understood how we might be "in the right" but very, very wrong. "Keep me from wrath," he prayed, "even when it seems ever so right; my wrath will never work thy righteousness."

Consider his prayer—a prayer much needed today, yet so rare: "Give me the power to let my rag-rights go."

"Rag-rights"? What does he mean?

We hear endless arguments about human rights and how to ensure for all people peace, health, and security. That's a good and biblical goal. Yet the idea that we have all sorts of rights and should aggressively agitate and sue to protect and enforce them fosters a society of litigation and bitter conflict.

When we stand on our rights, we can create all sorts of unintended consequences, from road rage to retaliatory insults. There's a fine line between standing strong on principle and asserting our rights without the Holy Spirit's guidance.

It's the human condition to be intensely concerned about getting our own rights without caring nearly as much about others' rights. But when we kneel before the Lord and do a spiritual inventory, we get a comprehensive understanding of our "rights."

MacDonald invited God to carry his rag-rights away in God's "great wind." He prayed his heart would handle the wrongs against him the way God had forgiven him his wrongs. "Lord, in the Spirit's hurricane, I pray, strip my soul—dress it then thy way. Change for me all my rags to cloth of gold."

Lord Jesus Christ, Son of God, have mercy on me, a sinner. When I consider all you endured for me, I don't ask that you'll give me all my rights but cleansing and strengthening to serve you and others.

Never let loyalty and kindness leave you! . . . Don't be impressed with your own wisdom. Instead, fear the LORD and turn away from evil. PROVERBS 3:3, 7, NLT

A CHANGE OF CLOTHES

JILL BRISCOE tells of a time when she had a very bad night. She went to bed with a sense of great heaviness, and when she awoke, she didn't feel she had slept at all.

Why? A fellow Christian once close to her had done something against her—and now the very sight of that person robbed her of all spiritual victory. She just couldn't get past her feelings. She felt drowned in despondency.

What delivered her? She came upon Isaiah 61:1, 3: "The LORD has anointed Me . . . to console those who mourn in Zion, to give them beauty for ashes, the oil of joy for mourning, the garment of praise for the spirit of heaviness" (NKJV).

What struck her was that she had been wearing heaviness as a garment she had put on herself. She recognized she needed to allow God to dress her spirit with praise.

What seems particularly fascinating is Briscoe's comment that it was praise *for her adversary* that released her.

When we're really mad at someone, or when someone we love and trust has betrayed us, the last thing we feel like doing is giving God praise for that person. Yet we've all heard it's in forgiving those who have done terrible things to us that we ourselves find release.

But how do we both forgive and praise?

Jill Briscoe somehow praised God for her adversary. Such forgiveness and praise requires a special work of the Holy Spirit. But he is ready to aid us.

Romans 8:26-27 tells us, "The Holy Spirit helps us in our weakness. For example, we don't know what God wants us to pray for. But the Holy Spirit prays for us with groanings that cannot be expressed in words. And the Father who knows all hearts knows what the Spirit is saying, for the Spirit pleads for us believers in harmony with God's own will" (NLT).

---

*Lord Jesus, sometimes my emotions are like a heavy,
wet raincoat dragging me down. Infuse me with
praise despite my feelings. Help me to fling off my
soggy garments! Put your song within me.*

Sing a new song of praise to him. PSALM 33:3, NLT

A CONDUIT

October 26

FRED SMITH often spoke of our being the pipe for God's power to flow through and not the source of the power itself. "When I get out of the way and let God work through me," he says, "I am the pipe. . . . The pipe never gets tired. When I try to be the pump as well as the pipe, it takes way more than I have."

With his pipe and pump illustration, Smith gives us a word picture of the apostle Paul's declarations about our weaknesses and God's strength. We read in 2 Corinthians 12:9-10, "I am glad to boast about my weaknesses, so that the power of Christ can work through me. That's why I take pleasure in my weaknesses, and in the insults, hardships, persecutions, and troubles that I suffer for Christ. For when I am weak, then I am strong" (NLT).

Paul's strength was extraordinary. In fact, his endurance of shipwreck, beatings, and stonings seems superhuman. In many ways it was, for his strength came from above.

"When I try to substitute my power for God's," Fred says, "I become powerless, dissatisfied, even frantic and defeated."

In contrast, Paul said he could do all things through Christ who strengthened him.

Sometimes it may seem we can't do even one thing well, let alone *all* things. Yet whatever our variety of experiences and challenges as we go through our seasons of life, God is faithful. He is the one who pumps out the power when we come to him and seek his will.

Properly aligned with God's will, we can become the pipe—the delivery system—for his grace, love, and blessings.

Father above, sometimes I feel overwhelmed. I have plenty of weaknesses for you to transform into strengths. Please guide and strengthen me as I open myself to be a conduit for your grace.

You will receive power when the Holy Spirit comes upon you. ACTS 1:8, NLT

LITTLE FAITH, BUT . . .

D. L. MOODY admitted, "When I first became a Christian, I thought I would be glad when I got further on, and got established. I thought I would be so strong there would not be any danger. But the longer I live, the more danger I see there is."

After he learned that strength and capacity to meet dangers come from God alone he also admitted, "The moment we lean on ourselves, down we go. The moment we get self-contented and think we are able to stand and overcome, we are on dangerous territory. We are standing on the edge of a precipice."

Yet God can keep us from plunging into the canyon below—when we call to him for help. Moody urges us to realize that our strength and help come from on high. He emphasizes nothing in heaven or on earth is too hard for God. Rather, he is able to do "above and beyond whatever we can imagine." Yet, we must be patient and let God do it his way, in his time.

Moody uses as an illustration the story of a woman in Scotland who was complimented on being a woman of great faith: "No," she replied, "I am a woman of little faith. But I have got a great God."

When we see the dangers Moody saw—as we move further along on our spiritual journeys and become dismayed at our weakness and the forces threatening us—encouragement comes as we realize we have a great God who loves us.

The Lord reaches down to the precipice and helps us scramble not only to safety but to fresh beginnings.

Father of all creation, help me to be filled with a sense of wonder and praise at your love and grace. Flood my mind and soul so that impurities drain away. Protect me from myself, and fill me with your Holy Spirit.

If you think you are standing strong, be careful not to fall. The temptations in your life are no different from what others experience. And God is faithful.
I CORINTHIANS 10:12-13, NLT

THE COMPLETE PACKAGE

FRANÇOIS FÉNELON says that when we cry out to God in our troubles, he often sends his help in unexpected, mysterious ways—and that his responses help us in more ways than simply coming to our rescue.

He lists as *most valuable* the following characteristics of God's responses:

That which most exercises our faith
That which shows us the limits of human wisdom
That which keeps us simple and humble
That which reminds us of our dependence on God

We are all on a spiritual journey, and God's engagement with us includes seeding, pruning, and cultivating our growth. The Lord has his own agenda, and someday we will see the full effectiveness and wonder of his responses to our prayers.

"God's ways of providing for us are both beautiful and mysterious," Fénelon writes. "He puts what he pleases where he pleases."

Sometimes—in fact, many times—we may not see any beauty or perceive any meaning in what we're going through. We search for answers to prayer that fit what we're longing to have happen. Yet as we wait, Fénelon's little list of contributions to our spiritual growth may be quietly at work in us. All that is happening is preparing us for glory to come.

"Even if the present is bitter," he assures us, "it is enough for us if it is the will of God. His will is our only treasure."

Fénelon urges us to accept what God allows and to invite him to do his work in us. "Open your heart to the riches of God's grace."

Lord, sometimes it is confusing that I pray and
yet don't see your responses. Please open my eyes
and understanding to how you are at work, both
in me and in all that's going on around me.

Let all that I am wait quietly before God, for my hope is in him. PSALM 62:5, NLT

WHO'S IN CHARGE?

PHILIP YANCEY says that when he's in a time of spiritual dryness, he asks God to use it to prepare him for future growth.

When we experience such dryness, instead of asking why it's happening, we can cultivate a spirit of expectancy: how might the Lord use it to stretch us toward deeper maturity?

Yancey describes what many of us experience—we sometimes feel as if we're on a spiritual high, and other times we feel as if we're in a spiritual desert. Then he shares a personal experience:

"On the hill behind my mountain home, each spring a pair of red foxes raises a litter of kits. Once, when a visitor from New Zealand stopped by, I took him to the den, warning him that he may see and hear nothing at all. 'They are wild animals, you know,' I said. 'We're not in charge.'"

Later Yancey received a letter from his friend saying that his comment about the foxes had helped him. The New Zealander sometimes felt God close and other times did not sense his presence. "He is wild, you know," he wrote. "We're not in charge."

We are at God's beck and call, not the other way around. That means we do our duty and leave the rest to him. "Out of duty comes joy," Mother Teresa said, but we well know that she did not always feel joy. She experienced mostly spiritual desert but knew the joy of obedience in her long spiritual journey of very different seasons.

Martin Luther insisted we must realize God is free to do as he will and is not subject to limitations. The Holy Spirit sometimes gives us a sense of his presence and sometimes he does not.

God is sovereign. We're not in charge.

Holy Spirit, I know that you are like the wind,
which comes without prompting. I open myself to you
now. Empower me to soldier on and care for others,
whatever the challenges and whatever my feelings.

You are God, O Sovereign LORD. Your words are truth, and you have promised these good things to your servant. 2 SAMUEL 7:28, NLT

THE OTHER KIND OF POWER

October 30

RAY STEDMAN writes that God does just two things in history. "Everything in the whole universe gathers around these two. God creates and God redeems."

Stedman describes the breadth of God's work: "He is our Maker and our Healer. God makes things live, and God heals what is broken. God is life, and God is love."

Then he gives an astounding application: "That is what you will be if you become godly."

Stedman draws attention to Ephesians 5:1: "Be imitators of God, as beloved children" (NASB).

We're to follow God's example—to be like him, to be *godlike*. That word and that idea may make us uncomfortable; but the truth is, we are called to be godlike.

That's not to say we become little gods—like Superman or a New Age personification of deity. We have new life from Christ, and we are to reflect the one true, holy God.

Ray Stedman challenges every one of us: "Be a godlike man. Be a godlike woman. What will you be like if you are godlike? Would you be strong? Yes. Filled with power? Yes, but be careful. It's a different kind of power than the world desires—quieter, less apparent, but far mightier.

"Will you be happy if you are godlike? Yes, but not the world's kind of happiness. Will you be wise and kind? Of course, more than you have ever been, because that is what God is.

"If you become godly, you will learn to love and to heal, to restore and bring together. You will learn to live to the fullest capacity of your humanity."

God creates. God redeems. "Imitate God, therefore, in everything you do, because you are his dear children" (Ephesians 5:1, NLT).

Lord, help me to receive all that you desire to pour
into me. Help me to live to my fullest capacity
because you are guiding and you are giving me
your power to do your work in your way.

Let the Spirit renew your thoughts and attitudes. Put on your new nature, created to be like God—truly righteous and holy. EPHESIANS 4:23-24, NLT

D. L. MOODY gives some wonderful homespun stories and insights about heaven. He describes going home to visit his mother, hoping to take her by surprise. Quietly going from room to room and then through the whole house, he was disappointed to find she didn't happen to be there. Just then, he says, "Home lost its charm, for mother made home sweet to me. And it's loved ones who will make heaven sweet for us. Christ is there; God the Father is there; many who are dear to us are there."

Moody quotes a believer who remembered that as a boy heaven was to him a great, shining city with walls, domes, and spires and cold, white-robed angels he didn't know. But his little brother died, and then he knew one little fellow in the great city above. Another brother died, and there were two loved ones there. Much later in life, one of his little children died. Then a second, a third, and a fourth of his beloved children went to heaven. This made him feel a part of himself was already there. He no longer thought of it as walls and domes and spires.

From Matthew 18:10, Moody points out that children's angels always behold the face of the Father in heaven. Angels are not cold strangers.

The evangelist received a card from a friend in England who had lost his beloved mother. This friend, instead of the customary black border on the card, had printed a wide *gold* border to indicate she had gone to the golden city.

"To me it is a sweet thought that death does not separate us from the Master," says Moody. "Many live in the bondage and fear of death. If I have eternal life, death cannot touch that." He quotes missionary Hannah More, who said on her deathbed, "It is a glorious thing to die."

He also quotes 1 John 3:2: "Beloved, now are we the sons of God, and it doth not yet appear what we shall be: but we know that, when he shall appear, we shall be like him; for we shall see him as he is" (KJV).

---

*Lord Jesus Christ, thank you for your promise that
you are preparing a place for us. Grant me your
comfort as I think of loved ones now in your golden
city. Pour into my mind your heavenly thoughts.*

Store your treasures in heaven, where moths and rust cannot destroy, and thieves do not break in and steal. Wherever your treasure is, there the desires of your heart will also be.
MATTHEW 6:20-21, NLT

BEYOND GUILT

MARTIN LUTHER famously said, "If I fail to spend two hours in prayer each morning, the devil gets the victory through the day. I have so much business, I cannot go on without spending three hours daily in prayer."

John Wesley spent two hours daily in prayer, starting at four o'clock in the morning. Robert McCheyne reserved the hours from six to eight for his "noblest and most fruitful employment, communion with God." Billy Graham, when faced with his gargantuan challenges, would pray all night.

Really? When we hear such stories, how do we respond? Does it make us feel guilty? defensive? intrigued? Is it possible we're missing something by not spending more time in prayer?

The best response may well be to celebrate the rich heritage of power and joy experienced by men and women of great prayer. Instead of goads for guilt, let's view this heritage as a gilded invitation.

Let's face it, all Christians struggle to "pray without ceasing." We long to engage in prayer that cleanses, empowers, and equips; yet life ebbs and flows, and so do our prayer lives. We are all different. Charles Spurgeon and D. L. Moody both found that short, dynamic prayers were most effective for them.

William Wilberforce, who tirelessly and successfully led the fight to abolish slavery, struggled to find adequate time for prayer. He lamented the way the "perpetual hurry of business and company ruins me in soul." He longed for more solitude and earlier hours for prayer. "All may be done through prayer," he said. "O then, pray, pray, pray!"

Life is demanding, and twenty-four hours a day never seem enough. The invitation to prayer is always there. So are the cautions about ignoring it, such as this one from Luther: "If I should neglect prayer but a single day, I should lose a great deal of the fire of faith."

Lord, teach me to pray. Enable me to pray. Draw me to prayer today, for I have so many distractions. Purify my mind and soul, and let me rejoice that you hear and respond.

Those who trust in the LORD will find new strength. They will soar high on wings like eagles. They will run and not grow weary. They will walk and not faint.
ISAIAH 40:31, NLT

GLORIOUS OPPORTUNITIES?

OSWALD CHAMBERS made an intriguing statement: "If you are to live to God, he will never take from you the amazing mercy of having something to put to death."

What does that mean? For most of us, I suspect, the idea of putting our desires to death doesn't feel like an "amazing mercy." Self-denial is difficult.

Chambers followed that observation with an equally-mixed message: "Jesus sacrificed his natural life and made it spiritual by obeying his Father's voice, and we have any number of glorious opportunities of proving how much we love God by the delighted way we go to sacrifice for him."

Glorious opportunities? Delighted way? Sacrifice? More likely, when we read passages in Scripture about putting our old nature to death, we may feel dread or guilt.

Chambers was aware of that. He noted Jesus always talked about discipleship as an option so that we're free to say, "No thank you, that's a bit too stern for me." He said many have heard Jesus' call to a life of liberty and gladness but not his second call to deny ourselves and to put to death what violates the life of Christ in us.

Jesus says, "All who love me will do what I say. My Father will love them, and we will come and make our home with each of them. Anyone who doesn't love me will not obey me" (John 14:23-24, NLT).

So it boils down to love, and what an incredible love Jesus is describing: he and his Father making their home in us. What glorious opportunities we have to obey him, putting to death whatever would wreck our relationship with him.

Says Chambers, "Being born again from above is a perennial, perpetual, and eternal beginning; a freshness all the time in thinking and in talking and in living, the continual surprise of the life of God."

Lord, the thought that you live within me is far beyond my comprehension. Cleanse me of all that would corrupt our relationship. Help me to make choices that bring you joy and delight.

I am leaving you with a gift—peace of mind and heart. And the peace I give is a gift the world cannot give. So don't be troubled or afraid. JOHN 14:27, NLT

BEYOND CHEERY SELF-RELIANCE

JAY KESLER says that, for some time, he had the concepts of spiritual self-control and self-reliance confused. He saw self-control, part of the fruit of the Holy Spirit, as something he had to work on. However, he came to believe self-control and self-reliance are exact opposites.

We can turn in self-reliance to our own capacities when we're tempted or in threatening circumstances. However, spiritual self-control kicks in only when we turn to another source—the Holy Spirit—for control.

Jay points out that Jesus was in a weakened condition when he was in the desert being tempted by the devil. "He offered Jesus jeweled dreams of power and recognition," Jay says. "If he had been self-reliant, Jesus would have accepted Satan's offers, for Satan appealed to his independence. He wanted Jesus to stand up against the Father and grab his own realm of authority. Jesus refused. He turned immediately to the Bible and drove off Satan's attack with blistering arguments from Scripture."

If Satan is prowling around "looking for whom he may devour," we need more than our own powers of self to elude him. We need God's help.

Shirley Temple, in one of her films as a little girl, boldly raises herself up and with cheery, endearing confidence declares, "I'm very self-reliant!" It's a delightful scene, and we find such self-reliance admirable. Yet as we grow spiritually, we learn we need far more than self-reliance.

Kesler says, "I used to think it was a sign of weakness to say, 'I need help.' But that should be one of the distinctions of the Christian. Self-control is when I tenaciously, deliberately cling to Christ as the Source."

Father, more and more I realize that I can't experience
the fruit of your presence without surrendering
control of my life to your Holy Spirit. Help me to
give up self-reliance in favor of godly self-control.

The high and lofty one who lives in eternity, the Holy One, says this: "I live in the high and holy place with those whose spirits are contrite and humble. I restore the crushed spirit of the humble and revive the courage of those with repentant hearts."
ISAIAH 57:15, NLT

AUTHENTIC HEROES

KING DAVID says to the Lord in Psalm 16:3, "The godly people in the land are my true heroes! I take pleasure in them!" (NLT).

David had plenty of evildoers and antiheroes around to contend with, and he often prayed against them in his psalms. But here he acknowledges those who follow the Lord as a significant source of inspiration for him.

Whom do we look to as heroes?

In our culture, we have done such a thorough job of debunking heroes that we are largely bereft of them. The Bible in its realism tells us that all men and women are flawed, and only God is perfect. Yet that doesn't mean we cannot look for inspiration to Abraham, David, Daniel, Gideon, Deborah, Mary, John, Paul, and others.

Down through the centuries, and in our day as well, we can find examples of heroes of the faith—both famous and unknown—who have passionately sought to serve God.

When a Christian leader fails spectacularly, we hear all about it. Yet, as we worship and serve in community, we connect with a great many Christians who strive to live godly lives—and they inspire us.

David says, "Troubles multiply for those who chase after other gods" (Psalm 16:4, NLT), but he also exults, "LORD, you alone are my inheritance, my cup of blessing" (Psalm 16:5, NLT).

His ultimate pleasure and inspiration, then, is in God, and he goes on to proclaim, "I will bless the LORD who guides me; even at night my heart instructs me. I know the LORD is always with me. I will not be shaken, for he is right beside me. No wonder my heart is glad, and I rejoice" (Psalm 16:7-9, NLT).

---

*Lord, help me to rejoice that you love me despite
my failings. Thank you for the privilege of serving
with others who love you. Help me today to lighten
their loads and to be an inspiration to them.*

Since we are surrounded by such a huge crowd of witnesses to the life of faith, let us strip off every weight that slows us down, especially the sin that so easily trips us up.
HEBREWS 12:1, NLT

THE MYSTERY OF THE UNIVERSE   *November 5*

SHERWOOD WIRT tells us that the French poet Paul Claudel once remarked, after listening to Beethoven's Fifth Symphony, "Now I know that at the heart of the universe is joy."

That's a hopeful and optimistic perspective, but it seems to be contradicted by the vast emptiness of outer space and the agonies of humankind. To echo Einstein's question, Is the universe friendly?

In response, Wirt turns to the Scriptures where, amid the Bible's rugged realism, he finds repeated affirmations of joy. The psalmist speaks of "God my exceeding joy" (Psalm 43:4, KJV). Isaiah urges, "Sing, O heavens! Be joyful, O earth!" (Isaiah 49:13, NKJV). Jesus promised his disciples joy, and Peter writes of "inexpressible and glorious joy" (1 Peter 1:8, NIV).

The psalms are songs full of rejoicing and calls to rejoice. Woody observes that the words *gladness, joyousness, delight,* and *jubilation* appear 108 times. In the Psalms we find the full range of human experience, including despair and desperation. Yet the theme throughout is the call to "shout for joy . . . all the earth, burst into jubilant song with music" (Psalm 98:4, NIV).

Wirt turns to the word *celebrate* to capture the meaning for our times. "Let the heavens celebrate, and let the earth be glad." He calls for an injection of a spirit of jubilation. "The gospel is a message of grace and deliverance from sin by the death and resurrection of Jesus Christ, a call to repentance, commitment, and new life in the Spirit. It is a life not only victorious, but filled with the joy of heaven."

What is at the heart of the universe? The Bible affirms that "God is love" (1 John 4:8, 16, NLT) and that he lives in glory and joy. In our tragic, sinful world, that's often hard to comprehend.

Sherwood Wirt points us to the Good News: "The church has been given a joyful message, the greatest news that ever came to the human race."

Father in heaven, your salvation and joy are far beyond
my comprehension. Infuse my mind and spirit, I pray,
with the rejoicing and celebration that comes from
you. Purify me, Lord, and draw me into your joy.

You will show me the way of life, granting me the joy of your presence and the pleasures of living with you forever. PSALM 16:11, NLT

LEARNING TO BE HOPEFUL

LEWIS SMEDES describes the person who turns hope into a habit this way: "She looks for hope the way an artist looks for light. You can count on her every time to inject hope into a frightening situation."

He describes how such people function in the nitty-gritty challenges of life: "They often do the hoping for their families, their children, and their friends, and pull the others through the tough times by the infectious forces of their hopes."

Smedes admits that he is not one of these people; instead, he sets his mind on the belief that better things are possible. "It's a tug-of-war, I'll admit, and my heels are dug in for a long pull before hope has a firm and steady grip on my spirit."

Sometimes nothing seems hopeful about what's happening—and what is about to happen may look worse. In addition, we may not be hopeful about ourselves. Maybe we're discouraged about our faltering discipleship and lukewarm love for the Lord. We long for faith to move mountains, but our mountains don't budge.

When life's tempests and troubles drag on our spirits and we find it hard to have a natural sense of hope, we can still take action. Smedes challenges us to move beyond our feelings. "We can look for and find positive ways of developing the habit of hope, of becoming a more hopeful person and living the productive and courageous and cheerful life that only hopeful people can live."

John Chrysostom, the fourth century bishop of Constantinople, challenges us: "Christ is risen! Open the doors of your comfortable despair, that the great storms of hope may blow life into us again."

Father in heaven, here are my feelings and my fears—and
my hopelessness about things that never seem to change.
I know you want me to be a change agent. Please pour
hope and faith into my heart as I seek to trust you.

Be strong and courageous, all you who put your hope in the LORD! PSALM 31:24, NLT

DARKNESS AND DAWN

HENRI NOUWEN recounts the old Hasidic tale of a rabbi who asked his students how they could discern the dawn—when night ends and day begins. The students answered it might be when you can distinguish between a sheep and a dog, or a fig tree and a grapevine.

The rabbi had a far more significant definition: "Dawn is when you look into the face of another human being and you have enough light in you to recognize your brother or your sister."

What do we see when we look into the faces of others? How does God see them? If we were looking through God's eyes, what would we see?

Nouwen emphasizes that community depends on our seeing as God sees. "If we do not know we are the beloved sons and daughters of God, we're going to expect others to make us feel special and worthy. Ultimately they cannot. True community is not loneliness grabbing onto loneliness."

Instead, only God can fill the loneliness. When we see one another as beloved of God—whether we feel close and warm or not—we can be faithful to one another. Of course, that's seldom easy, for we are so very, very human. We have to admit our own faults and forgive the faults of others, even when they hurt us. It starts with having enough light to recognize our brothers and sisters.

"We are called to God's table together," Henri says, "not by ourselves. In community we discover what it means to let go of our self-will and to really live for others. We learn true humility."

O God who loves us, shine your light so I can truly
see the faces of those around me. Help me to love
them as you love them, especially the ones who seem
unlovable. Open my eyes, Lord, to see as you see.

This is [God's] commandment: We must believe in the name of his Son, Jesus Christ, and love one another, just as he commanded us. I JOHN 3:23, NLT

THE DINAH DISASTER

JILL BRISCOE sketches the story of Jacob's daughter in Genesis 34 with this description: "Dinah was young and daring and wanted to see how the women in the rest of the world lived. She went to the annual Canaanite festival of nature worship, even though this was forbidden for an Israelite. Dinah, so young and naïve, roamed around the festival awestruck, no doubt, by the town girls' oriental garments."

The story progresses to deep tragedy. Prince Shechem saw Dinah and raped her. Dinah's brothers were furious and plotted revenge. They murdered Shechem and his father and all the men in their town.

Jacob was appalled. "You have ruined me!" he said to his sons.

Jill writes, "Dinah had let curiosity lead her into disaster, and the little escapade caused suffering and death to many." She adds, "There is a Dinah in all of us. Suspicious that God is withholding fun and happiness from us, we go to the party either in our heads or in actual fact, just to see what the world has to offer."

The point here is not to blame the victim, but to emphasize the spiritual dangers of being lured into things that may seem just a bit edgy, things that we know God would be displeased with. A little wandering can trigger a cascade of tragedy.

In these days of 24/7 Internet access, media visuals, and temptations of all sorts assaulting our eyeballs, it's almost impossible to avoid invitations and images that ignite desires.

Temptations come in many forms, and when the tempter knocks, writes François Fénelon, everything depends on blocking his first advance. If he's not stopped at the door, we may find compulsions awakened in our hearts that flare into conflagrations.

We must be alert. The Holy Spirit prays for us and empowers us as we stay in tune with him. We can lay before him all our curiosities and desires.

Lord, images and ideas from the world assault me constantly, and I'm often tempted to pay too much attention. Grant me your spirit of discernment. Cleanse me and equip me to faithfully serve you.

Don't let us yield to temptation, but rescue us from the evil one. MATTHEW 6:13, NLT

THE SPIRITUAL GYM

FRANÇOIS FÉNELON writes, "It's amazing how strong we can become when we begin to understand what weaklings we are."

What does he mean?

If we go to the gym fully aware of our weakness, we can find ways to make our muscles strong. When we're aware of our weaknesses, we can take corrective action. We can position ourselves to learn and grow.

Fénelon unpacks the benefits of understanding our weaknesses. When we're weak, he says,

We admit and confess mistakes and correct them.
We're ready to learn from others.
We don't pretend to know everything, but say things clearly and simply, with sensitivity to others.
We more easily accept criticism and correction and less often criticize others.
We offer advice only to those who want it, without being dogmatic.
We try from our own weakness to simply help rather than come off as sophisticated and wise.

This list could go on and on. No matter how much we know, or even how much we've prayed and sought God, when we're in touch with reality, we're acutely aware of our weaknesses. It's then we turn to the Holy Spirit for his empowerment and wisdom, which we can humbly share with others.

We will also find it liberating to laugh at our own pretensions. We're all so very human, and we're healthiest when we can confess our faults to God. When we recognize them, we can say with at least a touch of lightness, "There I go again!"

Fénelon urges us to be patient with ourselves, because spiritual growth does not happen overnight. "Let this spiritual work be done in us quietly and peacefully."

---

*Lord, I want to keep growing deeper, stronger, and
wiser in my faith. Help me to recognize my weaknesses
and to invite you to do your work in bringing me
to greater maturity, wisdom, and obedience.*

[The Lord said,] "My grace is all you need. My power works best in weakness."
2 CORINTHIANS 12:9, NLT

BIGGER THAN GOLIATH?

EUGENE PETERSON says, "There are times when our grand human plans to do something for God are seen, after a night of prayer, to be a huge human distraction from what God is doing for us."

He is referring to the prophet Nathan's night of prayer after King David announced he wanted to build a house for God. At first, Nathan told the king to go ahead with his plans; but then, that night, God told Nathan David wasn't the one to build the Temple.

"Do you know what I think?" Peterson asks. "I think David was just about to cross over a line from being full of God to being full of himself."

As a highly successful king, David wanted to do something big for God. When Nathan brought him the jarring news that he shouldn't do it, how did he react?

He sat before the Lord.

Gene sees this as perhaps David's greatest act, more significant than killing Goliath or honoring his enemy Saul. Although David was the king, bursting with ambition and plans, he let himself be stopped by God. He sat before the Lord.

We naturally get caught up in our enterprises, whatever they may be, and God can bless them as we constantly pray for his guidance and strength. But when we taste success, we can forget who ultimately gives that success. God becomes an afterthought instead of the architect.

This story of Nathan and David tells us something about handling critics and disappointments. We all experience both, and for most of us, our bodies and minds churn with unpleasant reactions. Yet those are often times for greater understanding and spiritual growth. Those are times to sit before the Lord.

Eugene Peterson says that when David sat before the Lord, it wasn't passivity. "It was entering into the presence of God, becoming aware of God's word and trading in his plans for God's plans."

Lord, I have lots of plans. Help me to realize that your blessing on them is more important than my sorting out pros and cons. Help me to sit before you and to listen carefully, even when you tell me what I'd rather not hear.

The LORD says, "I will guide you along the best pathway for your life. I will advise you and watch over you." PSALM 32:8, NLT

EDGY, POINTED QUESTIONS

JONI EARECKSON TADA, when she learned she would always be a quad-riplegic, was desperate for answers to her questions. She turned to the book of Job and found that it raised more questions than it answered.

She was surprised by the nature of Job's agonizing questions. "Job's questions to God weren't of the polite, Sunday school variety," she says. "They were pointed, sharp, and at times on the border of blasphemy."

Here are some of the questions Job bluntly asked God:

Why didn't you let me die at birth?
Why do you keep wretched people like me alive?
How do you expect me to have hope and patience?
What did I ever do to you that I became the target for your arrows?
Why do you favor the wicked?
You're the one who created me, so why are you destroying me?
Since you've already decided I'm guilty, why should I even try?
Why do you hide your face and consider me your enemy?

Despite the fact Job had a very high view of God's majesty and justice, these are obviously in-your-face, insistent questions.

In discovering Job's honesty, Joni in her own suffering found great comfort. Job could say all these things and God didn't condemn him! The Lord listened and was ready to take on Job's wrenching, extreme questions.

As we pray, we need not be reluctant to place everything before the Lord. He already knows all about our anger, our bewilderment, our desires, our frustrations—and our need for a sense of getting through to him. He listens to all our prayers.

Joni was comforted as she read about Job's candor and persistence. She realized that, in her outbursts during times of suffering and doubt, she wasn't insulting God but reaching out to him.

Father in heaven, you know what brings me pain
and distress. Here are all my troubles and all the
ways I'm struggling. Help me, like Job, to see your
glory and to experience your strength and grace.

Don't worry about the wicked or envy those who do wrong. For like grass, they soon fade away. Like spring flowers, they soon wither. PSALM 37:1-2, NLT

WHEN DAD LISTENS

TIM STAFFORD says that when we pray for someone with cancer, we need to get rid of the idea that we're bringing the concern to God. He's already engaged. We're not asking him to join us—we're joining him. In fact, he's been waiting for us, and his concern is deeper than ours.

One of the astounding aspects of intercessory prayer is that we become partners with God in his concerns. We join him in his love and travail for others. We have the privilege of calling out to our Father in heaven, who is full of compassion and grace, for his healing, restoring, redeeming touch. We do not always see outward results, but we know the Father has heard and he is engaged.

Tim says that people might address him as Mr. Stafford or Tim, and he responds to everyone in a respectful way. But what really gets his attention is when he's addressed by another name: Dad.

"When we say 'Our Father,'" he says, "we are calling on God the way Jesus did. We have an innate longing to know God, our Creator. We crave this the way abandoned children yearn to know their fathers."

Tragically, many people have extremely poor models for fatherhood—yet the intense longing for a loving father burns within them. Everyone can turn to our heavenly Father, who has shown his extreme love for us.

Jesus invites us to pray as he did: "Our Father in heaven, may your name be kept holy. May your Kingdom come soon. May your will be done on earth, as it is in heaven" (Matthew 6:9-10, NLT).

When we pray that the Father's will be done on earth, we may not see the results. Yet his will means evil is overcome and his righteousness, love, and grace prevail. When we pray, "Our Father," he hears us as his children. We become channels of helping to bring his will to bear in our suffering world.

Father in heaven, thank you for your fatherly love.
Help me to join you in your love and compassion
for the world. Let your agenda become my agenda
and open my eyes to what you are doing.

Don't let evil conquer you, but conquer evil by doing good. ROMANS 12:21, NLT

ANOTHER SIDE OF HOLINESS

PAUL TOURNIER presents us with an intriguing statement: "Holiness proves to be the greatest adventure of all."

We each have our personal responses to the word *holiness*. We may be lifted by singing hymns about it and rejoicing in the majesty and righteousness of God. We may feel guilty and unclean, the way Isaiah did when brought into God's holy presence. Or we may think of media caricatures of people in severe dark clothes, sour and sanctimonious, proclaiming their own "holiness."

Holiness involves being filled with the Spirit—not at all a dark, sour, or sanctimonious experience. The fruit of the Spirit is "love, joy, peace, patience, kindness, goodness, faithfulness, gentleness, and self-control" (Galatians 5:22-23, NLT).

Tournier describes the surrendered, holy life as an adventure because "it is always on the alert, listening to God, to his voice and to his angels. It is an absorbing puzzle, an exciting search for signs of God."

Examples of such listening and searching abound throughout the Bible, from Abraham, Samuel, Gideon, Jeremiah, and David to John, Peter, Paul—and Jesus. They listened intently for the Father's guidance and welcomed his presence and his holiness.

We embrace the adventure of holiness without illusions. Obstacles, confusions, and doubts lie ahead. We know troubles may jolt us, but they also stimulate new growth. We lay our doubts before the Lord, study the Scriptures, and pray with listening ears.

When we embrace God's holiness, we turn from our calling the shots to asking him to take charge. We move from duty and guilt to a spirit of adventure.

Tournier sums it up: "Saying 'yes' to God is saying 'yes' to life."

Lord, here is my will, here are my doubts, here is the key
to all my decision making. Fill me with your holiness
and a spirit of adventure. Absorb my weakness into
your strength as I trust you for the road ahead.

Honor the LORD for the glory of his name. Worship the LORD in the splendor of his holiness. PSALM 29:2, NLT

NOT ME?

NANCY GUTHRIE says she was shocked and shaken when she heard that a lifelong friend who had always been a person of integrity and a pillar of the church had left her husband and children and moved in with another man. One reason Nancy was so shaken was that she wanted to think she herself was above some sins. This news made her realize that attitude was dangerous.

When we've done something so wrong it makes us want to hide in shame, Guthrie says we think, *How could I have done that? That isn't like me.* Instead we should think, *That's exactly like me. This just reveals the core of who I am.*

One gifted and powerful man who succumbed to a sexual liaison that destroyed his career and wounded his marriage used the same words of shamed astonishment: "How could I have done that?"

Sometimes only the enormous consequences of our sins awaken us to the truth about ourselves. We are both Dr. Jekyll and Mr. Hyde. Until we recognize our sinful condition, we are vulnerable.

As Paul warned the Corinthians, "Let him who thinks he stands take heed lest he fall" (1 Corinthians 10:12, NKJV). We must contend with both our fallen nature and the enemy of our souls.

Jesus told Peter that Satan desired to sift him like wheat. What a fascinating, but chilling, revelation of the unseen war! Satan wants to sift us like wheat. He will use temptation, suffering, bitterness, or any other weapon he can to try to trip us up.

Jesus' promise to Peter in light of Satan's desire is equally fascinating: "I have pleaded in prayer for you, Simon, that your faith should not fail" (Luke 22:32, NLT). Scripture tells us that Jesus prays for us, too, so we know how high the stakes are for each of us. We must therefore be prayerful and constantly alert.

---

*Lord, sometimes I get a chilling glimpse of how
Satan is after me and tempts me. Please garrison
my soul and protect me against temptation, for I
understand my weakness and call for your strength.*

Humble yourselves before God. Resist the devil, and he will flee from you. Come close to God, and God will come close to you. JAMES 4:7-8, NLT

LOVE THAT LEAPS AND RUNS

November 15

THOMAS À KEMPIS obviously read with awe and delight Paul's great love chapter, 1 Corinthians 13. He becomes rhapsodic as he expands on its soaring themes, saying, "Love is a mighty power. It bears every hardship. The love of Jesus inspires us to great deeds. Love flies, runs, and leaps for joy—free and unrestrained."

When we read Paul's remarkable and oft-quoted chapter on love, we may feel such awe ourselves. Yet even though we may be lifted and inspired by these descriptions of magnificent love, it can seem far from our personal experience. What, really, is this love the apostle Paul and Thomas à Kempis are so rapturous about?

The apostle John tells us that "God is love" (1 John 4:8, 16, NLT). That's counter-intuitive—a revelation in light of the tragedy and misery in this world. Yet this is what Scripture reveals as the truly Good News, as announced by the angels when Jesus was born.

So how does all this affect us in the nitty-gritty of our lives? Thomas à Kempis says, "Love rests in the One above all things, not caring about things but turns to the Giver of all good gifts."

Only God can put within us this love that conquers all and leaps for joy. We surely can't conjure it up on our own.

That's particularly true when it comes to demonstrating love to others. In John's second epistle, he writes that we should love one another. "This is not a new commandment, but one we have had from the beginning. Love means doing what God has commanded us, and he has commanded us to love one another" (2 John 1:5-6, NLT).

When faced with that commandment and all the other challenges of our spiritual journey, we turn to the one who is the Giver of all good gifts.

Heavenly Father, I boldly ask you for this gift of love. Put within me the love that you have shown in your Word. Help me to feel your freedom, and to share your love with others.

May you experience the love of Christ, though it is too great to understand fully. Then you will be made complete with all the fullness of life and power that comes from God.
EPHESIANS 3:19, NLT

OUR WORK OR HIS?

JESUS says to his disciples in John 4 when they urge him to eat, "I have a kind of food you know nothing about. . . . My nourishment comes from doing the will of God, who sent me, and from finishing his work" (verses 32, 34, NLT).

Jesus was totally intent on one thing: doing the work his Father had sent him to do. We all have work. Are we intent on doing the work that comes from our heavenly Father?

"I tell you the truth," Jesus said, "the Son can do nothing by himself. He does only what he sees the Father doing. Whatever the Father does, the Son also does. For the Father loves the Son and shows him everything he is doing" (John 5:19-20, NLT).

If Jesus can do nothing by himself, what does that say about us?

We are invited through Jesus to have this same relationship with the Father because, Jesus tells us, the Father loves us. When we are in harmony with the Father, we draw on the nourishment he provides; when we drift away and ignore him, we may find ourselves very busy in "our own work" but spiritually hungry.

Jesus said, "I have come down from heaven to do the will of God who sent me, not to do my own will" (John 6:38, NLT).

His next words should fill us with great hope: "And this is the will of God, that I should not lose even one of all those he has given me, but that I should raise them up at the last day" (John 6:39, NLT).

---

*Father in heaven, help me to focus on what your work is
for me to do today. Please show me what you are doing
and how I can be obedient to your will, not my own.
Let me be an instrument of your peace and love.*

Always pray and never give up. LUKE 18:1, NLT

FROM DREAD TO JOY

ELLEN VAUGHN writes that the day she had dreaded all her life—the day when she stood by her mother's bedside staring at her mother's no-longer-warm hand—dramatically changed her. "To my wonder, it opened the door to a flood of fresh grace." She says she was "lifted by the buoyant gift of a grateful heart."

Gratitude in this moment of death?

Ellen says she found herself saying thank you over and over and over. Her thanks were for God's freeing her mother from pain and also for her own clear sense that her mother truly was alive and she would see her again.

The dreaded day became the door into a new beginning. Ellen had fearfully tiptoed up to the dark gate and "it burst open with untrammeled freedom and joy." Gratitude to God rushed over her life.

Few of us experience such an epiphany when a loved one passes away. Yet the reality of gratitude's remarkable power is available to us all. Throughout Scripture, we're commanded to praise and thank the Lord. "Give thanks in all circumstances" (1 Thessalonians 5:18, NIV).

In her book *Radical Gratitude*, Ellen explores how the simple habit of constantly giving thanks connects us to God, creating a "rhythm of divine renewal in grateful hearts." As we keep thanking him, we more and more see from his perspective.

In 1 Thessalonians, we're told to always be joyful and never stop praying—to be thankful in all circumstances. Philippians tells us not to worry about anything but to pray about everything and to thank God for all he's done—and then we'll experience his peace. Colossians 3:15 urges us to *always* be thankful. Psalm 107 repeatedly exhorts us, "Oh that men would praise the LORD . . . for his wonderful works" (KJV).

Ellen says that every day we're alive is "an opulent gift" from the Lord. For life itself, for his many gifts and blessings, and for his great love and redemption, we can be thankful even in times of grief and great loss.

Father and Creator, please pour into me a spirit of gratitude.
Help me to rejoice in you and your many blessings. Grant
me your perspective about all that goes wrong, and show
me how I can respond in harmony with your Spirit.

Praise the LORD, for he has shown me the wonders of his unfailing love.
PSALM 31:21, NLT

THE WAY TO HANDLE SIN

KING DAVID, in Psalm 32, demonstrates how we're to deal with our sins before the Lord. First David declares, "Oh, what joy for those whose disobedience is forgiven, whose sin is put out of sight! Yes, what joy for those whose record the LORD has cleared of guilt, whose lives are lived in complete honesty!" (verses 1-2, NLT).

Then David gives us a personal example: "When I refused to confess my sin, my body wasted away, and I groaned all day long. Day and night your hand of discipline was heavy on me. My strength evaporated like water in the summer heat" (verses 3-4, NLT).

The conviction of sin can sap our energy, even when our culture or the devil's sly lies may be telling us we've done nothing wrong. David was close enough to the Lord that conviction came and drained him of spiritual strength.

David prays, "Finally, I confessed all my sins to you and stopped trying to hide my guilt. I said to myself, 'I will confess my rebellion to the LORD.' And you forgave me! All my guilt is gone" (verse 5, NLT).

This removal of guilt is so wonderful to David that he wants everyone to have the same experience of God's mercy and forgiveness: "Therefore, let all the godly pray to you while there is still time, that they may not drown in the floodwaters of judgment. For you are my hiding place; you protect me from trouble. You surround me with songs of victory" (verses 6-7, NLT).

Then he gives us this counsel: "The LORD says, 'I will guide you along the best pathway for your life. I will advise and watch over you. Do not be like a senseless horse or mule that needs a bit and bridle to keep it under control'" (verses 8-9, NLT).

David concludes this psalm with rich and enduring promises: "Many sorrows come to the wicked, but unfailing love surrounds those who trust the LORD. So rejoice in the LORD and be glad, all you who obey him! Shout for joy, all you whose hearts are pure!" (verses 10-11, NLT).

Father in heaven, keep me from being senseless.
Open my eyes to all that I do that grieves your
Spirit. Cleanse me and equip me to serve you. Show
me the ways that I should follow you today.

I prayed to the LORD, and he answered me. He freed me from all my fears.
PSALM 34:4, NLT

THOUGHTS CREEPING
IN THE BASEMENT

November 19

JOHN HENRY JOWETT warns that, no matter how well we scheme, we can't find a hiding place to sin in secret. He quotes the psalmist, "You understand my thought afar off" (Psalm 139:2, NKJV). That, Jowett says, fills him with awe. God knows not only what we do but also what we're thinking.

That can be very good or very sobering. Jowett starts with this disconcerting fact: "I cannot wrap my jealousy up in flattery and keep it unknown. He knows the bottom thought that creeps in the basement of my being. Nothing surprises God. He sees all my sin."

One of the scariest Judgment Day scenarios is being forced to watch—projected on the big screen for all to see—everything God has been seeing in our thoughts and imaginations. Our duplicities, our lusts, our desires for revenge, and our self-centered focus—all would be revealed in vivid detail.

Fortunately, we are promised that, in Christ, all our sins are cast into the depths and will be remembered no more. Scratch the wide-screen scenario! What a relief!

Jowett says the fact that God knows our thoughts should fill us not only with awe but also with hope. "He sees the faintest, weakest desire aspiring after goodness. He sees the smallest fire of affection burning uncertainly in my soul. He sees every movement of penitence that looks toward home. He sees every little triumph."

He also assures us, "My God is not like a policeman, only looking for crimes; He is the God of grace, looking for graces, searching for jewels to adorn His crown. So am I filled with hope and joy."

Heavenly Father, thank you that I can come in confidence
and celebrate you as the God of grace. Help me not to
be lulled by that assurance into drifting from you. Fill
me with your Holy Spirit so that I might honor you.

Taste and see that the LORD is good. Oh, the joys of those who take refuge in him!
PSALM 34:8, NLT

A SATANIC IDEA

HELMUT THIELICKE expresses wonder at the contrast of Jesus' responses to Peter in Matthew 16. First, when his disciple recognized him as the Messiah, Jesus responded that this was surely revealed to him by God. He went on to say, "You are Peter, the rock."

But then comes what Thielicke calls a "totally unexpected catastrophe" and a "shocking reprimand." Here Peter had just been praised and a powerful future predicted for him. But when Jesus explained his upcoming crucifixion and Peter rebuked him for talking like that, Jesus said to him, "Away with you, Satan."

How could this be?

Jesus said Peter was thinking man's thoughts, not God's. Peter had very human ideas about what the Messiah would be like. Says Thielicke, "Peter hadn't the foggiest notion of what he really said in his confession, 'You are the Messiah, the Son of the living God.' He had meant a Christ without suffering, and therefore he had not meant Christ at all."

Jesus saw that it was Satan tempting Peter to believe he didn't have to suffer—and Satan whispers the same lies to us. Many of us are largely insulated from hunger, homelessness, and persecution. No one wants to suffer, and we do everything we can to avoid it. Yet it's inevitable. Suffering is part of the human condition, and we must endure it on this pilgrim path.

We recognize that suffering is for us the way to growth and depth. For Jesus, it was the path to our redemption.

Christ therefore understands our pain. Thielicke, who suffered persecution under the Nazis, declares that "in the witches' cauldron of our misery, Jesus is with us and the Father holds us by his hand. Here in the midst of our sorrow and anxiety, we grip the hand that will be scorched along with ours."

Lord Jesus, your suffering was far greater than mine. Help me to think your thoughts rather than my own about what I must endure. Grant me strength and courage for all that is ahead.

Wait patiently for the LORD. Be brave and courageous. Yes, wait patiently for the LORD.
PSALM 27:14, NLT

PRAYER AS A WARM-UP

PHILIP YANCEY met with a woman who took prayer very seriously, and he was surprised when she talked mostly not about her designated prayer closet but about the other hours of her day.

"I'm a painter," she told him. "I pray as I paint, and my painting becomes a kind of prayer. If someone asks me for help in prayer, I say to find what they most enjoy and do that, only do it for the glory of God. Start with what really energizes you. Ask God to remind you, as you do it, that you're doing it for him."

Her counsel resonates with what Brother Lawrence experienced and advised centuries ago. We may set aside specific times to pray and meditate on God's Word, yet those times can be a springboard to making all our hours a form of prayer. Brother Lawrence amazed his contemporaries because, in his simple focus of being always in a spirit of prayer, he found peace and joy whatever his tasks.

When we simply recognize during our normal activities that we're spending time with God, we will then act in harmony with his will and his Word. When we continually keep God in mind and try to perceive his viewpoint, it colors all our attitudes and actions. Whether we're sweeping the floor, leading a meeting, or running a company, a godly perspective changes everything.

Yancey says he now sees his designated times of prayer not as ends in themselves, but as "something like a warm-up exercise: to increase awareness of God at all other times."

Lord, whatever happens today, draw my thoughts toward you. Keep me from becoming distracted. Even when I'm focused on what's at hand, let me have a spirit of enjoying you and doing all for your sake.

We keep on praying for you, asking our God to enable you to live a life worthy of his call. May he give you the power to accomplish all the good things your faith prompts you to do.
2 THESSALONIANS 1:11, NLT

OLE HALLESBY warns that a great and common mistake made in prayer is to command God to do our bidding, but God doesn't permit us to issue orders.

Hallesby turns to the story of Mary at the wedding in Cana for a model of how to pray. When Mary told Jesus that the wedding party had no more wine, his answer was not encouraging: "My hour is not yet come."

Jesus lived in obedience to his Father and "could do nothing of himself." He would not intervene before the Father's time. Likewise, in answer to our prayers, God's timing and will transcend our understanding and concerns.

Mary made no attempt to command Jesus; his answer did not shake her conviction that he would do what was right and necessary. She told the servants to follow his instructions. She didn't know *what* would happen, but she knew that *something* would.

We must leave to Jesus the when and how of answering our prayers. Even when the need is urgent and we expect him to intervene at once—when it's obvious to us what he needs to do—we must patiently wait for and accept his timing and response.

"We arise from our holy meeting with God in prayer," says Hallesby, "we expect a real answer, and we look for it hour by hour. But nothing happens. The illness and distress take their natural course. What disappointments! What discouragement! What weariness descends upon our prayer lives."

Yet he says we've had the wrong expectations of prayer. God indeed hears us, but he reserves to himself the right to decide when and how the answer will be given. In his own time, the answer comes.

Hallesby says we get many answers from God we don't recognize, answers for which we're not grateful because we don't see them as answers. He emphasizes that when the Spirit teaches us, there's no danger in leaving with him the time and means of his responses. If we entrust our prayers to the Holy Spirit, our prayer times will become seasons of rest.

---

*Lord, you know what I long for in my prayers . You've
told us that with enough faith we can move mountains.
Please grant me both faith and complete trust in you.*

The LORD has heard my plea; the LORD will answer my prayer. PSALM 6:9, NLT

HUMBLE IN SUCCESS

BILLY GRAHAM, at the groundbreaking ceremony for the new Billy Graham Evangelistic Association headquarters, paraphrased John the Baptist: "Jesus must increase, and I must decrease. I cringe when I hear my name called in something that has been the work of God through these years."

"*Cringe!*" That word shows how seriously he identifies with John the Baptist's words. Throughout his years of ministry, Graham remained focused on returning all the glory to God. He often said that if he took the credit, his lips would turn to clay.

"He never did take any credit," says longtime associate Allan Emory. "He never let anybody make him a big shot. It's humility I have never seen in anybody else."

Thomas à Kempis observed that those who are most esteemed are exposed to the greatest peril. Billy Graham knew that. He saw himself simply as God's messenger boy, bringing the Good News to countless people. "The Holy Spirit is the communicating agent," he told David Frost in an interview. "People are not really listening to *me*."

The more we open ourselves to God as the Source of our power and "success," the more we realize our only honest response is to reflect the glory back to him.

Who was the most humble man in the entire Bible? It was Moses, liberator of his people from the powerful Egyptian empire and conveyor of the Ten Commandments. We read in Numbers 12:3: "Moses was very humble—more humble than any other person on earth" (NLT).

We also read in the same chapter that God said of Moses, "Of all my house, he is the one I trust. I speak to him face to face" (verses 7-8, NLT).

The closer we get to God, the more we realize how magnificent he is! We recognize his glory and that our role is to continually respond to what he wants to do in and through us.

Heavenly Father, I don't think it has ever occurred to
me to cringe when I'm greatly honored in some way.
Help me to rejoice in the talents you've given me but
to recognize that you are the Source of everything
good and are worthy of all glory and honor.

Honor the LORD for the glory of his name. Worship the LORD in the splendor of his holiness. PSALM 29:2, NLT

THE WONDERS OF FELLOWSHIP *November 24*

A. W. TOZER, known for emphasizing the holiness and grandeur of God, observes, "How good it would be if we could learn that God is easy to live with."

Tozer says God understands how frail we are. Even when he must chasten us, he is a loving Father. He looks on us with pleasure as an earthly father would a promising child. As we continue in the faith, he is pleased when each day we grow more and more into the family likeness.

Tozer maintains God is quick to see every simple effort we make to please him. When we fail even though we meant to do his will, he is equally quick to overlook our imperfections. He loves us for ourselves. In that context, Tozer calls our times of prayer "easy, uninhibited fellowship that is restful and healing to the soul."

All that is not to say Tozer downplays God's holiness and grandeur. "Christ can never be known without a sense of awe," he says. "He is the Lord high and mighty. He is the friend of sinners, but he is also the terror of devils." He warns we can never be flippant in God's presence.

In fact, in many sermons and books, Tozer comes down hard on depictions of Jesus that make him out to be an amiable buddy keeping us happy in an entertainment-focused culture. In contrast, he points to the shepherds who came to Jesus in fear and wonder and awe.

We worship God by inviting the fire of the Holy Spirit to purify us, and his presence to lift our hearts in praise.

We adore God, Tozer emphasizes, and we love him "with fear and wonder and yearning and awe." When we do that, we find the yoke of Jesus is easy and his burden light.

Lord, it's refreshing to know that you think of me as a promising child, even though I have so far to go and grow. Help me today to have that easy, healing fellowship with you and to praise you for your wonderful works.

Imitate God, therefore, in everything you do, because you are his dear children.
EPHESIANS 5:1, NLT

PEACE AT THE HEART OF THINGS *November 25*

GEORGE MACDONALD emphasizes the extraordinary love between God the Father and God the Son. He envisions them in the Father's house now, and he urges us to take heart if we feel like outsiders here on earth.

If we feel we're on the outside looking in at God's wonderful love for his Son, MacDonald asks, "Why should we mind standing in the dark for a minute outside his window?"

With his vivid imagination, MacDonald sees us looking in the window and saying to the Lord, "Jesus, are you loving the Father in there?"

Outside in the wind and rain, he says, we can be patient, knowing we are destined one day to be in the home of God's love. We know that Jesus is alive and that all is well. We do the Father's will as Jesus did and anticipate going to that loving home.

MacDonald sees Jesus as full of empathy for us, because when he was on earth, he, too, endured the wind and rain outside his Father's house. MacDonald envisions the Father encouraging the Son to comfort us in our world, which is so different from their celestial home.

We often need lots of comfort and a full dosage of hope. We are assured in Scripture that if we genuinely believe, when we get to the door of the Father's house we'll be welcomed into shelter from the wind and the rain—and into the love of the heavenly family.

"In a word," writes MacDonald, "let us be at peace, because peace is at the heart of things—peace and utter satisfaction between the Father and Son—peace they call us to share.

"Before us, then, lies a bliss unspeakable."

Father, Son, and Holy Spirit, help me to turn boldly into
the wind and rain and do your will as you guide, equip,
and empower me. Guide my mind and will so that I can get
beyond myself and into service that gladdens your heart.

We have heard of your faith in Christ Jesus and your love for all of God's people, which come from your confident hope of what God has reserved for you in heaven.
COLOSSIANS 1:4-5, NLT

YOU, THE MASTERPIECE

RAY STEDMAN, in teaching Ephesians 2, explores what it means for us to have been designed by the Master Craftsman. "God is working out in our lives a tremendous exhibition of his wisdom, his power, his love, his life, his character, his peace, and his joy."

Really? Can all that actually be happening in *us*? In fact, Stedman says, "We are his masterpiece."

If you're like me, you might be thinking, *If I'm a masterpiece, I'm at the extremely messy stage!* Marble chips are flying or the paint is splattering and the art is largely indistinguishable.

But Ray Stedman would say that's just fine. "He is teaching us, training us, bringing us along, applying the paint in just the right places, producing a marvelous masterpiece to put on display. This is to result in good works: kindness, love, mercy, compassion, help to one another, meeting another's needs."

Ray tells of a time when he and a colleague flew to Albuquerque. As the plane was landing, they prayed together, and Ray was struck by the way his colleague prayed: "Father, thank you for the good works already prepared for us in Albuquerque, for the fact that they are waiting for us to step into them and experience them."

Sure enough, in Albuquerque, those good works began to unfold. A missionary from the Amazon, greatly upset and ready to quit, came alive and with a light on his face said he was going back, revolutionized in his approach. A young pastor facing church dissension found wisdom and guidance. "All these good works had been prepared beforehand," he says. "All we did was step into them."

Today, good works are ready for us to step into. "We are God's masterpiece," Paul declares in Ephesians 2:10. "He has created us anew in Christ Jesus, so we can do the good things he planned for us long ago" (NLT).

Father, so often I don't feel like a masterpiece. Help me, Lord, to see the work you're doing in my life and the good works that you've set before me. Help me to walk in step with your Spirit.

We look forward with hope to that wonderful day when the glory of our great God and Savior, Jesus Christ, will be revealed. TITUS 2:13, NLT

THE HOSPICE BIRTH

JILL BRISCOE was touring new hospice facilities that were beautiful and made as much like home as possible. *But these people aren't "home" yet,* Jill thought. *This is the start, not the finish; the beginning, not the end.*

She shared the thought with the doctor and others with her that this was really a "birthing wing." Here was where people were going to be ushered into eternity.

What a marvelous image: the place of death transformed into the scene where anguish and pain and fears suddenly change into the triumph of birth and all the joys of new life. That is the firm hope of the gospel for every hospice.

Yet death is still a merciless enemy. We experience its ugliness. The horrific accident that suddenly rips a loved one away from us or the slow, often painful, process of dying can feel like a nightmare from which we cannot escape.

Jill says it was in just such a "bitter, despairing time" that she was greatly consoled by 1 Corinthians 15:

> Christ has been raised from the dead. He is the first of a great harvest of all who have died. . . . Our earthly bodies are planted in the ground when we die, but they will be raised to live forever. Our bodies are buried in brokenness, but they will be raised in glory. They are buried in weakness, but they will be raised in strength. . . . When our dying bodies have been transformed into bodies that will never die, this Scripture will be fulfilled: "Death is swallowed up in victory. O death, where is your victory? O death, where is your sting?" (1 Corinthians 15:20, 42-43, 54-55, NLT)

Lord Jesus Christ, Redeemer, grant me the faith to believe that your promises of new life beyond the grave are true. Help me to live here and now with that lively hope that enables me to live in your strength and love.

I pray that God, the source of hope, will fill you completely with joy and peace because you trust in him. Then you will overflow with confident hope through the power of the Holy Spirit. ROMANS 15:13, NLT

STEPPING UP TO STRESS

FRED SMITH maintains that stress and tension are vital forces in our lives. "Power, zeal, and creative energy are the result of valuable tensions. I have always been grateful for the extra punch tension brings. My family has often heard me say, 'There is nothing wrong with me that a little excitement can't cure.'"

We all recognize that tension is a natural part of life, but it's also natural that we shrink back from unpleasant tension. However, instead of dividing stress into pleasant (a thrill ride at an amusement park) and unpleasant (a root canal treatment), Smith points us to psychological research that divides stress into *vertical* and *horizontal*. Horizontal stresses pull us apart; vertical ones lift us.

One of the best vertical tensions, according to Smith, is the fear of God. The Bible refers to it often. The fear of God ultimately does not make us cringe. It lifts us into confession, cleansing, and empowerment.

In contrast, fear of man is a horizontal stress. "When we substitute the fear of man for the fear of God," Fred says, "we worry about the judgment of man, not the judgment of God. Havoc replaces holiness."

Fred also highlights selflessness as a vertical tension that produces creativity and productivity. We have only to study the fruit of the Spirit to see the powerful, uplifting effect of vertical tensions. In contrast, selfishness fills us with unsatisfied desires.

Praying to be an instrument of God's peace in the world—and then acting on what the Spirit leads us to do—may bring stress, but it's vertical stress. "When the Christian life is real, it releases power," Fred asserts. "It brings challenge, promotes healthy tensions, and increases vitality."

Lord Jesus, you certainly lived with plenty of stress when you were here on earth. Help me to have your attitude of stepping up to the challenges in the "fear of the Lord" and to act humbly, with your strength and courage.

My child, listen to what I say, and treasure my commands. . . . Then you will understand what it means to fear the LORD, and you will gain knowledge of God.
PROVERBS 2:1, 5, NLT

GREAT THINGS IN BATTLE

November 29

D. L. MOODY asserts, "The fiercest attacks are made on the strongest forts."

He's referring to those who have found strength in the Lord and are serving him well. "The more useful a man becomes, the better target he is for the devil."

Moody was speaking from personal experience. He said that early in his Christian life he thought his commitments meant the battle was won and the victory his. "I thought that old things had passed away, that all things had become new, that my old corrupt nature, the Adam life, was gone. But I found out that conversion was only like enlisting in the army—that there was a battle on hand."

Satan, with exquisite shrewdness, attacks our blind sides. His flaming arrows are shot with precision into just the spot where we're vulnerable.

For inspiration for the battle, Moody looked to biblical heroes. "Caleb and Joshua are great favorites of mine," he says. "They have got a ring about them. They were not all the time looking at the hindrances and obstacles in their way: they got their eyes above them."

He singles out Joshua as an example of courage, urging us to have confidence in what we can be and do through Christ. As God told Joshua, "Be strong and of good courage; do not be afraid, nor be dismayed, for the LORD your God is with you wherever you go" (Joshua 1:9, NKJV). In God's power, Joshua led Israel to great victories.

"We must believe that God is willing and ready to help," Moody says. "We need courage. If we are full of faith, we will not be full of fear and distrust the Lord."

Moody called for perseverance instead of a faith that burns brightly and then flickers. What's needed is "the long and steady pull" of constant communion with the Holy Spirit.

"Dear friends," he once preached, "let us expect that God is going to help us. Let us have courage and go forward, looking to God to do great things."

Lord, every day that goes by only proves that the battles never stop. Give me the courage and faith to persevere.

We live with great expectation, and we have a priceless inheritance—an inheritance that is kept in heaven for you, pure and undefiled, beyond the reach of change and decay.
I PETER 1:3-4, NLT

TWO PATHS WHEN GUILTY

CALVIN MILLER suggests something we're unlikely to think of as true. He says that as believers we may actually have a feeling in common with fallen angels. He's referring to Milton's depiction in *Paradise Lost* of the host of exiles from heaven bewailing all they have lost.

We may have feelings akin to theirs when we feel we've let God down in a big way. When we experience the feeling of estrangement from God, Miller says we have two courses open to us. We can nurse our spiritual remorse, which will fester into self-absorption. That's what Judas did. Or, we can repent, as Peter did.

Nursing guilt simply sucks us ever deeper into despair and cynicism. The devil would love to have us share his sense of estrangement from God. He'd happily supply all sorts of satanic replacements for God's love and grace. In contrast, breaking the dark, corrosive hold of remorse by confessing our sins and receiving God's cleansing sets us on the path Peter took. His path led to marvelous fellowship with the risen Savior and a life of victory and ultimate joy.

Miller expresses the plain truth about spiritual warfare: "Everyone here and there serves Satan." But then he says, "Remorse over our spiritual failures never needs to be terminal."

Why is that true? "Our temporary flights of permissiveness into the will of Satan grieve God, and grief is a love word."

Now that's an interesting thought—grief is a love word. So God doesn't hate us when we sin—he loves us and wants to cover us with his grace as we willingly turn to him.

"The only way to win in spiritual warfare," Miller tells us, "is to wrap ourselves in grace."

---

*Lord, help me to be like Peter and recognize my
sins and failures, then confess them to you. Put me
on the path of your purpose and blessing. Help me
to share your love and care with others today.*

---

*Be truly glad. There is wonderful joy ahead, even though you have to endure many trials
for a little while.* I PETER 1:6, NLT

FREUD AND LIBERATION

PAUL TOURNIER took the time to read and reread Freud's 260 clinical cases detailed in *The Psychopathology of Everyday Life* and came to a surprising conclusion: Freud's work confirms Christian teaching.

Tournier found that every case Freud included fell into one of four categories of sin described in the Sermon on the Mount: dishonesty, impurity, self-centeredness, and lack of love. He concludes, "Freud gives a detailed demonstration of the basic dishonesty of man. He shows that psychological conflicts stem from violation of God's commands." Further, Tournier sees the inner conflict Freud addresses as the same that the apostle Paul describes in Romans 7.

Paul Tournier asserted that the denial of sin destroys our sense of moral responsibility. Yet the longer we live and the more honestly we look, the more we recognize sin exists. Many of us experience the personal conviction of sin, which turns out not to be repressive but to be liberating because of God's grace in redemption.

In his medical practice, Tournier invited patients looking for spiritual relief to make lists of everything in their lives they sensed was contrary to God's commands. They brought extensive lists that included lies, jealousy, rancor, selfish ambitions, hostility, and hatreds. The results of the patients listing their personal sins and the process of bringing them into the open in a form of confession were fascinating and instructive. Tournier observes, "I have never seen anyone attempt it without feeling a real conviction of sin and winning a spiritual victory."

"If we claim we have no sin, we are only fooling ourselves and not living in the truth," writes the apostle John. "But if we confess our sins to him, he is faithful and just to forgive us our sins and to cleanse us from all wickedness" (1 John 1:8-9, NLT).

Then he flatly refutes the denial of sin: "If we claim we have not sinned, we are calling God a liar and showing that his word has no place in our hearts" (1 John 1:10, NLT).

Lord, I bring to you all my "dirty laundry," all my many
failures to listen to you and to obey. Help me to identify
what grieves you, and then enable me to repent and to
open myself to the cleansing power of your Spirit.

I am writing to you who are God's children because your sins have been forgiven through Jesus. I JOHN 2:12, NLT

JESUS says in John 6, "The Spirit alone gives eternal life. Human effort accomplishes nothing. And the very words I have spoken to you are spirit and life. But some of you do not believe me" (verses 63-64, NLT).

What an amazing mystery that people could listen to Jesus in the flesh and yet some would believe and some would reject him; some would hear the Spirit and some would not.

The next verse says Jesus knew from the beginning those who didn't believe and who would betray him. He explains, "That is why I said that people can't come to me unless the Father gives them to me" (verse 65, NLT).

At that point many of his disciples deserted him. He asked the Twelve, "Are you also going to leave?" (verse 67, NLT).

Peter said, "Lord, to whom would we go? You have the words that give eternal life. We believe, and we know you are the Holy One of God" (verses 68-69, NLT). So Peter, in contrast to those who left, was one in whom the Father was at work.

Then Jesus, speaking of Judas, who would betray him, said, "I chose the twelve of you, but one is a devil" (verse 70, NLT).

What a sobering reality! The drama of life with eternal consequences carries such heavy mysteries of belief and unbelief, devils and angels. The heavenly warfare the Bible so often refers to is waged in our souls and in our responses to the Father.

The words of Jesus proclaimed in John 7 resonate now as then: "My message is not my own; it comes from God who sent me. Anyone who wants to do the will of God will know whether my teaching is from God or is merely my own" (verses 16-17, NLT).

---

*Heavenly Father, open my eyes to your truths and help me
to live today as your Son did, in obedience to you. Help
me to have compassion for those estranged from you, and
to realize that only you can draw people to your Son.*

---

*Love the LORD, all you godly ones! For the LORD protects those who are loyal to him, but
he harshly punishes the arrogant.* PSALM 31:23, NLT

WILDERNESS WHISPERS

NANCY GUTHRIE made a discovery that surprised her as she read about Satan's temptation of Jesus. Matthew 4:1 reads, "Jesus was led by the Spirit into the wilderness to be tempted there by the devil" (NLT). Like many people, perhaps, Nancy hadn't previously noticed it was the Holy Spirit who led Jesus into the wilderness.

Why would the Spirit do that? What's this all about? The Holy Spirit led him to the place of temptation? What are the implications for you and me?

Here are a few:

The Holy Spirit is full of surprises. He is truly a wild wind.

What Satan intended for evil God turned into extreme good, because ultimately, God is sovereign.

Jesus, who prays for us in our temptations, empathizes with us. So does the Holy Spirit.

In times of temptation, the Holy Spirit is right there with us.

We have the same weapons that Jesus had to use against Satan: the Word of God, the Holy Spirit, and faith in our heavenly Father.

Satan whispers that none of this is true. He argues that we deserve what we crave and that giving in to temptation is natural and will be no big deal. He tries to make us question whether God cares about us at all, let alone loves us.

The Holy Spirit whispers that God does love us and that the consequences of giving in to temptation will be great, but obedience will lead to joy. The Holy Spirit was in the wilderness with Jesus, who triumphed over evil. He is with us in our own wilderness of temptations.

---

*Holy Spirit of God, as you led Jesus and were with him
all through his temptations, pour your courage and
determination into me. Fill me with your strength and
purpose so I can resist the devil and cause him to flee.*

"Get out of here, Satan," Jesus told him. "For the Scriptures say, 'You must worship the LORD your God and serve only him.'" MATTHEW 4:10, NLT

DANGERS IN GOD'S GRACE?

THOMAS À KEMPIS counsels us, as recipients of God's grace, to be wise and prudent when we experience it.

His caution is this: If God has given you rich spiritual blessings, don't boast about them. In fact, conceal them as an aid to humility.

Conceal them? We may rightly object that sharing the grace and blessing of the Lord is biblical and encourages others. Brother Lawrence certainly didn't conceal his blessings. Yet the dangers à Kempis warns of are clear: we can develop a sense of pride, as if we're spiritually superior to others. We can also offend others who struggle spiritually and feel dry and empty. What's called for is great sensitivity and honest humility.

He then gives us another caution—to not depend on feelings of grace because they can quickly change. When we're enjoying the sense of God's love and presence, we should fully enjoy it; yet, as we live out a lifetime of faithfulness to the Lord, it's inevitable our feelings will come and go.

We're not in control. God gives his grace and comfort when and to whom he wills.

"Progress in the spiritual life," à Kempis writes, "consists not so much in enjoying the grace of consolation, as in bearing its withdrawal with humility, resignation, and patience, never growing weary in prayer."

As C. S. Lewis and others have emphasized, our prayers when we are spiritually dry and full of anxiety may well mean more in the eyes of heaven than those that spring from a robust faith. "Pray without ceasing," the Bible tells us, and that includes during every spiritual state and every emotion.

"When the spirit of devotion is aflame in your heart," à Kempis says, "consider how you will fare when the light leaves you."

But then he adds this hopeful note: "When this happens, remember that this light will one day return."

---

*Lord, as I contrast the times you poured your grace
into my soul with times I've felt deserted, I see that this
adventure of faith is full of dramatic changes. Help
me, Lord, to be faithful whatever my feelings.*

The LORD is faithful; he will strengthen you and guard you from the evil one.
2 THESSALONIANS 3:3, NLT

GOD'S SILENCE AND MERCY

HABAKKUK lived in a degenerate culture, in many ways like our own. He cried out to God, "How long, O LORD, must I call for help? But you do not listen! 'Violence is everywhere!' I cry. . . . Why must I watch all this misery? Wherever I look, I see destruction and violence" (Habakkuk 1:2-3, NLT).

In our day, wherever we look, we also see violence and destruction. When we read Habakkuk's prayer, we can identify: "I am surrounded by people who love to argue and fight. . . . There is no justice in the courts. The wicked far outnumber the righteous" (Habakkuk 1:3-4, NLT).

Much has been written about the silence of God and why he doesn't intervene to stop injustice and tragedy. With a sense of bewilderment, Habakkuk complains that God isn't doing anything: "I cry, but you do not come to save. Must I forever see these evil deeds?" (Habakkuk 1:2-3, NLT).

God does answer Habakkuk, but his message stuns the prophet: "Look and be amazed! . . . I am raising up the Babylonians, a cruel and violent people. They will march across the world and conquer. . . . On they come, all bent on violence" (Habakkuk 1:5-6, 9, NLT).

Whoa! The Babylonians will conquer and pillage his people? Habakkuk is horrified. "Surely you do not plan to wipe us out?" he pleads. "Should you be silent while the wicked swallow up people more righteous than they? . . . Must we be strung up on their hooks?" (Habakkuk 1:12-13, 15, NLT).

What if God answered our prayers like that?

When we pray for God to act, we might also praise him for his mercy in holding back judgment. Whatever happens, though, Habakkuk shows us how to pray despite the worst: "Though the fig trees have no blossoms . . . and the fields lie empty and barren . . . yet I will rejoice in the LORD! I will be joyful in the God of my salvation! The Sovereign LORD is my strength!" (Habakkuk 3:17-19, NLT).

Father, despite all the bad news in the world, help me to live by faith and to rejoice in you. Truly, your ways are beyond my comprehension. Help me to bring hope and peace to others.

I am filled with awe by your amazing works. In this time of our deep need, help us again. HABAKKUK 3:2, NLT

UNRESCUED HEROES

JONI EARECKSON TADA longed to be healed of her paralysis. She desperately wanted out of her wheelchair, to walk and run as she had before her accident. She was impressed that Jesus opened blind eyes and deaf ears and raised up the paralyzed. Jesus, she read, promised he would give whatever was asked in his name. "Ask and you will receive, and your joy will be complete" (John 16:24, NIV).

So she asked.

To show her faith, she told friends she'd soon be on her feet. She prayed in Jesus' name, convinced that God would heal her, to his glory.

But nothing happened.

In Hebrews 11, she noticed that among the list of heroes of the faith who conquered kingdoms, escaped the sword, and received the dead back to life were also those who weren't delivered—heroes who were imprisoned, tortured, and executed without miracles to rescue them. Joni eventually concluded she was among those who would suffer and not be rescued. She was to be like those who were commended for their faith.

"It's taken me years to understand," she says, "but the deep and enduring joy I have has far outlived whatever immediate joy I would have experienced had I been healed."

She asks if we should expect an easier life than Jesus, who was "a man of sorrows and acquainted with grief" (Isaiah 53:3, NASB). Our prayers might not be answered with miraculous healings and dramatic rescues, but with our becoming more like Christ in faith, patience, and endurance.

What has Joni gained from praying for healing in Jesus' name? "His deep and lingering peace in the midst of turmoil and pain and loneliness and disappointments."

Sometimes we pray earnestly for something we desperately long for, and it seems that no answer—let alone a miracle—comes in response. Joni concludes, "When we pray in his name, we can be sure of this answer: God will bless us with every spiritual blessing. Now that's a big answer to prayer!"

Father, I bring my troubles to you. Please do one of your "mighty works" of deliverance! But whatever your response to this prayer, let me experience the "deep and lingering peace" that Joni Eareckson Tada found in the midst of her turmoil and pain.

Whatever is good and perfect comes down to us from God our Father, who created all the lights in the heavens. JAMES 1:17, NLT

WILD WEATHER

EUGENE PETERSON recounts a favorite story he used to tell when he and his wife and three children would huddle together on the porch to watch thunderstorms. Once, during a fierce storm, the naturalist John Muir decided to do something out of the ordinary. Despite the rain, he left his cozy cabin to ascend a giant Douglas fir tree. At its pinnacle, he relished the colors of the storm and the sting of the lashing winds and rain.

The story of Muir atop a tree in the storm became for Peterson's family "a standing rebuke against becoming a mere spectator to life, preferring creature comforts to Creator confrontations."

In one sense, we all spend our lives attempting to build cozy cabins in which to enjoy comfort, safety, and love. Not that comfort and safety and love are bad things—we need walls and a roof against the storms of life. Yet at times we must also brave the elements, with their fierce demands and possible rewards. We can do so with timidity or with a spirit of adventure—enthusiastically engaged—as John Muir did.

When we read Eugene Peterson's rendering of the Scriptures titled *The Message*, we sense just that sort of energy and verve throughout. That's because the ultimate source of enthusiasm for life is the Holy Spirit, who inspired the Scriptures and who brings vibrancy into our lives as we welcome his presence. It is then we become, as Peterson expresses it, "participants in the extravagant prodigality of the life, visible and invisible, that is Spirit created."

We live in our cozy cabins, but we must go in and out through the storms of life. From the Holy Spirit, we draw the inner resources to welcome the "weather," whatever its nature, and to live not as bystanders, but with courage and vitality.

Father in heaven, your creation fills me with wonder—
yet I don't always want to risk being up in a tree
when the lightning flashes. Grant me courage to take
risks—or to step back into the cabin as you lead.

It is not by force nor by strength, but by my Spirit, says the LORD of Heaven's Armies.
ZECHARIAH 4:6, NLT

TAKE A DEEP BREATH

FRANÇOIS FÉNELON encourages us to "live in peace without worrying about the future. Unnecessary worrying and imagining the worst possible scenario will strangle your faith. God alone knows what will happen to you. You really don't even own the present moment, for even this belongs to God."

Aren't we prone to worrying and imagining worst-case scenarios? As we hear about all the things going wrong in the world, we know painful things may be just ahead. As we meet the demands of each new day, we realize reversals and confrontations may come.

In light of all that, many have found great comfort in Fénelon's advice: "Each day there is just enough that God gives you to take care of—nothing more or less is expected of you."

So, we take a deep breath and focus on the tasks at hand.

"The future is not yet yours—perhaps it never will be," says Fénelon. "And when tomorrow comes it will probably be different from what you had imagined."

That's certainly the way things usually turn out. Worrying does us no good at all. Yet when the media bombard us every day with bad news of every sort, it's hard not to worry about the "other shoe" and when it might fall—perhaps on our own toes.

We must prepare for the future in various ways, but that's part of today's task. We plan and work hard, but place our worries in God's hands. We've done what we could, and we trust God to provide grace for the moment and for the future.

To live in both peace and vitality, we're invited to trust God and simply let his will unfold. That way, we go through each day in a spirit of worship, not being concerned whether we will have answers to our every question.

"Above all," Fénelon advises, "live in the present moment and God will give you all the grace you need."

Heavenly Father, help me to prayerfully receive whatever comes today. Let me see through your eyes what is really happening, with mind and heart fully open to your Holy Spirit.

The LORD God is our sun and our shield. He gives us grace and glory. The LORD will withhold no good thing from those who do what is right. PSALM 84:11, NLT

THE HOUSEGUEST

OSWALD CHAMBERS says, "The Holy Spirit cannot be located as a Guest in a house. He invades everything."

Chambers's analogy starts us thinking about all our "rooms." We are complex beings with a lot going on. Which rooms do we invite the Spirit to settle in? Which do we quietly lock and hope to keep private?

"He takes charge of everything," Chambers continues. "My part is to walk in the light and to obey all that he reveals."

Though the Holy Spirit is prepared to take charge of everything in the house, he does so only by our invitation. His gentle, quiet voice is easy to ignore. He can be grieved by our doing the opposite of what he whispers. When grieved, he may seem to have slipped away, but he waits patiently for us to invite him back.

On the other hand, when the Spirit has full access to all the rooms, we experience genuine friendship with God. Chambers describes it as "a life of freedom and liberty and delight. You decide things in perfect friendship with God, knowing that if your decisions are wrong, he will always check. When he checks, stop at once."

Yet the Spirit's invasion of all the rooms of our souls is not a sedate tea party. The liberty and delight ebb and flow. Spiritual battles abound. Victories or defeats hinge on our presenting our wills to God and asking him to direct us toward joyful obedience.

Chambers urges us to get alone with God and fight out the battles before him. "We either go toward a more and more dilatory and useless type of Christian life, or we become more and more ablaze for the glory of God—My Utmost for *His* Highest."

Father, sometimes the internal spiritual battles are intense. Here is my will. Shape it and direct it, Lord, to be in full harmony with your will. Help me today to be an effective instrument, fit for your use.

Obey me, and I will be your God, and you will be my people. Do everything as I say, and all will be well! JEREMIAH 7:23, NLT

THE CURE FOR COLD PRAYERS December 10

MARTIN LUTHER writes that Christians, by and large, are stuck in the mud of hoping our good works will allow us to bargain with God. Because it's hard to fully accept God's mercy when we know how much we fail, we do good works and hope they count. "The mud still sticks and clings to us," Luther says. "We want God to look at our lives and, because of what we have done, to change the judgment seat into the mercy seat."

Luther says flatly, "Nothing will come of this. Remember that you are appealing for grace, not justice."

Yes, we are called to good works, and plenty of Scripture passages tell us exactly that. Yet, no matter how many good works we pull off, without the mercy and grace of God, they are not enough.

Instead, we are to live by faith.

Luther, of course, had lots to say about faith. "Faith is active and powerful. The Holy Spirit gives us faith that transforms the mind and attitudes. It's a process that changes the heart. It creates an entirely new person."

When our faith is weak and we're stuck in the mud of our failures, what are we to do?

According to Luther, we should shake off what he calls unchristian thoughts and pray, "God, have mercy on me." He points to David, who cries out in Psalm 51:1, "Have mercy on me, O God, because of your unfailing love. Because of your great compassion, blot out the stain of my sins" (NLT).

Luther admits that he at times found this difficult. "Because I was worried about my own unworthiness, I often prayed coldly, 'God, have mercy on me.' Yet the Holy Spirit convinced me, 'No matter how you feel, you must pray!'"

David's prayer in Psalm 51 continues, "Purify me from my sins, and I will be clean; wash me, and I will be whiter than snow. Oh, give me back my joy again" (verses 7-8, NLT).

Lord, cleanse me of all the mud and muck of my failures.
Create a clean heart in me and let me sense new energy
from you. Strengthen my faith and my determination
to take on today's challenges in your Spirit.

Give thanks to the LORD, for he is good! His faithful love endures forever.
I CHRONICLES 16:34, NLT

VIPS?

THOMAS HOWARD, in his book *Splendor in the Ordinary*, asserts that in God's creation, when we lift up ordinary things to the Holy One, we perceive them in their true light—"as bearers of the divine mysteries to us."

We do not usually think of ordinary things that way. However, when we live with a spirit of worship and gratitude for God's provisions, we hallow them. We become most aware of the divine mysteries as we hold up our fellow humans, who are made in the image of God.

"It has to do with seeing and honoring the excellence of the other," Howard writes, "to treat all other selves as though they were kings."

That's a tall order! We might be ready to treat a few select persons with great deference, but to treat all others as royalty seems inconceivable. In fact, we might feel some deserve to be treated like trash.

Yet people long to be treated with high respect. Years ago, drivers could purchase a bumper sticker with the following message for the backs of their cars: "*Very Important Person*: *Pass with Awe*."

We may smile at the idea of passing drivers "with awe," but the truth is they are far more than VIPs. They are eternal souls, part of the ultimate drama being played out by the principalities and powers. We are faced with the great paradox that we mortals are incredibly weak and flawed, yet God has given us the dignity and responsibility of choice, with eternal consequences.

Thomas Howard calls for an awareness that we are dealing with persons made in God's image and that our connections with them are somehow part of the divine mysteries we encounter each and every day.

Father and Creator, help me to see through your eyes not only the people I love but all those who annoy or frustrate me. Put your love within me for these eternal beings. Help me to be a conduit for your grace and goodwill.

If you love only those who love you, why should you get credit for that? Even sinners love those who love them! LUKE 6:32, NLT

A GOLDEN PSALM

KING DAVID, in Psalm 19, gives us a rich feast of spiritual truths to study and to savor. It brings us soaring depictions of God's creation, and familiar but powerful affirmations, prayers, and wise counsel:

> The heavens proclaim the glory of God. The skies display his craftsmanship. Day after day they continue to speak; night after night they make him known. They speak without a sound or word; their voice is never heard. Yet their message has gone throughout the earth, and their words to all the world.

> God has made a home in the heavens for the sun. It bursts forth like a radiant bridegroom after his wedding. It rejoices like a great athlete eager to run the race. The sun rises at one end of the heavens and follows its course to the other end. Nothing can hide from its heat.

> The instructions of the LORD are perfect, reviving the soul. The decrees of the LORD are trustworthy, making wise the simple. The commandments of the LORD are right, bringing joy to the heart. The commands of the LORD are clear, giving insight for living. Reverence for the LORD is pure, lasting forever. The laws of the LORD are true; each one is fair. They are more desirable than gold, even the finest gold. They are sweeter than honey, even honey dripping from the comb. They are a warning to your servant, a great reward for those who obey them.

> How can I know all the sins lurking in my heart? Cleanse me from these hidden faults. Keep your servant from deliberate sins! Don't let them control me. Then I will be free of guilt and innocent of great sin.

> May the words of my mouth and the meditation of my heart be pleasing to you, O LORD, my rock and my redeemer. (NLT)

Lord, help me to savor the messages of this psalm so that they permeate every facet of my life. Help me to rejoice in you, to taste the goodness of your words, to obey you, and to receive the fullness of your Spirit.

All Scripture is inspired by God and is useful to teach us what is true and to make us realize what is wrong in our lives. 2 TIMOTHY 3:16, NLT

THE LEAP OF FAITH

SHERWOOD WIRT tells the story of a man with a rope on a steep, rugged cliff in southern England gathering the eggs of seabirds nesting in the rocks. With a basket on his back, he lowered himself over a precipice until he was dangling near a narrow ledge. To reach the ledge and the eggs, he had to swing himself in.

As he landed on the ledge and removed the basket, he accidentally let go of the rope. It swung away and out of reach.

The rope in its returning arc did not quite reach the ledge. He was stuck!

He knew his cries would be unheard. He had little hope of being rescued. Each time the rope swung back toward him, it was slightly farther away.

That rope is my one chance to save myself, he thought. *If I wait, it will be out of reach. It's nearer now than it ever will be again.*

As the rope swung toward him, he forgot about the basket and the eggs and leaped from the ledge, catching the rope in midair. Gripping it tightly, he pulled himself to safety.

In his book on Psalms 42 and 43, *A Thirst for God,* Wirt says the psalmist is "through with letting his fears run his life. He sees a rope and is reaching out. 'Why are you casting yourself down?' he asks himself. 'Nothing is down there but rocks. Put your hope in God.'"

At times, we find ourselves on a rocky ledge with no good options. Like the psalmists, we feel desperate until we finally come to realize that we have only one realistic hope—and the sooner we act, the better.

Wirt emphasizes that the psalmists longed for God, and as we, too, reach out to him, "we can be spiritually filled. We can know contentment and praise and joy and peace and love."

Father, when I feel trapped by circumstances and by my own foolishness or sinfulness, grant me the will and energy to leap from the ledge and into your arms of mercy. You are my unfailing hope, Lord.

As the deer longs for streams of water, so I long for you, O God. I thirst for God, the living God. PSALM 42:1-2, NLT

THE BEST THING ABOUT HEAVEN December 14

LEWIS SMEDES, after writing eloquently about the wonders we will experience in heaven, tells us that the best thing about it won't be what we will find there. The best thing is what *we* will be like. We'll be transformed!

Smedes cautions against trying to imagine what form we'll take but proposes that we concentrate, instead, on "the quality of persons" we'll become.

Our yearning for love may become the capacity to love fully. From "our nodding acquaintance with goodness" on earth, we may become good to the core. We have a portrait of Jesus in the New Testament, and Smedes says that each of us in our own fashion will be a good deal like Christ.

To imagine what it will be like, we might start with what gives us pleasure here on earth. "Have a thigh-thumping laugh at a ridiculous story," Smedes suggests, "and you get a sharp snap of yourself happy in heaven. Let a piece of soul music send shivers down your spine, and you have an image of your capacity for beauty in heaven. Watch a giggling two-year-old toddle into its mother's arms, and you get a fairly good image of yourself in heaven with God. Maybe the happiest memories of ourselves on earth are our clearest images of what we shall be in heaven."

When discouraged by our failures and foolishness, we can rejoice in good news: a great day of transformation is coming!

Smedes concludes his thoughts about heaven this way: "Remember that the best part of getting to heaven is becoming the sorts of persons we were always meant to be, and in our better moments wanted to be, in the loving company of God and all his children."

---

*Lord, I'm hoping for a big transformation in
heaven. But I pray you'll start that process now!
Help me to grow in ways that are more like you so
that I truly will be "getting ready for glory."*

Dear friends, we are already God's children, but he has not yet shown us what we will be like when Christ appears. But we do know that we will be like him, for we will see him as he really is. I JOHN 3:2, NLT

REMBRANDT AND THE PRODIGAL *December 15*

HENRI NOUWEN wrote numerous times about Rembrandt's painting *The Return of the Prodigal Son* because it spoke powerfully and personally to him.

"With his son safe within his outstretched arms," Henri says of the painting, "the father's expression seems to say, 'I am not going to ask you any questions. Wherever you have gone, whatever you have done, and whatever people say about you, you're my beloved child. I hold you safe in my embrace. I hug you. I gather you under my wings. You can come home to me.'"

In prayer, we kneel before the Father just as the Prodigal Son did. Nouwen says that, in a sense, we are held against God's chest and we hear his heartbeat. In prayer, we're led to an inner place where we're safe.

Jesus promised, "If anyone loves Me, he will keep My word; and My Father will love him, and We will come to him and make Our abode with him" (John 14:23, NASB). Nouwen, commenting on those words with amazement, says, "I am God's home!"

Yet, how do we act in response to Jesus' call to make our homes in him as he makes his home in us? It's as if Jesus has sent us an engraved invitation with the instructions that God will make his home in us if we love him and keep his word. Sounds simple and straightforward—but what a towering challenge!

We are invited as prodigals to come to the Father and finally to know that our sins and failures are past. But the struggle here is not over. Our spiritual journeys are more like a rugged game of football than a stroll in the park.

Jesus endured all "for the joy set before him" (Hebrews 12:2, NIV). The joy offered to us transcends any earthly reward. We are given the extraordinary invitation to come in prayer to the Father's embrace.

Our Father in heaven, revive your Spirit within me
so that I can be your home. Embrace me with your
forgiveness and love. Show me, Lord, how I can
obey you and walk with you and rejoice in you.

Peace be with you, dear brothers and sisters, and may God the Father and the Lord Jesus Christ give you love with faithfulness. EPHESIANS 6:23, NLT

LIFE, LONG AND SHORT

JILL BRISCOE says when she struggles with the discouragements of aging, her husband, Stuart, helps her (with a wry smile) by saying she needs to get her theology straight—that she was born at the right moment and will be "dead on time." She recognizes that life has been good to her, and she naturally wants to stay alive—yet what does that desire say about her view of God and heaven?

She contrasts the attitudes of two women dying of cancer. One was a friend who said she wasn't angry about her life being cut short. She had had a marvelous life and expected heaven to be even better. "It's my time and it's all right."

The other woman, who was young, said that when she'd discovered she had cancer, "I hit out at everyone in sight. It was so unfair. I hadn't had time to do everything I wanted to do. Mostly I was mad at God."

Dead on time. Trust in God. Mad at God. Those phrases start to describe the mixed emotions most of us have when it comes to our deaths or the deaths of our loved ones. Death is an enemy and a terrible rending of the fabric of our lives. Then again, do we really believe all the promises of salvation and eternal life?

It's an interesting commentary that people today pay enormous sums to gain just an additional week or month of life. For many, life has indeed been very good, and they will spare nothing to prolong it.

In faith, we access modern medicine with as much wisdom as we can muster. Yet at times we need restraint because we know that death is inevitable and heaven is sure. Stuart Briscoe is right that we were born on time, we will have adequate time to fulfill the roles God gives us on earth, and we will be "dead on time."

Then comes eternal glory.

Lord, help me to get my theology straight. Let my brief time on this earth be spent fully in step with your Spirit, starting right now. Guide me so that what I do will be fruitful and will honor you.

Everything comes from him and exists by his power and is intended for his glory. All glory to him forever! Amen. ROMANS 11:36, NLT

NATURAL AND GRACIOUS GRATITUDE

ELLEN VAUGHN reviews for us Jonathan Edwards's perspective on two types of gratitude. One is obvious. We thank the Lord for his many blessings, from morning coffee to evening dinner, for shelter, health, family, the sunshine that provides life, and the beauties and wonders of creation. We cultivate an attitude of gratitude for God's innumerable gifts. Edwards calls that "natural gratitude."

Edwards's second category of gratitude is actually the most transformational. He calls it "gracious gratitude." It is being thankful not just for God's gifts and blessings but for God himself and who he is.

Albert Einstein once said that the essential question is whether or not the universe is friendly. What if God were not friendly at all? What if he were cruel and capricious and decidedly *unfriendly* and vindictive?

What wonderful news that the God we worship is full of love and compassion toward us! In fact, his compassion in sending his Son to rescue us stretches credulity.

We thank God for his gifts, but what about times when his gifts disappear? Do we keep thanking him when the streams of health and wealth dry up and we find ourselves in a physical, emotional, and spiritual desert? Yes. There is still life itself for which to thank him. Constant through our lives can be the "gracious gratitude" that rises in thanks to God for who he is, what he has done, and what he has prepared for us in glory.

Thanks to God runs throughout the pages of the Old Testament, despite often horrific circumstances, and in the New Testament, despite persecutions, beatings, and mortal danger. In that context we can say with Job, "Though you slay me, yet will I trust you."

We embrace two kinds of thanksgiving: natural gratitude and gracious gratitude. The two work together in perpetual dialogue. Ellen says, "Thanksgiving for who he is mingles with daily thanks for all good gifts. Relishing who God is and all he's given is the secret of remaining connected to him."

---

*Lord, thank you that life is not meaningless, even though
so often it seems to be. Bring your purpose into our lives
today. Let your will be done as it is in heaven, and
help me to have a continuous spirit of gratitude.*

Let every created thing give praise to the LORD, for he issued his command, and they came into being. PSALM 148:5, NLT

VISCERAL DESPERATION

KING DAVID, in the Psalms, often cries out in helplessness for God to rescue him. When God pulls through for him, David bursts out in praise. In Psalm 34 he declares, "I will praise the LORD at all times. I will constantly speak his praises. I will boast only in the LORD; let all who are helpless take heart" (verses 1-2, NLT).

David had enemies and experienced helplessness in visceral, life-threatening ways. We, too, have enemies of the soul and body, and if we're at all in touch with reality, we recognize our helplessness and dependence on the Lord.

"Come," David says after telling the helpless to take heart, "let us tell of the LORD's greatness; let us exalt his name together" (verse 3, NLT). David invites us to join him in praising God and then gives his personal testimony:

"I prayed to the LORD, and he answered me. He freed me from all my fears. Those who look to him for help will be radiant with joy; no shadow of shame will darken their faces. In my desperation I prayed, and the LORD listened; he saved me from all my troubles. For the angel of the LORD is a guard; he surrounds and defends all who fear him. Taste and see that the LORD is good. Oh, the joys of those who take refuge in him!" (verses 4-8, NLT).

Life is difficult—at times desperately difficult—but as David found, that is when we are driven to seek God for help.

From his own experience, David encourages all who are in the depths of grief: "The LORD is close to the brokenhearted; he rescues those whose spirits are crushed" (verse 18, NLT).

Lord, fill my heart with praise! Change my feelings
of discouragement into confidence in your guidance.
Grant me a spirit of gratitude for your blessings. Help
me, I pray, to humbly serve you and others today.

I will be glad and rejoice in your unfailing love, for you have seen my troubles, and you care about the anguish of my soul. PSALM 31:7, NLT

BLESSED COINCIDENCES

JOHN HENRY JOWETT puts forward that sometimes the Lord sets the "impossible" before us. He marvels at the story of the poor widow who had only a handful of meal, yet was willing to feed Elijah, who was on the run from Jezebel. "Our road is full of surprises," he says. "The poor widow sacrificed her handful of meal and received an unfailing supply. This, too, is the way of the Lord."

Sometimes we are called upon to meet needs we sense will overwhelm us. Then, through "blessed coincidences" and unique circumstances, we endure, and we meet the needs.

Again and again in *The Hobbit* and *The Lord of the Rings*, Frodo and his companions experience their own jarring, impossible challenges. Nevertheless, they are committed to the adventure and the call—and they prevail against terrifying, evil forces. In the adventure of following Christ, we require courage and faith to take on the vast, often thankless, tasks and drudgeries of our lives.

Sometimes we see miracles, as did the widow who was surely astounded at how her meal was multiplied. Many have found that the more they pray and sense the leading of the Holy Spirit, the greater the flow of "coincidences." Yet, on our life's journey, it's also true that we may have to slog forward through deserts without seeing any miracles at all.

Sometimes we're called to stretch ourselves beyond our normal capacities. We also must be realistic about what we take on as we seek God's leading.

Let's face it. Sometimes we really are overwhelmed, and there's no rescuer at hand. There are no guarantees of miracles. But we are called to the adventure, one just as dangerous spiritually as the one in which Frodo faced his evil enemies. So we pray for courage and endurance.

Jowett says, "We see the frowning, precipitous hill, and we fear it, but when we arrive at its base we find a refreshing spring. This, too, is the way of the Lord."

Lord Jesus Christ, have mercy on me, a sinner. When you were on earth, you faced overwhelming needs and limitations. You understand it all; prepare me for what's ahead. Help me discover your refreshing springs.

O LORD, do not stay far away! You are my strength; come quickly to my aid!
PSALM 22:19, NLT

FAITH IN THE WAVES

HELMUT THIELICKE tells the story of a time when Otto von Bismarck looked at a heroic portrait of himself and asked, "Is that how I am supposed to look? That's not me." On an opposite wall, he saw a picture of the disciple Peter walking on water and sinking beneath the waves. Pointing to it, Bismarck said, "That's me."

If the "Iron Chancellor" who united Germany could feel that way, what about you and me? Sometimes we may appear strong and in control, yet we're deeply worried about how vulnerable we are. We look at the waves coming at us and get that sinking sensation.

Peter was full of bravado when he saw Jesus walking on the water and asked if he could too. He stepped out of the boat with his eyes on his Lord and started walking.

What went wrong?

Peter took his eyes off the Lord. Instead, looking at the roiling waves under his feet, he felt fear.

Life has plenty of wind-whipped waves that rush at us. Mostly they break harmlessly at our feet, but some rise high and can soak us or even plunge us into the depths. The truth is, we could catalog an endless list of "what ifs."

When Jesus told us not to have an anxious spirit, he was doing more than merely offering stress-avoidance advice. He wanted us to know that, when we keep our eyes on him instead of looking at the threatening waves, we are safe despite the sting of the spray.

When Peter took his eyes off Jesus and began to sink, Jesus seized him and rescued him. Peter's faith was small and easily shaken, yet, writes Thielicke, "This minimum is sufficient for Jesus Christ to enter the picture and enfold him in his rescuing arms. For Jesus Christ is greater than our faith."

Lord, when my faith falters and it feels as if I'm sinking in the waves of life, please grip my hand. Pull me up to your confidence and grace so that, with my eyes steadily on you, I can walk on whatever is beneath my feet.

Let your roots grow down into him, and let your lives be built on him. Then your faith will grow strong in the truth you were taught, and you will overflow with thankfulness.
COLOSSIANS 2:7, NLT

THE BEAUTIFUL FIGHT

GARY THOMAS tells us that the Orthodox fathers had a different way of looking at 2 Timothy 4:7. Instead of the familiar reading found in most modern English translations—"I have fought the good fight, I have finished the race"—they translated the verse: "I have fought the beautiful fight . . ."

Thomas says that putting the words *beautiful* and *fight* together creates a "mesmerizing twist." In fact, he was so taken with the phrase "beautiful fight" that he wrote a book with that title. And why not? It's the fight we all find ourselves in throughout our lives.

"In the Christian life of transformation and sacrificial service," writes Thomas, "there is drama, passion, struggle, and vision—everything our souls need to feel alive."

Everything our souls need to feel alive! That phrase may not mesmerize us, but it wonderfully captures one of our core needs—the need to feel alive inside. So much of what we do—in our work, our play, our relationships, and our involvement in society—we do in order to feel alive inside.

The Christian life can supply the drama and meaning that make us continually come alive. Yet Gary is realistic enough to say that it can also be disappointing. "The Beautiful Fight is filled with what appears to be constant failure," he writes. "Every time someone has experienced a 'splash of glory' through me, they have had to put up with ten sessions of my own inflated sense of importance."

What keeps Gary in the fight? He says, "Because Jesus reigns, we have hope." We look at our weaknesses and defeats through the lens of Christ's ascension. Jesus is not simply watching us; he gives us his Holy Spirit so that he can live through us.

Father above, please equip me for the spiritual struggles I have now. Let your Holy Spirit bring a sense of engagement that makes me feel alive with your energy, strength, and purpose.

The LORD your God fights for you, just as he has promised. So be very careful to love the LORD your God. JOSHUA 23:10-11, NLT

WORKSHOP PRAYER

OLE HALLESBY describes our times of prayer when the Spirit works in us as wonderful times of rest we can anticipate with joy. He also says the time of prayer should be not only a resting place but also a workshop.

Power and grace from heaven come through prayer, and Hallesby urges us to avail ourselves of what God wants to give. He paints a picture of Jesus after his ascension to heaven, reaching his arm so far down to us that we who are small and sinful can reach it every time we pray. "Whenever we touch his almighty arm, some of his omnipotence streams in upon us, into our souls and into our bodies. And not only that, but through us, it streams out to others."

When Hallesby gets specific about prayer's workshop practicality, it cuts close to the bone: "We should say to God as we mingle with our dear ones each day, 'God, give them each thy blessing. They need it, because they live with me, and I am very selfish and unwilling to sacrifice very much for them, although I do love them.'"

Whatever we may feel about that self-indicting prayer, his prediction that such prayers would bring "a good spirit to our homes" rings true.

Hallesby points out something we'll seldom admit—we sometimes make critical remarks in our minds about people we see. He challenges us with this exhortation: "Just think if the Spirit of God could make the new nature within us so strong that we would automatically lift our hearts in prayer to God every time we met someone."

Instead of critical thoughts, we would pray God's blessing on others. "Wherever we go," Hallesby says, "we meet people who are in need of something. If the Spirit could give us that open eye of love, we would turn to the Lord and tell him the needs of both our friends and of our enemies. That is how he would like to have us pray."

Father, as I meet people today, help me to see them with
your eyes. I pray for your Spirit to love them through me.
Instead of judging others, help me to pray for them.

We love each other because he loved us first. I JOHN 4:19, NLT

PROTECTION IN THE STORMS

December 23

JONI EARECKSON TADA writes about her childhood tree house fortress, in which she felt safe from the wind, rain, and storms. She was protected, dry, and cozy.

"The storms don't stop as we grow up, do they?" she asks. "The clouds become darker than we ever imagined and the wind can shake us with a fury that seems more than we can endure. Sometimes, we long for a hiding place."

She then refers to David's longing in the Psalms for a shelter from the storms of life.

"Oh, that I had wings like a dove," David writes, "then I would fly away and rest! . . . How quickly I would escape—far from this wild storm of hatred" (Psalm 55:6, 8, NLT).

David found the shelter that we all find ourselves looking for. He proclaims: "I love you, LORD; you are my strength. The LORD is my rock, my fortress, and my savior; my God is my rock, in whom I find protection. He is my shield, the power that saves me, and my place of safety. I called on the LORD, who is worthy of praise, and he saved me from my enemies" (Psalm 18:1-3, NLT).

David's life was tumultuous and full of danger. He was capable of tragic sins, yet he was a man after God's own heart. In the Psalms, we see David's passionate heart of seeking and finding God, of confessing and yearning and rejoicing in him.

When storms battered David, his first thought was to seek God's direction and protection.

Referring to God as a rock and a fortress, Joni asks, "What better place could there be? What better shelter for anxious hearts and weary minds?"

---

*Lord, here I am with rain pelting down and winds
tearing at me. Help me to experience you as my
shelter, as David did. Please be my rock, my fortress,
and my salvation in the wild storms that come.*

---

*"LORD, help!" they cried in their trouble, and he saved them from their distress. He
calmed the storm to a whisper and stilled the waves.* PSALM 107:28-29, NLT

MOTHER TERESA gives us this inspiration: "Every time we let Jesus love others through us, it is Christmas."

Love, of course, is what Christmas is all about. For God so loved the world that he gave his Son to be born as a babe, to bring good tidings of love and great joy.

But how in our embittered world are we to let the love of Jesus flow through us?

"Love, to be genuine, must bring some suffering with it," Mother Teresa says. "Jesus suffered in order to love us. He still suffers. He became our bread of life to satisfy our hunger for his love, our hunger for God, because it was for this love we were created."

To experience this love in our fallen world, we pray. In our disappointments, sorrows, and temptations, we turn first of all to the one who is love, the one who can fill us with his love and his truth.

"If you pray," Mother Teresa promises, "you will be able to overcome the tricks of the devil. Don't believe all the thoughts he puts into your mind."

Instead of hearing the devil's suggestions, we must listen in silence for the thoughts of the Holy Spirit. And when we feel we cannot pray, we can simply ask Jesus to pray for us.

Is life too hectic to pray? We need not interrupt our activities to pray. We ask continually that we be with God, and he with us, in all we do—with little checks all through the day as we ask for his blessing and guidance.

Mother Teresa urges us to pray that, just as Mary welcomed the baby in the manger, we would welcome Jesus at Christmas and at all times.

"Love to pray," she said. "When we do, Jesus softens our hearts with his own humility and love."

---

*Lord, I have all sorts of feelings associated with
Christmas. Help me most of all to welcome you into
my heart and life. Let Christmas be authentic because
I seek you at the center of celebrating your birth.*

Mary responded, "Oh, how my soul praises the Lord. How my spirit rejoices in God my Savior!" LUKE 1:46-47, NLT

THE GLORIOUS CHRISTMAS December 25

J. I. PACKER writes that there's nothing in fiction so fantastic as the Incarnation. He points to 2 Corinthians 8:9 as the key text: "You know the generous grace of our Lord Jesus Christ. Though he was rich, yet for your sakes he became poor, so that by his poverty he could make you rich" (NLT).

Christ laid aside his glory to endure extreme limitations and hardships. "This Christmas message," says Packer, "is that there is hope for a ruined humanity—hope of pardon, hope of peace with God, hope of glory."

What unimaginable glory the Lord Jesus set aside to come here! We get just a glimpse in Luke's account of the angels' announcement to the shepherds: "Suddenly, an angel of the Lord appeared among them, and the radiance of the Lord's glory surrounded them" (Luke 2:9, NLT).

We can barely imagine the shock felt by these ordinary shepherds. Luke writes they were terrified. The angel told them not to be afraid and said, "I bring you good news that will bring great joy to all people" (Luke 2:10, NLT).

What happened next ripped open a brief sighting of the vast glory that Jesus was setting aside. A host of thousands of angels—the armies of heaven—appeared, praising God and saying, "Glory to God in highest heaven, and peace on earth to those with whom God is pleased" (Luke 2:14, NLT).

A vast host of angels! The Son of God who commanded them all had humbled himself to become an infant. The armies of heaven rejoiced at the proclamation of this mind-boggling good news. Yet, most people were unaware of history's most incredible moment.

The King of Glory came not to dazzle the world with his grandeur but to redeem it in obscurity and humility. Jesus laid aside his glory for us. "The Christmas message," writes Packer, "is the most wonderful message the world has ever heard."

Lord Jesus, as we celebrate this most wonderful event
in history—your coming to earth as a baby—bring
to us, we pray, that sense of wonder that Mary and
the shepherds had. Birth within us praise and joy.

The angel reassured them. "Don't be afraid!" he said. "I bring you good news that will bring great joy to all people." LUKE 2:10, NLT

GOD'S SILENCE AND WONDERS December 26

ASAPH, in Psalm 77, laments, "I cry out to God; yes, I shout. Oh, that God would listen to me!" (verse 1, NLT).

Does God reply? Asaph senses no response at all. He is like a modern playwright depicting the absence of God: "When I was in deep trouble, I searched for the Lord. All night long I prayed, with hands lifted toward heaven, but my soul was not comforted. I think of God, and I moan, overwhelmed with longing for his help" (verses 2-3, NLT).

He feels God has deserted him despite his long, intense pleadings. He complains, "I think of the good old days, long since ended, when my nights were filled with joyful songs. I search my soul and ponder the difference now. Has the Lord rejected me forever? Will he never again be kind to me? Is his unfailing love gone forever? . . . Has he slammed the door on his compassion?" (verses 5-9, NLT). The gritty realism of the Psalms resonates with human experience. We may have once felt God's vital presence, yet in great trouble we pray and sense no response or comfort. Our prayers for relief don't change our situation.

Asaph doesn't record that he broke through to God. Instead, the turning point is his own change of thought. He prays: "But then I recall all you have done, O LORD. I remember your wonderful deeds of long ago. They are constantly in my thoughts" (verses 11-12, NLT).

Our lifetime spiritual journey will often include times of dryness and deep dismay. Like Asaph, we may feel abandoned and that God is not listening. Yet, as we pray, thinking about all God has done for us through Christ, his promises provide wisdom and comfort.

"O God, your ways are holy," Asaph prays. "You are the God of great wonders!" (verses 13-14 , NLT).

Lord, I call out to you to work in my life right now,
whatever my feelings. Help me to think about your
magnificent creation and your wonderful love for
me—and that you love all those I'll meet today.

I know the LORD is always with me. I will not be shaken, for he is right beside me. No wonder my heart is glad. PSALM 16:8-9, NLT

THE POWER OF GRATITUDE

ELLEN VAUGHN describes "a mustard seed of life-changing power" that appears when we develop a habit of constantly whispering thanks to God—no matter what our circumstances are. Even though this practice may seem small and insignificant, she says, "It has the power to change our lives and blow our socks off."

Does that sound like an audacious and inflated claim? Well, Ellen builds her case on Scripture and unpacks it with an illustration:

A friend was going through a prickly patch of trouble with her teenage daughter. Gone was their once-close friendship, replaced by angry confrontations. The mother decided to tenaciously thank God in the midst of these conflicts, even though she surely didn't feel grateful for the sparks and the anger. Rather than focus on the conflict, she thanked God for the gift of her daughter, for her daughter's quick mind and health, and for the promise that God was with them. She kept up a barrage of thanks, one thank-you after another.

The results? She began thinking of her daughter as also being God's daughter. She gained resilience. "Oddly enough," Ellen writes, "she couldn't wait for her daughter to get home from school every day, so she could lavish love on her. My friend's act of obedience to God—thanking him in all things—actually changed not only her mind but also her emotions."

We find ourselves in all sorts of situations, ones that are exasperating, scary, disappointing, or even devastating. Sometimes, life is not only difficult but even crushing. Thanking God in all circumstances may seem irrelevant—yet we are urged to do so throughout the Bible.

Psalm 106:1-2 exclaims, "Praise the LORD! Give thanks to the LORD, for he is good! His faithful love endures forever. Who can list the glorious miracles of the LORD? Who can ever praise him enough?" (NLT).

We reap enormous benefits and bring glory to God when we praise in all circumstances.

Lord, you are worthy of my praise. Fill me, I pray,
with gratitude for the many blessings in my life.
Show me how to be grateful in all circumstances.

The heavens proclaim the glory of God. The skies display his craftsmanship. Day after day they continue to speak; night after night they make him known. PSALM 19:1-2, NLT

HOPE IN THE FOG

FRED SMITH maintains that "hope is the healthy mental condition of the normal Christian." He says that if we are to live as Christians, we do so with hope—even when situations seem hopeless.

Fred recounts a time when the president of a large corporation facing bankruptcy came to him to talk about the pressures he was under. Many of the factors that had wrecked the company were beyond his control, and he faced tough, divisive meetings. Fred reminded this executive of the dangers of hopelessness. "We are never to be without hope," he told him, "because we are never without help."

On more than one occasion, Fred visited a friend who saw nothing good ahead and was considering suicide. He challenged the man to demonstrate hope, emphasizing that hope is not in productivity or material wealth.

Enemies of hope invade our lives like toxic fog. A spouse deserts the family. Job losses devastate another family. An accident takes a loved one on whom many had pinned their hopes. The tragedies of our lives are endlessly various and painfully unique to each soul.

For inspiration, Fred turned to Romans 5, with its ringing declaration of our lively hope. When we feel hope has deserted us, we would do well to read and reread these verses: "We can rejoice, too, when we run into problems and trials, for we know that they help us develop endurance. And endurance develops strength of character, and character strengthens our confident hope of salvation. And this hope will not lead to disappointment. For we know how dearly God loves us, because he has given us the Holy Spirit to fill our hearts with his love" (verses 3-5, NLT).

Fred declares from the promise of Scripture and long experience, "Hope is the birthright of the Christian."

Heavenly Father, enable me to put all my hope in you instead of focusing on my circumstances. Please grow in me the kind of endurance and character that strengthens my hope, and let me be one who brings hope to others.

Always be humble and gentle. Be patient with each other, making allowance for each other's faults because of your love. . . . For there is one body and one Spirit, just as you have been called to one glorious hope for the future. EPHESIANS 4:2, 4, NLT

DESPITE THE SOOT

D. L. MOODY believed that if people could only understand that God is love, they would be irresistibly drawn to him. Yet he sensed that most people saw God as an angry judge or too distant to care about them.

Moody was so anxious to burn this truth into people's minds that he set up gas jets right above the pulpit—yes, gas jets!—to spell out the words GOD IS LOVE.

A man walking by glanced in and saw the words. As he walked on, he thought, *God is not love. God does not love me, a miserable sinner.* Yet the words burned into his soul. He later came back to the meeting, and afterward Moody found him weeping. When the evangelist told the man that God had loved him from the beginning of his life, the light of the gospel finally broke through to him.

Despite all our sins and failures, God still loves us. Like the father in Jesus' parable of the Prodigal Son, God waits with open arms, whether we've been scrubbed clean or come fresh from the pigsty.

Moody told a true story reminiscent of Jesus' parable. A boy in London had been stolen from his family and forced to work for years as a chimney sweep. His grieving mother prayed constantly for her little boy, but years went by with no word of him. One day, the boy came down the wrong chimney—and it turned out to be the right one! He found himself standing in a room that looked strangely familiar.

As he stood in his rags, covered with soot, his mother entered the room. When she saw her boy, she took him in her arms, all dirty and smoky, and hugged him while shedding tears of joy.

Moody said that's what God is like toward each of us. He quoted God's assurance in Jeremiah 31:3, "I have loved thee with an everlasting love; therefore with loving-kindness have I drawn thee" (KJV).

---

*Lord, fill me with your Holy Spirit so that I may
experience your love and share your love with others.
So often I don't feel your love; help me to obey and act
in ways that open the gates for your love to flow.*

May you have the power to understand, as all God's people should, how wide, how long, how high, and how deep his love is. May you experience the love of Christ.
EPHESIANS 3:18-19, NLT

THE DEVIL'S TERMITES

CALVIN MILLER says, "Never forget that, just as God is the Creator who wants to make your life and testimony beautiful, Satan is the destroyer. He is out to smash every beautiful thing God created you to be and achieve."

Strong stuff. Mostly we don't think much about our enemy, who hates us and wants to ruin us—though it's also true we can think about him too much. Yet Jesus himself said plenty about the devil, and the words he used are not pretty: *murderer, deceiver, accuser, evil one, prince of demons.*

When Satan tempted Jesus, showing him all the kingdoms of the world and their glory and said he would give them all to him, Jesus didn't refute his capacity to do so. Think about that. Jesus didn't say, "This is my Father's world—who are you to promise me the kingdoms?" That was because Satan, in one sense, does rule the world.

So, how does he subtly attempt to ruin us? "He is not a 'wrecker-ball' destroyer," writes Miller. "He is the Lord of the termites." He then gives a graphic picture of the devil's termites producing unseen decay that "makes Pharisees seem alive when they are only the hollow dead."

The hollow dead! It's sobering to think that the Pharisees were Bible believers, yet their faith and spirits were dead. Satan wants to make us into the hollow dead as well—to eat away at our spiritual vitality until we're lifeless inside.

The devil won't come around with a contract for our souls the way he does in literature or the movies. He'll keep day by day lying about God and why we don't need to obey him. He'll lure us with promises about where the real action and satisfaction is.

James 4:7 has it right: "Resist the devil, and he will flee from you" (NLT).

Father, it's hard to know why you made mosquitoes, and far worse, the devil. What a difficult and tragic world we find ourselves in! Help me to embrace the wonders of your creation and to reject all Satan's lures.

Be strong in the Lord and in his mighty power. Put on all of God's armor so that you will be able to stand firm against all strategies of the devil. EPHESIANS 6:10-11, NLT

THE SHROUD FLUNG AWAY December 31

ISAIAH foresees a magnificent event still to come. In chapter 25 of his prophetic book, he says that the Lord of Heaven's Armies will one day spread a wonderful feast for all the people of the world. He describes it as a "delicious banquet" (verse 6, NLT).

What he foresees will be far more than merely a feast that surpasses a Sunday brunch. Isaiah says that God will do what we all long for: remove the shroud of death that hangs over the earth. "He will swallow up death forever!" Isaiah declares. "The Sovereign LORD will wipe away all tears" (verse 8, NLT).

The prophet's vision transcends ethnic and national loyalties, for this banquet and this global promise are for "all people." How can this possibly be? In our fallen world, it's hard to imagine. But Isaiah proclaims it, and in the New Testament we're told the same story: that the whole creation groans in travail, that a new creation is coming, and that death will be no more.

In the meantime, we live beneath the dark shroud of inevitable death and the grief that invades our lives with unexpected force and tragic disruption.

Yet, Christ in his sacrifice has fulfilled the vision of that shroud flung away and death disarmed and defeated.

Isaiah gives this ringing affirmation: "Those who die in the LORD will live; their bodies will rise again! Those who sleep in the earth will rise up and sing for joy! For your life-giving light will fall like dew on your people in the place of the dead!" (Isaiah 26:19, NLT).

Heavenly Father, all our lives we've been haunted by the realization that those we love will someday die, and we will too. Thank you for the glorious hope of resurrection. Fill me with joy and faith in your everlasting life.

With eager hope, the creation looks forward to the day when it will join God's children in glorious freedom from death and decay. . . . We, too, wait with eager hope.
ROMANS 8:20-21, 23, NLT

SOURCES/BIBLIOGRAPHY

Treasure hunt. That's the way this devotional was developed. Books, periodicals, sermons, Web postings, and personal interactions were all rich soil in which to find nuggets of gold for the soul.

In the listings below, no attempt has been made to link quotes to specific pages and sources. At times, quotes for one day were cobbled together from different pages scattered throughout a book—or even from several books and/or sermons. Communicators typically revisit themes and illustrations, so a particular quote might be found in several sources.

Because many of these classic books have been published by more than one publisher, or in more than one edition over the years, only titles are listed here. In the case of past spiritual writers such as Thomas à Kempis, Brother Lawrence, François Fénelon, and Martin Luther, sometimes several translations contributed to a condensed rendering of their ideas.

What follows includes sources and bibliography—but it's far from an exhaustive list. For instance, Oswald Chambers's classic *My Utmost for His Highest* was one source, yet his dozens of other books provided context and additional material.

Today, all that's needed is a name and Web access to find biographical information and content. My hope is that the brief listings below will serve as an invitation to a personal treasure hunt.

Jill Briscoe: *Prayer That Works; Faith Enough to Finish; By Hook or by Crook; Wings; The One Year Book of Devotions for Women; God's Front Door; The Garden of Grace*

Rosemary Budd: *Journey of Prayer; Moving Prayer*

Amy Carmichael: *Gold by Moonlight; Rose from Brier; If*

Oswald Chambers: *My Utmost for His Highest; Not Knowing Whither; Baffled to Fight Better; If Thou Wilt Be Perfect; Conformed to His Image; Disciples Indeed*

Ed Dobson: *Prayers and Promises When Facing a Life-Threatening Illness*; articles in *Christianity Today*

François Fénelon: various translations of his writings and letters, including *The Seeking Heart*; *Let Go*; *Selections from Fénelon*

Billy Graham: *Hope for the Troubled Heart*; *Approaching Hoofbeats*; *The Leadership Secrets of Billy Graham*; *Just as I Am*; articles in *Christianity Today*

Nancy Guthrie: *The One Year Book of Hope*; *Holding on to Hope*; *When Your Family's Lost a Loved One*; *Hearing Jesus Speak into Your Sorrow*

Ole Hallesby: *Prayer*; *God's Word for Today*; *Under His Wings*

Thomas Howard: *Splendor in the Ordinary*; *Christ the Tiger*

John Henry Jowett: *My Daily Meditation*; sermon Web sites

Thomas à Kempis: various translations of *The Imitation of Christ*, including those by E. M. Blaiklock, Leo Sherley-Price, and Joseph N. Tylenda

Jay Kesler: *Growing Places*; *Being Holy, Being Human*; speeches; personal correspondence and conversation

Brother Lawrence: various translations of *Practicing the Presence of God*, including those by E. M. Blaiklock, The Seedsowers, Whitaker House, Revell

C. S. Lewis: *Mere Christianity*; *Miracles*; *The Weight of Glory*; *A Grief Observed*; *A Mind Awake* (Clyde Kilby, editor)

Martin Luther: *Faith Alone* (James C. Galvin, editor); *Come Thou Long-Expected Jesus* (Nancy Guthrie, editor); various Luther Web sites

George MacDonald: *Diary of an Old Soul*; *Your Life in Christ* (Michael Phillips, editor); several of MacDonald's novels and fantasies

Calvin Miller: *Disarming the Darkness*; *The Singer*; *The Song*

D. L. Moody: *D. L. Moody on Spiritual Leadership* (Steve Miller, editor); Moody Web sites and sermon Web sites

Henri J. M. Nouwen: *With Open Hands*; *The Way of the Heart*; *Spiritual Direction* (with Michael Christensen and Rebecca Laird); *Beyond the Mirror*; *The Inner Voice of Love*; articles in *Leadership Journal*

John Ortberg: *Living the God Life*; *Everybody's Normal Till You Get to Know Them*; *The Life You've Always Wanted*; articles and columns in *Leadership Journal*

J. I. Packer: *Knowing God*; *I Want to Be a Christian*; articles in *Christianity Today*

Alan Paton: *Instrument of Thy Peace*; *Cry, the Beloved Country*; *Alan Paton: A Biography* by Peter F. Alexander

Ben Patterson: *He Has Made Me Glad*; *Deepening Your Conversation with God*; *Waiting*; *God's Prayer Book*; articles in *Leadership Journal*

Eugene Peterson: *Leap Over a Wall*; *Run with the Horses*; *Reversed Thunder*; *A Long Obedience in the Same Direction*; *A Year with the Psalms*; *Eat This Book*; articles and interviews in *Leadership Journal*

Francis Schaeffer: *The Mark of the Christian*; *The God Who Is There*; *Escape from Reason*; *How Should We Then Live?*

Luci Shaw: *The Crime of Living Cautiously*; *Water My Soul*; *The Secret Trees*; *God in the Dark*

Lewis Smedes: *Standing on the Promises*; *Union with Christ*; *Forgive and Forget*

Fred Smith: *Breakfast with Fred*; www.breakfastwithfred.com; *You and Your Network*; articles in *Leadership Journal*; interviews; personal correspondence and conversations

Charles Haddon Spurgeon: sermon Web sites and collections; *Encounter with Spurgeon* by Helmut Thielicke

Tim Stafford: *Personal God*; *Knowing the Face of God*; *Surprised by Jesus*; articles in *Christianity Today*

Ray Stedman: *Body Life*; *The Power of His Presence* (Mark Mitchell, editor); www.raystedman.org

Joni Eareckson Tada: *The God I Love*; *Joni*; *A Quiet Place in a Crazy World*; *Holiness in Hidden Places*; *A Step Further*; *Choices . . . Changes*

Corrie ten Boom: *The Hiding Place*; *Amazing Love*; *Tramp for the Lord*

Mother Teresa: *Something Beautiful for God* by Malcolm Muggeridge; books of her writings and talks; journal articles

Helmut Thielicke: *Our Heavenly Father*; *The Waiting Father*; *Life Can Begin Again*; *How to Believe Again*; *Notes from a Wayfarer*

Gary Thomas: *The Beautiful Fight*; *Authentic Faith*; articles in *Christianity Today*

Paul Tournier: *The Adventure of Living*; *The Meaning of Persons*; *The Healing of Persons*; *Guilt and Grace*; *The Strong and the Weak*

A. W. Tozer: *The Knowledge of the Holy*; *The Pursuit of God*; *Tozer on Worship and Entertainment*

Ellen Vaughn: *Radical Gratitude*; books and articles coauthored with Charles Colson

John Wesley: *Fire of Love*; *The John Wesley Reader*; various Wesley sermon Web sites

Sherwood Wirt: *Jesus, Man of Joy*; *A Thirst for God*; *Afterglow*; articles in *Decision*; sermons, personal correspondence, and conversations

Philip Yancey: *Prayer*; *What's So Amazing About Grace?*; *Reaching for the Invisible God*; *Rumors of Another World*; *The Jesus I Never Knew*; articles in *Christianity Today, Books & Culture*, and *Leadership Journal*

Sometimes we need to know that there is *Hope.*

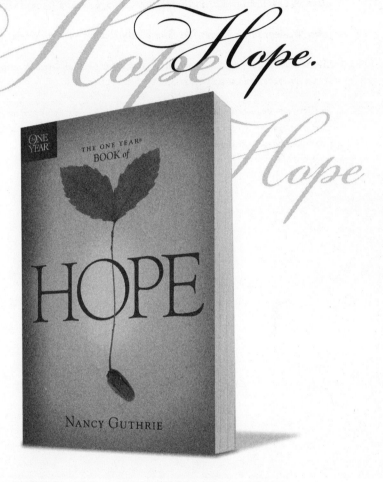

Pain and disappointment are real. Some losses you can never fully recover from. There are wounds that never quite heal. Nancy Guthrie, no stranger to seemingly hopeless situations, offers remarkable insights into the hope that God gives and *not* trite answers or quick fixes. Let *The One Year Book of Hope* guide you toward healing, peace, and most of all, the God of all comfort and hope.

Mr Joanna

252-799-7284